European Community Law
in the United Kingdom

European Community Law in the United Kingdom

FOURTH EDITION

Lawrence Collins
MA, LLB (Cantab), LLM (Columbia Univ, NY); *Solicitor, London; Fellow, Wolfson College, Cambridge; Visiting Professor, Queen Mary and Westfield College, London; Associé de l'Institut de Droit International.*

Butterworths
London, Dublin, Edinburgh
1990

United Kingdom	Butterworth & Co (Publishers) Ltd 88 Kingsway, LONDON WC2B 6AB and 4 Hill Street, EDINBURGH EH2 3JZ
Australia	Butterworths Pty Ltd, SYDNEY, MELBOURNE, BRISBANE, ADELAIDE, PERTH, CANBERRA and HOBART
Canada	Butterworths Canada Ltd, TORONTO and VANCOUVER
Ireland	Butterworth (Ireland) Ltd, DUBLIN
Malaysia	Malayan Law Journal Sdn Bhd, KUALA LUMPUR
New Zealand	Butterworths of New Zealand, WELLINGTON and AUCKLAND
Puerto Rico	Equity de Puerto Rico, Inc, HATO REY
Singapore	Malayan Law Journal Pte Ltd, SINGAPORE
USA	Butterworth Legal Publishers, AUSTIN, Texas; BOSTON, Massachusetts; CLEARWATER, Florida (D & S Publishers); ORFORD, New Hampshire (Equity Publishing); ST PAUL, Minnesota; and SEATTLE, Washington

All rights reserved. No part of this publication may be reproduced in any material form (including photocopying or storing it in any medium by electronic means and whether or not transiently or incidentally to some other use of this publication) without the written permission of the copyright owner except in accordance with the provisions of the Copyright, Designs and Patents Act 1988 or under the terms of a licence issued by the Copyright Licensing Agency Ltd, 33–34 Alfred Place, London, England WC1E 7DP. Applications for the copyright owner's written permission to reproduce any part of this publication should be addressed to the publisher.

Warning: The doing of an unauthorised act in relation to a copyright work may result in both a civil claim for damages and criminal prosecution.

© Butterworth & Co (Publishers) Ltd 1990

A CIP Catalogue record for this book is available from the British Library

ISBN 0 406 59200 4 (Hardcover)
     0 406 59201 2 (Softcover)

Typeset by Phoenix Photosetting, Chatham, Kent
Printed by Biddles Ltd, Guildford, Surrey

Preface

Since its first edition in 1975 this book has dealt with four main areas: the general relationship between Community law and the law of the United Kingdom; the operation of directly applicable and effective Community law in the United Kingdom; the relationship between United Kingdom courts and the European Court in the interpretation of Community law; and avenues of challenge to Community acts.

There have been almost four hundred relevant decisions of the European Court and of United Kingdom courts since the last edition in 1984. There can be no doubt that the involvement of United Kingdom lawyers and courts with Community law has increased dramatically in recent years, and that the single European market will strongly reinforce this tendency. This edition endeavours to take account of such developments as the approach of the House of Lords in *Pickstone v Freemans* and *Litster v Forth Dry Dock* to the interpretation of United Kingdom legislation implementing Community law; the relationship between the direct effect of Community law and remedies in national law, including the decisions of the Court of Appeal in *Bourgoin* and of the House of Lords in *Factortame*; and the power of national courts to rule on the validity of Community acts in the light of the *Foto-Frost* decision. In Chapter 4 I have added a section on *locus standi* in state aid cases.

There have now been about seventy decisions of the European Court on references from United Kingdom courts. But the delays in litigation caused by references are very serious. Although the European Court is able to produce statistics which suggest that the average time for art 177 references is about seventeen months (and even this cannot be regarded as a short period for an interlocutory matter), a study of the more important references from United Kingdom courts frequently reveals a delay of between two and three years. The European Court of Human Rights in Strasbourg has held that proceedings which took four years were capable of amounting to a breach of the fundamental right to a fair hearing within a reasonable time (see *H v France*, Ser A, vol 162, 1989). The delays in the Luxembourg Court (which will only be partially alleviated by the creation of the Court of First Instance) are little short of scandalous.

For this edition I have benefited from the advice of Anthony Lester

QC and David Vaughan QC, and the efforts of Sarah Baker, Susan Bone and Helen Spiegel, as well as from the inspiration of E K Ellington and Eleanora Fagan and the continued support of Chief Justice and Mrs F Iacobucci. Maureen Higgins, my secretary, has given invaluable assistance. The idea for this book came originally from Mr E Lauterpacht QC.

This edition is dedicated to my wife, Sarah, and to Hannah and Aaron.

London, April 1990   Lawrence Collins

Contents

Preface v
Table of statutes xi
Table of European Communities legislation xiii
Table of cases:
   Alphabetical xvii
   Numerical xli

Chapter 1
Introduction 1
Community law and its relationship with national law and
   international law 1
   1 The nature of Community law 1
   2 Community law and international law 2
   3 Community law and individuals 7
   4 Community law and fundamental human rights 8
   5 Community law and national law 14
   6 The supremacy of Community law—the position according to
      Community law 15
   7 The supremacy of Community law—the national viewpoint—
      the problem of 'sovereignty' 22
   8 Treaties as the source of Community law 23
   9 The mode of incorporation and the sovereignty of
      Parliament 26
      (i) Section 2(4) of the European Communities Act 1972 28
      (ii) The views of Lord Denning 30
      (iii) Section 2(4) in the House of Lords 35
      (iv) Conclusions 39

Chapter 2
Community law as part of United Kingdom law 44
I. The direct applicability and effect of Community law and
      section 2(1) of the European Communities Act 1972 46
   1 Direct effect of Treaty provisions 46
      (i) The provision must not concern member states
         only 48

viii *Contents*

        (ii) The provision must be clear and precise 49
        (iii) The provision must be unconditional and unqualified and not subject to any further measures on the part of member states or of the Community 53
        (iv) The provision must not leave substantial discretion to member states or to the Commission 56
        (v) Alternative remedies for breach of the provision are irrelevant to direct effectiveness 59
      Temporal effect 60
      Remedies 62
    2 Direct effect of other treaties 67
    3 Direct applicability and effect of regulations, decisions and directives 69
      (i) Regulations 69
      (ii) Decisions 77
      (iii) Directives 83
    4 Directly applicable or effective Community law—its operation in the United Kingdom 99
II. The European Communities Act 1972, section 2(2) 112
    1 Subordinate legislation and the implementation of Community law 114
      (i) Procedural aspects 116
      (ii) Limits on power 116
      (iii) Interpretation of and challenge to delegated legislation 117
      (iv) Scrutiny of European legislation 120
    2 Subordinate legislation in practice 121
III. Directly effective provisions of the EEC Treaty—a summary 122

Chapter 3
The national court and the European Court 127
I   The 1972 Act: the status of Community law 128
II. Interpretation of Community law and the European Court 130
III. Interpretation of United Kingdom legislation giving effect to Community law which is not directly applicable 135
    1 Statutes and treaties 135
    2 Statutes and Community law 137
IV. Preliminary rulings by the European Court 142
    1 The purpose of article 177 143
    2 The national courts which may refer questions to the European Court 144
      (i) Administrative tribunals 145

(ii) Disciplinary tribunals   147
   (iii) Arbitral tribunals   148
  3 The national courts which must make references under article 177   150
   (i) Identification of the final court   150
   (ii) Final courts and interlocutory appeals   155
   (iii) Acte clair   156
  4 The questions which may be referred   162
   (i) Relevance   163
   (ii) Interpretation and application   165
   (iii) Compatibility of national law with Community law   166
  5 Refusal of the European Court to give preliminary rulings   169
   Foglia v Novello   170
 V The exercise of the national court's discretion to refer   172
  1 The European Court's guidelines   172
  2 The role of article 177 before lower courts   174
  3 When a decision is necessary and Lord Denning's guidelines—*Bulmer v Bollinger*   176
  4 The operation of article 177 in United Kingdom practice   183
  5 The role of article 177 in interlocutory proceedings   189
  6 Appeals from decisions of lower courts to refer   194
  7 Procedural aspects   200
   (i) Order 114—references by the High Court   200
   (ii) The reference and its form   201
   (iii) The role of the parties   203
   (iv) Costs and legal aid   207
  8 The effect and authority of a ruling on an article 177 reference   209
  9 Validity rulings: special considerations   211

Chapter 4
Challenging Community acts   215
I. Introduction   215
II. Remedies against member states under Community law   216
III. The relationship between article 169 and the remedies available to private parties   227
IV. Actions to annul Community acts   229
  1 The types of act which are open to challenge   230
  2 The standing of private persons   234
   (i) Article 173(2) and the annulment of regulations   236
   (ii) Decisions addressed to member states   240
   (iii) Locus standi principles: restrictive practices, anti-dumping investigations, and state aids   244

           (iv) Conclusions   255
        3 The substantive grounds for review   256
           (i)   Lack of competence   257
           (ii) Infringement of essential procedural
                 requirement   259
           (iii) Infringement of the Treaty or of a rule of law relating
                 to its application   266
           (iv) Misuse of powers   270
        4 The time element   271
        5 The effects of annulment   272
        6 Interim measures   273
V.   The relationship between challenge under article 173 and
        references by national courts under article 177   274
VI.   The plea of illegality—article 184   276
VII.   The remedy against refusal to act—article 175   278
VIII.   Damages against Community institutions   282

Appendix
European Communities Act 1972   289

Index   297

Table of statutes

References in this Table to *Statutes* are to Halsbury's Statutes of England (Fourth Edition) showing the volume and page at which the annotated text of the Act may be found.

Page references printed in **bold** type indicate where the section of an Act is set out in part or in full.

	PAGE
Agriculture Act 1970	122
Arbitration Act (2 *Statutes* 608)	149, 150
Civil Evidence Act 1968 (17 *Statutes* 155)	
s 14	102
Civil Jurisdiction and Judgments Act 1982 (11 *Statutes* 903)	
s 1 (1)	200
Sch 2	203
Colonial Laws Validity Act 1865 (7 *Statutes* 211)	292
Companies Act 1985 (8 *Statutes* 107)	
s 35–35B	141
36 (4)	140
Companies Act 1989	
s 108	141
Criminal Justice Act 1982 (27 *Statutes* 321)	
s 40, 46	296
Criminal Law Act 1977 (12 *Statutes* 690)	
s 32 (3)	296
65 (10)	296
Crown Proceedings Act 1947 (13 *Statutes* 16)	109
s 21 (1)	120
Customs and Excise Duties (General Reliefs) Act 1979 (13 *Statutes* 450)	
s 19 (1)	296
Sch 2	296
Equal Pay Act 1970 (16 *Statutes* 187)	31, 32, 33, 34, 35, 36, 37, 38, 84, 97, 118, 138, 141

	PAGE
Equal Pay Act 1970—*contd*	
s 1 (4)	31
European Assembly Elections Act 1978 (15 *Statutes* 463)	
s 6 (1)	24
European Communities Act 1972 (10 *Statutes* 617)	8, 26, 29, 33, 34, 40, 44
s 1	128, **289**
(2), (3)	115
2	33, 43, 44, 73, 77, 99, 100, 114, 115, 121, 128, 137, **291**
(1)	26, 28, 32, 33, 36, 37, 38, 39, 40, 44, 46, 50, 69, 73, 77, 99, 100, 103, 106, 113, 121, 122, 128, 130
(2)	26, 27, 37, 38, 73, 100, 112, 114, 116, 117, 118, 121, 128, 130
(4)	27, 28, 32, 33, 34, 35, 36, 37, 38, 39, 40, 128, 130
3	128, 129, 211, **293**
(1)	27, 44, 48, 128, 129, 130, 138, 211
(2)	27, 128
4	27
5, 6	27, 116
7, 8	27
9	27
(1)	141
(2)	140
10	27

xi

Table of statutes

	PAGE
European Communities Act 1972—contd	
s 11	294
Sch 1	289, 290
Sch 2	27, 112, 113, 116, 117, 118, 291, 292, 295
European Communities (Amendment) Act 1986	115, 128
s 1	291
2	293, 295
European Communities (Finance) Act 1988	115
s 1	291
European Communities (Greek Accession) Act 1979 (17 *Statutes* 64)	115
s 1	290
European Communities (Spanish and Portuguese Accession) Act 1985	115
s 1	291
False Oaths (Scotland) Act 1933	
s 1	294
Fisheries Act 1981 (18 *Statutes* 311)	122
Food Act 1984	122
Insurance Companies Act 1982 (22 *Statutes* 153)	100
Interpretation Act 1978 (41 *Statutes* 899)	
s 25 (1)	290
Sch 3	290
Interpretation Act (Northern Ireland) 1954	
s 41 (6)	296
Local Government (Miscellaneous Provisions) Act 1982:	193

	PAGE
Magistrates' Courts Act 1980 (27 *Statutes* 157)	154
Medicines Act 1968 (28 *Statutes* 344)	184, 185
Merchant Shipping Act 1988	38, 108, 109, 193, 224, 225
Northern Ireland Constitution Act 1973 (31 *Statutes* 302)	
s 41 (1)	292
Sch 6	292
Official Secrets Act 1911 (12 *Statutes* 176)	27, 295
Official Secrets Act 1939 (12 *Statutes* 222)	27, 295
Opticians Act 1958 (28 *Statutes* 46)	153
Perjury Act 1911 (12 *Statutes* 165)	27
s 1 (1)	294
Prosecution of Offences Act 1985 (12 *Statutes* 933)	
s 31 (2), (6)	295
Sch 2	295
Sex Discrimination Act 1975 (6 *Statutes* 696)	31, 32, 35, 84, 89, 97, 102, 141
s 6 (4)	96
Sex Discrimination Act 1986	35, 36, 97, 141
Statute of Westminster 1931 (7 *Statutes* 12)	29
Supreme Court Act 1981 (11 *Statutes* 756)	
s 31 (3)	234
Tribunals and Inquiries Act 1958:	154
Tribunals and Inquiries Act 1971 (10 *Statutes* 364)	154
Weights and Measures Act 1963	168

Table of European Communities legislation

TREATIES

	PAGE
Act of Accession (1972)	
art 152	78
ECSC Treaty (1951)	
art 14	142
(1), (2)	78
(3)	83
15 (2)	78
33 (2)	229
41	200, 203
64	77
65, 66	245
88	216
89 (1)	226
Protocol on the Statute of the Court of Justice of the European Coal and Steel Community	
art 33	273
EEC Treaty (1957) (Treaty of Rome)	
art 2	52, 114, 115
3	115
(h)	111
5	16, 52, 62, 63, 67, 84, 98, 114
(2)	79
7	52, 53, 65, 167
8a	116
9	52, 54, 55, 56, 115
11	114
12	41, 49, 53, 54, 59, 157, 163, 165
13	55, 62, 63
(2)	55, 56
14	192
16	21, 54, 55, 63
27	114
30	40, 56, 57, 105, 106, 107, 129, 133, 159, 160, 167, 169, 182, 185, 193, 205, 219

	PAGE
EEC Treaty (1957) (Treaty of Rome)—*contd*	
art 31	56, 57, 133
32	56, 57, 133
(1), (2)	57
33	56, 57, 133
(1)	57
(2)	57, 77
34, 35	133
36	40, 129, 133, 159, 160, 167, 168, 185, 273
37	50, 51, 133, 156
(2)	50, 51, 54
39	116
43 (2)	77
48	132
52	38, 51
53	50, 51, 53
54–57	51
58	38, 51
71	52
74	79
80 (1)	79
85	7, 58, 100, 102, 104, 157, 165, 166, 198, 202, 244, 245, 246, 248, 250, 258, 283
(1)	230
(3)	166, 230, 231, 245, 246, 248, 260
86	30, 58, 103, 104, 106, 156, 232, 235, 244, 245, 246, 248, 250, 281, 283
87, 88	58, 245
89	58, 70, 245
(2)	77
90	58, 60, 245
(2)	58
(3)	77
91	58

xiii

xiv Table of European Communities legislation

EEC Treaty (1957) (Treaty of Rome)—*contd*

Article	Page
art 92	58, 79, 105, 254
(1)	59
93	50, 58, 59, 105, 254
(2)	59, 282
(3)	105
94	58, 59
95	41, 55, 62, 64, 68, 170, 220, 221, 228
(2)	58
97	57, 58
99	116
100	112, 114, 121
100A, 100B	217
101	114
102	49, 50, 59
103	116
106	110, 111
110	116
113, 114	3
119	31, 32, 33, 34, 37, 38, 53, 60, 101, 102, 160, 166
164	232
169	21, 32, 54, 59, 60, 161, 166, 215, 216, 217, 219, 220, 221, 222, 223, 224, 225, 227, 228, 229, 230, 280
170	59, 215, 226, 227
171	21, 22, 32, 225, 226
172	247
173	80, 82, 213, 214, 215, 223, 227, 228, 229, 230, 231, 232, 233, 234, 235, 239, 246, 247, 253, 256, 257, 272, 274, 275, 276, 277, 278, 279, 281, 282, 285, 286, 288
(1)	279
(2)	232, 233, 234, 235, 236, 237, 245, 248, 249, 250, 276, 286
(3)	271, 276
174	230
(2)	272
175	215, 227, 228, 229, 250, 278, 279, 280, 281, 282, 286, 288
(2), (3)	280

EEC Treaty (1957) (Treaty of Rome)—*contd*

Article	Page
art 177	17, 19, 21, 32, 44, 49, 50, 54, 55, 74, 76, 94, 96, 100, 129, 132, 142, 143, 144, 145, 146, 147, 148, 149, 150, 152, 154, 155, 156, 157, 158, 160, 161, 162, 163, 165, 166, 167, 168, 169, 170, 171, 172, 173, 174, 176, 177, 178, 180, 181, 183, 185, 186, 188, 189, 190, 191, 192, 193, 194, 195, 196, 197, 198, 199, 200, 201, 202, 203, 204, 205, 207, 208, 210, 211, 212, 213, 214, 215, 222, 223, 225, 240, 252, 257, 272, 274, 275, 277, 278, 287
(2)	153, 174, 191, 194, 203
(3)	144, 150, 151, 152, 153, 154, 155, 156, 157, 158, 174, 175, 184, 190, 194, 203
178	282
184	223, 276, 277, 278
185, 186	273
189	17, 18, 19, 45, 69, 73, 74, 75, 77, 78, 79, 80, 81, 82, 85, 89, 99, 122, 140, 232, 237
(3)	83, 84, 98
(4)	78, 82
190	259, 262, 264, 265
191	78, 82
(2)	259
210, 211	3
214	284
215	229, 272, 282, 283, 284, 286, 287, 288
(2)	282, 286, 288
220	111
226	271
228	217
(2)	217
234	49, 69
235	114, 115

	PAGE		PAGE
EEC Treaty (1957) (Treaty of Rome)—contd		Euratom Treaty (1957)—contd	
236	217	156	278
237	169	Protocol on the Statute of the Court of Justice of the European Atomic Energy Community	
238	3		
Protocol on the Statute of the Court of Justice of the European Economic Community		art 37	273
art 20	198, 201, 203, 205, 206, 207	Single European Act (signed at Luxembourg on 17 February 1986 and at The Hague on 28 February 1986)	116, 122, 217
35	207		
36	273	preamble	13
43	288	Treaty establishing a single Council and a single Commission of the European Communities (Brussels, 8th April 1965) (the Merger Treaty)	
Euratom Treaty (1957)			
art 141	216		
142	226		
146 (2)	229		
art 150	142, 200, 203	art 28	4

SECONDARY LEGISLATION

DECISIONS
EEC Council Decision [1989] 3 CMLR 458
art 3 (1) 245
4 273

DIRECTIVES
EEC Council Directive 64/221 ... 97
EEC Council Directive 67/227 ... 79
art 17 86
EEC Council Directive 69/463 ... 79
EEC Council Directive 75/117 ... 36
art 1 32
EEC Council Directive 76/207 ... 35
art 6 .... 11, 63, 92, 93, 94
EEC Council Directive 77/187 ... 139
EEC Council Directive 77/388 ... 94, 95

REGULATIONS
EEC Council Regulation 17 of 1962 .... 102, 231, 232, 233, 245, 247, 248, 260, 261, 262, 264, 281, 282
art 2 246
3 246
(2) 246
4, 6, 7, 11 246
14, 16, 17, 19 246

EEC Council Regulation 17 of 1962—contd
art 14 262
15 (6) 231
EEC Council Regulation 19 ..... 75, 82
EEC Council Regulation 22/62 .. 18
EEC Commission Regulation 99/63 .... 245, 246, 260, 261
art 6 249
EEC Commission Regulation 102/64 70
EEC Council Regulation 120/67 70
EEC Commission Regulation 473/67 70
EEC Council Regulation 816/70: 176
EEC Council Regulation 817/70: 176
EEC Council Regulation 3017/79: 253
EEC Council Regulation 2423/88: 250
art 5 250
7, 9, 10 251
Rules of Procedure of the Court of Justice
r 83 273
95 142
104 209
(3) 207

Table of cases—alphabetical

Decisions of the European Court of Justice are listed both alphabetically and numerically. The numerical table follows the alphabetical.

	PAGE

A

Absence in Ireland, Re: 7/76: [1977] 1 CMLR 5 32
ACF Chemiefarma v Commission: 41/69 [1970] ECR 661 .... 257, 258, 260
AKZO Chemie BV v Commission: 5/85 [1986] ECR 2585, [1987] 3 CMLR 716 . 10
AKZO Chemie BV v Commission: 53/85 [1986] ECR 1965, [1987] 1 CMLR 231: 247
AM and S Europe Ltd v Commission: 155/79 [1982] ECR 1575, [1982] 2 CMLR 264 .... 247, 257, 267
APESCO v Commission: 207/86 [1989] 3 CMLR 687 242
ARPOSOL v Council: 55/86 [1988] ECR 13, [1989] 2 CMLR 508 238
ASSIDER v High Authority: 3/54 [1955] ECR 63 270
Adams v Commission: 145/83 and 53/84 [1985] ECR 3540, [1986] 1 CMLR 507 . 283
Administration des Douanes v Vabre [1975] 2 CMLR 336 41
Adoui and Cornuaille v Belgium: 115 and 116/81 [1982] ECR 1665, [1982] 3 CMLR 631 .... 173, 204
Advocate (Lord) v Scotsman Publications Ltd [1989] 2 All ER 852, [1989] 3 WLR 358, HL 12
Agricola Commerciale Olio Srl v Commission: 232/81 [1984] ECR 3881, [1987] 1 CMLR 363 239
Ahlstrom Oy v Commission: 89, 104, 114, 116–117, 125–129/85 [1988] 4 CMLR 901 7
Albini v Council and Commission: 33/80 [1981] ECR 2141 278
Albion Shipping Agency v Arnold [1982] ICR 22, EAT 32
Alcan v Commission: 69/69 [1970] ECR 385, [1970] CMLR 337 .... 241, 271
Alderblum v Caisse Nationale d'Assurance Vieillesse des Travailleurs Salariés de Paris: 93/75 [1975] ECR 2147, [1976] 1 CMLR 236 169
Allen and Hanbury's Ltd v Genenics (UK) Ltd: 434/85 [1988] 2 All ER 454, [1989] 1 WLR 414 181
Allgemeine Gold- und Silbersheideanstalt v Customs and Excise Comrs [1980] QB 390, [1980] 2 All ER 138, CA 12
Alliance des Belges de la CE v Belgium [1979] 3 CMLR 175 13
Allied Corpn v Commission: 239, 275/82 [1984] ECR 1005, [1985] 3 CMLR 572 252
Alusuisse Italia SpA v Council and Commission: 307/81 [1982] ECR 3463, [1983] 3 CMLR 388 251
American Cyanamid v Ethicon [1975] AC 396, [1975] 1 All ER 504 155
Amministrazione delle Finanze v Denkavit Italiana Srl: 61/79 [1980] ECR 1205, [1981] 3 CMLR 394 .... 62, 63, 64
Amministrazione delle Finanze dello Stato v Ariete SpA: 811/79 [1980] ECR 2545, [1981] 1 CMLR 316 .... 62, 63

xvii

Table of cases—alphabetical

	PAGE
Amministrazione delle Finanze dello Stato v Essevi SpA and Salengo: 142 and 143/80 [1981] ECR 1413	62, 63
Amministrazione delle Finanze dello Stato v San Giorgio SpA: 199/82 [1983] ECR 3595, [1985] 2 CMLR 658	64, 66, 77, 146
Amministrazione delle Finanze dello Stato v Salumi Meridionale Industria Srl: 66, 127 and 128/79 [1980] ECR 1237, [1981] 1 CMLR 1	62, 63
Amministrazione delle Finanze dello Stato v Simmenthal SpA: 106/77 [1978] ECR 629, [1978] 3 CMLR 263	19, 31, 67, 69, 197
Amministrazione delle Finanze dello Stato v Società Petrolifera Italiana SpA: 267–269/81 [1983] ECR 801, [1984] 1 CMLR 354	5, 69, 162
Amsterdam Bulb v Produktschap voor Siergewassen: 50/76 [1977] ECR 137, [1977] 2 CMLR 218	75, 76
Amylum v Council and Commission: 116 and 124/77 [1979] ECR 3497, [1982] 2 CMLR 590	285
Amylum v Council (Isoglucose): 108/81 [1982] ECR 3107	265, 268
An Bord Bainne Co-operative Ltd (Irish Dairy Board) v Milk Marketing Board [1984] 2 CMLR 519	100
An Bord Bainne Co-operative Ltd v Milk Marketing Board [1988] 1 CMLR 605	45, 107
An Bord Bainne Co-operative Ltd v Milk Marketing Board (No 2) [1985] 1 CMLR 6	183, 184, 187
An Bord Bainne Co-operative Ltd v Minister for Agriculture: 92/77 [1978] ECR 497, [1978] 2 CMLR 567	265
Apple and Pear Development Council v Customs and Excise Comrs [1987] 2 CMLR 634	137, 140
Apple and Pear Development Council v Lews: 222/82 [1983] ECR 4083, [1984] 3 CMLR 733	62
Application des Gaz SA v Falks Veritas [1974] Ch 381, [1974] 3 All ER 51	103, 131
Application of Kloppenburg, Re [1988] 3 CMLR 1	95, 211
Application of Wünsche. Re [1987] 3 CMLR 225	2, 11, 41, 72
Argyll Group plc v Distillers Co Ltd [1986] 1 CMLR 764	104
Asteris AE v Commission: 194–206/83 [1985] ECR 2815	284
Asteris AE v Commission: 97 etc/86 [1988] 3 CMLR 493	235, 236, 237, 238, 280
Asteris AE v Greece: 106–120/87 (27 September 1988, unreported)	284, 287
A-G v BBC [1981] AC 303, [1980] 3 All ER 161, HL	12
A-G v Burgoa: 812/79 [1980] ECR 2787, [1981] 2 CMLR 193	6, 49, 69
A-G v Guardian Newspapers Ltd [1987] 3 All ER 316, [1987] 1 WLR 1248	12
A-G v Guardian Newspapers Ltd (No 2) [1988] 3 All ER 545, [1988] 2 WLR 805	12
A-G v Nissan [1970] AC 179, [1969] 1 All ER 629, HL	3
A-G v Wilts United Diaries (1922) 127 LT 822	119
A-G for Canada v A-G for Ontario [1937] AC 326	14, 25
Auer v Ministère Public (No 2): 271/82 [1983] ECR 2727, [1985] 1 CMLR 123	87
Autexpo SpA v Commission: 82/87R [1987] ECR 2131, [1988] 3 CMLR 541	273, 242
Azo-Maschinenfabrik Adolf Zimmermann GmbH v Customs and Excise Comrs [1987] 3 CMLR 462	90

B

BP v Commission: 77/77 [1978] ECR 1513, [1978] 3 CMLR 174	235
Bakaert v Procureur de la République Rennes: 204/87 [1988] 2 CMLR 655	173
Balkan-Import-Export v Hauptzollamt Berlin-Packhof: 118/76 [1977] ECR 1177	76
Bank voor Handel en Scheepvaart v Slatford [1953] 1 QB 248, [1952] 2 All ER 956	24

Table of cases—alphabetical

	PAGE
Barge v High Authority: 18/62 [1963] ECR 259, [1965] CMLR 330	265
Barkworth v Customs and Excise Comrs [1988] 3 CMLR 759	140, 186
Barra v Belgium: 309/85 [1988] 2 CMLR 409	61, 65
BayWa AG v Bundesanstalt für Landwirtschaftliche Marktordnung: 146 and 192–193/81 [1982] ECR 1503	76
Bearra Fisheries and Shipping Ltd v Minister for the Marine Ireland [1989] 1 CMLR 840	110
Becher v Commission: 30/66 [1967] ECR 285, [1968] CMLR 169	283
Becker v Finanzamt Münster-Innenstadt: 8/81 [1982] ECR 53, [1982] 1 CMLR 499	45, 74, 86, 87, 95, 159
Bela-Mühle v Grows-Farm (Skimmed Milk Powder): 114/76 [1977] ECR 1211, [1979] 2 CMLR 83	269
Belgische Radio en Televisie v SABAM: 127/73 [1974] ECR 51, [1974] 2 CMLR 238	103, 199
Belgium v Commission: 40/85 [1986] ECR 2321, [1988] 2 CMLR 301	261
Belgium v Commission: 142/87R [1988] 2 CMLR 601	254, 255
Bell Concord Educational Trust Ltd v Customs and Excise Comrs [1989] 1 CMLR 845	138, 140
Bellenden (formerly Satterthwaite) v Satterthwaite [1948] 1 All ER 343	195
Benedetti v Munari: 52/76 [1977] ECR 163	67, 204, 209
Bernstein v Immigration Appeal Tribunal [1988] 3 CMLR 445, CA	186
Bertini v Regione Lazio: 98 etc/85 [1986] ECR 1885, [1987] 1 CMLR 774	164, 172
Bethell (Lord) v Commission: 246/81 [1982] ECR 2277, [1982] 3 CMLR 300:	233, 249, 280
Bethell (Lord) v Sabena [1983] 3 CMLR 1	180
Beus v Hauptzollamt München: 5/67 [1968] ECR 83, [1968] CMLR 131	265, 275
Binderer v Commission: 147/83 [1985] ECR 257	237, 240, 288
Biovilac NV v EEC: 59/83 [1984] ECR 4057	283
Birra Würher SpA v Council and Commission: 256, 257, 265 and 267/80 and 5/81 [1982] ECR 85	285, 288
Blackburn v A-G [1971] 2 All ER 1380, [1971] 1 WLR 1037, [1971] 1 CMLR 784	24, 25, 29, 30, 33
Blaizot v University of Liège: 24/86 [1989] 1 CMLR 57	53, 61, 65
Bock v Commission: 62/70 [1971] ECR 897, [1972] CMLR 160	241, 243
Boehringer v Commission: 7/72 [1972] ECR 1281, [1973] CMLR 864	270
Bollman v Hauptzollamt Hamburg-Waltershof: 62/72 [1973] ECR 269	207
Bork International A/S v Foreningen af Arbejdsleder Danmark [1989] IRLR 41	139
Borker, Re: 138/80 [1980] ECR 1975, [1980] 3 CMLR 638	147
Borromeo v Commission: 6/70 [1970] ECR 815, [1970] CMLR 436	279, 280
Bourgoin SA v Ministry of Agriculture, Fisheries and Food [1986] QB 716, [1985] 3 All ER 585, CA	105, 107, 282
Boussac Saint-Frères SA v Gerstenmeier: 22/80 [1980] ECR 3427, [1982] 1 CMLR 202	167
Bozzetti v Invernizzi SpA: 179/84 [1985] ECR 2301	63
Brack v Insurance Officer: 17/76 [1976] ECR 1429, [1976]) 2 CMLR 592	133, 146
Bresciani v Amministrazione Italiana delle Finanze: 87/75 [1976] ECR 129, [1976] 2 CMLR 62	68, 162
Brewery Solus Agreement, Re [1975] 1 CMLR 611	211
British Airways Board v Laker Airways Ltd [1985] AC 58, [1984] 3 All ER 39	14
BBC v Johns (Inspector of Taxes) [1965] Ch 32, [1964] 1 All ER 923, CA	91
British Coal Corpn v R [1935] AC 500	29
British Leyland Motor Corpn Ltd v Armstrong Patents Co Ltd [1986] AC 577, [1986] 1 All ER 850, HL	187

xx Table of cases—alphabetical

	PAGE
British Leyland Motor Corpn Ltd v TI Silencers Ltd [1981] 2 CMLR 75, CA . . .	187
British Railways Board v Pickin [1974] AC 765, [1974] 1 All ER 609	27, 29

Broekmeulen v Huisarts Registratie Commissie: 246/80 [1981] ECR 2311, [1982] 1 CMLR 91 . . . . 147, 148
Bruce (Lord) of Donington v Aspden: 208/80 [1981] ECR 2205, [1981] 2 CMLR 506. 147
Buchanan (James) & Co Ltd v Babco Forwarding and Shipping (UK) Ltd [1977] QB 208, [1977] 1 All ER 518; affd. [1978] AC 141, [1977] 3 All ER 1048. . . . . 131, 135, 136, 137
Bulgarian Dessert Grapes, Re [1967] CMLR 156. 274
Bulk Oil (Zug) AG v Sun International Ltd [1984] 1 All ER 386, [1984] 1 WLR 147, CA. 149
Bulk Oil (Zug) AG v Sun International Ltd (No 2): 174/84 [1986] 2 All ER 774, [1986] ECR 559, [1986] 2 CMLR 732 150
Bulmer v Bollinger [1974] Ch 401, [1974] 2 All ER 1226 . . . . 152, 174, 176, 177, 178, 191 195, 205
Bulmer v Bollinger [1975] 2 CMLR 479; revsd. [1977] 2 CMLR 625, CA: 131, 184, 205
Burchell v Adjudication Officer: 377/85 [1987] ECR 3329, [1987] 3 CMLR 757 . 146
Burton v British Railways Board: 19/81 [1982] ECR 555, [1982] 2 CMLR 136, [1982] QB 1080; subsequent proceedings [1983] 1 All ER 1094 . . . . 88, 147, 208
Bussone v Italian Ministry of Agriculture and Forestry: 31/78 [1978] ECR 2429, [1978] 3 CMLR 18 76
Buttes Gas and Oil Co v Hammer (Nos 2 and 3) [1982] AC 888, [1981] 3 All ER 616. . . . . 24, 168

C

CAM SA v Commission: 100/74 [1975] ECR 1393 239
CFDT v European Communities: 8030/77 [1979] 2 CMLR 229 13
CICCE v Commission: 298/83 [1985] ECR 1105, [1986] 1 CMLR 486 249
CIDA v Council: 197/86 [1989] 3 CMLR 851 . . . . 240, 244
CILFIT Srl v Ministry of Health: 283/81 [1982] ECR 3415, [1983] 1 CMLR 472. . . . . 131, 144, 158, 159, 204, 209
CNTA v Commission: 74/74 [1975] ECR 533, [1977] 1 CMLR 171; [1976] ECR 797. . . . . 268, 284
COFAZ v Commission: 169/84 [1986] ECR 391, [1986] 3 CMLR 385 . . . . 227, 255
Cadillon v Höss: 1/71 [1971] ECR 351, [1971] CMLR 420 202
Calpak SpA v Commission: 789/79 [1980] ECR 1949, [1981] 1 CMLR 26 . . . . 237, 238
Camera Care Ltd v Commission: 792/79R [1980] ECR 119, [1980] 1 CMLR 334. . . . . 246, 274, 279
Camera Care Ltd v Hasselblad [1986] 1 FTLR 348, CA 103
Campus Oil Ltd v Minister for Industry and Energy: 72/83 [1984] ECR 2727, [1984] 3 CMLR 544 173
Campus Oil Ltd v Minister for Industry and Energy [1984] 1 CMLR 479 197
Canon Inc v Council: 277 and 300/85 [1989] 1 CMLR 915 252
Capalongo v Maya: 77/72 [1973] ECR 611, [1974] 1 CMLR 230 . . . . 55, 59, 123
Carl-Zeiss-Stiftung v Herbert Smith & Co [1969] 1 Ch 93, [1968] 2 All ER 1002 . 178
Casati: 203/80 [1981] ECR 2595, [1982] 1 CMLR 365 172
Casteels Pvba v Commission: 40/84 [1985] ECR 667, [1986] 2 CMLR 475 . . . . 237, 240
Cayne v Global Natural Resources Plc [1984] 1 All ER 225, CA 155, 194
Champlor SA v Commission: 233–235/86 [1987] ECR 2251 . . . . 236, 238
Chanel v Cepeha: 31/68 [1970] ECR 403, [1971] CMLR 403. . . . . 198, 206
Chelmkarm Motors Ltd v Esso Petroleum Co Ltd [1979] 1 CMLR 73 194
Chemial Farmaceutici Spa v DAF SpA: 140/79 [1981] ECR 1, [1981] 3 CMLR 350. 172

Table of cases—alphabetical xxi

	PAGE
Cheney v Conn [1968] 1 All ER 779, [1968] 1 WLR 242	42, 135
Chevalley v Commission: 15/70 [1970] ECR 975	231, 279
Chung Chi Cheung v R [1939] AC 160, [1938] 4 All ER 786	15
Church of Scientology of California v Customs and Excise Comrs [1981] 1 All ER 1035, [1981] STC 65, CA	47, 187
Cie d'Approvisionnement v Commission: 9 and 11/71 [1972] ECR 391, [1973] CMLR 529	286
Cie Française Commerciale v Commission: 63–65/69 [1970] ECR 205, [1970] CMLR 369	238
Cimenteries v Commission: 8–11/66 [1967] ECR 75, [1967] CMLR 77	230, 258, 264, 265
Cinéthèque SA v FNCF: 60, 61/84 [1985] ECR 2604, [1986] 1 CMLR 365	11
Civilian War Claimants v R [1932] AC 14	25
Clarke v Chief Adjudication Officer: 384/85 [1987] ECR 2865, [1987] 3 CMLR 277	146
Clin-Midy SA v Belgium: 301/82 [1984] ECR 251, [1985] 1 CMLR 443	87
Clymo v Wandsworth London Borough Council [1989] ICR 250, EAT	142
Comet v Produktschap voor Siergewassen: 45/76 [1976] ECR 2043, [1977] 1 CMLR 533	63
Commission v Belgium: 77/69 [1970] ECR 237, [1974] 1 CMLR 203	220
Commission v Belgium: 156/77 [1978] ECR 1881	223, 275, 276
Commission v Belgium: 102/79 [1980] ECR 1473, [1981] 1 CMLR 282	83, 88
Commission v Belgium: 68–71/81 [1982] ECR 153	221
Commission v Belgium: 301/81 [1983] ECR 467, [1984] 2 CMLR 430	83
Commission v Belgium: 52/84 [1986] ECR 89	223
Commission v Belgium: 85/85 [1986] ECR 1149, [1987] 1 CMLR 787	219
Commission v Belgium: 293/85 [1989] 2 CMLR 527	219
Commission v Belgium: 9/86 [1987] ECR 1331	221
Commission v Belgium: 134/86 [1987] ECR 2415	221
Commission v Belgium: 255/86 [1989] 3 CMLR 91	74
Commission v Belgium: 298/86 (14 July 1988, unreported)	220
Commission v Council: 22/70 [1971] ECR 263, [1971] CMLR 335	4, 231, 232, 257, 265
Commission v Council: 81/72 [1973] ECR 575, [1973] CMLR 639	257, 270, 272
Commission v Council: 45/86 [1987] ECR 1493, [1988] 2 CMLR 131	265
Commission v Denmark: 143/83 [1985] ECR 427, [1986] 1 CMLR 44	84
Commission v France: 6 and 11/69 [1969] ECR 523, [1970] CMLR 43, 15 Rec 523	229, 271
Commission v France: 26/69 [1970] ECR 565, [1970] CMLR 444	220
Commission v France: 167/73 [1974] ECR 359, [1974] 2 CMLR 216	220
Commission v France: 232/78 [1979] ECR 2729, [1980] 1 CMLR 418	222, 226
Commission v France: 152/78 [1980] ECR 2299, [1981] 2 CMLR 743	224
Commission v France: 24/80R and 97/80R [1980] ECR 1319, [1981] 3 CMLR 25:	226
Commission v France: 42/82 [1983] ECR 1013, [1984] 1 CMLR 160	220
Commission v France: 52/83 [1983] ECR 3707, [1985] 3 CMLR 278	223
Commission v Germany: 29/84 [1985] ECR 1661, [1986] 3 CMLR 579	84
Commission v Germany: 74/86 (26 April 1988, unreported)	83
Commission v Germany: 94/87 [1989] 2 CMLR 425	64
Commission v Greece: 194 and 241/85 (25 February 1988, unreported)	217
Commission v Greece: 147/86 (15 March 1988, unreported)	47
Commission v Greece: 240/86 [1989] 3 CMLR 578	220
Commission v Greece: 226/87 [1989] 3 CMLR 569	223
Commission v Greece: 63/87 (7 June 1988, unreported)	223
Commission v Ireland: 61/77 [1978] ECR 417, [1978] 2 CMLR 466	5, 42

xxii *Table of cases—alphabetical*

	PAGE
Commission v Ireland: 249/81 [1982] ECR 4005, [1983] 2 CMLR 104	222
Commission v Ireland: 45/87R [1987] ECR 783, [1987] 2 CMLR 197	224
Commission v Italy: 7/61 [1961] ECR 317, [1962] CMLR 39	219, 220, 229
Commission v Italy: 45/64 [1965] ECR 857, [1966] CMLR 97	220
Commission v Italy: 7/68 [1968] ECR 423, [1969] CMLR 1	21, 226
Commission v Italy: 7/69 [1970] ECR 111, [1970] CMLR 97	220
Commission v Italy: 31/69 [1970] ECR 25, [1970] CMLR 175	220, 222
Commission v Italy: 38/69 [1970] ECR 47, [1970] CMLR 77	80
Commission v Italy: 8/70 [1970] ECR 961	55, 221
Commission v Italy: 48/71 [1972] ECR 527, [1972] CMLR 699	21, 54, 221, 225
Commission v Italy: 39/72 [1973] ECR 101, [1973] CMLR 439	220
Commission v Italy: 172/73 [1974] ECR 475	42
Commission v Italy: 52/75 [1976] ECR 277, [1976] 2 CMLR 320	222
Commission v Italy: 69/77 [1978] ECR 1749, [1979] 1 CMLR 206	220
Commission v Italy: 159/78 [1979] ECR 3247, [1980] 3 CMLR 446	47, 220
Commission v Italy: 136/81 [1982] ECR 3547	221
Commission v Italy: 300/81 [1983] ECR 449, [1984] 2 CMLR 430	83
Commission v Italy: 145/82 [1983] ECR 711, [1984] 1 CMLR 148	83
Commission v Italy: 103/84 [1986] ECR 1759, [1987] 2 CMLR 825	220
Commission v Italy: 166/82 [1984] ECR 459, [1985] 2 CMLR 615	220
Commission v Italy: 17/85 [1986] ECR 1199	221
Commission v Italy: 154/85 [1987] ECR 2717, [1988] 2 CMLR 951	220
Commission v Italy: 154/85R [1985] ECR 1753, [1986] 2 CMLR 159	227
Commission v Italy: 168/85 [1986] ECR 2945, [1988] 1 CMLR 580, ECJ	47, 83
Commission v Italy: 262/85 [1987] ECR 3073	83
Commission v Italy: 364/85 [1987] ECR 487	221
Commission v Italy: 69/86 [1987] ECR 773	226
Commission v Italy: 116/86 (3 March 1988, unreported)	83
Commission v Italy: [1989] 3 CMLR 25	42, 66
Commission v Luxembourg and Belgium: 90 and 91/63 [1964] ECR 625, [1965] CMLR 58	6, 222
Commission v Netherlands: 96/81 [1982] ECR 1791	83
Commission v Netherlands: 97/81 [1982] ECR 1819	83
Commission v Netherlands: 160/82 [1982] ECR 4637, [1984] 1 CMLR 230	83
Commission v United Kingdom: 128/78 [1979] ECR 419, [1979] 2 CMLR 45	218
Commission v United Kingdom: 231/78 [1979] ECR 1447, [1979] 2 CMLR 427	133, 218
Commission v United Kingdom: 804/79 [1981] ECR 1045, [1982] 1 CMLR 543	218
Commission v United Kingdom: 61/81 [1982] ECR 2601, [1982] 3 CMLR 284	37, 118, 138
Commission v United Kingdom: 40/82 [1982] ECR 2793, [1982] 3 CMLR 497:	105, 218
Commission v United Kingdom: 124/81 [1983] ECR 203, [1983] 2 CMLR 1	218
Commission v United Kingdom: 170/78 [1983] ECR 2265, [1983] 3 CMLR 512	218
Commission v United Kingdom: 207/83 [1985] ECR 1201, [1985] 2 CMLR 259	218, 219
Commission v United Kingdom: 23/84 [1986] ECR 3581, [1987] 1 CMLR 607	218
Commission v United Kingdom: 100/84 [1985] ECR 1169, [1985] 2 CMLR 199	134, 218
Commission v United Kingdom: 93/85 [1986] ECR 4011, [1987] 1 CMLR 895	218
Commission v United Kingdom: 261/85 [1988] 2 CMLR 11	218
Commission v United Kingdom: 353/85 (1988) Times, 24 February	218
Commission v United Kingdom: 60/86 [1988] 3 CMLR 437	84, 218
Commission v United Kingdom: 246/89R [1989] 3 CMLR 601	109, 225

Table of cases—alphabetical xxiii

	PAGE
Commune de Differdange v Commission: 222/83 [1984] ECR 2889, [1985] 3 CMLR 638	241
Compagnie Alitalia [1990] 1 CMLR 248	94
Concorde Express Ltd v Traffic Examiner Metropolitan Area [1980] 2 CMLR 221	218

Concrete Reinforcement Bars, Re: SpA Ferriera Valsabbia v Commission. *See* Ferriera Valsabbia SpA v Commission

Conegate Ltd v Customs and Excise Comrs: 121/85 [1986] ECR 1007, [1986] 1 CMLR 739	6
Consorzio Cooperative d'Abruzzo v Commission: 15/85 [1987] ECR 1005, [1988] 1 CMLR 841	223

Continental Can Case. *See* Europemballage and Continental Can v Commission: 6/72

Control Data Belgium NV v Commission: 294/81 [1983] ECR 911, [1983] 2 CMLR 357	240, 243, 264
Cooperativa Veneta Allevatori Equini v Commission: 191/87 [1989] 3 CMLR 420	237
Copyright Owners Reproduction Society Ltd v EMI (1958) 100 CLR 597	29
Corocraft v Pan American Airways [1969] 1 QB 616, [1969] 1 All ER 82	137
Costa v ENEL: 6/64 [1964] ECR 585, [1964] CMLR 425; further proceedings [1968] CMLR 267	2, 4, 17, 22, 31, 49, 50, 51, 53, 59, 151, 164, 165, 202
Council of Civil Service Unions v Minister for the Civil Service [1985] AC 374, [1984] 3 All ER 935, HL	268
Council v Parliament: 34/86 [1986] ECR 2155, [1986] 3 CMLR 94	234
Cowan v Le Trésor Public: 186/87 (1989) Times, 13 February	53
Cremonini and Vrankovich: 815/79 [1980] ECR 3583, [1981] 3 CMLR 49	45
Crotty v An Taoiseach [1987] IR 713, [1987] 2 CMLR 666	22
Cunningham v Milk Marketing Board for Northern Ireland [1988] 3 CMLR 815	74, 134
Customs and Excise Comrs v ApS Samex [1983] 1 All ER 1042	131, 133, 144, 181, 184
Customs and Excise Comrs v Cure & Deeley Ltd [1962] QB 340, [1961] 3 All ER 641	120, 276
Customs and Excise Comrs v Fine Art Developments plc [1989] AC 914, [1989] 1 All ER 502, HL	104
Cutsforth v Mansfield Inns Ltd [1986] 1 All ER 577, [1986] 1 WLR 558	104

D

DEFI v Commission: 282/85 [1986] ECR 2469, [1988] 2 CMLR 156	242, 254
Da Costa v Nederlandse Belastingadministratie: 28–30/62 [1963] ECR 31, [1963] CMLR 224	157, 209
Danzig Railway Officials Case (1928) PCIJ, Series B. No. 15, pp. 19–23	8
David (Lawrence) Ltd v Ashton [1989] ICR 123	155
Debayser v Commission: 12, 18 and 21 [1978] ECR 553, [1978] 3 CMLR 361	287
De Bloos v Bouyer: 59/77 [1977] ECR 2359, [1978] 1 CMLR 511	230, 275
De Cicco v Landesversicherungsanstalt Schwaben: 19/68 [1968] ECR 473, [1969] CMLR 67	206
Decker v Hauptzollamt Landau: 99/78 [1979] ECR 101	271
Defrenne v Sabena (No 2): 43/75 [1976] ECR 455, [1976] 2 CMLR 98	53, 60
Defrenne v Sabena: 149/77 [1978] ECR 1365, [1978] 3 CMLR 312	8
De Geus v Bosch: 13/61 [1962] ECR 45, [1962] CMLR 1	143, 165, 198, 207
Delhaize Frères 'Le Lion' SA v Belgium: 2–4/82 [1983] ECR 2973, [1985] 1 CMLR 561	198

Table of cases—alphabetical

PAGE

Delkvist v Anklagemyndigheden: 21/78 [1978] ECR 2327, [1979] 1 CMLR 372: 88
Demirel v Stadt Schwäbisch Gmünd: 12/86 [1987] ECR 3719, [1989] 1 CMLR 412 .... 11, 45, 68, 162
Demo-Studio Schmidt v Commission: 210/81 [1983] ECR 3045, [1984] 1 CMLR 63 .... 233, 248
Demouche v Fonds de Garantie Automobile: 152/83 [1987] ECR 3833 ...... 163, 198
Denkavit v Commission: 14/78 [1978] ECR 2497 229
Denkavit Futtermittel GmbH v Germany: 233/81 [1982] ECR 2933 76
Denkavit Nederland v Produktschap voor Zuivel: 35/80 [1981] ECR 45 265
Deportation of Aliens, Re [1977] 2 CMLR 255 211
Detergents Directive, Re, Commission v Italy: 91/79 [1980] ECR 1099, [1981] 1 CMLR 331 6
Deutsche Milchkontor GmbH v Germany: 205–215/82 [1983] ECR 2633 64
Deutz und Gelderman v Council: 26/86 [1987] ECR 941, [1988] 1 CMLR 668 .. 237
Développement SA v Commission 267/82 [1986] ECR 1907, [1989] 1 CMLR 309 283
Deville v Administration des Impôts 240/87 [1989] 3 CMLR 611 65
Diamantarbeiders v Brachfeld: 2–3/69 [1969] ECR 211, [1969] CMLR 335 ... 54, 123
Dietz v Commission: 126/76 [1977] ECR 2431, [1978] 2 CMLR 608 287
Direct Cosmetics Ltd v Customs and Excise Comrs: 5/84 [1985] ECR 617, [1985] 2 CMLR 145 .... 87, 147
Direct Cosmetics v Customs and Excise Comrs: 138–139/86 [1988] 3 CMLR 333 .... 147, 211
Direct Cosmetics Ltd v South Hampshire Area Health Authority [1986] QB 401 95
DPP v Sidney Hackett Ltd: 91–92/84 [1985] ECR 1139, [1985] 2 CMLR 213 ... 218
Distillers Co Ltd v Commission: 30/78 [1980] ECR 2229, [1980] 3 CMLR 121 .. 262
Draft Agreement Establishing a European Laying-Up Fund for Inland Waterways: 1/76 [1977] ECR 741, [1977] 2 CMLR 279 5
Draft Convention of the IAEA on the Physical Protection of Nuclear Materials, Facilities and Transports: 1/78 [1978] ECR 2151, [1979] 1 CMLR 131 5
Draft International Agreement on Natural Rubber: 1/78 [1979] ECR 2871, [1979] 3 CMLR 639 5
Duke v GEC Reliance Ltd [1988] AC 618, [1988] 1 All ER 626, HL 35, 49, 91, 97, 98, 141, 142
Dumortier Frères SA v Council: 64 etc/76, 239/78, 27 etc/79 [1979] ECR 3091 .. 285
Dürbeck v Hauptzollamt Frankfurt. *See* Firma Anton Dürbeck
Dyestuffs Case. *See* ICI v Commission: 48/69

E

EMI Records Ltd v CBS United Kingdom Ltd [1975] 1 CMLR 285 .... 184, 191
ERTA, Re: Commission v Council. *See* Commission v Council: 22/70
Eier-Kontor v Council and Commission: 44/76 [1977] ECR 393 .... 285, 288
Einberger v Hauptzollamt Freiburg: 240/81 [1982] ECR 3699, [1983] 2 CMLR 170 209
Ellerman Lines v Murray [1931] AC 126 135
Enka v Inspecteur der Invoerrechten en Accijnzen: 38/77 [1977] ECR 2203, [1978] 2 CMLR 212 88
Entreprises Garoche v Société Striker Boats (Nederland) [1974] 1 CMLR 469 .. 211
Eridania v Commission: 10 and 18/68 [1969] ECR 459 .... 241, 242, 279, 281
Esso Petroleum Co Ltd v Kingswood Motors (Addlestone) Ltd [1974] QB 142, [1973] 3 All ER 1057, [1973] CMLR 665 .... 44, 194
Eunomia di Porro v Ministry of Education: 18/71 [1971] ECR 811, [1972] CMLR 4 .... 21, 54, 59, 123

Table of cases—alphabetical xxv

	PAGE
European School in Brussels, Re [1987] 2 CMLR 57	13
Europemballage and Continental Can v Commission: 6/72 [1973] ECR 215, [1973] CMLR 199	259
Exécutif Régional Wallon v Commission: 62 and 72/87 [1989] 2 CMLR 771	254
Expatriate United Kingdom Citizen, Re An [1979] 3 CMLR 172	13
Exportation des Sucres v Commission: 88/76 [1977] ECR 709	235
Exportation des Sucres v Commission: 132/77 [1978] ECR 1061, [1979] 1 CMLR 309	286
Express Dairy Foods Ltd v Intervention Board for Agricultural Produce: 130/79 [1980] ECR 1887, [1981] 1 CMLR 451	76

F

FEDESA v Council: 160/88R [1988] 3 CMLR 534	238, 273
FEDETAB v Commission [1980] ECR 3125, [1981] 3 CMLR 134	10
FEDIOL v Commission: 191/82 [1983] ECR 2913, [1984] 3 CMLR 244	253, 267
FIVA v Mertens [1963] CMLR 141	211
Factortame Ltd v Secretary of State for Transport. See R v Secretary of State for Transport, ex p Factortame Ltd.	
Fa Karl-Heinz Neumann v BALM: 299/84 [1985] ECR 3663, [1987] 3 CMLR 4	204
Fees for Examination of Imported Oranges, Re [1975] 2 CMLR 415	41
Felicitas Rickmers-Linie KG & Co v Finanzamt Hamburg: 270/81 [1982] ECR 2771, [1982] 3 CMLR 447	86
Felixstowe Dock and Rly Co v British Transport Docks Board [1976] 2 CMLR 655	30
Ferriera Valsabbia SpA v Commission: 154 etc/78 and 39 etc/79 [1980] ECR 907, [1981] 1 CMLR 613	10
Ferwerda BV v Produktschap voor vee en Vlees: 265/78 [1980] ECR 617, [1980] 3 CMLR 737	77
Fink-Frucht v Hauptzollamt München: 27/67 [1968] ECR 223, [1968] CMLR 228	58
Firma Anton Dürbeck v Hauptzollamt Frankfurt am Main-Flughafen: 112/80 [1981] ECR 1095, [1982] 3 CMLR 314	5, 268
Foglia v Novello (No 1): 104/79 [1980] ECR 745, [1981] 1 CMLR 45	144, 146, 170, 204
Foglia v Novello (No 2): 244/80 [1981] ECR 3045, [1982] 1 CMLR 585	172
Ford of Europe Inc v Commission: 228 and 229/82 [1984] ECR 1129, [1984] 1 CMLR 649	240, 246, 258
Ford Werke AG v Commission: 228–229/82R [1982] ECR 3091, [1982] 3 CMLR 673	274
Foster v British Gas plc [1988] 2 CMLR 697, CA	91
Fothergill v Monarch Airlines Ltd [1981] AC 251, [1980] 2 All ER 696, HL	136
Foto-Frost v Hauptzollamt Lübeck-Ost: 314/85 [1988] 3 CMLR 57	213
Fragd v Amministrazione delle Finanze dello Stato: 33/84 [1985] ECR 1605	272
France v United Kingdom: 141/78 [1979] ECR 2923, [1980] 1 CMLR 6	227
Fratelli Pardini SpA v Ministry of Foreign Trade: 338/85. (21 April 1988, unreported)	146
French Widow's Pension Settlement, Re [1971] CMLR 530	157
Frimodt Pedersen v Commission: 30/86 [1987] ECR 3123	252
Fromançais SA v FORMA: 66/82 [1985] ECR 395, [1983] 3 CMLR 453	269
Fromme v Bundesanstalt für Landwirtschaftliche Marktordnung: 54/81 [1982] ECR 1449	76
Frontini v Minister of Finance [1974] 2 CMLR 372	42

G

	PAGE
GEMA v Commission: 125/78 [1979] ECR 3173, [1980] 2 CMLR 177	250, 281
Galli: 31/74 [1975] ECR 47, [1975] 1 CMLR 211	73
Garden Cottage Foods Ltd v Milk Marketing Board [1984] AC 130, [1983] 2 All ER 770, [1983] 3 WLR 143, HL	48, 100, 103, 156, 194
Garland v British Rail Engineering Ltd: 12/81 [1983] 2 AC 751, [1982] 2 All ER 402, [1982] ECR 359, [1982] 1 CMLR 696, HL	35, 43, 45, 129, 136, 137, 160, 211
Gauff v Commission: 182/80 [1982] ECR 799, [1982] 3 CMLR 402	234, 279
Gebroeders Beentjes BV v Netherlands: 31/87 (20 September 1988, unreported)	84, 87
General Medical Council v Spackman [1943] AC 627, [1943] 2 All ER 337	262
German Property Administrator v Knoop [1933] Ch 439	25
Germany v Commission: 24/62 [1963] ECR 63, [1963] CMLR 347	263, 264
Germany v Commission 34/62 [1963] ECR 131, [1963] CMLR 369	257, 263, 271
Germany v Commission: 52 and 55/65 [1966] ECR 159, [1967] CMLR 22	230, 270
Germany v Commission: 2/71 [1971] ECR 669, [1972] CMLR 431	271
Germany v Commission: 819/79 [1981] ECR 21	76, 266
Germany v Commission: 44/81 [1982] ECR 1855, [1983] 2 CMLR 656	234, 272
Germany v Commission: 181 etc/85 [1987] ECR 3203, [1988] 1 CMLR 11	271
Getreide-Import v Commission: 38/64 [1965] ECR 203, [1965] CMLR 276	240, 242, 243
Gibson v Lord Advocate 1975 SLT 134, [1975] 1 CMLR 563	45
Giménez Zaera v Instituto Nacional de la Seguridad Social: 126/86 [1987] ECR 3697, [1989] 1 CMLR 827	52, 164
Giordano v Commission: 11/72 [1973] ECR 417	288
Giuffrida and Campogrande v Council: 64/80 [1981] ECR 693	238
Glucoseries Réunies v Commission: 1/64 [1964] ECR 413, [1964] CMLR 596:	240, 242
Grad v Finanzamt Traunstein: 9/70 [1970] ECR 825, [1971] CMLR 1	78, 84
Granaria v PVV: 18/72 [1972] ECR 1163, [1973] CMLR 596:	75
Granaria BV v Council and Commission: 90/78 [1979] ECR 1081	280
Granaria BV v Hoofdproduktschap voor Akkerbouwprodukten: 101/78 [1979] ECR 623, [1978] 3 CMLR 124	169, 275
Grand Duchy of Luxembourg v European Parliament: 230/81 [1983] ECR 255, [1983] 2 CMLR 726	7
Grands Moulins v Commission: 99/74 [1974] ECR 1531	287
Grands Moulins de Paris v Council and Commission: 50/86 [1987] ECR 4833	285
Grasselli v Commission: 23/80 [1980] ECR 3709	272
Gravier v City of Liège: 293/83 [1985] ECR 593, [1985] 3 CMLR 1	61
Greek Canners Association v Commission: 250/81 [1982] ECR 3535, [1983] 2 CMLR 32	238
Greis Unterweger: 318/85 [1986] ECR 955	145
Grendel GmbH v Finanzamt Hamburg: 255/81 [1982] ECR 2301, [1983] 1 CMLR 379	87, 95, 159
Grosoli: 131/73 [1973] ECR 1555, [1974] 2 CMLR 40	76
Group of the European Right v Parliament: 78/85 [1986] ECR 1753, [1988] 3 CMLR 645	234
Groupement des Agences de Voyages Asbl v Commission: 135/81 [1982] ECR 3799	235, 243

H

HNL v Council and Commission: 83 and 94/76, 4, 15 and 40/77 [1978] ECR 1209, [1978] 3 CMLR 566	285
Haage (Friedrich) GmbH: 32/74 [1974] ECR 1201, [1975] 1 CMLR 32	146
Hadmor Productions Ltd v Hamilton [1983] 1 AC 191, [1982] 1 All ER 1042	155, 196

Table of cases—alphabetical xxvii

	PAGE
Haegeman v Commission: 96/71 [1972] ECR 1005, [1973] CMLR 365	287
Haegeman Sprl v Belgium: 181/73 [1974] ECR 449, [1975] 1 CMLR 515	162
Hagen v Einfuhr- und Vorratsstelle für Getreide: 49/71 [1972] ECR 23, [1973] CMLR 35	75
Hagen v Fratelli D and G Moretti SNC [1980] 3 CMLR 253	152, 187
Harrison v Tew [1990] 1 All ER 321	27
Harz v Deutsche Tradax GmbH: 79/83 [1984] ECR 1921	63, 92
Haselhorst v Finanzamt Düsseldorf: 23/70 [1970] ECR 881, [1971] CMLR 1	78
Hasley v Fair Employment Agency [1989] IRLR 106, NICA	32
Hasselblad (GB) Ltd v Commission: 86/82 [1984] 1 CMLR 559	264
Hauer v Land Rheinland-Pfalz: 44/79 [1979] ECR 3727, [1980] 3 CMLR 42	72, 268
Haug-Adrion v Frankfurter Versicherungs AG: 251/83 [1984] ECR 4277	173
Haughton v Olau Line (UK) Ltd [1986] 2 All ER 47, [1986] 1 WLR 504, CA	142
Hauptzollamt Bremen v Bremer Handelsgesellschaft: 72/69 [1970] ECR 427, [1970] CMLR 466	75
Hauptzollamt Bremen v Krohn: 74/69 [1970] ECR 427, [1970] CMLR 466	18, 75
Hauptzollamt Hamburg v Bollmann: 40/69 [1970] ECR 69, [1970] CMLR 141:	74
Hauptzollamt Hamburg-Jonas v Krucken: 316/86 (26 April 1988, unreported)	269
Hauptzollamt Mainz v C A Kupferberg & Cie KG: 104/81 [1982] ECR 3641, [1983] 1 CMLR 1	68, 162, 217
Hayward v Cammell Laird Shipbuilders Ltd [1988] AC 894, [1988] 2 All ER 257, HL	119, 140
Healey's Habeas Corpus Application, Re [1984] 3 CMLR 575	152
Heineken Brouwerijen BV v Inspecteurs der Vennootschapsbelasting: 127/83 [1984] ECR 3435, [1985] 1 CMLR 389	167
Heintz van Landewyck Sarl (FEDETAB) v Commission: 209–215 and 218/78 [1980] ECR 3125, [1981] 3 CMLR 134	10, 264
Henn and Darby v DPP [1981] AC 850, [1980] 2 CMLR 229, sub nom. R v Henn [1980] 1 All ER 166, HL; *see also* R v Henn and Darby: 34/79	40, 47, 101, 131, 133, 152, 159, 160, 185, 188
Herpels v Commission: 54/77 [1978] ECR 585	272
Hessische Knappschaft v Singer: 44/65 [1965] ECR 965, [1966] CMLR 82	205, 277
Hoechst AG v Commission: 46/87, 227/88 (1989) Times, 23 October	10, 267
Hoechst AG v Commission: 46/87R [1987] ECR 1549, [1988] 4 CMLR 430	273
Hoffmann-La Roche v Centrafarm: 107/76 [1977] ECR 957, [1977] 2 CMLR 334	156, 190
Hoffmann-La Roche v Commission: 85/76 [1979] ECR 461, [1979] 3 CMLR 211	261, 283
Hoffmann-La Roche v Secretary of State for Trade and Industry [1975] AC 295, [1974] 2 All ER 1128	282
Holdijk: 141 to 143/81 [1982] ECR 1299, [1983] 2 CMLR 635	172
Holiday in Italy, Re a [1975] 1 CMLR 184	154
Holleran v Daniel Thwaites plc [1989] 2 CMLR 917	104
Holtz and Willemsen GmbH v Council: 134/73 [1974] ECR 1	280
Holtz and Willemsen GmbH v Council and Commission: 153/73 [1974] ECR 675, [1975] 1 CMLR 91	286
Howell v Falmouth Boat Construction [1951] AC 837, [1951] 2 All ER 278	119
Hugh-Jones v St John's College. Cambridge [1979] ICR 848, EAT	88
Humblet v Belgium: 6/60 [1960] ECR 559	63
Humblot v Directeur des Services Fiscaux: 112/84 [1985] ECR 1367, [1986] 2 CMLR 338	64
Hurd v Jones (Inspector of Taxes): 44/84 [1986] ECR 29, [1986] 2 CMLR 1	147, 162

xxviii *Table of cases—alphabetical*

PAGE

I

IBC v Commission: 46/75 [1976] ECR 65 287
IBM v Commission: 60/81 [1981] ECR 2639, [1981] 3 CMLR 635 ...... 232, 233, 247
IBM v Commission: 60 and 190/81R [1981] ECR 1857, [1981] 3 CMLR 93 274
ICI v Commission: 48/69 [1972] ECR 619, [1972] CMLR 557 ..... 257, 258, 259, 267
IFG v Commission: 68/77 [1978] ECR 353, [1978] 2 CMLR 733 285
Iannelli v Meroni: 74/76 [1977] ECR 557, [1977] 2 CMLR 688 .... 57, 73
Ilford v Commission: 1/84R [1984] 2 CMLR 475 243
Import Duties on Mutton Case. See Germany v Commission: 52 and 55/65
Import Duties on Sweet Oranges Case. See Germany v Commission: 34/62
Import of Milk, Re: Commission v Luxembourg and Belgium. See Commission v Luxembourg and Belgium: 90 and 91/63
Industria Molitoria Imolese v Council: 30/67 [1968] ECR 115 238
IRC v Collco Dealings Ltd [1962] AC 1, [1961] 1 All ER 762................. 42, 135
IRC v National Federation of Self-Employed and Small Businesses Ltd [1982] AC 617, [1981] 2 All ER 93 .... 235, 278
Interagra SA v Commission: 217/81 [1982] ECR 2233 287
Intermills SA v Commission: 323/82 [1984] ECR 3809, [1986] 1 CMLR 614.... 254
International Chemical Corpn SpA v Amministrazione delle Finanze dello Stato: 66/80 [1981] ECR 1191, [1983] 2 CMLR 593 .... 212, 275
International Fruit Co v Commission: 41–44/70 [1971] ECR 411, [1975] 2 CMLR 515 239
International Fruit Co NV v Produktschap voor Groenten en Fruit: 21–24/72 [1972] ECR 1219, [1975] 2 CMLR 1 .... 5, 162
International Sales and Agencies Ltd v Marcus [1982] 3 All ER 551, [1982] 2 CMLR 46 140
International Tin Council, Re [1987] Ch 419, [1987] 1 All ER 890; affd [1989] Ch 309, [1988] 3 All ER 257, CA 15
Internationale Handelsgesellschaft v Einfuhr-und Vorratsstelle für Getreide: 11/70 [1970] ECR 1125, [1972] CMLR 255 .... 8, 19, 70
Internationale Handelsgesellschaft v Einfuhr-und Vorratsstelle für Getreide: [1972] CMLR 177 2
Internationale Handelsgesellschaft mbH v Einfuhr-und Vorratsstelle für Getreide: [1974] 2 CMLR 540 2
Intervention Buying, Re [1978] 2 CMLR 644 72
Ireks-Arkady GmbH v Council and Commission: 238/78 [1979] ECR 2955..... 285, 287
Ireland, an Absence in, Re [1977] 1 CMLR 5 32
Irish Cement Co Ltd v Commission: 166 and 220/86 [1989] 2 CMLR 57 282
Irish Creamery Milk Suppliers Association v Ireland: 36 and 71/80 [1981] ECR 735, [1981] 2 CMLR 455 .... 166, 172, 197
Italy v Commission: 13/63 [1963] ECR 165, [1963] CMLR 289 271
Italy v Commission: 32/64 [1965] ECR 365, [1967] CMLR 207 271
Italy v Commission: 12/78 [1979] ECR 1731, [1980] 2 CMLR 573 268
Italy v Commission: 1251/79 [1981] ECR 205, [1981] 3 CMLR 110 266
Italy v Council and Commission: 32/65 [1966] ECR 389, [1969] CMLR 39 ..... 271, 276, 278

J

Japanese Ball Bearing Cases: 113, 118–121/77 [1979] ECR 1185, [1979] 2 CMLR 257.. 252
Japanese Ball Bearings (Nippon Seiko): 119/77R [1977] ECR 1867; 119/77 [1979] ECR 1303, [1979] 2 CMLR 257 .... 273, 287
Jeffrey v Evans [1964] 1 All ER 536, [1964] 1 WLR 505 154

Table of cases—alphabetical   xxix

PAGE
Jenkins v Kingsgate (Clothing Productions) Ltd: 96/80 [1981] ECR 911, [1981]
2 CMLR 24 .... 147, 209
Jensen v Corpn of the Trinity House of Deptford [1982] 2 Lloyd's Rep 14,
CA 45, 47, 52, 53, 101, 103, 123
Johnson and Firth Brown Ltd v Commission: 3/75R [1975] ECR 1, [1975] 1
CMLR 638 273
Johnston v Chief Constable of the Royal Ulster Constabulary: 222/84 [1987] QB
129, [1986] 3 All ER 135, [1986] ECR 1651, [1986] 3 CMLR 240 .... 10, 84, 89, 93,
94, 95
Just (Hans) v Danish Ministry for Fiscal Affairs: 68/79 [1980] ECR 501   65

K
Kampffmeyer v Commission: 5, 7 and 13–24/66 [1967] ECR 245 .... 283, 287, 288
Kampffmeyer v Commission and Council: 56–60/74 [1976] ECR 711 .... 285, 288
Kenny v National Insurance Comr [1978] ECR 1489, [1978] 3 CMLR 651, ECJ: 53
King-Emperor v Benoari Lal Sarma [1945] AC 14, [1945] 1 All ER 210 119
Kloppenburg v Finanzamt Leer: 70/83 [1984] ECR 1075, [1985] 1 CMLR 205.... 87,
94, 95
Komponistenverband v Commission: 8/71 [1971] ECR 705, [1973] CMLR 902 .. 281,
282
Könecke v Commission: 76/79 [1980] ECR 665 271
Koninklijke Scholten Honig NV v Council and Commission: 101/76 [1977]
ECR 797 .... 236, 237, 238, 275
Koninklijke Scholten Honig v Hoofdproduktschap voor Akkerbouwprodukten:
125/77 [1978] ECR 1991, [1979] 1 CMLR 675 275
Krohn & Co v Commission: 175/84 [1986] ECR 753, [1987] 1 CMLR 745 ..... 286, 287
Kühne v Finanzamt München: 50/88 (1989) Times, 2 August   87
Kwekerij Gebr Van der Kooy BV v Commission: 67 etc/85 [1989] 2 CMLR 804: 255

L
Lansing Bagnall Ltd v Buccaneer Lift Parts Ltd [1984] 1 CMLR 224, CA 187
Lapeyre v Administration des Douanes [1967] CMLR 362 157
Lawlor v Minister for Agriculture [1988] 3 CMLR 22 131
Lee v Minister of Agriculture: 152/79 [1980] ECR 1495, [1980] 2 CMLR 682 209
L'Etoile Commerciale v Commission: 89 and 91/86 [1987] ECR 3005, [1988] 3
CMLR 564 .... 241, 278, 286, 287
Leonesio v Italian Ministry of Agriculture: 93/71 [1972] ECR 287, [1973]
CMLR 343   75
Lerose Ltd v Hawick Jersey International Ltd [1973] CMLR 83 194
Les Fils de Jules Bianco SA v Directeur Général des Douanes [1989] 3 CMLR
36   66
Lesage v Hauptzollamt Freiburg: 20/70 [1970] ECR 861, [1971] CMLR 1   78
Lesieur Cotelle v Commission: 67–85/75 [1976] ECR 391, [1976] 2 CMLR 185: 287
Levantina Agricola Industrial SA v Council: 35/86 [1988] 2 CMLR 420......... 283
Leverton v Clwyd County Council [1989] IRLR 239; affd [1989] AC 706, [1989]
1 All ER 78, HL... 53, 140
Lion and Loiret & Haentjens v FIRS: 293/81 [1982] ECR 3887 265
Lion Laboratories Ltd v Evans [1985] QB 526, [1984] 2 All ER 417, CA   12
Litster v Forth Dry Dock and Engineering Co Ltd [1989] 1 All ER 1134, [1989]
2 WLR 634, HL..................................... 38, 43, 99, 118, 139
Livestock Sales Transport Ltd v Intervention Board for Agricultural Produce:
162/86 [1988] 2 CMLR 186.. 211
Löwenbraü München v Grunhalle Lager International Ltd [1974] 1 CMLR 1 176,
191

xxx Table of cases—alphabetical

PAGE

Ludwigshafener Walzmühle v Council and Commission: 197 to 200, 243, 245
and 247/80 [1981] ECR 3211 .... 284, 286, 287
Lütticke v Commission: 48/65 [1966] ECR 19, [1966] CMLR 378 ...... 228, 230, 280
Lütticke v Commission: 4/69 [1971] ECR 325 286
Lütticke v Hauptzollamt Saarlouis: 57/65 [1966] ECR 205, [1971] CMLR 674 .. 55,
57, 210
Luxembourg v European Parliament: 230/81 [1983] ECR 255, [1983] 2 CMLR
726 229

M

M (Miss) v Commission: 155/78 [1980] ECR 1797 267
Maas & Co NY v BALM: 21/85 [1986] ECR 3537, [1987] 3 CMLR 794 269
Macarthys Ltd v Smith [1979] 3 All ER 325, [1979] ICR 785, [1979] 1 WLR
1189, [1979] 3 CMLR 44, CA; 129/79 [1980] ECR 1275, [1980] 2 CMLR 205,
ECJ; [1981] QB 180, [1981] 1 All ER 111, CA 32, 33, 45, 53, 166
McDermott and Cotter v Minister for Social Welfare and A-G: 286/85 [1987]
ECR 1453, [1987] 2 CMLR 607 89
Mackprang v Commission: 15/71 [1971] ECR 797, [1972] CMLR 52 280
MacMahon v Department of Education and Science [1983] Ch 227, [1982] 3
WLR 1129 183
McWhirter v A-G [1972] CMLR 882 .... 24, 26
Madzimbamuto v Lardner-Burke [1969] 1 AC 645, [1968] 3 All ER 561 .... 15, 29
Magnavision NV v General Optical Council [1987] 1 CMLR 887 .... 153, 186
Magnavision NV v General Optical Council (No 2) [1987] 2 CMLR 262 186
Maizena GmbH v BALM: 137/85 [1987] ECR 4587, [1989] 2 CMLR 336 9
Malone v Metropolitan Police Commissioner (No 2) [1979] Ch 344, [1979] 2 All
ER 620, [1979] 2 WLR 700 .... 12, 24
Mannesmann-Röhrenwerke AG v Council: 333/85 [1987] ECR 1381, [1988] 2
CMLR 627 238
Manuel v A-G [1983] 1 Ch 77, [1982] 3 All ER 786; affd [1982] 3 All ER 822 27
Manzoni v FNROM: 112/76 [1977] ECR 1647, [1978] 2 CMLR 416 275
Mareva Compania Naviera SA v International Bulk-carriers SA [1975] 2 Lloyd's
Rep 509 112
Marshall v Southampton and South West Hampshire Area Health Authority:
152/84 [1986] QB 401, [1986] 2 All ER 584, [1986] ECR 723 .... 35, 89
Marshall v Southampton and South West Hampshire Area Health Authority
(No 2) [1988] 3 CMLR 389 97
Mattheus v Doego: 93/78 [1978] ECR 2203, [1979] 1 CMLR 551 .... 169, 204
Maxim's Ltd v Dye [1978] 2 All ER 55, [1977] 1 WLR 1155, [1977] 2 CMLR
410 .... 194, 205, 208
Meijer BV v Department of Trade [1978] 2 CMLR 563; 118/78 [1979] ECR
1387, [1979] 2 CMLR 398 218
Merkur v Commission: 43/72 [1973] ECR 1055 .... 286, 287
Metro SB-Grossmärkte GmbH & Co KG v Commission: 26/76 [1977] ECR
1875, [1978] 2 CMLR 1 .... 233, 248
Metro SB-Grossmärkte GmbH & Co KG v Commission: 75/84 [1986] ECR
3021, [1987] 1 CMLR 188 248
Metzger v DHSS [1977] 3 All ER 444, [1978] 1 WLR 1046 172
Meyer-Burckhardt v Commission: 9/75 [1975] ECR 1171 229
Milchkontor v Hauptzollamt Saarbrücken: 29/68 [1969] ECR 165, [1969]
CMLR 390 209
Miliangos v George Frank (Textiles) Ltd [1976] AC 443, [1975] 3 All ER 801 ... 111
Minister for Economic Affairs v SA Fromagerie Franco-Suisse Le Ski [1972]
CMLR 330 241

Table of cases—alphabetical xxxi

	PAGE
Minister of Agriculture, Fisheries and Food, ex p Jaderow Ltd: C-216/87 (1990) Times, 19 January	181
Minister of the Interior v Daniel Cohn-Bendit [1980] 1 CMLR 543	94, 95
Ministère Public v Asjes: 209–213/84 [1986] ECR 1425, [1986] 3 CMLR 173	172, 173
Ministère Public v Déserbais: 286/86 [1989] 1 CMLR 516	6
Ministère Public v Gauchard: 20/87 [1987] ECR 4879	173
Ministère Public v Grunert: 88/79 [1980] ECR 1827	86
Ministère Public v Kugelmann: 108/80 [1981] ECR 433	86
Ministère Public v Lefèvre: 188/86 [1987] ECR 2963	166
Ministère Public v Mathot: 98/86 [1987] ECR 809, [1988] 1 CMLR 411	167
Ministère Public v Mutsch [1985] ECR 2681, [1986] 1 CMLR 648	45
Ministère Public v Traen: 372–374/85 [1987] ECR 2141, [1988] 3 CMLR 511	86, 90
Ministère Public Luxembourgeois v Müller: 10/71 [1971] ECR 723	56, 58, 60
Minnesota Mining and Manufacturing Co v Geerpres Europe Ltd [1973] CMLR 259	194
Moksel v Commission: 45/81 [1982] ECR 1129	238
Molkerei-Zentrale Westfalen v Hauptzollamt Paderborn: 28/67 [1968] ECR 143, [1968] CMLR 187	52, 57, 58, 59, 63, 210
Morris (Phillip) Holland BV v Commission: 730/79 [1980] ECR 2671, [1981] 2 CMLR 321	254
Morson and Jhanjan v Netherlands: 36/82 [1982] ECR 3723, [1983] 2 CMLR 221	155
Moser v Land Baden-Württemberg: 180/83 [1984] ECR 2539, [1984] 3 CMLR 720	164, 172
Moulins Pont-à-Mousson v Office Interprofessional des Céréales (Gritz): 124/76 and 20/77 [1977] ECR 1795, [1979] 2 CMLR 445	269
Murphy v An Bord Telecom Eireann [1988] 1 CMLR 879	45
Murphy v An Bord Telecom Eireann [1988] 2 CMLR 753	20
Musique Diffusion Française SA v Commission: 100–103/80 [1983] ECR 1825, [1983] 3 CMLR 221	10, 247, 261
Mutasa v A-G [1980] QB 114, [1979] 3 All ER 257	12

N

NTN Tokyo Bearing Co Ltd v Council: 240/84 [1987] ECR 1809, [1989] 2 CMLR 76	252
NWL Ltd v Woods [1979] 3 All ER 614, [1979] 1 WLR 1294	194
National Panasonic (UK) Ltd v Commission: 136/79 [1980] ECR 2033, [1980] 3 CMLR 169	10, 247, 262, 264
National Smokeless Fuels Ltd v IRC [1986] 3 CMLR 227, [1986] STC 300	90, 95, 133, 140
Nederlandse Spoorwegen v Minister Verkeer en Waterstaat: 36/73 [1973] ECR 1299, [1974] 2 CMLR 148	146
Netherlands v Commission: 13/72 [1973] ECR 27, [1974] 1 CMLR 161	266
Netherlands v FNV: 71/85 [1986] ECR 3855, [1987] 3 CMLR 767	89
Netherlands and Leeuwarder Papierwaren-Fabriek v Commission: 296 and 318/82 [1985] ECR 809, [1985] 3 CMLR 380	266
Neumann v Hauptzollamt Hof: 17/67 [1967] ECR 441	18, 22
Newstead v Department of Transport 192/85 [1987] ECR 4753, [1988] 1 CMLR 19	147, 181
Nicolo, Re [1990] ICMLR 173	41
Nissan v A-G [1970] AC 179, [1969] 1 All ER 629	24
Nold v Commission: 4/73 [1974] ECR 491, [1974] 2 CMLR 338	9
Noordwijks Cement Accoord Case. See Cimenteries v Commission: 8–11/66	

xxxii *Table of cases—alphabetical*

	PAGE
Nordgetreide v Commission: 42/71 [1972] ECR 105, [1973] CMLR 177	229, 281
Nordsee v Reederei Mond: 102/81 [1982] ECR 1095	148, 149
North Kerry Milk Products Ltd v Minister for Agriculture and Fisheries [1976] 2 CMLR 680; 80/76: [1977] ECR 425, [1977] 2 CMLR 769	134
Norwest Holst Ltd v Secretary of State for Trade [1978] Ch 201, [1978] 3 All ER 280, CA	262

O

OCE v Samavins: 74/79 [1980] ECR 239	169
OECD Understanding on a Local Cost Standard: 1/75 [1975] ECR 1355, [1976] 1 CMLR 85	5
O'Brien v Sim-Chem Ltd [1980] 2 All ER 307, [1980] 1 WLR 734, CA; revsd [1980] 3 All ER 132, [1980] 1 WLR 1011, HL	95
Office National des Pensions pour Travailleurs Salariés v Damiani: 53/79 [1980] ECR 273, [1981] 1 CMLR 548	164
Officier van Justitie v Kolpinghuis Nijmegen BV: 80/86 [1987] ECR 3969, [1989] 2 CMLR 18	45, 84, 90
Officier van Justitie v Kramer: 3, 4 and 6/76 [1976] ECR 1279, [1976] 2 CMLR 440	5
Open University v Customs and Excise Comrs [1982] 2 CMLR 572	137
Openbaar Ministerie v Bout: 21/81 [1982] ECR 81, [1982] 2 CMLR 371	268
O'Reilly v Mackman [1983] 2 AC 237, [1982] 3 All ER 1124	216
Osman v Customs and Excise Comrs [1989] STC 596	140

P

Pabst and Richarz KG v Hauptzollamt Oldenburg: 17/81 [1982] ECR 1331, [1983] 3 CMLR 11	45, 68
Pan American World Airways v Department of Trade [1976] 1 Lloyd's Rep 257	24
Papiers Peints de Belgique v Commission: 73/74 [1975] ECR 1491, [1976] 1 CMLR 589	263
Parlement Belge, The (1878–9) 4 PD 129; revsd. (1880) 5 PD 197	24
Parliament v Council: 302/87 (1988) Times, 17 October	229
Partie Ecologiste Les Verts v Parliament: 294/83 [1986] ECR 1339, [1987] 2 CMLR 343	229, 234, 240, 241
Patented Feedingstuffs. Re [1989] 2 CMLR 902	161
Paterson v Weddell & Co Ltd: 90/83 [1984] ECR 1567, [1984] 2 CMLR 540	134
Patrick v Ministre des Affaires Culturelles: 11/17 [1977] ECR 1199, [1977] 2 CMLR 523	47
Pecastaing v Belgian State: 98/79 [1980] ECR 691	11
Pesca Valentia Ltd v Minister for Fisheries [1985] IR 193, 201	110
Pesca Valentia v Minister for Fisheries and Forestry [1987] 1 CMLR 856	42
Pfizer International Inc v Commission: 65/87R [1987] ECR 1691	273
Phoenix General Insurance Co of Greece SA v Halvanon Insurance Co Ltd [1988] QB 216, [1987] 2 All ER 152	118
Phonogram Ltd v Lane [1982] QB 938, [1981] 3 All ER 182	140
Pickering v Liverpool Daily Post and Echo Newspapers plc [1990] 1 All ER 335, CA	144
Pickstone v Freemans plc [1989] AC 66, [1988] 2 All ER 803, HL	46, 84, 118, 138, 139, 142, 153
Pigs and Bacon Commission v McCarren: 177/78 [1979] ECR 2161, [1979] 3 CMLR 389	76
Pigs Marketing Board v Redmond [1978] 2 CMLR 697; 83/78 [1978] ECR 2347, [1979] 1 CMLR 177; subsequent proceedings [1979] 3 CMLR 118	29, 202, 205

Table of cases—alphabetical xxxiii

	PAGE
Pinna v Caisse d'Allocations Familiales de la Savoie: 41/84 [1986] ECR 1, [1988] 1 CMLR 350	62, 272
Pioneer Shipping Ltd v BTP Tioxide Ltd [1982] AC 724, [1981] 2 All ER 1030:	149
Piraiki-Patraiki Cotton Industry v Commission [1985] ECR 207, [1985] 2 CMLR 4	244
Plaumann & Co v Commission: 25/62 [1963] ECR 95, [1964] CMLR 29	240, 242, 257, 270, 272, 276, 285, 286
Politi SAS v Ministero delle Finanze: 43/71 [1971] ECR 1039, [1973] CMLR 60	18, 68, 69, 164
Polydor Ltd v Harlequin Record Shops Ltd and Simons Records Ltd [1980] 2 CMLR 413, CA; 270/80 [1982] ECR 329, [1982] 1 CMLR 677	184, 186, 187, 192
Portsmouth City Council v Richards [1989] 1 CMLR 673, CA	192, 194, 205
Potato Marketing Board v Drysdale [1986] 3 CMLR 331	187
Prais v Council: 130/75 [1976] ECR 1589, [1976] 2 CMLR 708	9
Pretore di Salò v X: 14/86 [1987] ECR 2545, [1989] 1 CMLR 71	90, 146, 167, 172
Prince v Secretary of State for Scotland 1985 SLT 74	183
Prince v Younger [1984] 1 CMLR 723	187
Procureur de la République v Chatain Laboratories Sandoz: 65/79 [1980] ECR 1345, [1981] 3 CMLR 418	76
Procureur de la République v Chiron: 27–274/84 and 6–7/85 [1986] ECR 529, [1988] 1 CMLR 735	211
Procureur de la République v Giry and Guerlain SA: 253/78 and 1–3/79 [1980] ECR 2327, [1981] 2 CMLR 99	166
Procureur de la République v Waterkeyn: 314 to 316/81 and 83/82 [1982] ECR 4337, [1983] 2 CMLR 145	47, 224
Procureur du Roi v Debauve: 52/79 [1980] ECR 833, [1981] 2 CMLR 362	53
Procureur du Roi v Dechmann: 154/77 [1978] ECR 1573, [1979] 2 CMLR 1	197
Procureur Général v Arbelaiz-Emazabel: 181/80 [1981] ECR 2961	5, 69
Producteurs de Fruits et Légumes v Council: 16–17, 19–22/62 [1962] ECR 471, [1963] CMLR 160	236, 237, 257
Producteurs de Vins de Table et Vins de Pays v Commission: 59 and 60/79 [1979] ECR 2425	279, 280
Pubblico Ministero v Manghera: 59/75 [1976] ECR 91, [1976] 1 CMLR 557	55
Pubblico Ministero v Ratti: 148/78 [1979] ECR 1629, [1980] 1 CMLR 96	45, 86, 87, 88
Publishers Association v Commission: 56/89R [1989] 4 CMLR 816	273

R

R v A-G, ex p ICI plc [1987] 1 CMLR 72, CA	105, 235
R v Board of Inland Revenue, ex p MFK Underwriting Agencies [1990] 1 All ER 91	269
R v Bouchereau [1977] 3 All ER 365, [1977] 1 WLR 414, [1977] 1 CMLR 269	208
R v Bouchereau: 30/77 [1978] QB 732, [1977] ECR 1999, [1977] 2 CMLR 800	132, 134, 189, 222
R v Bow Street Metropolitan Stipendiary Magistrate, ex p Noncyp Ltd [1989] 3 WLR 467	186
R v Chief Immigration Officer, ex p Salamat Bibi [1976] 3 All ER 843, [1976] 1 WLR 979	24
R v Fishing Department of Ministry of Agriculture, Fisheries and Food, ex p Agegate Ltd [1987] 3 CMLR 939	187
R v Goldstein [1983] 1 All ER 434, [1983] 1 WLR 151, HL	40, 44, 47, 101, 129, 269

xxxiv *Table of cases—alphabetical*

	PAGE
R v Governor of Pentonville Prison, ex p Budlong [1980] 1 All ER 701, [1980] 1 WLR 1110	185
R v Halliday, ex p Zadig [1917] AC 260	119
R v Henn. See Henn and Darby v DPP	
R v Henn and Darby: 34/79 [1979] ECR 3795, [1980] 1 CMLR 246	133, 167
R v HM Customs and Excise Comrs, ex p Imperial Tobacco Ltd: 141/86 [1988] 2 CMLR 43	211
R v HM Customs and Excise Comrs, ex p National Dried Fruit Association: 77/86 [1988] 2 CMLR 195	211
R v HM Treasury, ex p Daily Mail and General Trust plc [1987] 2 CMLR 1	183
R v Home Secretary, ex p Bhajan Singh [1976] QB 198, [1975] 2 All ER 1081	24, 135
R v Home Secretary, ex p Brind [1990] 2 WLR 787, CA	12, 15, 269
R v Home Secretary, ex p Muhammad Ayub [1983] 3 CMLR 140	95
R v Home Secretary, ex p Narin (1989) Independent, 18 December	68
R v HM Treasury, ex p Smedley [1985] 1 CMLR 665: affd [1985] QB 657, [1985] 1 All ER 589, CA	115, 235
R v IRC, ex p National Federation of Self-Employed and Small Businesses Ltd [1982] AC 617, [1981] 2 All ER 93	216
R v ILEA, ex p Hinde [1985] 1 CMLR 716	186
R v Intervention Board for Agricultural Produce, ex p ED&F Man (Sugar) Ltd: 181/84 [1985] ECR 2889, [1985] 3 CMLR 759	211, 213, 269
R v Intervention Board for Agricultural Produce, ex p Fish Producers' Organisation Ltd [1988] 2 CMLR 661, CA	183, 187
R v Johnson [1978] 1 CMLR 390	208
R v Kirk: 63/83 [1984] ECR 2689, [1985] 1 All ER 453, [1984] 3 CMLR 522	10, 168
R v Lancashire County Council, ex p Huddleston [1986] 2 All ER 941	216
R v London Boroughs Transport Committee, ex p Freight Transport Association Ltd [1990] 1 CMLR 229	84, 91
R v Metropolitan Borough Council, ex p Wirral Licensed Taxi Owners Association [1983] 3 CMLR 150	185
R v Metropolitan Police Comr, ex p Blackburn [1968] 2 QB 118, [1968] 1 All ER 763, CA	90
R v Miah [1974] 2 All ER 377, [1974] 1 WLR 683	117
R v Minister of Agriculture, Fisheries and Food, ex p Agegate Ltd (1990) Times, 19 January	47, 109
R v Minister of Agriculture, Fisheries and Food, ex p Bell Lines Ltd [1984] 2 CMLR 502	104, 105
R v Minister of Agriculture, Fisheries and Food, ex p FEDESA [1988] 3 CMLR 207	210, 214
R v Minister of Agriculture, Fisheries and Food, ex p Jaderow Ltd: C-216/87 (1990) Times, 19 January	109
R v National Joint Council for the Craft of Dental Technicians, ex p Neate [1953] 1 QB 704, [1953] 1 All ER 327	148
R v Pharmaceutical Society of Great Britain, ex p Association of Pharmaceutical Importers [1987] 3 CMLR 951, CA	153, 183, 186, 205
R v Pieck: 157/79 [1980] ECR 2171, [1980] 3 CMLR 220	188
R v Plymouth Justices, ex p Rogers [1982] QB 863, [1982] 2 All ER 175; *see* Rogers v Darthenay: 87/82	184, 188, 198
R v Saunders: 175/78 [1979] ECR 1129, [1979] 2 CMLR 216	189, 202
R v Secretary of State for Home Affairs, ex p Tombofa [1988] 2 CMLR 609	186
R v Secretary of State for Social Security, ex p Bomore Medical Supplies Ltd [1986] 1 CMLR 228, CA	104, 186
R v Secretary of State for Social Services, ex p Clarke [1988] 1 CMLR 279	104

Table of cases—alphabetical xxxv

PAGE

R v Secretary of State for Social Services, ex p Wellcome Foundation Ltd [1987] 2 All ER 1025, [1987] 1 WLR 1166, CA; affd sub nom. Wellcome Foundation Ltd v Secretary of State for Social Services [1988] 2 All ER 684, [1988] 1 WLR 635, HL 184
R v Secretary of State for the Home Department, ex p Ruddock [1987] 2 All ER 518, [1987] 1 WLR 1482 268
R v Secretary of State for the Home Department, ex p Santillo: 131/79 [1980] ECR 1585, [1980] 2 CMLR 308, [1981] QB 778 .... 46, 73, 85, 95, 96, 101
R v Secretary of State for the Home Department, ex p Thakrar [1974] QB 684, [1974] 2 All ER 261... 15
R v Secretary of State for the Home Office, ex p Weeks (1988) Times, 15 March: 12
R v Secretary of State for Transport, ex p Factortame Ltd [1989] 2 CMLR 353, CA; on appeal sub nom Factortame Ltd v Secretary of State for Transport [1989] 2 All ER 692, [1989] 2 WLR 997, HL 38, 39, 108, 120, 183, 193, 194, 225
R v Thomas Scott & Sons (Bakers) Ltd: 133/83 [1984] ECR 2863, [1985] 1 CMLR 188 218
R v Thompson [1978] 1 CMLR 390; 7/78: [1978] ECR 2247, [1979] 1 CMLR 47... 132, 188, 202
R v Trinity House London Pilotage Committee, ex p Jensen [1985] 2 CMLR 413... 52, 103
R v Tymen [1981] 2 CMLR 544; 269/80 [1981] ECR 3079, [1982] 2 CMLR 111 .. 101, 188, 205
R v Warry [1976] 1 CMLR 494; 41/77 [1977] ECR 2085, [1977] 2 CMLR 783 ... 133
R v Wells Street Stipendiary Magistrate, ex p Deakin [1980] AC 477, [1979] 2 All ER 497, HL 12
RAR v Council and Committee: 250/86 and 11/87 (29 June 1989, unreported) .. 237
RSV v Commission: 223/85 [1987] ECR 4617, [1989] 2 CMLR 259 .... 254, 269
Racke v Hauptzollamt Mainz: 98/78 [1979] ECR 69 .... 172, 268
Radio Telefís Éireann v Commission: 76 etc/89R [1989] 4 CMLR 816 273
Rainey v Greater Glasgow Health Board [1987] AC 224, [1987] 1 All ER 65, HL: 137
Ransburg-Gema AG v Electrostatic Plant Systems Ltd [1989] 2 CMLR 712 187
Rau v BALM: 133–136/85 [1987] ECR 2289 275
Rau v De Smedt: 261/81 [1982] ECR 3961, [1983] 2 CMLR 496.............. 169
Rayner (JH) (Mincing Lane) Ltd v Department of Trade and Industry [1989] Ch 72, [1988] 3 All ER 257, CA; affd [1989] 3 All ER 523, [1989] 3 WLR 969, HL 3, 4, 15, 127, 136
Razanatsimba: 65/77 [1977] ECR 2229, [1978] 1 CMLR 246 .... 147, 197
Reina v Landeskreditbank Baden-Württemberg: 65/81 [1982] ECR 33, [1982] 1 CMLR 744 150
Reparation for Injuries Case 1949 ICJ Rep 174........................... 3
Republic of Italy v Hambros Bank [1950] Ch 314, [1950] 1 All ER 430........ 24
Restrictions on Imports of Lamb (No 2), Re: Commission v France. See Commission v France: 24/80R and 97/80R
Rewe v Hauptzollamt Kiel: 158/80 [1981] ECR 1805, [1982] 1 CMLR 449 .... 67, 87, 92, 265
Rewe v Hauptzollamt Landau: 45/75 [1976] ECR 181, [1976] 2 CMLR 1 55
Rewe v Landwirtschaftskammer Saarland: 33/76 [1976] ECR 1989, [1977] 1 CMLR 533 .... 63, 64, 123
Rewe-Zentrale: 37/70 [1971] ECR 23, [1971] CMLR 238 264
Reyners v Belgium: 2/74 [1974] ECR 631, [1974] 2 CMLR 305 55
Rheinmühlen v Einfuhr- und Vorratsstelle für Getreide: 6/71 [1971] ECR 823, [1972] CMLR 401 76

Table of cases—alphabetical

PAGE

Rheinmühlen-Düsseldorf v Einfuhr- und Vorratsstelle für Getreide: 146/73 [1974] ECR 33, [1974] 1 CMLR 523 .... 180, 196
Rheinmühlen-Düsseldorf v Einfuhr-und Vorratsstelle für Getreide: 166/73 [1974] ECR 33, [1974] 1 CMLR 523 .... 158, 196
Rhenania v Commission: 103/63 [1964] ECR 425, [1965] CMLR 82 228
Richez-Parise v Commission: 19, 20, 25 and 30/69 [1970] ECR 325 283
Riff, Re [1985] CMLR 29 157
Rijksdienst voor Werknemerspensionen v Vlaeminck: 132/81 [1982] ECR 2953.. 165
Rio Tinto Zinc Corpn v Westinghouse Electric Corpn [1978] AC 547, [1977] 3 All ER 703, CA; revsd [1978] AC 547, [1978] 1 All ER 434, HL 44, 101
Robards v Insurance Officer: 149/82 [1983] ECR 171, [1983] 2 CMLR 37 171
Rochdale Borough Council v Anders [1988] 3 CMLR 431.................. 194, 205
Rogers v Darthenay: 87/82 [1983] ECR 1579, [1984] 1 CMLR 135............ 73, 188
Rolls-Royce plc v Doughty [1988] 1 CMLR 569, EAT 91
Roquette v Commission: 26/74 [1976] ECR 677.......................... 76, 287
Roquette v France: 29/77 [1977] ECR 1835 266
Roquette Frères v Council: 138/79 [1980] ECR 3333 .... 239, 259
Roquette Frères v Council: 242/81 [1982] ECR 3213 238
Rothschild (J) Holdings Plc v IRC [1989] 2 CMLR 621, CA 140, 186
Royal Scholten-Honig (Holdings) Ltd v Intervention Board for Agricultural Produce [1977] 2 CMLR 449; 103/77 [1979] ECR 2037, [1979] 1 CMLR 675... 202, 265, 285
Ruckdeschel & Co v Hauptzollamt Hamburg-St Annen: 117/76 and 16/77 [1977] ECR 1753, [1979] 2 CMLR 445 269
Russo v AIMA: 60/75 [1976] ECR 45 63
Rustomjee v R (1876) 1 QBD 487; affd 2 QBD 69 .... 24, 25
Rutili v Minister for the Interior: 36/75 [1975] ECR 1219, [1976) 1 CMLR 140 .. 9

S

SACE v Italian Ministry for Finance: 33/70 [1970] ECR 1213, [1971] CMLR 123... 55, 59, 84
SAFA v Amministrazione delle Finanze [1973] CMLR 152 211
SAP Vicente Nobre v Council: 253/86 [1990] 1 CMLR 105................... 237
Salaman v Secretary of State for India [1906] 1 KB 613 24
Salerno v Commission and Council: 87 etc/83 and 9 and 10/84 [1985] ECR 2523... 239, 278
Salgoil SpA v Italian Ministry for Foreign Trade: 13/68 [1968] ECR 453, [1969] CMLR 181 .... 56, 63, 164, 207
Salomon v Customs and Excise Comrs [1967] 2 QB 116, [1966] 3 All ER 871, CA... 14, 127, 135, 136
Salonia v Poidomani and Giglio: 126/80 [1981] ECR 1563, [1982] 1 CMLR 64 .. 164, 204
Salumificio di Cornuda SpA v Amministrazione delle Finanze dello Stato: 130/78 [1979] ECR 867, [1979] 3 CMLR 561 82
Schering Chemicals Ltd v Falkman Ltd [1982] QB 1, [1981] 2 All ER 321, CA .. 12
Schiavello v Nesci [1975] 2 CMLR 198..................................... 157
Schlüter v Hauptzollamt Hamburg: 94/71 [1972] ECR 307, [1973] CMLR 113: 76
Schlüter v Hauptzollamt Lörrach: 9/73 [1973] ECR 1135 .... 52, 123
Schorsch Meier v Hennin [1975] QB 416, [1975] 1 All ER 152 .... 44, 110, 131
Schroeder v Germany: 40/72 [1973] ECR 125, [1973] CMLR 824 270
Schwarze v Einfuhr- und Vorratsstelle für Getreide: 16/65 [1965] ECR 877, [1966] CMLR 172 263
Sermes v Commission: 279/86 [1987] ECR 3109 252

Table of cases—alphabetical xxxvii

PAGE
Secretary of State for Employment v Levy [1989] IRLR 469, EAT 91
Sgarlata v Commission: 40/64 [1965] ECR 215, [1966] CMLR 314.......... 238, 257
Shell-Berre, Re [1964] CMLR 462 156
Shields v E Coomes (Holdings) Ltd [1979] 1 All ER 456, [1978] 1 WLR
 1408... 20, 26, 31, 48, 95, 101, 102
Silver Seiko Ltd v Council: 273/85R [1985] ECR 3475, [1986] 1 CMLR 214 273
Simmenthal SpA v Amministrazione delle Finanze dello Stato (No 3): 70/77
 [1978] ECR 1453, [1978] 3 CMLR 670 .... 146, 191, 204
Simmenthal SpA v Commission: 92/78 [1979] ECR 777, [1980] 1 CMLR
 25... 235, 243, 272, 277
Sirdar Ltd v Les Fils de Louis Mulliez [1975] 1 CMLR 378 194
Siskina, The [1979] AC 210, [1977] 3 All ER 803 .... 111, 112
Smit Transport BV v Commissie Grensoverschrijdend Beroepsgoederenver-
 voer: 126/82 [1983] ECR 73, [1983] 3 CMLR 106 88
Smith Kline and French Laboratories Ltd, Re [1989] 1 All ER 578, [1989] 2
 WLR 397, HL 185
Snoxell and Davies v Vauxhall Motors Ltd [1978] QB 11, [1977] 3 All ER 770 .. 102
Sociale Verzekeringsbank v Van der Vecht: 19/67 [1967] ECR 345, [1968]
 CMLR 151 134
Società Italiana per l'Oleodotto Transalpino (SIOT) v Ministero delle Finanze:
 266/81 [1983] ECR 731, [1984] 2 CMLR 231 .... 5, 69, 162,
 250
Société Ateliers de Construction de Compiègne SA v Fabry [1980] 3 CMLR
 647... 41
Société Bessin et Salson v Administration des Douanes: 386/87 (9 November
 1989, unreported) 63
Société Coopérative Providence Agricole de la Champagne v ONIC: 4/79 [1980]
 ECR 2823 .... 62, 272
Société des Produits de Maïs SA v Administration des Douanes: 112/83 [1985]
 ECR 719, [1988] 1 CMLR 459...................................... 62, 272
Société des Usines de Beauport v Council: 103–109/78 [1979] ECR 17, [1979] 3
 CMLR 1 239
Société pour Exportation des Sucres v Commission: 88/76 [1977] ECR 709 239
Southampton and South-West Hampshire Area Health Authority v Marshall
 (No 2) [1989] 3 CMLR 771, EAT 20, 102
Spijker Kwasten BV v Commission: 231/82 [1984] 2 CMLR 284 242
Staatsanwalt Freiburg v Keller: 234/85 [1986] ECR 2897, [1987] 1 CMLR 875 .. 9, 72
State v Cornet [1967] CMLR 351 157
Stauder v City of Ulm: 29/69 [1969] ECR 419, [1970] CMLR 112.......... 8, 70, 134
Steinike und Weinlig v Bundesamt für Ernährung und Forstwirtschaft [1980] 2
 CMLR 531 72
Sucrimex SA v Commission: 133/79 [1980] ECR 1299, [1981] 2 CMLR
 479... 234, 287
Surjit Kaur v Lord Advocate [1980] 3 CMLR 79 12
Syndicat Général de Fabricants de Semoules [1970] CMLR 395............. 41
Syndicat National des Fabricants Raffineurs d'Huile de Graissage v Interhuiles:
 172/82 [1983] ECR 555, [1983] 3 CMLR 485 223
Syndicat National des Importateurs Français en Produits Laitiers et Agricoles,
 Re [1968] CMLR 81 157

T
TCB Ltd v Gray [1986] Ch 621, [1986] 1 All ER 587; affd [1987] Ch 458n, [1988]
 1 All ER 108, CA 141

Table of cases—alphabetical

	PAGE
Tachographs, Re: Commission v United Kingdom. See Commission v United Kingdom: 128/78	
Tariff Quota on Wine, Re: German Federal Republic v Commission. See Germany v Commission: 24/62	
Taxation of Foreign Workers, Re [1977] 1 CMLR 659	157
Technointorg v Council: 77/87R [1987] ECR 1793, [1987] 3 CMLR 491	274
Tezi Textiel BV v Commission: 59/84 [1986] ECR 887, [1987] 3 CMLR 64	271, 286
Timex Corpn v Council and Commission [1985] ECR 849, [1985] 3 CMLR 550:	253
Toepfer v Commission: 106–107/63 [1965] ECR 405, [1966] CMLR 111	82, 241, 243, 271
Toepfer v Commission: 112/77 [1978] ECR 1019	239, 286
Tradax BV v Commission: 64/82 [1984] ECR 1359	286
Transocean Marine Paint Association v Commission: 17/74 [1974] ECR 1063, [1974] 2 CMLR 459	247, 260, 261
Trendtex Trading Corpn v Central Bank of Nigeria [1977] QB 529, [1977] 1 All ER 881	111

U

UDIDFA v Comune di Carpaneto Piacentino: 231/87 and 129/88 (17 October 1989, unreported)	87
UNICME v Council: 123/77 [1978] ECR 845	239
Unifrex v Council and Commission: 281/82 [1984] ECR 1969	287
Union Deutsche Lebensmittelwerke v Commission: 97/85 [1987] ECR 2265	214, 242, 276
Union Laitière Normande v French Dairy Farmers Ltd: 244/78 [1979] ECR 2663, [1980] 1 CMLR 314	168, 172
Union Syndicale v Council: 72/74 [1975] ECR 401, [1975] 2 CMLR 181	187
United Kingdom v Commission: 84/85 [1987] ECR 3765, [1988] 1 CMLR 113	269
United Kingdom v Commission: 114/86 [1989] 1 CMLR 32	234
United Kingdom v Council: 68/86 [1988] 2 CMLR 543	214
Universität Hamburg v Hauptzollamt Hamburg: 216/82 [1983] ECR 2771	264, 275

V

VBVB v VBBB: 43, 63/82 [1984] ECR 19, [1985] 1 CMLR 27	10
Vaassen v Beambtenfonds Mijnbedrijf: 61/65 [1966] ECR 261, [1966] CMLR 508	145
Valor International Ltd v Application des Gaz SA [1978] 3 CMLR 87	103
Valsabbia v Commission: 154 etc/78, 39 etc/79 [1980] ECR 907, [1981] 1 CMLR 613	266
Value Added Tax Exemption, Re [1989] 1 CMLR 113	95, 159
Van Den Bergh en Jurgens v Commission: 265/85 [1987] ECR 1169	283
Van Duyn v Home Office [1974] 3 All ER 178, [1974] 1 WLR 1107	176
Van Duyn v Home Office: 41/74 [1975] Ch 358, [1975] 3 All ER 190, [1974] ECR 1337, [1975] 1 CMLR 1	7, 74, 85, 87, 101, 132
Van Gend en Loos v Nederlandse Administratie der Belastingen: 26/62 [1963] ECR 1, [1963] CMLR 105	2, 16, 22, 48, 49, 59, 143, 145, 157, 163, 165, 209, 210
Variola v Italian Ministry of Finance: 34/73 [1973] ECR 981	75, 122
Verbond van Nederlandse Ondernemingen v Inspecteur der Invoerrechten en Accijnzen: 51/76 [1977] ECR 113, [1977] 1 CMLR 413	86
Vinal SpA v Orbat SpA: 46/80 [1981] ECR 77, [1981] 3 CMLR 524	172
Virdee, Re [1980] 1 CMLR 709	185
Volvo (AB) v Erik Veng (UK) Ltd: 238/87 [1989] 4 CMLR 122	147

Table of cases—alphabetical xxxix

	PAGE
Von Colson v Land Nordrhein-Westfalen: 14/83 [1984] ECR 1891, [1986] 2 CMLR 430	63, 84, 92, 98, 138
Von Kempis v Geldof [1976] 2 CMLR 152	41

W

Wagner v Commission: 12/79 [1979] ECR 3657 .... 239, 287
Walker v Baird [1892] AC 491 24
Waltham Forest London Borough v Scott Markets Ltd [1988] 3 CMLR 773.... 187
Weissgerber v Finanzamt Neustadt: 207/87 (14 July 1988, unreported) 87
Welding v Hauptzollamt Hamburg-Waltershof: 87/78 [1978] ECR 2457 265
Werhahn v Council: 63–69/72 [1973] ECR 1229 283
Westinghouse Uranium Contract, Re. See Rio Tinto Corpn v Westinghouse Electric Corpn
Who Group Ltd, The v Stage One (Records) Ltd [1980] 2 CMLR 429......... 194
Wilhelm v Bundeskartellamt: 14/68 [1969] ECR 1, [1969] CMLR 100 2
Wilson, Smithett & Cope Ltd v Terruzzi [1976] QB 683, [1975] 2 All ER 649 ... 137
Wöhrmann v Commission: 31 and 33/62 [1962] ECR 501, [1963] CMLR 152 .... 205, 207, 271, 277
Worringham and Humphreys v Lloyds Bank Ltd: 69/80 [1981] ECR 767, [1981] 2 CMLR 1 .... 53, 61, 88
Wörsdorfer née Koschniske v Raad van Arbeid: 9/79 [1979] ECR 2717, [1980] 1 CMLR 87 134
Wünsche v Germany [1986] ECR 947 .... 162, 210
Wünsche Handelsgesellschaft GmbH & Co v Germany: 345/82 [1984] ECR 1995.. 210
Wychavon District Council v Midland Enterprises (Special Event) Ltd [1988] 1 CMLR 397 194

Y

Yoga for Health Foundation v Customs and Excise Comrs [1985] 1 CMLR 340: 95
Yoga Fruit Juices, Re [1969] CMLR 123 157

Z

Zerbone v Amministrazione delle Finanze dello Stato: 94/77 [1978] ECR 99.... 75
Zuckerfabrik Bedburg AG v Council and Commission: 281/84 [1987] ECR 49.. 284, 287
Zuckerfabrik Schöppenstedt v Council: 5/71 [1971] ECR 975 284
Zuckerfabrik Watenstedt GmbH v Council: 6/68 [1968] ECR 409, [1969] CMLR 26 .... 238, 257

Table of cases—numerical

Decisions of the European Court of Justice are listed below numerically. These decisions are also included in the preceding alphabetical table.

	PAGE
3/54	270
6/60	63
7/61	228, 229
13/61	143, 165, 198, 207, 219
16–17, 19–22/62	236, 257
18/62	265
24/62	263, 264
25/62	240, 242, 257, 270, 276, 286
26/62	2, 16, 22, 48, 53, 59, 143, 145, 157, 163, 209, 272, 285
28–30/62	157, 209
31 and 33/62	205, 207, 271, 277
34/62	257, 263, 271
13/63	271
90 and 91/63	6, 222
103/63	228
106–107/63	82, 241, 243, 271
1/64	240, 242
6/64	2, 4, 22, 31, 49, 50, 54, 59, 151, 164, 165, 202
32/64	271
38/64	240, 242, 243
40/64	238, 257
45/64	220
16/65	263
32/65	271, 276, 278
44/65	205, 220, 277
48/65	228, 230, 280
52 and 55/65	230, 270
57/65	55, 57, 210
61/65	145
5, 7 and 13–24/66	283, 287, 288
8–11/66	230, 258, 264, 265
30/66	283
5/67	265, 275
17/67	18, 22
19/67	134
27/67	58
28/67	52, 57, 58, 59, 63, 210
30/67	238
6/68	238, 257
7/68	21, 54, 226
10 and 18/68	241, 242, 279, 281
13/68	56, 63, 164, 207
14/68	2
19/68	206
29/68	206, 209
31/68	198, 206
2–3/69	54
4/69	286
6 and 11/69	229, 271
7/69	220
19, 20, 25 and 30/69	283
26/69	134, 220
29/69	8, 70
31/69	220, 222
38/69	80
40/69	18, 74
41/69	257, 258, 260
48/69	257, 258, 259, 267
63–65/69	238
69/69	241, 271
72/69	75
74/69	75
77/69	220
6/70	279, 280
8/70	55, 221
9/70	78, 84
11/70	8, 19, 70
15/70	231, 279
20/70	78
22/70	4, 231, 257, 265
23/70	78
33/70	55, 59, 84
37/70	264

xlii Table of cases—numerical

Case	PAGE
41–44/70	239
62/70	241, 243
1/71	202
2/71	271
5/71	284
6/71	76
8/71	281, 282
9 and 11/71	286
10/71	56, 58, 60
15/71	280
18/71	21, 54, 59
42/71	229, 281
43/71	69, 164
48/71	21, 54, 221, 225
49/71	75
93/71	75
94/71	75, 76
96/71	287
6/72	259
7/72	270
11/72	286, 288
13/72	266
18/72	75
21–24/72	5, 162
39/72	220
40/72	270
43/72	286, 287
62/72	207
63–69/72	283, 285
77/72	55, 59
81/72	257, 270, 272
4/73	9
9/73	52
34/73	75, 122
36/73	146
127/73	103, 199
131/73	76
134/73	280
146/73	196
153/73	286
166/73	158, 180, 196
167/73	220
172/73	42
181/73	162
2/74	55
17/74	247, 260
26/74	76, 287
31/74	73
32/74	146
41/74	7, 74, 85, 87, 101, 132
56–60/74	285, 288
73/74	284
74/74	268
99/74	287
100/74	239
1/75	5
3/75R	273
9/75	229
36/75	9
43/75	53, 60
45/75	55
46/75	287
52/75	222
59/75	55
60/75	63, 67
67–85/75	287
87/75	68, 162
93/75	169
130/75	9
1/76	5
3, 4 and 6/76	5
17/76	133, 146
26/76	233, 248
33/76	63
35/76	19
44/76	285, 288
45/76	63
50/76	75, 76
51/76	86
52/76	67, 209
64 etc/76, 239/78, 27 etc/79	285
74/76	57, 73
80/76	134
83 and 94/76, 4, 15 and 40/77	285
85/76	261, 283
88/76	235, 239
101/76	236, 237, 238, 275
107/76	155, 190
112/76	275
114/76	269
117/76 and 16/77	269
118/76	76
124/76 and 20/77	269
126/76	287
11/77	47
12, 18 and 21/77	287
29/77	266
30/77	132, 134, 189, 222
31 and 53/77R	224
38/77	88
41/77	133
54/77	272
59/77	230, 275
61/77	5, 42
65/77	147, 197
68/77	285
69/77	220
70/77	146, 191, 204

Table of cases—numerical

Case	PAGE
77/77	235
87/77	239
92/77	265
94/77	75
103/77	202, 265, 285
106/77	19, 31, 42, 67, 69, 164, 197
112/77	239, 286
113, 118–121/77	252
116 and 124/77	285
119/77	287
119/77R	273
123/77	239
124/77	285
125/77	275
132/77	286, 287
145/77	265
149/77	8
154/77	197
156/77	223, 275, 276
1/78	5, 53
1/78R	5
7/78	132, 188, 202
12/78	268
14/78	229
21/78	88
23/78	285
30/78	262
31/78	76
83/78	202
87/78	265
90/78	280
92/78	235, 243, 277
93/78	169, 204
98/78	268
99/78	271
101/78	169, 275
103–109/78	239
118/78	218
125/78	281
128/78	218
130/78	82
141/78	227
148/78	45, 86, 87, 88
152/78	224
154 etc/78 and 39 etc/79	10, 266
155/78	267
159/78	47, 220
162/78	239
170/78	218
175/78	189, 202
177/78	76
209–215 and 218/78	10, 264
231/78	133, 218
232/78	222, 226
238/78	285, 287
244/78	168, 172
253/78 and 1–3/79	166
265/78	77
4/79	62, 272
9/79	134
12/79	287
34/79	133, 167
41, 121 and 796/79	10
44/79	9, 72, 268
52/79	53
53/79	164
59 and 60/79	279, 280
61/79	62, 63, 64
65/79	76
66, 127 and 128/79	62, 63
68/79	65
74/79	169
76/79	271
88/79	86
91/79	6
98/79	11
102/79	83, 88
104/79	144, 146, 204
105/79	169
129/79	32, 45, 53, 166
130/79	76
131/79	46, 73, 85, 87, 95, 97, 101
133/79	234, 287
136/79	10, 247, 262, 264
138/79	147, 239, 259
140/79	172
152/79	209
155/79	247, 257, 267
157/79	188
730/79	254
789/79	237, 238
792/79R	246, 274, 279
804/79	218
811/79	62, 63
812/79	6, 49, 69
815/79	45
819/79	76, 266
1251/79	266
22/80	167
23/80	272
24/80R and 97/80R	226
33/80	278
35/80	265
36 and 71/80	166, 172, 197
46/80	172
64/80	238

xliv Table of cases—numerical

Case	Page
66/80	212, 275
69/80	53, 61, 88
96/80	53, 147, 209
100–103/80	10, 247, 261
108/80	86
112/80	5, 268
126/80	164, 204
142 and 143/80	62, 63
158/80	67, 87, 92, 265
170/80	218
181/80	5, 69
182/80	234, 279
197 to 200, 243, 245 and 247/80	286, 287
203/80	52, 172
208/80	147
244/80	170, 172
246/80	147
256, 257, 265 and 267/80 and 5/81:	285, 288
269/80	101, 188
270/80	68, 186
8/81	45, 74, 86, 87, 95, 159
12/81	45, 166
17/81	45, 68
19/81	88, 147, 208
21/81	268
44/81	234, 272
45/81	238
54/81	76
60/81	232, 247
60, 190/81R	274
61/81	37, 118, 138
65/81	150
68–71/81	221
96/81	83
97/81	83
102/81	148
104/81	6, 68, 162, 217
108/81	265, 268
115 and 116/81	173, 204
124/81	218
132/81	165
135/81	235, 243
136/81	221
141 to 143/81	172
146 and 192–193/81	76
210/81	233, 248
217/81	287
230/81	7, 229
232/81	239
233/81	76
240/81	209
242/81	238
246/81	233, 249, 280
249/81	222
250/81	238
255/81	87, 95, 159
261/81	169, 172
266/81	5, 69, 162, 250
267–269/81	5, 69, 162
270/81	86
283/81	131, 133, 144, 158, 204, 209
292 and 293/81	265
294/81	240, 243, 264
300/81	83
301/81	83
307/81	251
314 to 316/81 and 83/82	47, 224
2–4/82	198
35 and 36/82	155
40/82	105, 218
42/82	220
43, 63/82	10
64/82	286
66/82	269
86/82	264
87/82	73, 188
126/82	88
145/82	83
149/82	171
160/82	83
166/82	220
172/82	223
191/82	253, 267
199/82	64, 66, 77, 146
205–215/82	64
216/82	264, 275
222/82	62
228 and 229/82	240, 246, 258, 274
231/82	242
239, 275/82	252
264/82	253
267/82	282
271/82	87
281/82	287
296 and 318/82	266
301/82	87
323/82	254
345/82	210
14/83	63, 84, 92, 98, 138
22/83	239
52/83	223
53/83	252
59/83	283
63/83	10, 168
70/83	87, 94, 95

Table of cases—numerical

Case	Page
72/83	173
79/83	63, 92
87 etc/83 and 9, 10/84	278
90/83	134
91 and 127/83	167
112/83	62, 272
133/83	218
143/83	84
145/83	283
147/83	237, 288
152/83	163, 198
180/83	164, 172
194–206/83	284
207/83	218, 219
222/83	241
251/83	173
293/83	61, 65, 241, 249
294/83	229, 234, 240
1/84R	243
5/84	87, 95, 147
9–10/84	239
23/84	218
29/84	83
33/84	272
40/84	237, 240
41/84	62, 272
44/84	123, 147, 162
53/84	283
59/84	271, 286
60, 61/84	8, 11
75/84	248
91–92/84	218
100/84	134, 218
103/84	220
112/84	64
137/84	45
152/84	35, 89, 95
169/84	227, 255
174/84	150
175/84	286, 287
179/84	63
181/84	211, 269
190/84	234
298–213/84	172, 173
222/84	84, 89, 93, 95
240/84	252
251/84	287
271–274/84	211
281/84	284
209/84	204
5/85	10
6–7/85	211
15/85	223
17/85	221
21/85	269
40/85	261
53/85	247
67/85	255
69/85	162, 210
71/85	89
78/85	234
84/85	269
85/85	219
89, 104, 114, 116–117, 125–129/85:	7
93/85	218
97/85	214, 238, 242, 276
98/85	164, 172
121/85	6
133–136/85	214
137/85	9
154/85	220
154/85R	227
168/85	47, 83
181 etc/85	271
192/85	181
194/85	217
223/85	254, 269
234/85	9, 72
241/85	217
261/85	218
262/85	83
265/85	283
273/85R	273
277 and 300/85	252
282/85	242, 254
286/85	89
293/85	219
309/85	65
314/85	213
318/85	145
331, 376, 378/85	66
333/85	238
338/85	146
353/85	218
364/85	221
372–374/85	86, 90
377/85	146
384/85	146
422/85	211
434/85	181
9/86	221
11/86	234
12/86	11, 68, 162
14/86	90, 146, 167, 172
24/86	53, 61, 65
26/86	237, 238
45/86	265
50/86	285

xlvi *Table of cases—numerical*

Case	PAGE
55/86	238
60/86	84, 218
68/86	214
69/86	226
74/86	83
77/86	211
80/86	45, 84, 90
89, 91/86	241, 278, 287
97 etc/86	235, 236, 237, 286
98/86	167
104/86	66
116/86	83
126/86	52, 164
134/86	221
138–139/86	147, 211
141/86	211
157/86	45
162/86	211
166 and 220/86	282
188/86	166
197/86	244
207/86	242
233–235/86	236, 238
240/86	220
250/86	237
253/86	237
255/86	74
279/86	252
286/86	6
297/86	240
298/86	220
301/86	252
316/86	269
C-3/87	109
11/87	237
20/87	173
31/87	84, 87
45/87	224
45/87R	224
46/87 and 227/88	10
46/87R	273
62 and 72/87	254
63/87	223
65/87R	273
76/87	267
77/87R	274
82/87R	242, 273
94/87	64
101/87	139
106–120/87	284, 287
142/87R	254, 255
186/87	53
204/87	173
207/87	87
C-216/87	109, 181
226/87	223
231/87	87
238/87	147
240/87	65
302/87	229
386/87	63
50/88	87
129/88	87
277/88	267
160/88R	238, 273
206 etc/88	138
56/89R	273
76 etc/89R	273
188/89	91
246/89R	109, 225

Chapter 1

Introduction

COMMUNITY LAW AND ITS RELATIONSHIP WITH NATIONAL LAW AND INTERNATIONAL LAW

It is neither possible nor desirable to deal in detail within the confines of this book with the purely theoretical aspects of the complex problems which are inevitably presented by the question of the true nature of Community law and its relationship with other systems of law. It is not possible for reasons of space. Those problems are merely a part of a long-standing and richly documented doctrinal dispute as to the nature of law and the relationship between different legal systems. It is not desirable because this book is concerned with the application of Community law within the context of the legal system of one of the member states and that legal system itself gives practical pointers to the solution of these theoretical problems.

1 The nature of Community law

Community law may for present purposes be defined as a body of law comprising rights, duties, powers and remedies created by and under the treaties setting up the three communities, the European Coal and Steel Community, Euratom and the European Economic Community.[1]

Community law is a system of law created by Treaty. This independent system has been given effectiveness by the creation of Community institutions, by its recognition within the national legal systems of the member states, and by its development in the decisions of the European Court. Community law and the legal systems of the member states operate in overlapping spheres. Community law is superior in the sense, as will be shown below, that it restricts the sovereignty of member states. There is hardly a phrase in the preceding sentences which would not require elaboration or qualification if this book were concerned primarily with theoretical questions.

The theoretical and doctrinal disputes have often had a largely verbal character and frequently the problems so hotly disputed in the

---

1 On which see generally Wyatt and Dashwood *Substantive Law of the EEC* (2nd edn 1987); Halsbury's *Laws of England* (1986) vols 51 and 52.

2 *Introduction*

academic literature have had no practical significance. It will suffice to refer to and quote from some decisions of the European Court and of national courts to show how judges who operate within the system view that system themselves. The European Court said in the pioneering decision in which it held that nationals of member states could derive direct rights from Community law:

> ... the Community constitutes a new legal order of international law, for the benefit of which the states have limited their sovereign rights, albeit within limited fields, and the subjects of which comprise not only member states but also their nationals.[2]

and

> By contrast with ordinary international treaties, the EEC Treaty has created its own legal system which, on the entry into force of the Treaty, became an integral part of the legal system of the member states and which their courts are bound to apply.[3]

The Belgian Cour de Cassation, in an historic decision asserting the supremacy of Community law, said:

> ... the treaties which have created Community law have instituted a new legal system in whose favour the member states have restricted the exercise of their sovereign powers in the areas determined by those treaties[4]

and a German court, when asserting the subjection of Community rules to German constitutional standards, described EEC regulations as 'legal provisions of the European Economic Community which constitute neither public international law nor national law of the member states'.[5]

2 Community law and international law

Community law has been created by the treaties setting up the European Communities in the sense that those treaties have created not only institutions which have a separate legal personality in inter-

---

2 Case 26/62 *Van Gend en Loos v Nederlandse Administratie der Belastingen* [1963] ECR 1 at 12, [1963] CMLR 105 at 129.
3 Case 6/64 *Costa v ENEL* [1964] ECR 585 at 593, [1964] CMLR 425 at 455. See also Case 14/68 *Wilhelm v Bundeskartellamt* [1969] ECR 1 at 14, [1969] CMLR 100 at 119: 'the EEC Treaty has established its own system of law, integrated into the legal systems of the member states, and which must be applied by their courts'.
4 *Minister for Economic Affairs v SA Fromagerie Franco-Suisse Le Ski* [1972] CMLR 330 at 373.
5 *Internationale Handelsgesellschaft v Einfuhr- und Vorratsstelle für Getreide* [1972] CMLR 177 at 185. According to the German Federal Constitutional Court, Community law is neither part of the national legal structure nor international law but an autonomous body of laws flowing from an autonomous source of law: [1974] 2 CMLR 540. See also *Re Application of Wünsche* [1987] 3 CMLR 225 at 251.

national law but also a system of law within which those institutions, the member states *and* their nationals have rights and duties.

There is no inherent novelty in the creation of an international institution which is not a state but has legal personality both in international law and national law. Whether an institution has personality in international law is a question to be determined by international law. It is now a commonplace of international law that states may create institutions having international personality. The landmark decision was the advisory opinion of the International Court of Justice in the *Reparation for Injuries* case[6] on the status of the United Nations, in which it held that the member states had created an international person, the United Nations, with a legal personality distinct from that of its members and which could pursue claims for injuries done to itself and its employees, although that was:

> not the same thing as saying that it is a state which it certainly is not, or that its legal personality and rights and duties are the same as those of a state.[7]

This important point seems to have eluded the House of Lords in relation to the United Nations.[8] But it is clear from the decision of the House of Lords in the International Tin Council cases[9] that the law of the United Kingdom recognises the concept of an international organisation with legal capacity and personality under international law, which is a legal person in its own right, independent of its members, and not simply an association of the member states with no separate legal existence.

The states which create an international institution must show an intention (expressly or impliedly) to confer international legal personality on it. Article 210 of the EEC Treaty provides that 'the Community shall have legal personality'. This is not of itself conclusive because it could (and does) equally refer to legal personality within the legal systems of the member states.[10] But taken together with the provisions which expressly provide for the treaty-making powers of the Community (eg arts 113, 114 and 238) there can be no doubt that, accompanied by recognition by other states, the original six founder members created an international institution with a separate legal

---

6 1949 ICJ Rep 174. On the relationship between Community law and international law see Jacot-Guillarmod *Droit communautaire et droit international public* (1979); Wyatt (1982) 2 EL Rev, 147; Schermers and Waelbroeck *Judicial Protection in the European Communities* (4th edn 1987) pp 89–95.
7 1949 ICJ Rep at 178–179. See, for further references, Brownlie *Principles of Public International Law* (3rd edn 1979) pp 676–86.
8 *A-G v Nissan* [1970] AC 179 at 222 (per Lord Morris) and 723 (per Lord Pearce), [1969] 1 All ER 629 at 646 and 647, HL.
9 *J H Rayner (Mincing Lane) Ltd v Department of Trade and Industry* [1989] 3 WLR 969, [1989] 3 All ER 523, HL.
10 As to which, see art 211.

personality, which means 'that in its external relations the Community enjoys the capacity to establish contractual links with third countries over the whole field of objectives' of the Treaty.[11]

Thus in the litigation arising out of the insolvency of the International Tin Council, the members of the Tin Council who were sued by the creditors included a number of sovereign states as well as the EEC. It was held that the members of the Tin Council were not liable for the Tin Council's debts because the Tin Council was a legal entity separate and distinct from its members. But the EEC's argument that it was *immune* from suit was rejected by the Court of Appeal. Kerr LJ said:[12]

> There can be no doubt that the EEC has legal personality in international law.... Next, there is equally no doubt that the EEC exercises powers and functions which are analogous to those of sovereign states. In particular it has the jus missionis in the sense that it has permanent delegations in many non-member states and receives permanent representatives from many countries, and that all these missions have diplomatic status. Furthermore, apart from the right of legation, the EEC also has the jus tractatus as instanced by [the Sixth International Tin Agreement] itself, ie the power to conclude or participate in treaties with sovereign states and international organisations. This power has also been widely used. Finally, the EEC enjoys certain sovereign powers to the extent to which these have been ceded to it by its members under the various EEC treaties, and from this cession it has derived its own legislative, executive and judicial organs whose acts and decisions take effect within the member states. On the other hand, the EEC differs from sovereign states in that it has no sovereignty over territory as such and no nationals or citizens.

The claim of the EEC to immunity was rejected as 'ill-judged' and 'untenable' because it was justified neither by art 28 of the Merger Treaty (which sets out the immunities of the EEC, but without any suggestion of immunity from suit) nor by any domestic legislation.

The power of the Community in the external relations aspects of the common commercial policy is an exclusive one, in the sense that it is the Community, and not the member states, which has the power to

---

11 Case 22/70 *Re ERTA: Commission v Council* [1971] ECR 263 at 274, [1971] CMLR 335 at 354. In Case 6/64 *Costa v ENEL* [1964] ECR 585, [1964] CMLR 425, the Court referred to the 'personality' and 'capacity' of the Community. The German Federal Constitutional Court indicated that the Community is not a state, in particular not a federal state, but a community *sui generis* in the process of progressive integration and an international organisation: [1974] 2 CMLR 540.
12 *J H Rayner (Mincing Lane) Ltd v Department of Trade and Industry* [1989] Ch 72 at 198, [1988] 3 All ER 257 at 317, CA; affd on other grounds [1989] 3 WLR 969, [1989] 3 All ER 523, HL.

conclude agreements with third countries.[13] As for recognition of the international personality of the Communities by non-member states, it is sufficient to refer to a decision of the European Court in which it noted that since the entry into force of the EEC Treaty and the adoption of the common customs tariff, the conferment of powers on the European Community had been recognised by the states party to the General Agreement on Tariffs and Trade (GATT). The Court said:[14]

> In particular, since that time, the Community, acting through its own institutions, has appeared as a partner in the tariff negotiations and as a party to the agreements of all types concluded within the framework of the General Agreement.

In 1978 the European Parliament adopted a resolution on the position of the European Communities in public international law[15] in which it lent its support to the body of case law[16] developed by the European Court where the Court held that the powers of the Communities to enter into commitments with third countries derived implicitly from the treaties, and that the Community powers to conclude trade agreements with third countries precluded the exercise of any concurrent powers by the member states.

The relationship between the rules of European law and those of customary international law has given rise to much discussion,[17] not all of which has properly distinguished between two questions. A first question is whether Community institutions and member states are bound by and may take advantage of rules of international law. The answer to this question is obviously in the affirmative. Thus the

---

13 See note 11, supra, and Opinion 1/75 *OECD Understanding on a Local Cost Standard* [1975] ECR 355, [1975] 1 CMLR 85; Opinion 1/76 *Draft Agreement Establishing a European Laying-Up Fund for Inland Waterways* [1977] ECR 741, [1977] 2 CMLR 279; Cases 3, 4 and 6/76 *Kramer* [1976] ECR 1279, [1976] 2 CMLR 440; Case 61/77 *Commission v Ireland* [1978] ECR 417, [1978] 2 CMLR 466; Ruling 1/78 *Draft Convention of the IAEA on the Physical Protection of Nuclear Materials, Facilities and Transports* [1978] ECR 2151, [1979] 1 CMLR 131; Opinion 1/78 *Re Draft International Agreement on Natural Rubber* [1979] ECR 2871, [1979] 3 CMLR 639; Case 181/80 *Procureur Général v Arbelaiz-Emazabel* [1981] ECR 2961. See Temple Lang (1986) 6 Yb Eur L 183.
14 Cases 21–24/72 *International Fruit Co NV v Produktschap voor Groenten en Fruit* [1972] ECR 1219 at 1227, [1975] 2 CMLR 1 at 21. This important decision also deals with the relationship of EEC and GATT at the national level; see also Case 112/80 *Firma Anton Dürbeck v Hauptzollamt Frankfurt am Main-Flughafen* [1981] ECR 1095, [1982] 3 CMLR 314; Case 266/81 *Società Italiana per l'Oleodotto Transalpino (SIOT) v Ministero delle Finanze* [1983] ECR 731, [1984] 2 CMLR 231; Cases 267–269/81 *Amministrazione delle Finanze dello Stato v Società Petrolifera Italiana SpA* [1983] ECR 801, [1984] 1 CMLR 354.
15 OJ 1978 C239/16.
16 See cases cited at note 13, supra.
17 See literature at n 6, p 3, supra.

European Court has recognised that 'in conformity with the principles of public international law' Community institutions which negotiate international treaties may agree with the other contracting parties what effect the provisions of the agreement are to have in the national legal system of the parties; and that 'according to the general rules of international law there must be bona fide performance of every agreement'.[18] It has also recognised that, in accordance with the principles of international law, the application of the EEC Treaty does not affect the duty of a member state to respect the rights of non-member states under a prior treaty and to perform its obligations thereunder.[19]

A second set of questions relates to the use of the rules of public international law as a source of Community law and to the identity or similarity of rules of public international law and Community law. Here there has been much misunderstanding. There have been several cases in the European Court in which a party has put forward a proposition of public international law as justifying its conduct. Instead of considering whether the rule of international law had been properly invoked or properly formulated, the Court or the Advocate General has rejected the argument on the basis that the purported rule is not part of Community law. Thus in *Commission v Luxembourg and Belgium*[20] the European Court rejected the argument of the defendant states that their breach of the EEC Treaty was justified by the principle of international law that breach by another party (the Commission) suspended their obligations; the Court rejected the argument not on the correct ground that the general principle did not apply where the treaty yields a contrary intention, but (it seems) because the relevant principle of international law 'cannot be recognised under Community law'.[1] In *Re Detergents Directive: Commission v Italy*[2] the Italian Government sought to rely on a supposed principle of international law to suggest that in considering its liability for failure to implement Community law the Court should take into account the fact that it was hindered from implementing it due to difficulties in its internal legal system; instead of rejecting this argument on the ground that international law said precisely the opposite,[3] Advocate General

---

18 Case 104/81 *Hauptzollamt Mainz v CA Kupferberg & Cie KG* [1982] ECR 3641 at 3663–4, [1983] 1 CMLR 1 at 21.
19 Case 812/79 *A-G v Burgoa* [1980] ECR 2787, [1981] 2 CMLR 193; Case 121/85 *Conegate Ltd v Customs and Excise Comrs* [1986] ECR 1007, [1986] 1 CMLR 739; Case 286/86 *Ministère Public v Déserbais* [1989] 1 CMLR 516.
20 Cases 90 and 91/63 [1964] ECR 625, [1965] CMLR 58.
1 See Wyatt (1982) 7 EL Rev, 147, 159–60.
2 Case 91/79 [1980] ECR 1099, [1981] 1 CMLR 331.
3 See pp 20–21 and 220–221, infra.

Mayras merely treated it as irrelevant to the question of liability under Community law.[4]

Finally, there is no doubt that the EEC Treaty is to be interpreted so as to be in conformity with the rules of public international law. Thus in *Van Duyn v Home Office (No 2)*[5] the European Court indicated that it was a principle of international law, which the EEC Treaty could not be assumed to disregard, that a state was precluded from refusing its own nationals the right of entry or residence. In the *Wood Pulp Cartel* cases[6] the Commission decided that 41 wood pulp producers, all with places of business outside the European Community, had been guilty of restrictive practices in contravention of art 85 of the EEC Treaty, and imposed fines on most of them. On an application by several of the addressees for annulment of the decision, it was argued (inter alia) that the Commission had, in breach of the rules of public international law, assumed jurisdiction on the basis of the 'effects' doctrine, ie on the ground that the activities of the cartel *outside* the Community had produced economic effects *within* the Community. Advocate General Darmon, after an exhaustive discussion of the controversial nature of the 'effects' doctrine in international law, concluded that the Commission was entitled to exercise jurisdiction on the basis of effects within the Community provided that they were substantial, direct and foreseeable. But the European Court decided the case on a narrower ground. Even if the cartel had been formed outside the Community, the producers had *implemented* their cartel within the Community. The jurisdiction of the Community to apply its competition rules to that conduct was covered by the territoriality principle as universally recognised in public international law. But it is clear that both the Advocate General and the Court proceeded on the basis that the Community was bound by the rules of public international law as to jurisdiction to impose sanctions for breach of competition law, and that art 85 of the EEC Treaty was to be read subject to those rules.

3 Community law and individuals

Thus Community law is established by the treaties and has its own institutions including rule-making bodies, an executive and a court. The subjects of Community law are those institutions, the member

---

4 For reliance by a member state on a very odd view of the international law of estoppel see Case 230/81 *Grand Duchy of Luxembourg v European Parliament* [1983] ECR 255, [1983] 2 CMLR 726.
5 Case 41/74 [1974] ECR 1337 at 1351, [1975] 1 CMLR 1 at 17. This was, perhaps, an over-generalisation.
6 Cases 89, 104, 114, 116–117, 125–129/85 *Ahlstrom Oy v Commission* [1988] 4 CMLR 901. See Akehurst (1988) 59 BYIL 415.

8 Introduction

states, individuals and all other legal entities recognised by the national laws of the member states. There is no novelty in a treaty creating rights for individuals[7] and it is well settled in international law that a treaty can have that effect.[8] The treaties constituting the European Communities of course go further in this direction than any previous treaties and provide (expressly) that (1) regulations of the Council and Commission shall be *directly applicable* in all member states, and (2) decisions shall be binding on the persons to whom they are addressed, and, in many of their provisions (impliedly, as a result of decisions of the European Court), create direct rights for individuals which must be respected by national courts. This important question is discussed in relation to the European Communities Act 1972 in greater detail in chapter 2.

4 Community law and fundamental human rights

In response to misgivings about the lack of effective supervision over the executive organs of the Communities and to the problems created by the subjection of Community regulations to national constitutional standards,[9] the European Court has come to lay considerable stress on its role as guardian of respect for human rights. In 1970 it held that the German courts could not, as a matter of Community law, subject Community regulations to the guarantees laid down by the German constitution, but went on to say that:

> an examination should be made as to whether or not any analogous guarantee inherent in Community law has been disregarded. In fact, respect for fundamental rights forms an integral part of the general principles of law protected by the Court of Justice. The protection of such rights, whilst inspired by the constitutional traditions common to the member states, must be ensured within the framework of the structure and objectives of the Community.[10]

---

7 Wyatt (1982) 7 ELRev 147 agrees.
8 See eg *Case of the Danzig Railway Officials* (1928) PCIJ, Series B, No 15, and Oppenheim *International Law* (8th edn 1955, Sir H Lauterpacht) vol 1, pp 19–23. But whether individual rights can be conferred under United Kingdom law is a different question: cf cases cited at p 24, n 14, post.
9 See pp 70–73, post. The literature is now extensive: see eg Mendelson (1981) 1 Yb Eur L 125; Drzemcsewski (1981) 30 ICLQ 118; *The Protection of Fundamental Rights in the European Community*, Bulletin of the EC, Supplement 5/76; House of Lords Select Committee on the European Communities (1975–6), 53rd Report; Frowein, in *Integration Through Law* (ed Cappelletti et al) (1986) vol 1, book 3, p 300; Dauses (1985) 10 ELRev 398. For criticism of the European Court's application of human rights standards see Churchill and Foster (1987) 12 ELRev 430.
10 Case 11/70 *Internationale Handelsgesellschaft v Einfuhr- und Vorratsstelle für Getreide* [1970] ECR 1125 at 1134, [1972] CMLR 255 at 283. See also Case 29/69 *Stauder v City of Ulm* [1969] ECR 419 at 425, [1970] CMLR 112 at 119; Case 149/77 *Defrenne v Sabena* [1978] ECR 1365 at 1378, [1978] 3 CMLR 312 at 329; Cases 60, 61/84

In a number of cases the European Court has referred to the fundamental rights protected by the European Convention on Human Rights, to which all of the members of the European Communities are party. Thus in *Nold v Commission*, where the applicant alleged that restrictions imposed by the Commission violated (inter alia) the European Convention, the Court held that 'international treaties for the protection of human rights on which the member states have collaborated or of which they are signatories, can supply guidelines which should be followed within the framework of Community law'.[11] In *Prais v Council*[12] the applicant relied on the principles of freedom of religion in the European Convention. The Court held that the principles had not in fact been violated, but noted that the Council did not seek to deny that the right of freedom of religion embodied in the European Convention formed part of the fundamental rights recognised in Community law. In 1977 the European Parliament, the Council and the Commission adopted the following joint declaration:[13]

1. The European Parliament, the Council and the Commission stress the prime importance they attach to the protection of fundamental rights, as derived in particular from the constitutions of the member states and the European Convention for the Protection of Human Rights and Fundamental Freedoms.
2. In the exercise of their powers and in pursuance of the aims of the European Communities they respect and will continue to respect these rights.

In reliance on this declaration, the European Court in *Hauer v Land Rheinland-Pfalz*[14] reassured a German court that a Community regulation restricting the new planting of vines did not need to be tested against the fundamental rights of the German constitution because:

> The right to property is guaranteed in the Community legal order in accordance with the ideas common to the constitutions of the Member States, which are also reflected in the first Protocol to the European Convention for the Protection of Human Rights.

Cinéthèque SA v FNCF [1985] ECR 2604 at 2627, [1986] 1 CMLR 365 at 386; Case 234/85 *Staatsanwalt Freiburg v Keller* [1986] ECR 2897 at 2912, [1987] 1 CMLR 875 at 844; Case 137/85 *Maizena GmbH v BALM* [1987] ECR 4587 at 4607, [1989] 2 CMLR 336 at 350.

11 Case 4/73 [1974] ECR 491 at 507, [1974] 2 CMLR 338 at 354. See also Case 36/75 *Rutili v Minister for the Interior* [1975] ECR 1219 at 1232, [1976] 1 CMLR 140 at 155.
12 Case 130/75 [1976] ECR 1589, [1976] 2 CMLR 708.
13 OJ 1977 C103/1. The signatory on behalf of the Council was Dr David Owen, the Foreign Secretary, who was asked a question in the United Kingdom Parliament on the legal force of the declaration. The answer given on his behalf was that the declaration was 'a statement of policy which has no legal force' (942 HC Official Report (5th Series), 23 January 1978, written answers col 447).
14 Case 44/79 [1979] ECR 3727 at 3745, [1980] 3 CMLR 42 at 64.

After quoting Article 1 of the Protocol, the Court held that the restrictions placed on the pursuit of wine-growing were justified and were not contrary to the requirements flowing from the protection of fundamental rights in the Community.[15] The European Court has similarly considered Community procedures in relation to the fair hearing provisions of Article 6 of the European Convention on Human Rights,[16] in relation to the respect for correspondence provisions of Article 8,[17] and freedom of publication under Article 10.[18] In *R v Kirk*[19] the European Court recognised that the principle that penal provisions may not have retroactive effect is one which is common to all the legal orders of the member states and is enshrined in art 7 of the European Convention as a fundamental right; it takes its place among the general principles of law whose observance is ensured by the Court.

Johnston v Chief Constable of the Royal Ulster Constabulary[20] arose out of a change of policy with regard to the arming of police in Northern Ireland. After members of the RUC were equipped with guns in the normal course of their duties, the Chief Constable decided not to renew the contracts of women members of the full-time RUC Reserve. The reason for this was that the Chief Constable took the view that general police duties, which often involved operations requiring the carrying of firearms, would no longer be assigned to women and decided not to offer to renew any more contracts for women in the RUC Reserve except where they had to perform duties assigned only to women officers. As a result Mrs Johnston, who was a member of the full-time RUC Reserve, was dismissed. The industrial tribunal in Northern Ireland referred to the European Court a number of questions relating to whether national security and public safety could justify sex discrimination in employment. The Northern Ireland Sex Discrimination Order provided for the conclusiveness of a certificate of the Secretary of State that an act was done for the purpose of safeguarding national security or for protecting

---

15 See also Cases 41, 121 and 796/79 *Testa v Bundesanstalt für Arbeit Nürnberg* [1980] ECR 1979, [1981] 2 CMLR 552; Cases 154 etc/78 and 39 etc/79 *SpA Ferriera Valsabbia v Commission* [1980] ECR 907, [1981] 1 CMLR 613.
16 But the Commission is not a 'tribunal' for this purpose: Cases 209 to 215 and 218/78 *Heintz van Landewyck Sarl (FEDETAB) v Commission* [1980] ECR 3125, [1981] 3 CMLR 134; Cases 100–103/80 *Musique Diffusion Française SA v Commission* [1983] ECR 1825, [1983] 3 CMLR 221.
17 Case 136/79 *National Panasonic (UK) Ltd v Commission* [1980] ECR 2033, [1980] 3 CMLR 169; Case 5/85 *Akzo Chemie BV v Commission* [1986] ECR 2585, [1987] 3 CMLR 716; Cases 46/87 and 227/88 *Hoechst AG v Commission* (1989) Times, 23 October.
18 Cases 43, 63/82 *VBVB v VBBB* [1984] ECR 19, [1985] 1 CMLR 27.
19 Case 63/83 [1984] ECR 2689, [1984] 3 CMLR 522.
20 Case 222/84 [1987] QB 129, [1986] 3 All ER 135, [1986] ECR 1651, [1986] 3 CMLR 240.

public safety or public order. One of Mrs Johnston's complaints was that this provision was contrary to the principle embodied in the relevant EEC directive,[1] that all persons who considered themselves the victims of discrimination had a right to pursue their claims by judicial process. The European Court concluded that this principle of effective judicial control did not allow such a certificate to be treated as conclusive evidence so as to exclude the exercise of any power of review by the courts. The Court observed:[2]

> The requirement of judicial control stipulated by [the Directive] reflects a general principle of law which underlies the constitutional traditions common to the Member States. That principle is also laid down in Articles 6 and 13 of the European Convention on the Protection of Human Rights and Fundamental Freedoms of 4 November 1950. As the European Parliament, Council and Commission recognised in their Joint Declaration of 5 April 1977 . . . and as the Court has recognised in its decisions, the principles on which that Convention is based must be taken into consideration in Community law.

The European Court has not gone so far as to hold that the European Convention on Human Rights is part of European Community law[3] but the result of these decisions is that at the least the principles of the Convention may be taken to be identical with Community law. But the Court cannot examine the compatibility of *national* legislation with the European Convention.[4]

In 1986 these developments led the German Federal Constitutional Court to declare that it would no longer exercise its jurisdiction to test the constitutionality of secondary Community law against the Federal Constitution.[5] The Court held that a measure of protection of fundamental rights had been established within the sovereign jurisdiction of the European Communities which in its conception, substance and manner of implementation was essentially comparable with the standards of fundamental rights provided for in the German Constitution. All of the main institutions of the Community had acknowledged that in the exercise of their powers and the pursuit of the objectives of the Community they would be guided as a legal duty by respect for fundamental rights, in particular as established by the constitutions of member states and by the European Convention on Human Rights.

Even if some of the fundamental rights and guarantees had not been the subject of a judgment delivered by the European Court, its general

---

1 Council Directive 76/207, art 6.
2 [1986] ECR at 1682, [1986] 3 CMLR at 262.
3 Cf Case 98/79 *Pecastaing v Belgian State* [1980] ECR 691 at 716, [1980] 3 CMLR 685 at 708.
4 Cases 60, 61/84 *Cinéthèque SA v FNCF* [1985] ECR 2604, [1986] 1 CMLR 365; Case 12/86 *Demirel v Stadt Schwäbisch Gmünd* [1987] ECR 3719, [1989] 1 CMLR 421.
5 *Re Application of Wünsche* [1987] 3 CMLR 225.

attitude to the respect for fundamental rights, to the incorporation of fundamental rights in Community law as reflected in the constitution of member states and the European Human Rights Convention, and the declarations by the Community, showed that fundamental rights were now adequately protected in the Community. Accordingly, the German Federal Constitutional Court held that:

> So long as the European Communities, and in particular in the case law of the European Court, generally ensure an effective protection of fundamental rights as against the sovereign powers of the Communities, which is to be regarded as substantially similar to the protection of fundamental rights required unconditionally by the Constitution and insofar as they generally safeguard the essential content of fundamental rights, the Federal Constitutional Court . . . will no longer review [Community secondary] legislation by the standard of the fundamental rights contained in the Constitution . . .[6]

But the Convention on Human Rights has not become part of United Kingdom law.[7] Although on the international level the United Kingdom has ratified the European Convention on Human Rights and accepted the right of individual petition, the Convention is not part of the law of the United Kingdom as such,[8] with the result that the application of United Kingdom law may involve a breach of the Convention.[9] Thus a prisoner whose treatment has been held to be in breach of the Convention is not entitled to damages in the English court.[10] But the Convention does have a strong influence in the formulation of public policy and in the application of the presumption that statutory provisions must be interpreted so as to be in conformity with the international obligations of the United Kingdom.[11] Thus when the House of Lords considered whether to ban publication of *Spycatcher* it is clear that the freedom of speech provisions of art 10 of the European Convention (as interpreted by the European Court of Human Rights) were treated as being identical to English law, or subsumed in English law, or as a source of resolution of conflicting public interests.[12]

---

6 [1987] 3 CMLR at 265.
7 *Surjit Kaur v Lord Advocate* [1980] 3 CMLR 79; cf *Allgemeine Gold- und Silbersheideanstalt v Customs and Excise Comrs* [1980] QB 390, [1980] 2 All ER 138, CA.
8 *Malone v Metropolitan Police Comr (No 2)* [1979] Ch 344, [1979] 2 All ER 620; *Mutasa v A-G* [1980] QB 114, [1979] 3 All ER 257, and cases cited at n 7, ante.
9 See, eg *R v Wells Street Stipendiary Magistrate, ex p Deakin* [1980] AC 477, [1979] 2 All ER 497, HL.
10 *R v Secretary of State for the Home Office, ex p Weeks* (1988) Times, 15 March.
11 See *A-G v BBC* [1981] AC 303 at 354, [1980] 3 All ER 161 at 177, HL; *Schering Chemicals Ltd v Falkman Ltd* [1982] QB 1, [1981] 2 All ER 321, CA.
12 *A-G v Guardian Newspapers Ltd* [1987] 3 All ER 316, [1987] 1 WLR 1248; *(No 2)* [1988] 2 WLR 805, [1988] 3 All ER 545. See also *Lion Laboratories Ltd v Evans* [1985] QB 526, [1984] 2 All ER 417, CA; *Lord Advocate v Scotsman Publications Ltd* [1989] 3 WLR 358, [1989] 2 All ER 852, HL; *R v Home Secretary, ex p Brind* [1990] 2 WLR 787, CA.

Even if the principles of the European Convention are reflected in European Community law the Communities are not directly bound by it and the institutional machinery of the Convention is not applicable in European law.[13] Consequently there have been powerful moves toward effecting the accession of the European Communities to the Convention. In 1979 the Commission published a memorandum which concluded that the accession of the European Communities to the Convention was desirable, but that wide consultation was required before formal steps were taken.[14] In the same year the European Parliament resolved that it was in favour of accession by the Communities to the Convention and called on the Council and the Commission, in consultation with the Parliament, to make immediate preparations for accession.[15] But progress has been slow, and in 1982 the Parliament recognised that accession could involve considerable constitutional, political, legal and technical difficulties, but resolved that the accession of the Communities to the Convention would demonstrate to the outside world and to public opinion in the Community the determination of the Communities' institutions to reinforce the rule of law in the Communities, and requested the Commission to submit a proposal to the Council for accession.[16]

The preamble to the Single European Act signed in 1986 confirms adherence of the signatory states to the fundamental rights recognised in (inter alia) the constitutions of the member states and in the European Convention on Human Rights. On 12 April 1989 the European Parliament adopted a Declaration of fundamental rights and freedoms, the preamble to which recalled that fundamental rights derived from the Treaties establishing the European Communities, the constitutional traditions common to the member states, the European Convention and other international instruments, and had been developed in the case law of the European Court. The goal of the European Parliament is to see the Declaration adopted by other Community institutions and to see it endorsed by the European Court.

---

13 Cf *CFDT v European Communities* [1979] 2 CMLR 229, where the European Commission on Human Rights declared inadmissible a complaint brought by a French trade union because the European Communities were not party to the European Convention; see also Case 11055/84 *Re European School in Brussels* [1987] 2 CMLR 57. As to the application of the Convention to European elections see *Re An Expatriate United Kingdom Citizen* [1979] 3 CMLR 172; *Alliance des Belges de la CE v Belgium* [1979] 3 CMLR 175. See, generally, Mendelson (1983) 3 Yb Eur L 99.
14 *Accession of the Communities to the European Convention on Human Rights*, Bulletin of the EC, Supplement 2/79; House of Lords Select Committee on the European Communities (1979–80) 71st Report (with some very valuable memoranda and evidence); 418 HL Official Report (5th series) col 1354 (Lord Scarman); McBride and Brown (1981) 1 Yb Eur L 167.
15 OJ 1979 C127/69.
16 OJ 1982 C304/253.

5 Community law and national law

The problem of the relationship between Community law and national law is not a unique one. It is no different in kind from the problem of the relationship between international law and national law that has so exercised so many jurists for so long.[17] It is usually treated as a distinct and separate problem because Community law is much more like loose federal law than international law, because so many of its rules reflect national notions of administrative law and because it impinges so much more on private rights than is usual. Furthermore, the institutions of the Communities have sought to establish the unique character of Community law and therefore to minimise its relationship with traditional treaty law. But the rules of Community law derive their force from treaty law and therefore from the international obligations of the member states *inter se*. The question, therefore, of the primacy of Community law and the ways in which that primacy is to be given effect in national law is similar in character to certain aspects of the question of the relationship between international law and national law.[18] The extent to which *national law* must give effect to Community law is one aspect of the question of the extent to which *member states* must give effect to it, namely a question of treaty obligation.

There is, however, no need to resolve the great problem of the conflict between the theory of monism and the theory of dualism, namely, whether international law and municipal law are a single system in which the former has primacy (monism) or whether they are separate systems, the former binding states only and having effect in municipal law only when expressly incorporated (dualism). The reason there is no need to resolve this problem in the present context is that there is little doubt that, from the point of view of Community law, it is supreme and has to take effect in national law, but from the point of view of United Kingdom law, Community law derives from a treaty and its incorporation into United Kingdom law is necessary if it is to affect private rights. To put it differently, Community law adopts the monist approach—from the point of view of Community law it is supreme. But the law of the United Kingdom tends to the dualist approach. Thus, treaties are not self-executing in the United Kingdom and require legislation to achieve their result,[19] since, according to the traditional formula, the rules of international law

---

17 See, with references, Oppenheim *International Law* vol 1, pp 37–43.
18 On the problem in relation to Community law, see, eg Warner (1977) 93 LQR 349; Usher *European Community Law and National Law: The Irreversible Transfer?* (1981) ch 2; Bebr *Development of Judicial Control of the European Communities* (1981) ch 14.
19 See eg *A-G for Canada v A-G for Ontario* [1937] AC 326 at 347–8; *Salomon v Customs and Excise Comrs* [1967] 2 QB 116 at 143, [1966] 3 All ER 871 at 875; *British Airways Board v Laker Airways Ltd* [1985] AC 58, 83, [1984] 3 All ER 39, 47–48, HL.

are only part of the law of the United Kingdom in so far as they are accepted and adopted by the United Kingdom.[20] As Lord Oliver put it recently in the cases arising out of the collapse of the International Tin Council:[1]

> ... as a matter of the constitutional law of the United Kingdom, the Royal Prerogative, whilst it embraces the making of treaties, does not extend to altering the law or conferring rights upon individuals or depriving individuals of rights which they enjoy in domestic law without the intervention of Parliament. Treaties, as it is sometimes expressed, are not self-executing. Quite simply, a treaty is not part of English law unless and until it has been incorporated into the law by legislation.

A real and practical problem, however, can only arise when adequate statutory effect is not given in United Kingdom law to a rule of Community law or when United Kingdom law conflicts with Community law. Then the two systems are in conflict and, it is suggested, the resolution of that problem is a political question, since a deadlock would arise: the Community legal system would give effect to Community law, and the United Kingdom legal system would give effect to United Kingdom law. It is not unusual to have such a conflict between legal systems which is reconcilable only by political means.[2]

The question of the relationship between Community law and United Kingdom law will therefore be looked at from two points of view: *first*, that of the Community legal system and *second*, that of the United Kingdom legal system. It is suggested that not only is this approach sound in principle but that it also disposes of what have seemed to some to be problems but which do not in fact arise, particularly the so-called problem of sovereignty.

6 The supremacy of Community law—the position according to Community law

There is no doubt that, from the standpoint of Community law, it is Community law which is supreme, with the following results in *Community* law:

(1) Community law confers rights on individuals to which national law must give effect;
(2) municipal legislation cannot prevail over Community law, whichever is first in time;

---

20 *R v Secretary of State, ex p Thakrar* [1974] QB 684 at 701, [1974] 2 All ER 261 at 266, following *Chung Chi Cheung v R* [1939] AC 160, [1938] 4 All ER 786.
1 *J H Rayner (Mincing Lane) Ltd v Department of Trade and Industry* [1989] 3 WLR 969 at 1002, [1989] 3 All ER 523 at 544–545, HL. See also *Re International Tin Council* [1987] Ch 419, [1987] 1 All ER 890; affd [1989] Ch 309, [1988] 3 All ER 257, CA; *R v Home Secretary, ex p Brind* [1990] 2 WLR 797, CA.
2 Cf *Madzimbamuto v Lardner-Burke* [1969] 1 AC 645, [1968] 3 All ER 561, PC.

(3) the efficacy of Community law cannot vary from one member state to another;
(4) member states cannot take or maintain in force measures which are liable to impair the useful effect of the treaty;
(5) member states cannot give authoritative rulings (by legislation or otherwise) on the interpretation of Community regulations;
(6) Community law cannot be tested in municipal courts for compliance with the constitutions of member states;
(7) member states may not remove from ordinary courts the power to apply Community law;
(8) where the European Court declares legislation of a member state to be incompatible with Community law, the legislative authorities of the state are under a duty to amend or repeal the offending legislation and its courts are under a duty to ensure that the European Court's judgment is complied with;
(9) member states cannot excuse their non-performance of treaty obligations by relying on their domestic constitutions.

These propositions will be discussed later in detail but it must be emphasised that they are propositions of *Community law*. If, and to the extent that, they cannot be regarded also as propositions of the law of a particular member state there is a conflict between Community law and national law. In practice, however, the courts of member states have sought to avoid and to resolve conflicts by giving primacy to Community law to the extent that their constitutional systems have allowed it.[3]

Under art 5 of the EEC Treaty:

> Member states shall take all appropriate measures, whether general or particular, to ensure fulfilment of the obligations arising out of this Treaty or resulting from action taken by the institutions of the Community. They shall facilitate the achievement of the Community's tasks.
>
> They shall abstain from any measure which could jeopardise the attainment of the objectives of this Treaty.

It has already been seen that in the *Van Gend en Loos* case[4] the European Court referred to the creation of a new legal order in which 'the states have limited their sovereign rights' and went on to conclude:

> Independently of the legislation of member states, Community law therefore not only imposes obligations on individuals but is also intended to confer upon them rights which become part of their legal heritage.[5]

The Court thus emphasised that the rights of individuals under Community law were quite independent of implementing legislation.

---

3 See pp 41–42.
4 Case 26/62 [1963] ECR 1, [1963] CMLR 105.
5 [1963] ECR 1 at 12, [1963] CMLR 105 at 129.

In *Costa v ENEL*[6] the Court had to deal with an argument that it could not give a ruling under art 177 because Community law was irrelevant in the national court in the particular case, there being an applicable Italian law. The Court held that it was not debarred from ruling on a point of interpretation, although it did hold that it could not, in an art 177 reference, give a ruling on the compatibility of national law with Community law. It said:[7]

> The integration into the laws of each member state of provisions which derive from the Community, and more generally the terms and the spirit of the Treaty, make it impossible for the states, as a corollary, to accord precedence to a unilateral and subsequent measure over a legal system accepted by them on a basis of reciprocity. . . . The obligations undertaken under the Treaty establishing the Community would not be unconditional, but merely contingent, if they could be called in question by subsequent legislative acts of the signatories. . . . The precedence of Community law is confirmed by Article 189, whereby a regulation 'shall be binding' and 'directly applicable in all member states'. This provision, which is subject to no reservation, would be quite meaningless if a state could unilaterally nullify its effects by means of a legislative measure which could prevail over Community law. It follows from all these observations that the law stemming from the Treaty, an independent source of law, could not, because of its special and original nature, be overridden by domestic legal provisions, however framed, without being deprived of its character as Community law and without the legal basis of the Community itself being called into question. The transfer by the states from their domestic legal system to the Community legal system of the rights and obligations arising under the Treaty carries with it a permanent limitation of their sovereign rights, against which a subsequent unilateral act incompatible with the concept of the Community cannot prevail.

The Court thus emphasised (1) the restriction of sovereign rights, and (2) the creation of a new body of law applicable not only to member states but also to individuals, to reach the conclusion that it would be inconsistent with such a restriction of sovereignty and the creation of a new body of law if member states could nevertheless have power to legislate in a sense contrary to the rights and obligations created in that new body of law. There is nothing inherently unusual in this. What is unusual (which will be discussed in greater detail below) is the way in which the Court in these cases extended the area in which sovereignty is so restricted by extending the areas of the direct effect or applicability of Community law. What that means is that the Court was implying from express terms of the Treaty an obligation on the states to provide a domestic remedy and also assuming that the national law did or would give a remedy. In other words, from the standpoint of

---

6 Case 6/64 [1964] ECR 585, [1964] CMLR 425.
7 [1964] ECR 585 at 593–4, [1964] CMLR 425 at 455–6.

the Court, Community law was reaching into national law and providing a national remedy *whether or not national law in fact did so*. Whether the national law would recognise that incursion is another question. But for present purposes it suffices to say that from the standpoint of Community law national law was bound to recognise it.

In 1967 the European Court spoke of the way in which Regulations of the Council and Commission were, by art 189 of the Treaty, directly applicable in member states, and said:[8]

> According to Article 189, Regulation No 22, which established the system of levies, is 'binding in its entirety and directly applicable in all member states'. This system must therefore be applied with the same binding force in all the member states within the context of the Community legal system which they have set up and which, by virtue of the Treaty, has been integrated into their legal systems. The states have thus conferred on the Community institutions power to take measures fixing the levy such as those which form the subject-matter of Regulation No 22, thus submitting their sovereign rights to a corresponding limitation.

Thus the Court appears to have recognised that the limitation of 'sovereign rights' of the member states took effect by the incorporation of Community law into the legal systems of the member states. But once that had been done, Community law did not allow it to be undone, so that in a case concerning the interpretation of the same regulation the Court could say:[9]

> Since Regulation No 22/62, in conformity with the second paragraph of Article 189 of the Treaty, is directly applicable in all member states, the latter, unless otherwise expressly provided, are precluded from taking steps, for the purposes of applying the regulation, which are intended to alter its scope or supplement its provisions. To the extent to which member states have transferred legislative powers in tariff matters with the object of ensuring the satisfactory operation of a common market in agriculture they no longer have the power to adopt legislative provisions in this field.

The Court went on to hold that member states could not make internal provisions affecting the scope of the Regulation, and, in particular, in order to ensure uniformity throughout the Common Market, the Court held that they could not enact binding rules of interpretation of Community regulations.

The culmination of the line of cases re-enforcing the direct applicability of Community regulations pursuant to art 189 came with the judgment of the Court in 1970 when it asserted the supremacy of Community law over the constitutional law of member states. In a

---

8 Case 17/67 *Neumann v Hauptzollamt Hof* [1967] ECR 441 at 453. See also Case 43/71 *Politi v Ministero delle Finanze* [1971] ECR 1039, [1973] CMLR 60.
9 Case 40/69 *Hauptzollamt Hamburg v Bollmann* [1970] ECR 69 at 79, [1970] CMLR 141 at 153. See for the development of this principle pp 74–77, post.

judgment to be discussed in greater detail below in chapter 2[10] the Court said:[11]

> Recourse to the legal rules or concepts of national law in order to judge the validity of measures adopted by the institutions of the Community would have an adverse effect on the uniformity and efficacy of Community law. The validity of such measures can only be judged in the light of Community law. In fact, the law stemming from the Treaty, an independent source of law, cannot because of its very nature be overridden by rules of national law, however framed, without being deprived of its character as Community law and without the legal basis of the Community itself being called in question. Therefore the validity of a Community measure or its effect within a member state cannot be affected by allegations that it runs counter to either fundamental rights as formulated by the constitution of that state or the principles of a national constitutional structure.

In the celebrated *Simmenthal*[12] decision the Court went a stage further. In a previous reference the Court had ruled that charges made for veterinary and public health inspectors were charges equivalent to customs duties.[13] Following that reference the Italian court was faced with a conflict between a Council regulation on the common organisation of the market in beef and veal, and the Italian veterinary and public health laws, some of which were subsequent in time to the Council Regulation. Under Italian law Italian legislation contrary to EEC regulations may be held unconstitutional under art 11 of the Italian constitution,[14] but only by the Constitutional Court, and not by the ordinary courts. The Italian judge of first instance referred to the European Court under art 177 of the EEC Treaty the question whether the direct applicability of regulations under art 189 required national courts to disregard inconsistent subsequent national legislation without waiting for the relevant legislation to be eliminated by national action (either by repeal or by being declared invalid by the Constitutional Court).

The European Court held, first, that directly applicable regulations take precedence over both prior and subsequent national legislation, and consequently that:[15]

---

10 See pp 70–73, post.
11 Case 11/70 *Internationale Handelsgesellschaft v Einfuhr- und Vorratsstelle für Getreide* [1970] ECR 1125 at 1134, [1972] CMLR 255 at 283.
12 Case 106/77 *Amministrazione delle Finanze dello Stato v Simmenthal SpA* [1978] ECR 629, [1978] 3 CMLR 263.
13 Case 35/76 *Simmenthal v Italian Minister of Finance* [1976] ECR 1871, [1977] 2 CMLR 1.
14 Which has been interpreted to provide for the supremacy of Community obligations over national law: see p 41, post.
15 [1978] ECR 629 at 644. For a recent re-affirmation see Case 170/88 *Ford España SA v Spain* 11 July 1989.

any national court must, in a case within its jurisdiction, apply Community law in its entirety and protect rights which the latter confers on individuals and must accordingly set aside any provision of national law which may conflict with it, whether prior or subsequent to the Community rule.

The Court held, secondly, that any national law or practice which might impair the effectiveness of Community law by withholding from the national court the power to do everything necessary forthwith to set aside incompatible national legislation was itself incompatible with Community law. The solution of the conflict between national law and Community law should not be left to another body with a discretion of its own, even if there were only a temporary impediment to the full effectiveness of Community law. The question was accordingly answered in these terms:

> A national court which is called upon, within the limits of its jurisdiction to apply provisions of Community law, is under a duty to give full effect to those provisions, if necessary refusing of its own motion to apply any conflicting provision of national legislation, even if adopted subsequently, and it is not necessary for the court to request or await the prior setting aside of such provisions by legislative or other constitutional means.[16]

In the United Kingdom there is no special constitutional court, but the effect of the *Simmenthal* decision is that a system which does not allow courts to refuse to apply subsequent inconsistent legislation is incompatible with Community law. Whether the United Kingdom system is in this category is discussed below.[17] But it has been held that courts with special statutory functions have the duty to apply Community law just as much as courts of general jurisdiction.[18]

It follows from the primacy of Community law created by treaty that a member state cannot put forward as an excuse for its non-fulfilment of a treaty obligation that its executive has done what it could to comply with an obligation or to remedy a breach but that its legislature will not, or cannot, pass the necessary legislation. This principle, which is also an example of a general principle of international law,[19] is illustrated by the litigation relating to the Italian

---

16 [1978] ECR 629 at 645–6. By the time the Court gave its ruling the Italian law in question had been declared unconstitutional in other proceedings.
17 See pp 28–39, post.
18 *Shields v E Coomes (Holdings) Ltd* [1979] 1 All ER 456, [1978] 1 WLR 1408, CA; *Murphy v An Bord Telecom Eireann* [1988] 2 CMLR 753. Cf *Southampton and South-West Hampshire Area Health Authority v Marshall (No 2)* [1989] 3 CMLR 771 at 774, EAT.
19 The Permanent Court of International Justice said, in its Advisory Opinion in the case of *Treatment of Polish Nationals in Danzig* (1932), Series A/B, No 44, p 24; 'A state cannot adduce as against another state its own Constitution with a view to evading obligations incumbent upon it under international law or treaties in force.' For this principle in Community law see pp 220–221, post.

export tax on art treasures which was alleged to be in violation of Italy's obligation under art 16 to abolish customs duties (and charges having equivalent effect) on exports. In 1968 the European Court held that, by continuing to levy the tax, the Italian Government was in breach of art 16.[20] Legislation had been introduced in Italy to exempt exports to member states, but the Bill, introduced in 1967 and passed to the Chamber of Deputies, had lapsed on the dissolution of the Italian Parliament in March 1968. In 1971, in a case referred by the Turin court under art 177, the European Court held that art 16 constituted a directly effective rule of Community law with the result that Italian law had to provide a remedy for the refund to exporters of sums paid by way of export tax.[1]

Meanwhile, the Commission had instituted further proceedings under art 169 alleging that Italy had failed to take adequate measures to comply with the 1968 judgment of the Court. After argument had taken place in the further proceedings, the Italian Government informed the Court that legislation introduced in late 1971 had been adopted, abolishing the tax on exports to member states and providing for refunds of tax already paid. In argument, the Italian Government suggested that it had complied with the 1968 judgment by submitting the necessary legislation and that there had been no violation of the obligation under art 171 (to take necessary measures to comply with the judgment of the Court) because the delay had been due to circumstances independent of the will of the relevant authorities. The Court rejected this argument. It said:[2]

> Since it is a question of a directly applicable Community rule, the argument that the infringement can be terminated only by the adoption of measures constitutionally appropriate to repeal the provision establishing the tax would amount to saying that the application of the Community rule is subject to the law of each member state and more precisely that this application is impossible where it is contrary to a national law.

But the principle was not limited to directly applicable rules of Community law since:

> The grant made by member states of the Community of rights and powers in accordance with the provisions of the Treaty involves a definitive limitation on their sovereign rights and no provisions whatsoever of national law may be invoked to override this limitation.

The Court held that Italy had been in continuing breach of art 16 but

---

20 Case 7/68 *Commission v Italy* [1968] ECR 423, [1969] CMLR 1.
1 Case 18/71 *Eunomia di Porro v Ministry of Education* [1971] ECR 811, [1972] CMLR 4.
2 Case 48/71 *Commission v Italy* [1972] ECR 527 at 532, [1972] CMLR 699 at 708.

noted that its breach of the obligation to remedy it under art 171 had been terminated with the enactment of the legislation.

7 The supremacy of Community law—the national viewpoint—the problem of 'sovereignty'

It has been seen above that the European Court has said that the member states 'have limited their sovereign rights, albeit within limited fields'.[3] This is clearly so in the sense that the member states have contractually bound themselves in international law to do certain things and refrain from others. But the power to enter into treaties (and thereby undertake what may be restrictive obligations) is an exercise of the power of sovereignty. As the Permanent Court of International Justice put it in the case of the *SS Wimbledon*,[4] 'the right of entering into international engagements is an attribute of State sovereignty'.

'Sovereignty' is a word of many meanings.[5] It has already been used in two senses in the preceding paragraph. When the Government White Paper of 1971 said that there was 'no question of any erosion of essential national sovereignty'[6] and when Mr Rippon said that the European Communities Bill did not abridge 'the ultimate sovereignty of Parliament'[7] the word sovereignty was used in two further senses. When the Irish Supreme Court considered whether the Single European Act was compatible with the Irish Constitution and whether a referendum to amend the constitution was necessary it described sovereignty variously as 'the unfettered right to decide', and as including 'the freedom to formulate foreign policy',[8] and a bare majority decided that the Single European Act required member states to co-ordinate their foreign policy to such an extent as to restrict the freedom given by the Irish Constitution to the Government; ratification by Ireland could not take place until the Constitution had been amended following a referendum. Henchy J, one of the majority, said that:[9]

---

3 Case 26/62 *Van Gend en Loos v Nederlandse Administratie der Belastingen* [1963] ECR 1 at 12, [1963] CMLR 105 at 129; see also Case 6/64 *Costa v ENEL* [1964] ECR 585, [1964] CMLR 425; and Case 17/67 *Neumann v Hauptzollamt Hof* [1967] ECR 441.
4 PCIJ, Series A, No 1, p 15. See also McNair *Law of Treaties* (1969) pp 754 et seq.
5 See eg Hart *The Concept of Law* (1961) pp 70–6, 145–50, 215–21, 255–6; Wade *The Basis of Legal Sovereignty* [1955] CLJ 172; Heuston 'Sovereignty' in *Oxford Essays in Jurisprudence* (ed Guest 1961) pp 198–222, or *Essays in Constitutional Law* (2nd edn 1964) pp 1–31; Winterton (1976) 92 LQR 591.
6 The United Kingdom and the European Communities (Cmnd 4715) para 29.
7 831 HC Official Report (5th Series) col 278, 15 February 1972.
8 *Crotty v An Taoiseach* [1987] IR 713 at 769 and 783, [1987] 2 CMLR 666 at 713 and 723. See Temple Lang (1987) 24 CML Rev 709.
9 [1987] IR at 786 and 788, [1987] 2 CMLR at 725 and 728.

... although the approach to the ultimate aim of European Union is to be reached by a pathway of gradualism, each Member State will immediately cede a portion of its sovereignty and freedom of action in matters of foreign policy ... [I]f Ireland were to ratify the Treaty it would be bound in international law to engage actively in a programme which would trench progressively on Ireland's independence and sovereignty in the conduct of foreign relations.

The White Paper was probably speaking of the continuing political power of the United Kingdom to order its own affairs at home and abroad—clearly entry into the Common Market has, at least, while the United Kingdom remains a member, restricted that power, and whether the restriction has eroded 'essential national sovereignty' is a political question. When Mr Rippon spoke of the 'ultimate sovereignty of Parliament' he referred, no doubt, to the constitutional doctrine that there is nothing that, in the eyes of the law of the United Kingdom, a statute properly enacted cannot do.[10]

It is only in the sense last mentioned that the word has any useful meaning in relation to the national law of the United Kingdom. In the international sphere and in the political sphere there may have been a limitation of sovereignty but there is no reason to believe that there has as yet been any limitation on the sovereignty of the United Kingdom Parliament. This is made clear by the way in which Community law has been given effect in the United Kingdom, a way which is wholly orthodox and wholly consistent with the previous practice on the transformation of international obligations into the municipal sphere.

8 Treaties as the source of Community law

As has been shown above, the European Court has on numerous occasions stressed the treaties as being the source of the obligations of the member states to make changes to their national law and to give effect to the rights of individuals conferred by Community law.

According to the well-established constitutional law and practice of the United Kingdom, the treaty-making power is vested in the Crown. Entering into a treaty is an executive act and domestic ratification is not necessary for the United Kingdom to be bound internationally. This has two important consequences. The first is that the United Kingdom courts will not challenge or question the treaty-making power of the Crown. The second is that treaties have no effect as such on the existing domestic law—legislation is necessary if any alteration of domestic law is required, expressly or impliedly, by the treaty.

---

10 See eg Wade and Phillips *Constitutional and Administrative Law* (10th edn Bradley, 1985) ch 5, pp 28–39, post.

(1) The principle that the courts will not challenge or question the treaty-making power of the Crown is part of the wider principle that acts of state are not cognisable in the national courts.[11] When Mr Blackburn sought declarations in 1971 (before the United Kingdom had become a party to the Treaties) claiming (inter alia) that the Crown had no power to enter into the Treaty of Rome, Lord Denning MR said:[12]

> The general principle applies to this treaty as to any other. The treaty-making power of this country rests not in the courts, but in the Crown; that is, Her Majesty acting on the advice of her Ministers. When her Ministers negotiate and sign a treaty, even a treaty of such paramount importance as this proposed one, they act on behalf of the country as a whole. They exercise the prerogative of the Crown. Their action in so doing cannot be challenged or questioned in these courts.

A treaty may require ratification by the executive to make it fully binding in international law but it does not require ratification by Parliament.[13] But the European Assembly Elections Act 1978, s 6(1), provides that no treaty which provides for an increase in the powers of the United Kingdom Parliament is to be ratified by the United Kingdom unless it has been approved by an Act of Parliament.

(2) It is a commonplace of constitutional law and practice that if treaties are to affect private rights they cannot do so without more, and that only legislation can affect such rights.[14] If legislation is not enacted, there may be a breach of treaty, and the Crown may therefore be in breach of its treaty obligations in international law to the other contracting parties. It has been suggested that in certain exceptional

---

11 The English act of state doctrine is of somewhat uncertain scope (see *Nissan v A-G* [1970] AC 179, [1966] 1 All ER 629) but in this context there is no doubt that it applies so as to prevent the courts from questioning the exercise of the treaty-making power. See eg *Rustomjee v R* (1876) 1 QBD 487 affd. 2 QBD 69; *Walker v Baird* [1892] AC 491; *Salaman v Secretary of State for India* [1906] 1 KB 613; *Bank voor Handel en Scheepvaart v Slatford* [1953] 1 QB 248, [1952] 2 All ER 956; *Republic of Italy v Hambros Bank* [1950] Ch 314, [1950] 1 All ER 430; *Buttes Gas and Oil Co v Hammer (Nos 2 and 3)* [1982] AC 888, 930, [1981] 3 All ER 616, 628, HL.
12 *Blackburn v A-G* [1971] 2 All ER 1380 at 1382; [1971] 1 WLR 1037 at 1040; see also Salmon LJ 1041 at 1383. Cf *McWhirter v A-G* [1972] CMLR 882, CA.
13 Whether in international law a treaty requires ratification depends on the intention of the parties; art 14 of the Vienna Convention of 1969 on the Law of Treaties. A treaty will not require, or be conditional upon, ratification by a parliamentary body unless the treaty so provides (which it would rarely do). On the British practice, see McNair *Law of Treaties* pp 129–147.
14 *The Parlement Belge* (1878–9) 4 PD 129 at 154, reversed in part (1880) 5 PD 197, and for modern examples see *R v Chief Immigration Officer, ex p Salamat Bibi* [1976] 3 All ER 843 at 847, 848, [1976] 1 WLR 979 at 984, 986; *R v Home Secretary, ex p Bhajan Singh* [1976] QB 198 at 207, [1975] 2 All ER 1081 at 1083; *Pan-American World Airways v Department of Trade* [1976] 1 Lloyd's Rep 257 at 261; *Malone v Metropolitan Police Comr (No 2)* [1979] Ch 344, [1979] 2 All ER 620. Cf Cmnd 3301, para 22.

cases a treaty may be the basis of a cause of action in favour of a third party named as beneficiary,[15] but the authorities do not go beyond indicating that in very exceptional cases the Crown may contract as agent or trustee for its nationals.[16]

The most authoritative statement of the principle that treaties cannot as such confer rights or impose duties in national law is by Lord Atkin in *A-G for Canada v A-G for Ontario*:[17]

> Within the British Empire there is a well-established rule that the making of a treaty is an executive act, while the performance of its obligations, if they entail alteration of the existing domestic law, requires legislative action. Unlike some other countries, the stipulations of a treaty duly ratified do not within the Empire, by virtue of the treaty alone, have the force of law. If the national executive, the government of the day, decide to incur the obligations of a treaty which involve alteration of law they have to run the risk of obtaining the assent of Parliament to the necessary statute or statutes. To make themselves as secure as possible they will often in such cases before final ratification seek to obtain from Parliament an expression of approval. But it has never been suggested, and it is not the law, that such an expression of approval operates as law, or that in law it precludes the assenting Parliament, or any subsequent Parliament, from refusing to give its sanction to any legislative proposals that may subsequently be brought before it.

It is not necessary for present purposes to consider what may sometimes be regarded as exceptions to the general rule: treaties relating to cessation of territory, peace treaties, treaties affecting belligerent rights and treaties conferring immunities have been discussed in this connection, because they sometimes incidentally affect private rights. For example, an enemy alien cannot sue while a state of war subsists; a state of war commences as a result of the act of the prerogative and may end by a similar act exercised by means of a treaty of peace; the treaty turns the enemy alien who cannot sue into an alien who can; but no legislation is required to achieve this result.[18]

In the context of Community law, the principle has been recognised in two decisions of the Court of Appeal. In *Blackburn v A-G* Lord Denning MR said:[19]

---

15 Mann *Studies in International Law* (1973) pp 355–8.
16 In *Rustomjee v R* (1876) 2 QBD 69 at 72 it was said that where a treaty was concerned the 'Crown is not, and cannot be, either a trustee or an agent for any subject whatever'. But see *Civilian War Claimants v R* [1932] AC 14; *Administrator of German Property v Knoop* [1933] Ch 439, and McNair *Law of Treaties*, pp 328–31.
17 [1937] AC 326 at 347–8. For the re-affirmation of the principle see *British Airways Board v Laker Airways Ltd*, p 14, n 19; *J H Rayner (Mincing Lane) Ltd v Department of Trade and Industry*, p 15, ante; see also Higgins in *The Effect of Treaties in Domestic Law* (ed Jacobs and Roberts) (1987) p 123.
18 See Mann, *Studies in International Law* (1973) pp 334–6.
19 [1971] 2 All ER 1380 at 1382, [1971] 1 WLR 1037 at 1039, [1971] CMLR 784 at 789.

Even if a treaty is signed, it is elementary that these courts take no notice of treaties as such. We take no notice of treaties until they are embodied in laws enacted by Parliament, and then only to the extent that Parliament tells us.

Salmon LJ added that 'these courts are concerned only with the effect of such [political] decisions if and when they have been implemented by legislation.'[20] In *McWhirter v A-G* Lord Denning MR pointed out:

Even though the Treaty of Rome has been signed, it has no effect, so far as these Courts are concerned, until it is made an Act of Parliament. Once it is implemented by an Act of Parliament, these Courts must go by the Act of Parliament. Until that day comes, we take no notice of it.[1]

and Phillimore LJ said:

Whether [the Treaty of Accession] is ratified[2] or not depends, so far as this country is concerned, upon the present Bill before Parliament; it is that Bill which will or will not alter the law of this country; and unless and until that Bill becomes law this Court is not concerned with the provisions of the Treaty . . .[3]

9 The mode of incorporation and the sovereignty of Parliament

The European Communities Act 1972 will be examined in detail in the next chapter in so far as it relates to the incorporation of Community law into the law of the United Kingdom. At this point, therefore, it is necessary only to note that the technique of the Act is not revolutionary, whatever its effects may be. On the contrary, the technique is wholly consistent with traditional and orthodox notions of constitutional theory and practice.

The broad scheme of the Act[4] is as follows:

(1) those rights and duties which are, as a matter of Community law, directly applicable or effective are to be given legal effect in the United Kingdom (s 2(1));
(2) the executive is given power to make orders and regulations to give effect both to obligations of the United Kingdom and to deal with any incidental problems arising from those rights and duties which are directly applicable or effective (s 2(2));
(3) there are limitations on the power of delegated legislation conferred by the Act, most notably that the power does not include

---

20 [1971] 2 All ER 1380 at 1383, [1971] 1 WLR 1037 at 1041.
1 [1972] CMLR 882 at 886. Cf *Shields v E Coomes (Holdings) Ltd* [1979] 1 All ER 456 at 461, [1978] 1 WLR 1408 at 1414.
2 The word 'ratified' is used loosely in this context to mean 'given effect to'.
3 [1972] CMLR 882 at 887.
4 For the text of the significant provisions, see Appendix.

powers (a) to tax, (b) to legislate retrospectively, (c) to sub-delegate, or (d) to impose new criminal offences punishable by more than certain specified penalties (s 2(2) and Sch 2), but subject to those restrictions (and subject to any future Act of Parliament) the orders and regulations may include any provision as might be made by Act of Parliament (s 2(4));
(4) any existing or future enactments are to be construed and have effect subject to the above (s 2(4));
(5) any question as to the meaning or effect of the treaties is to be treated as a question of law to be determined in accordance with Community law, of which judicial notice is to be taken (s 3(1) and (2));
(6) specific alterations are made to existing law (statute and common law) to take account of specific Community obligations, especially in the area of customs duties, agriculture, company law and restrictive practices (ss 4–10);
(7) provision is made for extending the Perjury Act 1911 and the Official Secrets Act 1911–1939 to the European Court and Community institutions.

There is no suggestion in the 1972 Act that there has been any attempt on the part of the legislature to entrench all or any of its provisions, to protect them against repeal by a future Act of Parliament. The prevailing legal philosophy in the United Kingdom is that Parliament is supreme. This philosophy was re-affirmed in *Manuel v A-G*.[5] Megarry V-C said:[6]

> I have grave doubts about the theory of the transfer of sovereignty as affecting the competence of Parliament. In my view, it is a fundamental of the English Constitution that Parliament is supreme. As a matter of law the courts of England recognise Parliament as being omnipotent in all save the power to destroy its own omnipotence ...

and in the words of Lord Justice Slade:

> On the face of it, the ordinary, elementary rules of English constitutional law leave the court with no choice but to construe and apply the enactments of Parliament as they stand.[7]

Speaking for a unanimous House of Lords,[8] Lord Lowry quoted with evident approval the description by Wade and Bradley[9] of the doctrine of sovereignty or legislative supremacy of Parliament as consisting essentially of 'a rule which governs the legal relationship between the

---

5 [1983] Ch 77, [1982] 3 All ER 786 and [1982] 3 All ER 822, CA.
6 [1983] Ch 77 at 89.
7 At 103, citing *British Railways Board v Pickin* [1974] AC 765, [1974] 1 All ER 609.
8 *Harrison v Tew* [1990] 1 All ER 321 at 329.
9 *Constitutional and Administrative Law* (10th edn 1985) p 65.

courts and the legislature, namely that the courts are under a duty to apply the legislation made by Parliament'.

The 1972 Act proceeds on the basis of the legal sovereignty of Parliament, and is expressive of and subject to the principle of sovereignty of Parliament. It has been enacted but there is no fetter on Parliament—it can amend it or repeal it.

(i) Section 2(4) of the European Communities Act 1972

It is true that s 2(4) of the 1972 Act provides that 'any enactment passed or to be passed, other than one contained in this Part of this Act, shall be construed and have effect subject to the foregoing provisions of this section'. The 'foregoing provisions' include s 2(1), which provides that directly enforceable Community law is to be given effect in the United Kingdom. In so far as the sub-section relates to existing legislation it is effective to make such amendments (or confer power to make such amendments) as may be necessary to give effect to Community law.

The extent of its effect on subsequent legislation is more controversial. It has been suggested that s 2(4) has effected a degree of entrenchment by denying effectiveness to subsequent legislation inconsistent with Community law.[10] But it is submitted that the better view is that, in so far as it relates to future legislation, s 2(4) only expresses a rule of construction which must give way to a contrary intention.[11] Section 2(4) does therefore go part of the way to prevent legislation which would otherwise by implication be contrary to Community law. Its effect is that United Kingdom courts should interpret subsequent legislation in such a manner as to be consistent with Community law and may read subsequent inconsistent legislation as subject to Community law. It is therefore suggested that no theoretical or practical problem of sovereignty arises in this context. The considerable literature (mostly pre-accession) on the subject is largely devoted to a consideration of the ways in which Community law could have been entrenched if the executive and the legislature had thought it desirable.[12]

There is little room for a suggestion[13] that just in the way that

---

10 Mitchell, Kuipers & Gall (1972) 9 CML Rev 134 at 143–4. See also Trindade (1972) 35 MLR 375 at 393.
11 Cf Howe (1973) 49 Int Aff 1 at 7–10; Forman (1973) 10 CML Rev 39 at 49–52; Iaconelli (1979) 28 ICLQ 65; Bradley, in *The Changing Constitution* (ed Jowell and Oliver) (1985) p 23; Clarke and Sufrin, in *Effect on English Domestic Law of Membership of the European Communities* (ed Furmston) (1983) p 32.
12 See eg Wade (1972) 88 LQR 1; Martin (1968–9) 6 CML Rev 7; Mitchell (1967–8) 5 CML Rev 112; de Smith (1971) 34 MLR 597.
13 de Smith, ibid, p 613.

The mode of incorporation and the sovereignty of Parliament

Parliament lost the right to legislate for the former Dominions by the Statute of Westminster 1931 so it could lose the power to legislate contrary to Community law as a result of the enactment of legislation giving effect to the accession to the Treaties. In the first place, it is likely that *as a matter of law* (whatever may be the political position) legislation repealing, or inconsistent with, the Statute of Westminster would have to be given effect by the United Kingdom court. As Lord Reid put it in *Madzimbamuto v Lardner-Burke*:[14]

> It is often said that it would be unconstitutional for the United Kingdom Parliament to do certain things, meaning that the moral, political and other reasons against doing them are so strong that most people would regard it as highly improper if Parliament did these things. But that does not mean that it is beyond the power of Parliament to do such things. If Parliament chose to do any of them the courts could not hold the Act of Parliament invalid.

In the second place, there is nothing in the European Communities Act 1972 to suggest that it was intended to have this effect.

Similarly, there is little scope for the notion of a constitutional convention that Parliament will not enact legislation inconsistent with Community law.[15] First, even if there were such a convention it is almost certain that the courts would give effect to any contrary Act of Parliament.[16] Second, there is clearly no intention on the part of the executive to create such a convention and it is difficult to see how mere abstention on the part of the legislature from enacting inconsistent legislation could give rise to a binding convention. It does seem that the only theoretical basis for the notion that future inconsistent legislation could be held to be invalid would be that of a legal revolution, in the sense of a fundamental change in the legal order, or a change in the 'grundnorm'.[17] Whether the judiciary would participate in such a change is ultimately a political question, but the years since accession have shown no sign of a legal revolution.

---

14 [1969] 1 AC 645 at 723, [1968] 3 All ER 561 at 573. See also *British Railways Board v Pickin* [1974] AC 765 at 782 and 789, [1974] 1 All ER 609 at 614 and 619. But for a contrast between legal theory and political reality see Lord Denning MR in *Blackburn v A-G* [1971] 2 All ER 1380, 1382, [1971] 1 WLR 1037, 1040; Lord Sankey in *British Coal Corpn v R* [1935] AC 500 at 520; *Copyright Owners Reproduction Society Ltd v EMI* (1958) 100 CLR 597, 611.
15 See Martin (1968–9) 6 CML Rev 7 at 23–5.
16 Lord Reid in *Madzimbamuto v Lardner-Burke*, n 14, ante. This would include legislation repealing the European Communities Act 1972. See *Membership of the European Community, Report on Renegotiation* (1975) Cmnd 6003, para 135 and cf *Legal and Constitutional Implications of United Kingdom Membership of the European Communities* (1967) Cmnd 3301, paras 22–23.
17 See Winterton (1976) 92 LQR 591; Mitchell (1979) 55 Int Aff 33 at 40; Mitchell (1980) 11 Cambrian L Rev 69. Cf *Pigs Marketing Board v Redmond* [1979] 3 CMLR 118 at 121.

(ii) The views of Lord Denning

One of Mr Blackburn's complaints was that accession to the Treaty of Rome entailed an irreversible surrender of the sovereignty of Parliament. His action was dismissed on the ground that it disclosed no reasonable cause of action, and the question of sovereignty did not therefore arise for decision. Treasury counsel appearing for the Attorney General accepted that Parliament could repeal any legislation giving effect to accession. Lord Denning MR appeared to accept that 'the sovereignty of these islands' had been limited by accession to the Treaties, but he went on:[18]

> We have all been brought up to believe that, in legal theory, one Parliament cannot bind another and that no Act is irreversible. But legal theory does not always march alongside political reality . . . What are the realities here? If Her Majesty's Ministers sign this treaty and Parliament enacts provisions to implement it, I do not envisage that Parliament would afterwards go back on it and try to withdraw from it. But, if Parliament should do so, then I say we will consider that event when it happens. We will then say whether Parliament can lawfully do it or not . . . So whilst in theory Mr Blackburn is quite right in saying that no Parliament can bind another, and that any Parliament can reverse what a previous Parliament has done, nevertheless so far as this court is concerned, I think we will wait till that day comes. We will not pronounce upon it today.

Thus Lord Denning, while not deciding the point, appears to have inclined to the view that inconsistent subsequent legislation will be recognised by the courts. Salmon LJ went further and indicated a clear view:

> As to Parliament, in the present state of the law, it can enact, amend and repeal any legislation it pleases. The sole power of the courts is to decide and enforce what is the law and not what it should be—now, or in the future.[19]

Since accession, the point has not arisen directly for decision, but there have been some helpful, although not entirely consistent, dicta. In *Felixstowe Dock and Rly Co v British Transport Docks Board*[20] it was alleged that the proposed promotion by the Board of a private Bill to take over the Felixstowe Dock and Railway Co and the subsequent takeover would be an abuse of a dominant position by the Board contrary to art 86 of the EEC Treaty. Speaking of the proposed Bill, Lord Denning said:

---

18 [1971] 2 All ER 1380 at 1382, [1971] 1 WLR 1037 at 1040–1.
19 [1971] 2 All ER at 1383 and 1041. For a similar view, expressed extra-judicially, see Lord Diplock (1972) 6 The Law Teacher 3. But cf 10th Report of the House of Lords Select Committee on the European Communities (1974–1975) para 12, for a suggestion that this is a 'so far unsettled constitutional question'.
20 [1976] 2 CMLR 655.

It seems to me that once the Bill is passed by Parliament and becomes a Statute, that will dispose of all this discussion about the Treaty. These courts will then have to abide by the Statute without regard to the Treaty at all.[1]

In 1978 and 1979 Lord Denning reverted to the question in two decisions involving sex discrimination in relation to pay. In the United Kingdom the relevant legislation came into force on 29 December 1975 and consists of the Equal Pay Act 1970, as amended by the Sex Discrimination Act 1975. In European law the principle of equal pay for equal work is contained in art 119 of the EEC Treaty as supplemented by a series of Council Directives. In *Shields v E Coomes (Holdings) Ltd*[2] the applicant, a woman, was employed as a counterhand at a betting shop at a lower rate than a man employed at the same establishment; the employers justified the difference on the ground that the man's duties were different because he had a protective role in a 'troublesome area'; by s 1(4) of the 1970 Act the industrial tribunal was entitled to take into account whether differences in duties are of 'practical importance' and the tribunal had so found in this case. The Court of Appeal held unanimously that there had been unjustified discrimination, but reached that result through differing routes. Lord Denning, after referring to the supremacy of Community law,[3] went on:

> Suppose that the Parliament of the United Kingdom were to pass a statute inconsistent with article 119: as, for instance, if the Equal Pay Act 1970 gave the right to equal pay only to unmarried women. I should have thought that a married woman could bring an action in the High Court to enforce the right to equal pay given to her by article 119. I may add that I should have thought that she could bring a claim before the industrial tribunal also... If such a tribunal should find any ambiguity in the statutes or any inconsistency with Community law, then it should resolve it by giving the primacy to Community law.[4]

Orr LJ did not think that any question of Community law arose, and Bridge LJ adopted the conventional approach of accepting that the EEC directives could be prayed in aid to assist in resolving ambiguity

---

1 At 664–5. The Bill was not in the event passed. It is rather difficult to see how on any view an Act of Parliament could be regarded as void because it aids an abuse of a dominant position. No question of inconsistent legislation could really arise: cf Scarman LJ at 666.
2 [1979] 1 All ER 456, [1978] 1 WLR 1408.
3 Relying on Case 6/64 *Costa v ENEL* [1964] ECR 585, [1964] CMLR 425 and Case 106/77 *Amministrazione delle Finanze dello Stato v Simmenthal SpA* [1978] ECR 629, [1978] 3 CMLR 263.
4 [1979] 1 All ER 456 at 461, [1978] 1 WLR 1408 at 1415.

in the English statutes, but held that there was no such ambiguity, and it was therefore unnecessary to resort to the directives.[5]

Macarthy's Ltd v Smith[6] was another case involving pay discrimination. Mrs Smith was employed by Macarthy's as a stockroom manageress; her male predecessor in the job, who had left four months previously, was paid more than Mrs Smith. The short point was whether the Equal Pay Act 1970, as amended by the Sex Discrimination Act 1975, applied only where men and women were employed *contemporaneously* at different rates of pay, or whether it was broader in scope and applied in particular to a man and a woman employed in succession. Lord Denning thought that the Equal Pay Act was not limited to men and women working contemporaneously, but Lawton and Cumming-Bruce LJJ thought that it was. As a result the court thought there was a potential conflict between the legislation and art 119 of the EEC Treaty and art 1 of the first Council Directive on equal pay,[7] which prima facie were not so limited; accordingly, the Court of Appeal made a reference under art 177 to the European Court on the question (inter alia) whether art 119 and the Council Directives were so limited.

In fact the supposed conflict between the Equal Pay Act 1970 and art 119 of the EEC Treaty did not exist. Article 119 is directly effective, and Community law applies in the industrial tribunals; to the extent that it gave rights to Mrs Smith more extensive than the Equal Pay Act 1970 (as amended by the Sex Discrimination Act 1975), there was nothing in the 1970 Act forbidding the court from giving effect to those rights. It should follow that Mrs Smith would be entitled to rely on whichever legal rule, art 119 or the 1970 Act, gave her more extensive rights. But the Court of Appeal did treat the case as one of possible conflict, not merely a case of difference, between the two systems.

Lord Denning pointed out that if there were a conflict the Commission could take action against the United Kingdom under arts 169 and 171,[8] but it was unnecessary for the courts to wait for that procedure to be gone through; as a result of s 2(1) and (4) of the 1972 Act the courts

---

5 [1979] 1 All ER 456 at 469, [1978] 1 WLR 1408 at 1425. See also *Re an Absence in Ireland* [1977] 1 CMLR 5, where the National Insurance Commissioner applied a 1971 Council Regulation in apparent priority to a 1975 Act of Parliament.
6 (No 1) [1979] 3 All ER 325, [1979] ICR 785, [1979] 1 WLR 1189; Case 129/79 [1980] ECR 1275, [1980] 2 CMLR 205; (No 2) [1981] QB 180, [1981] 1 All ER 111. See also *Albion Shipping Agency v Arnold* [1982] ICR 22, EAT; *Hasley v Fair Employment Agency* [1989] IRLR 106 (N.I.CA) and cf *Prince v Secretary of State for Scotland* 1985 SLT 74, noted (1985) 101 LQR 149.
7 75/117.
8 See pp 216–225, post.

were bound to give effect to art 119 because it was directly applicable and also to any directive which was also directly applicable.[9] He went on:[10]

> We should, I think, look to see what those provisions require about equal pay for men and women. Then we should look at our own legislation on the point—giving it, of course, full faith and credit—assuming that it does fully comply with the obligations under the Treaty. In construing our statute, we are entitled to look to the Treaty as an aid to its construction: and even more, not only as an aid but as an overriding force. If on close investigation it should appear that our legislation is deficient—or is inconsistent with Community law—by some oversight of our draftsmen—then it is our bounden duty to give priority to Community law. Such is the result of section 2(1) and (4) of the European Communities Act 1972.

In this passage he was considering the effect of inconsistency due to an 'oversight'. Clearly a *deficiency* in United Kingdom law could be made good by Community law under the 1972 Act; an *inconsistency* is dealt with under s 2(4) by the notion that the subsequent legislation is to be regarded as having effect *subject* to Community law. He then considered the 'constitutional' point, and said:

> Thus far I have assumed that our Parliament, whenever it passes legislation, intends to fulfil its obligations under the Treaty. If the time should come when our Parliament deliberately passes an Act—with the intention of repudiating the Treaty or any provision in it—or intentionally of acting inconsistently with it—and says so in express terms—then I should have thought that it would be the duty of our courts to follow the statute of our Parliament. I do not however envisage any such situation. As I said in *Blackburn v A-G*,[11] 'But, if Parliament should do so, then I say we will consider that event when it happens.' Unless there is such an intentional and express repudiation of the Treaty, it is our duty to give priority to the Treaty.

Lawton LJ thought that the courts could not ignore art 119 and apply the plain meaning of the Act, since art 119 gave rise to individual rights which the courts must protect by virtue of s 2 of the European Communities Act 1972. After referring to s 2(1) and (4) of the 1972 Act he went on:[12]

> Parliament's recognition of European Community law and of the jurisdiction of the European Court of Justice by one enactment can be withdrawn by another. There is nothing in the Equal Pay Act 1970, as amended, to indicate that Parliament intended to amend the European Communities Act 1972, or to limit its application.

---

9 See pp 46 et seq, 83 et seq on the direct effect of treaty provisions and directives.
10 [1979] ICR 785 at 789.
11 [1971] 2 All ER 1380 at 1383, [1971] 1 WLR 1037 at 1040, [1971] CMLR 784 at 790.
12 [1979] ICR at 796.

Cumming-Bruce LJ said:[13]

> If the terms of the Treaty are adjudged in Luxembourg to be inconsistent with the provisions of the Equal Pay Act 1970, European law will prevail over that municipal legislation. But such a judgment in Luxembourg cannot affect the meaning of the English statute.

On the reference the European Court decided that the principle in art 119 that men and women should receive equal pay for equal work was not confined to situations in which they were working contemporaneously. The matter then came again before the Court of Appeal on the question of costs. Lord Denning said:[14]

> It is important now to declare—and it must be made plain—that the provisions of article 119 of the EEC Treaty take priority over anything in our English statute on equal pay which is inconsistent with article 119. That priority is given by our own law. It is given by the European Communities Act 1972 itself. Community law is now part of our law; and, whenever there is any inconsistency, Community law has priority. It is not supplanting English law. It is part of our law which overrides any other part which is inconsistent with it. . . . [The employers] ought throughout to have looked at the EEC Treaty as well. Community law is part of our law by our own statute, the European Communities Act 1972. In applying it, we should regard it in the same way as if we found an inconsistency between two English Acts of Parliament: and the court had to decide which had to be given priority.

The view of Lord Denning and Lawton LJ may be taken as being that a piece of legislation which was intended to be inconsistent with Community law would be given effect by United Kingdom courts notwithstanding the primacy of Community law in the Community legal system; but that s 2(4) would avoid this result by a process of interpretation in all cases except those cases where it could be said that Parliament had evinced an intention to legislate in a manner which was inconsistent with Community law, in Lord Denning's formulation, or with the European Communities Act 1972, in Lawton LJ's formulation. The latter approach is more consistent with theory, but it is not easy to envisage a case in which the different formulations would lead to a different result.[15]

---

13 At 798. Cumming-Bruce LJ subsequently, in answer to academic criticism of his formulation in the earlier proceedings (Hood Phillips (1980) 96 LQR 31), added that if he had been of the view that the English statute had been ambiguous it would have been appropriate to look at art 119 to resolve the ambiguity: [1981] QB at 201–2, [1981] 1 All ER at 121.
14 [1981] QB at 200–1, [1981] 1 All ER at 120.
15 See Hood Phillips (1982) 98 LQR 524.

(iii) Section 2(4) in the House of Lords

The House of Lords has not heard a case in which the constitutional effect of s 2(4) has been central to the decision. In *Garland v British Rail Engineering Ltd*[16] Lord Diplock indicated that the case was not one in which it was appropriate:

> ... to consider whether, having regard to the express direction as to the construction of enactments 'to be passed' which is contained in s 2(4), anything short of an express positive statement in an Act of Parliament passed after 1 January 1973 that a particular provision is intended to be made in breach of an obligation assumed by the United Kingdom under a Community treaty would justify an English court in construing that provision in a manner inconsistent with a Community treaty obligation of the United Kingdom however wide a departure from the prima facie meaning of the language of the provision might be needed in order to achieve consistency.

Section 2(4) has been considered in two subsequent sex discrimination cases. In *Duke v GEC Reliance Ltd*[17] Mrs Duke claimed that she had been the victim of unlawful discrimination because she had been compulsorily retired at the age of 60 by her employers, although a comparable male employee would have been allowed to work until the age of 65. In December 1975 the Equal Pay Act 1970 and the Sex Discrimination Act 1975 had come into force, but neither applied to provision in relation to retirement. In 1976 the EEC Council Directive on Equal Treatment[18] was adopted. The United Kingdom Government took the view that the Equal Treatment Directive permitted discrimination in retirement ages, but in 1986 the European Court held that that view was wrong, and that the United Kingdom had been in breach of the directive in not legislating to outlaw discriminatory retirement ages.[19] Following that decision, the Sex Discrimination Act 1986 was passed, and discriminatory retirement ages were made unlawful, but without retrospective effect. In the *Marshall* case it had been held that the Equal Treatment Directive had direct effect,[20] but not as against private employers. It was argued on behalf of Mrs Duke that the effect of s 2(4) was to make the Sex Discrimination Act 1975 (which was passed and came into effect after the European Communities Act 1972) subject to the Community obligation not to discriminate. But this argument was dismissed because section 2(4):[1]

---

16 [1983] 2 AC 751 at 771, [1982] 2 All ER 402 at 415, HL.
17 [1988] AC 618, [1988] 1 All ER 626, HL.
18 76/207.
19 Case 152/84 *Marshall v Southampton and South West Hampshire Area Health Authority* [1986] QB 401, [1986] ECR 723, [1986] 2 All ER 584.
20 See ch 2, p 89.
1 [1988] AC at 630, 639–640, [1988] 1 All ER at 629, 636, per Lord Templeman, with whose speech all members concurred.

... does no more than reinforce the binding nature of legally enforceable rights and obligations imposed by appropriate Community law ... [It] does not ... enable or constrain a British court to distort the meaning of a British statute in order to enforce against an individual a Community directive which has no direct effect between individuals. Section 2(4) applies and only applies where Community's provisions are directly applicable.

Lord Templeman's reasoning appears to rest on this basis: (a) s 2(4) provides that 'any enactment passed or to be passed ... shall be construed and have effect subject to the foregoing provisions of this section'; (b) the relevant 'foregoing provision' was s 2(1), which will be discussed in greater detail in the next chapter,[2] and in summary provides (inter alia) that all rights which 'in accordance with the Treaties are without further enactment to be given legal effect or used in the United Kingdom shall be recognised and available in law'; (c) the relevant provision of s 2(1) refers only to rights which are directly effective under Community law; (d) the right on which Mrs Duke relied was not a directly effective right; (e) accordingly, s 2(4) had no application. It has been suggested that to restrict the application of s 2(1) to directively effective or applicable Community law is too narrow an approach,[3] but if it is not so limited then the words 'in accordance with the Treaties are *without further enactment*' are deprived of all substance. It is not necessary to resort to s 2(1) or s 2(4) for the proposition that domestic legislation should where possible be construed so as to conform to Community law, since this is a general principle of statutory interpretation.[4] In any event, the *Duke* case did not raise the question of the constitutional effect of s 2(4). There was no legislation *subsequent* to the Equal Treatment Directive which was inconsistent with the directive. The Sex Discrimination Act 1986 had complied with Community law for the future, but had left untouched the prior legislation for the period before the 1986 Act.

In *Pickstone v Freemans plc*,[5] Lord Oliver (with whom Lords Keith, Brandon and Jauncey expressly concurred[6]) relied on s 2(4) to justify the court's interpretation of an amendment to the Equal Pay Act 1970, which had been made to implement the Council directive on equal pay,[7] which like the Equal Treatment Directive in *Duke*, was not directly effective as against a private employer. In *Pickstone* the applicants were female warehouse operatives who were paid the same as a male warehouse operative, but who claimed that their work was of

---

2 See pp 46 et seq.
3 Ellis (1988) 104 LQR 381; Foster (1985) 51 MLR 775, (1988) 25 CML Rev 629.
4 Pp 137–142, post.
5 [1989] AC 66, [1988] 2 All ER 803, HL.
6 Lord Templeman delivered a concurring judgment, which did not rely on s 2(4).
7 Council Directive 75/117.

equal value to a male warehouse checker who was paid more than they were. The question was whether a woman's claim to equal pay for work of 'equal value' was excluded if, notwithstanding that a man was doing work of equal value for higher pay, there was a man who was working on 'like work' for the same pay as the woman.

The Equal Pay Act 1970 in its original form did not allow an 'equal value' claim, but it was amended by statutory instrument in 1983 under the European Communities Act 1972, s 2(2),[8] after the European Court had held that the United Kingdom was in breach of the Equal Pay Directive by failing to legislate to enable all employees who considered themselves wronged by the failure to apply the principle of equal pay for men and women for work to which equal value is attributed.[9] The 1983 amendment was in terms of outstanding obscurity, and, in the words of Lord Oliver,[10] 'the strict and literal construction of the section does indeed involve the conclusion that the Regulations, although purporting to give full effect to the United Kingdom's obligations under article 119, were in fact in breach of those obligations'. It did not, therefore, achieve the object of allowing a claim for equal value in circumstances where there were some male employees doing the same work for the same pay. But the House of Lords held that in view of the directive, the decision of the European Court, and the statement made by the Government when presenting the draft regulations to Parliament, the Equal Pay Act 1970 as amended should be interpreted so as to achieve the desired objective. The case differed from *Duke* in that in *Pickstone* the relevant provision of the Equal Pay Act 1970 inserted in 1983 was intended to give effect to a Community directive; in *Duke* the relevant part of the legislation was not so intended.

Pickstone was essentially a decision on construction, but Lord Oliver relied on 'the compulsive provision of s 2(4)' of the European Communities Act 1972 in concluding that the words of the Equal Pay Act 1970 as amended were reasonably capable of bearing a meaning which would not put the United Kingdom in breach of its treaty obligations. In a passage which is by no means clear he referred to s 2(1) of the 1972 Act, and continued:[11]

> Although, at any rate on one construction, this may be said to apply only to rights which are clearly directly applicable, subsection (2) goes on to provide for a designated Minister to make provision by regulation 'for the purpose of implementing any Community obligation of the United Kingdom' and 'for the purpose of dealing with matters arising out of or related to any such obligation'. Subsection (4) provides that provision

---
8 See pp 112 et seq, post.
9 Case 61/81 *Commission v UK* [1982] ECR 2601, [1982] 3 CMLR 284.
10 [1989] AC at 127, [1988] 2 All ER at 818.
11 Ibid at 126, 817.

made under subsection (2) includes such provision as might be made by Act of Parliament, and that 'any enactment passed or to be passed . . . shall be construed and have effect subject to the foregoing provisions of this section . . .' One is thus thrown back to the provisions of subsection (1).

But if the case had been concerned solely with directly effective rights under art 119, s 2(4) would have had the effect of making the 1983 amendment to the Equal Pay Act 1970 unnecessary and the power to enact subordinate legislation under s 2(2) would have been irrelevant. If, as seems to be the case, the decision was concerned with provisions of the Equal Pay Directive which were not directly effective as against a private employer, the only effect of s 2(4) would have been to make it clear that the Equal Pay Act 1970 could be amended by subordinate legislation order s 2(2), which was not in doubt. It is not easy to see how s 2(4) was relevant to the question of construction.[12]

But this is not to underestimate the importance of the decision in *Pickstone*. For in that case the House of Lords held that the court could depart from the strict and literal application of the words of legislation by using the technique of implying words to fill a gap in order to conform to a Community law obligation; and the House of Lords, as will be seen below,[13] went far beyond the normal techniques of statutory interpretation in *Litster v Forth Dry Dock and Engineering Co Ltd*[14] in implying complex provisions into a statutory instrument in order to comply with a directive as interpreted by the European Court.

In *Factortame Ltd v Secretary of State for Transport*[15] the House of Lords was concerned with applications by United Kingdom companies, which were Spanish-owned, whose complaint was that the Merchant Shipping Act 1988 and regulations made thereunder were contrary to Community law to the extent that they prevented registration of fishing vessels as British if the shareholders of the companies which were owned by them were not British citizens or domiciled in Britain. The applicants sought interim relief on the basis that the restrictions under the 1988 Act were contrary (inter alia) to directly effective provisions of the EEC Treaty, including the freedom of establishment provisions of arts 52 and 58. The House of Lords referred to the European Court the question whether, pending trial,

---

12 Pp 138–139, post.
13 Ibid.
14 [1989] 2 WLR 634, [1989] 1 All ER 1134, HL. This case involved the interpretation of subordinate legislation to give effect to a Council directive on the approximation of laws relating to the safeguarding of employees' rights in the event of transfers of businesses. The House of Lords construed the regulations so as to be consistent with the meaning of the directive as interpreted by the European Court, but without reference to section 2(4) of the 1972 Act.
15 [1989] 2 WLR 997, [1989] 2 All ER 692. On the background see Churchill (1989) 14 EL Rev 470.

Community law gave a *right* to interim relief, and this aspect will be discussed in the next chapter,[16] but for present purposes it is only necessary to point out that Lord Bridge (with whom all members concurred) referred to s 2(4), and said that it had:

> ... precisely the same effect as if a section were incorporated in Part II of the Act of 1988 which in terms enacted that the provisions with respect to registration of British fishing vessels were to be without prejudice to the directly enforceable Community rights of nationals of any member state of the EEC.[17]

It was not suggested in this case that the 1988 Act might prevail over Community law. The only issue was as to the remedy, since it was common ground that, if the applicants were successful in the European Court in establishing their alleged rights under Community law, those rights would prevail over the restrictions in the 1988 Act, and the English court would be obliged to make appropriate declarations to give effect to those rights. Thus the reasoning clearly demonstrates (although it does not decide) that the effect of s 2(4) is to prevent the *implied* repeal of statutory rights, and in particular of s 2(1) of the European Communities Act 1972 itself.

(iv) Conclusions

It is suggested, therefore, that, at present, whatever may be the position in the future, the correct position in United Kingdom constitutional law is the orthodox one, that the courts must and will give effect to subsequent United Kingdom legislation, even if it is inconsistent with Community law, subject to the important rule of construction in s 2(4). If the United Kingdom remains in the European Communities, it will be under an obligation to repeal such legislation, but its judges will not be able to declare the legislation inapplicable unless they are satisfied that there is no intention to depart from the principles established by s 2(1) and s 2(4) of the 1972 Act. There will therefore be a breach of the principle in the *Simmenthal* case,[18] that a national court should not have to await the repeal of inconsistent legislation before giving full effect to Community law.

If this view be right, the following consequences ensue:

(1) While the European Communities Act 1972 remains in force, existing directly applicable or effective Community law will be the law in the United Kingdom, notwithstanding any legislation prior to the Act which is inconsistent with such directly

---

16 Pp 108–110, post.
17 [1989] 2 WLR at 1011, [1989] 2 All ER at 701. See also [1989] 2 CMLR 353 at 400–404, per Bingham LJ.
18 See pp 19–20, ante.

applicable or effective laws. Thus in *Henn and Darby v DPP*[19] and *R v Goldstein*[20] it was accepted in the House of Lords that if the United Kingdom pre-accession legislation, under which the accused had been convicted, had been contrary to the prohibition of restriction on imports under art 30, then the convictions could not have stood: but in the event the ban on pornography, in the former case, and on citizens' band radios, in the latter, was held to be justified by the public policy exception of art 36;

(2) Community law which is not directly applicable or effective will have no force in the United Kingdom until given effect by Act of Parliament or by order or regulation enacted pursuant to powers given by the European Communities Act 1972 or other legislation;

(3) Directly applicable or effective Community law will take effect in the United Kingdom, notwithstanding any legislation prior to the 1972 Act, or even after the Act but prior to the coming into effect of the Community rule;

(4) A subsequent Act of Parliament which is inconsistent with a rule of Community law will be read subject to the rule of construction in s 2(4) so that Community law can take effect notwithstanding the Act, at any rate if the Court is satisfied that the subsequent inconsistent legislation is not intended to repeal s 2(1) or (4) of the 1972 Act; but

(5) Any subsequent Act of Parliament inconsistent with the 1972 Act, including one which repeals the latter in whole or in part or one which is intended to limit the application of s 2(1) and (4), will be given effect by the United Kingdom courts.

These conclusions do not cast doubt on the importance of the changes effected by the accession of the United Kingdom to the Communities. Nor do they ignore the fact that the scope of the EEC Treaty is far wider than other treaties which have been given effect in United Kingdom law. But these conclusions are not, it is suggested, affected to any significant degree by the experience and practice of those other member states whose courts allow Community law to prevail over subsequent inconsistent legislation. The decisions and writings in the other member states, although of great interest with regard to Community law, cannot without considerable reservation be treated as even of persuasive authority in relation to the problem of the relationship of Community law and national law at the national level in the United Kingdom. This is a matter not primarily of Community

---

19 [1981] AC 850, [1980] 2 All ER 166, HL.
20 [1983] 1 All ER 434, [1983] 1 WLR 151, HL.

law, but of constitutional law. The practice illustrates the interaction between Community law and national law (including constitutional law) in each of the countries and is affected by (1) the terms of any relevant constitutional provision, (2) the role of the legislature in the treaty making or ratifying process, and (3) the extent to which treaties are part of national law.[1]

In Belgium a directly effective rule of Community law—art 12 of the EEC Treaty—has been held to prevail over a subsequent Parliamentary law, by virtue of the application of a rule newly developed by Belgian courts that 'in the event of a conflict between a norm of domestic law and a norm of international law which produces direct effects in the legal system, the rule established by the Treaty shall prevail.'[2] In France, art 55 of the 1958 Constitution provides that treaties ratified or approved duly have an authority superior to that of 'lois', and the Cour de Cassation has held that art 95 of the EEC Treaty prevailed over a subsequent custom statute.[3] But the Conseil d'Etat did not show the same acceptance of the supremacy of Community law. From 1968 it held that an administrative court could not accord precedence to Community law over inconsistent subsequent legislation.[4] But in the 1989 decision in *Re Nicolo*[5] the Conseil d'Etat appears to have accepted the submission that it was able to consider the compatibility of the 1977 French law on European elections with the EEC Treaty. But it held that the law was in conformity with the Treaty.

In Germany, the courts have held that Community law takes effect even against subsequent legislation.[6] Since the 1986 decision of the Federal Constitutional Court German courts cannot disapply Community regulations on the ground they are contrary to the German constitution.[7] In Italy, art 11 of the Constitution has been interpreted to allow the subordination of subsequent national legislation to directly applicable Community law. Until 1984, the position taken by the Italian Constitutional Court was that only the Constitutional Court itself could decide that national legislation inconsistent with

---

1 Among the very considerable literature, see especially the survey by Bebr *Development of Judicial Control of the European Communities* (1981) ch 15.
2 *Minister for Economic Affairs v SA Fromagerie Franco-Suisse Le Ski* [1972] CMLR 330 at 373. See Lenearts (1986) 23 CML Rev 253.
3 *Administration des Douanes v Vabre* [1975] 2 CMLR 336. See also *Société Ateliers de Construction de Compiègne SA v Fabry* [1980] 3 CMLR 647; *Von Kempis v Geldof* [1976] 2 CMLR 152; Simon (1976) 92 LQR 85.
4 *Syndicat Général de Fabricants de Semoules de France* [1970] CMLR 395.
5 [1990] 1 CMLR 173, on which see Dehaussy 1990 J Dr Int 5.
6 See cases discussed by Bebr *Development of Judicial Control of the European Communities* (1981) pp 697–701; and *Re Fees for Examination of Imported Oranges* [1975] 2 CMLR 415.
7 *Re Application of Wünsche* [1987] 3 CMLR 225, pp 72–73, post.

Community law was invalid.[8] But in 1984 the Constitutional Court decided that the ordinary courts could apply Community law in preference to conflicting national law without referring the validity of national law to the Constitutional Court. Community law could not be impaired by Italian national legislation, whether it was enacted prior to, or subsequent to, Community law.[9] In Luxembourg (as a result of judicial decisions on the supremacy of international law) and in the Netherlands (as a result of the provisions of its constitution providing for the supremacy of treaties) it is likely that subsequent national legislation will yield to Community law.[10]

When the 1967 White Paper said:

> It would also follow that within the fields occupied by the Community law Parliament would have to refrain from passing fresh legislation inconsistent with that law as for the time being in force[11]

it is suggested that it was merely restating the position in *international law*, namely, that a state should not pass legislation inconsistent with its treaty obligations. Whether the United Kingdom courts will come to accept, as the courts of the other member states have come to accept, the full implications of the supremacy of Community law remains open. They have certainly not yet accepted them, and the indications are that the orthodox view of Parliamentary supremacy will prevail for some time to come.

The point should not be confused with the problems of interpretation to be discussed below. Although in the United Kingdom there is no constitutional limitation on the power of legislation to override at the domestic level treaty obligations of the Crown,[12] there is a (rebuttable) presumption that Parliament does not intend to legislate in a sense contrary to the international obligations of the United Kingdom. If, therefore, a piece of legislation is ambiguous and one of the possible

---

8 *Frontini v Ministero delle Finanze* [1974] 2 CMLR 372; and see Case 172/73 *Commission v Italy* [1974] ECR 475, and cases discussed in Case 106/77 *Simmenthal*, p 19, n 12, ante.
9 *Granital*, Foro Italiano, 1984, I, p 2062, discussed by Petriccione (1986) 11 EL Rev 320. See also *Ministry of Finance v BECA*, Foro Italiano, 1985, p 1600; Case 104/86 *Commission v Italy* [1989] 3 CMLR 25.
10 See Waelbroeck *Traités Internationaux et Juridictions Internes* pp 246–53. For Denmark, see Due & Gilman (1972) 3 CML Rev 256, and Due (1973) 10 CML Rev 355; for Greece, Keremeus and Kremlis (1988) 25 CML Rev 141; and for Spain, see Gadea and Lage (1986) 23 CML Rev 11. On Ireland, see Lang (1972) 9 CML Rev 167, and Robinson (1973) 10 CML Rev 352 and 467 and (1979) 16 CML Rev 9; Cf also Case 61/77 *Commission v Ireland* [1978] ECR 417 at 442, [1978] 2 CMLR 466 at 511; *Pesca Valentia Ltd v Minister for Fisheries and Forestry* [1987] 1 CMLR 856.
11 Cmnd 3301, para 23.
12 *IRC v Collco Dealings Ltd* [1962] AC 1, [1961] 1 All ER 762; *Cheney v Conn* [1968] 1 All ER 779 at 781, [1968] 1 WLR 242 at 245.

meanings is consonant with a treaty obligation and the other is not, the meaning which is consonant is to be preferred. 'A fortiori is this the case where the treaty obligation arises under one of the Community treaties to which s 2 of the European Communities Act 1972 applies.'[13] As Lord Oliver put it recently:[14]

> If the legislation can reasonably be construed so as to conform with [Community] obligations—obligations which are to be ascertained not only from the wording of the relevant directive but from the interpretation placed on it by the European Court of Justice at Luxembourg—such a purposive construction will be applied even though, perhaps, it may involve some departure from the strict and literal application of the words which the legislature has elected to use.

---

13 *Garland v British Rail Engineering Ltd* [1983] 2 AC 751 at 771, [1982] 2 All ER 402 at 415, HL, per Lord Diplock. See chapter 3, pp 137–142, post.
14 *Litster v Forth Dry Dock and Engineering Co Ltd* [1989] 2 WLR 634 at 641, [1989] 1 All ER 1134 at 1140, HL.

Chapter 2

Community law as part of United Kingdom law

Section 2 of the European Communities Act 1972 draws a distinction between the treatment in the United Kingdom of rights and duties which under the Treaties are to have direct effect in the domestic law of member states and the treatment of that part of Community law which requires implementation by the member states. The scheme of the Act is that the former provisions are, without more, to have full effect in the United Kingdom. The latter provisions are to take effect by a process of delegated legislation enacted under the umbrella of the Act. The Act assumes that the latter provisions relate primarily to the rights and obligations of the United Kingdom, as distinct from the former provisions which concern primarily, it would seem, rights and obligations of individuals and corporations. But the line between the two is not in practice a clear one and there have been cases in the United Kingdom, as there have been in the original member states, where the main issue is whether a provision of Community law takes direct effect and can be relied upon in the courts without having been given the force of law by delegated legislation.

As s 2(1) of the Act leaves this issue to be determined under Community law, the English court may, and in some cases must, refer such a question to the European Court under art 177.[1] If the English court does not refer it, the court must interpret the provision according to Community law.[2]

There are two points of a general character which should be made at the outset. First, the European Communities Act 1972 does not incorporate the whole of EEC law into the law of the United Kingdom. Lord Denning MR, however, consistently took a broader view. Thus in *Re Westinghouse Uranium Contract*[3] he said that the EEC Treaty 'and all its provisions are now part of the law of England. That is clear from section 2

---

1 See chapter 3, post.
2 European Communities Act 1972, s 3(1), on which see *R v Goldstein* [1983] 1 All ER 434, [1983] 1 WLR 151, HL.
3 [1978] AC 547 at 564, [1977] 3 All ER 703 at 711. See also *Schorsch Meier v Hennin* [1975] QB 416 at 426, [1975] 1 All ER 152 at 157; cf Bridge J in *Esso Petroleum Co Ltd v Kingswood Motors (Addlestone) Ltd* [1974] QB 142 at 151, [1973] 3 All ER 1057 at 1064. See Bridge (1975) 1 EL Rev 13 at 14–15.

of the European Communities Act 1972. We have to give force to the Treaty as being incorporated—lock, stock and barrel—into our own law here.' But in fact EEC law has not been incorporated 'lock, stock and barrel' and it is clear that, except as specifically provided for by statute or subordinate legislation, only those provisions of EEC law which by EEC law are directly applicable or effective in member states have become directly part of the law of the United Kingdom. EEC law has become 'part of the corpus juris of the member states'.[4]

Secondly, there has been an increasing tendency in recent years, largely[5] but not exclusively confined to academic writers, to distinguish between direct applicability and direct effect, reserving for the former the consequence of the provision of art 189 of the EEC Treaty that regulations shall be 'directly applicable' in member states, and for the latter the notion of directly enforceable rights. According to this distinction, only regulations are directly applicable, in the sense that no national measures of implementation are required for them to come into force in the member states; regulations, treaty provisions and directives may be directly effective in the sense of conferring direct individual rights, but whether they have that effect will depend on whether they fulfil in the individual case the criteria laid down by the European Court for direct effectiveness.[6] It cannot be said that the distinction is observed by the European Court,[7] but it has been used by Advocates-General to show that (a) provisions in regulations are directly applicable under art 189 but not necessarily directly effective and that (b) directives are not directly applicable under art 189 but may be directly effective.[8] But in any event the concept of direct effect has nothing in common with the notion of a 'self-executing' treaty.

---

4 *Jensen v Corpn of the Trinity House of Deptford* [1982] 2 Lloyd's Rep 14, 26, CA, per Kerr LJ.
5 See Winter (1972) 9 CML Rev 425 at 435; Dashwood (1977–8) 16 Journal of Common Market Studies 229; Wyatt (1975) 125 NLJ 575; Steiner (1982) 98 LQR 229.
6 Cf *Gibson v Lord Advocate* 1975 SLT 134, [1975] 1 CMLR 563.
7 See eg Case 129/79 *Macarthys Ltd v Smith* [1980] ECR 1275, [1980] 2 CMLR 205; Case 12/81 *Garland v British Rail Engineering Ltd* [1982] ECR 359, [1982] 1 CMLR 696, [1983] 2 AC 751; Case 17/81 *Pabst and Richarz KG v Hauptzollamt Oldenburg* [1982] ECR 1331, [1983] 3 CMLR 11; Case 137/84 *Ministère Public v Mutsch* [1985] ECR 2681, [1986] 1 CMLR 648; Case 157/86 *Murphy v Bord Telecom Eireann* [1988] 1 CMLR 879; Case 12/86 *Demirel v Stadt Schwäbisch Gmünd* [1989] 1 CMLR 421, for cases where the distinction might have been, but was not, drawn.
8 See cases cited, p 73, n 16, infra, and also Case 148/78 *Pubblico Ministero v Ratti* [1979] ECR 1629 at 1650, [1980] 1 CMLR 96 at 101, per Reischl AG; Case 815/79 *Cremonini and Vrankovich* [1980] ECR 3583 at 3621, [1981] 3 CMLR 49 at 60, per Warner AG; Case 8/81 *Becker v Finanzamt Münster-Innenstadt* [1982] ECR 53 at 80, [1982] 1 CMLR 499 at 505, per Slynn AG; Case 80/86 *Officier van Justitie v Kolpinghuis Nijmegen BV* [1987] ECR 3969 at 3976–7, [1989] 2 CMLR 18 at 20–21 per Mischo AG; Warner (1977) 93 LQR 349 at 356–7. See also *An Bord Bainne Co-operative Ltd v Milk Marketing Board* [1988] 1 CMLR 605 at 609, CA.

The latter expression reflects constitutional problems (particularly in the United States) which are not relevant in this context.⁹

I. THE DIRECT APPLICABILITY AND EFFECT OF COMMUNITY LAW AND SECTION 2(1) OF THE EUROPEAN COMMUNITIES ACT 1972

Section 2(1) of the Act provides:

> All such rights, powers, liabilities, obligations and restrictions from time to time created or arising by or under the Treaties, and all such remedies and procedures from time to time provided for by or under the Treaties, as in accordance with the Treaties are without further enactment to be given legal effect or used in the United Kingdom shall be recognised and available in law, and be enforced, allowed and followed accordingly; and the expression 'enforceable Community right' and similar expressions shall be read as referring to one to which this subsection applies.

It is in this way that a whole complex of rights and duties has been incorporated into the law of the United Kingdom. The section is to the most casual observer widely drafted: first, rights and duties are listed as 'rights, powers, liabilities, obligations and restrictions'; secondly, they include 'remedies and procedures'; third, they are to be 'recognised and available in law' and 'enforced, allowed and followed accordingly'. But, most importantly, whether the right or power or liability or obligation or restriction is enforceable depends on Community law ('as in accordance with the Treaties are without further enactment to be given legal effect in the United Kingdom'). Thus, not only the Treaty provisions themselves and the secondary legislation made thereunder have to be taken into account, but also they are to have the effect ascribed to them by the European Court.[10]

1 Direct effect of Treaty provisions

In a series of decisions stretching over almost 30 years the European Court has established that as a matter of Community law, and from the standpoint of Community law, some of the provisions of the EEC Treaty confer individual rights which the national courts must respect and to which they must give effect. The complex constitutional questions to which this concept has given rise in other countries will not, it is hoped, arise in the United Kingdom because so long as s 2(1) of the Act is in force all rights are available in law in the United

---

9 Cf Case 131/79 *R v Secretary of State for Home Affairs, ex p Santillo* [1980] ECR 1585 at 1608–9, [1980] 2 CMLR 308 at 317, per Warner AG.
10 On the scope of s 2(1) see *Pickstone v Freemans plc* [1989] AC 66 at 126, [1988] 2 All ER 803 at 817, HL, per Lord Oliver, and cf *Duke v GEC Reliance Ltd* [1988] AC 618 at 630, [1988] 1 All ER 626 at 629, HL, per Lord Templeman.

Kingdom if they (1) are created or arise under the Treaties and (2) are in accordance with the Treaties to be given legal effect in the United Kingdom. If, therefore, it is established under Community law as reflected in the case law of the European Court that any particular provision is directly effective and is capable of giving rise to individual rights, then such a provision can be relied upon in proceedings in the United Kingdom. As the Court has made clear, if a provision is directly effective it is for the national courts to decide in what way they will give effect to it.[11] It is not essential that there be a judicial remedy available in national law if administrative officials are empowered to apply directly effective Community law.[12] But a member state is under a duty to repeal domestic legislation which is inconsistent with directly effective Community law even if that legislation is not applied in practice.[13] Where the European Court has held that a member state is in breach of a directly effective provision of the Treaty the courts of that state have an obligation to ensure that the European Court's judgment is complied with.[14]

The basic principle of direct effect is that nationals of member states may invoke certain provisions of the Treaties[15] as conferring direct rights, upon which the individuals concerned may rely in proceedings in national courts. A few examples from the case law may make the point clearer: in proceedings by or against the Commissioners of Customs and Excise a person may allege that a duty or tax has been applied in a way which is contrary to the Treaty or a directive;[16] or criminal proceedings may be defended on the ground that the law under which the accused is charged offends against the Treaty;[17] or a British architect may claim that he is being unlawfully excluded from practice in France on the ground of his nationality,[18] or a Danish ship's captain may claim that he is being unlawfully denied a pilot's certificate on the ground of his nationality;[19] or a company may

---

11 See pp 62–67, post.
12 *Jensen v Corpn of the Trinity House of Deptford* [1982] 2 Lloyd's Rep 14, CA.
13 Case 159/78 *Commission v Italy* [1979] ECR 3247, [1980] 3 CMLR 446; Case 168/85 *Commission v Italy* [1986] ECR 2945, [1988] 1 CMLR 580; Case 147/86 *Commission v Greece* 15 March 1988.
14 Cases 314 to 316/81 and 83/82 *Procureur de la République v Waterkeyn* [1982] ECR 4337, [1983] 2 CMLR 145.
15 And of associated treaties: pp 67–69, post. On provisions of the Spanish-Portuguese Act of Accession see Case C3/87 *R v Minister of Agriculture, Fisheries and Food, ex p Agegate Ltd* (1990) Times, 19 January.
16 See eg *Church of Scientology of California v Customs and Excise Comrs* [1981] 1 All ER 1035, CA.
17 *Henn and Darby v DPP* [1981] AC 850, [1980] 2 All ER 166; *R v Goldstein* [1983] 1 All ER 434, [1983] 1 WLR 151, HL.
18 Case 11/77 *Patrick v Ministre des Affaires Culturelles* [1977] ECR 1199, [1977] 2 CMLR 523.
19 *Jensen v Corpn of Trinity House of Deptford* [1982] 2 Lloyd's Rep 14, CA.

claim that it has been damaged by conduct contrary to the restrictive practices rules of the Treaty.[20]

It should be emphasised that the direct effect of Treaty provisions impinges on relations between private persons and is not limited to disputes with state agencies. This 'horizontal effect' is especially apparent in the fields of equal pay, restrictive practices, and freedom of movement of persons and goods.[1]

It was in 1963, in a reference from the Dutch courts, that the European Court first articulated a theoretical basis for the principle of direct effect.[2] As a result of that case and its successors, it is possible to indicate with some precision the criteria by which the European Court (and, because of s 3(1) of the Act, United Kingdom courts) will assess whether a provision of the Treaties has direct effect and can therefore be relied upon in proceedings in the United Kingdom. The case law is authority for the following propositions:

(i) the provision in question, if it is to confer individual rights, must not by its nature indicate that it concerns the member states only in their relations *inter se*;
(ii) the provision must be clear and precise;
(iii) the provision must be unconditional and unqualified and not subject to any further measures on the part of the member states or of the Community;
(iv) the provision must not be one which leaves any substantial latitude or discretion to member states;
(v) it is irrelevant that the Commission or other member states have alternative remedies for breach of the provision in question.

Although many of these propositions overlap in practice it will be convenient to consider the relevant decisions of the European Court under these headings.

(i) *The provision must not concern member states only*

This is really more a statement of the conclusion that a provision is not directly effective than a test for its direct effect. On their face almost all the treaty provisions appear to concern member states only,[3] but many have been held to be directly effective. If a provision is by its nature applicable only to inter-state relations it is not susceptible of

---

20 *Garden Cottage Foods Ltd v Milk Marketing Board* [1984] AC 130, [1983] 2 All ER 770, HL.
1 On the horizontal effect of art 30, see Quinn and MacGowan (1987) 12 EL Rev 163.
2 Case 26/62 *Van Gend en Loos v Nederlandse Administratie der Belastingen* [1963] ECR 1, [1963] CMLR 105.
3 Cf Lord Denning MR in *Shields v E Coomes (Holdings) Ltd* [1979] 1 All ER 456 at 460, [1978] 1 WLR 1408 at 1414.

conferring direct rights. Thus in *Costa v ENEL*,[4] in relation to art 102, the Court held that the member states:

> have undertaken an obligation to the Community which binds them as states, but which does not create individual rights which national courts must protect.[5]

This is not a test which has played any significant part in later decisions and it is well established that the fact that the provision in question mentions only member states and not individuals does not prevent it from having direct effect.[6] One case in which it became relevant was *A-G v Burgoa*[7] where the Court held that art 234 (which preserves the effect of treaties entered into by the member states prior to their entry into the Community) did not create individual rights; the Court emphasised that art 234 was essentially concerned with the application of the principle of international law that the EEC Treaty did not affect the duty of member states vis-à-vis third states; it did not create individual rights.

(ii) The provision must be clear and precise

In the *Van Gend en Loos* case[8] the plaintiff sought in the Dutch revenue courts to establish, by way of appeal against the imposition of import duty, that there had been an illegal increase of customs duty, contrary to art 12 ('the standstill clause')[9] of the EEC Treaty, on certain aminoplasts which it sought to import from Germany to the Netherlands. The Tariefcommissie, a Dutch administrative tribunal, referred to the European Court under art 177 the question (inter alia) whether art 12 had direct application within the territory of a member state and so enured to the benefit of citizens that their individual rights had to be protected by the national courts.

The Court held that art 12 did have direct effect. The following features of art 12 were emphasised:

(a) its text set out a clear and unconditional prohibition;
(b) the prohibition was imposed without any power in the states to subordinate the application of the prohibition to a positive act of internal law; and
(c) it did not require legislative intervention by the states in order for it to be carried out.

---

4 Case 6/64 [1964] ECR 585, [1964] CMLR 425.
5 [1964] ECR 585 at 595, [1964] CMLR 425 at 457.
6 Ibid.
7 Case 812/79 [1980] ECR 2787, [1981] 2 CMLR 193.
8 See n 2, supra.
9 Art 12 prohibits the introduction of new customs duties or the increase of existing ones as between member states.

As a matter of treaty interpretation, the Court thought that the prohibition was perfectly suited by its nature to produce direct effects; the fact that member states were designated by the article as subject to the duty did not imply that their nationals might not be the beneficiaries of it.

Costa v ENEL[10] was a decision rendered in a celebrated piece of litigation arising out of the nationalisation in 1962 in Italy of the production and distribution of electricity. The litigation involved complex questions of Italian constitutional law which will not be considered here because, as indicated above, s 2(1) of the Act will give effect to individual rights provided that they are conferred by Community law. The sole interest, therefore, of this fascinating case for present purposes is the light it sheds on the criteria for direct effect of Community law.

Signor Costa was a lawyer in Milan who was a shareholder in Edisonvolta, an Italian electricity company. From 1962 the Italian Government enacted legislation under which the production and distribution of electricity was nationalised. Among the electricity undertakings affected by this legislation was Edisonvolta, whose property (like that of similar undertakings) was transferred to a state organisation, the Ente Nazionale per l'Energia Elettrica (ENEL). In 1963 Signor Costa received an electricity bill from ENEL in the sum of 1925 lire, at the then rate of exchange the equivalent of just over £1. Signor Costa refused to pay the bill and contested his liability to pay it before the Giudice Conciliatore of Milan, a local magistrate.

Signor Costa claimed (inter alia) that the nationalisation laws were (a) contrary to the Italian constitution and (b) contrary to the various articles of the EEC Treaty, including two 'standstill' clauses, arts 53 and 37(2). He asked the magistrate to refer the case for preliminary opinions (a) to the Italian Constitutional Court and (b) under art 177 to the European Court. In the reference to the European Court, the Milan magistrate seised the Court of the question whether the Italian nationalisation laws violated arts 102, 93, 53 and 37 of the EEC Treaty. As reformulated by the Court the question became one of treaty interpretation, namely, whether those articles conferred individual rights which could be invoked in national courts.

Signor Costa's case was that the Treaty had been violated because the nationalisation laws were (a) a distortion of competition within art 102, (b) state aids incompatible with the Common Market and prohibited by art 93, (c) restrictions on the right of establishment and so prohibited by art 53 and (d) discrimination by means of State trading monopolies forbidden by art 37(2). The sole question for the

---

10 Case 6/64 [1964] ECR 585, [1964] CMLR 425. See also [1968] CMLR 267 for further proceedings.

Court was whether, as a matter of Community law, Signor Costa was entitled to rely, as an individual, on those provisions in the national courts.

By virtue of art 53, which is in the group of articles (52–58) dealing with the right of establishment:

> Member states shall not introduce any new restrictions on the right of establishment in their territories of nationals of other member states, save as otherwise provided in this treaty.

It was in relation to this provision that the Court indicated in the clearest terms that when a provision was (inter alia) complete and legally perfect it was capable of producing direct effects. The Court said:[11]

> By article 53 the member states undertake not to introduce any new restrictions on the right of establishment in their territories of nationals of other member states, save as otherwise provided in the Treaty. The obligation thus entered into by the states simply amounts legally to a duty not to act, which is neither subject to any conditions, nor, as regards its execution or effect, to the adoption of any measure either by the states or by the Commission. It is therefore legally complete in itself and is consequently capable of producing direct effects on the relations between member states and individuals. Such an express prohibition which came into force with the Treaty throughout the Community, and thus became an integral part of the legal system of the member states, forms part of the law of those states and directly concerns their nationals, in whose favour it has created individual rights which national courts must protect.

It should be noted that the fact that the Treaty provision came into immediate effect, although relied on, is shown by subsequent cases not to be a determining factor. In this case the clarity of art 53 was beyond question for the purpose of giving individual rights.

In relation to art 37, Signor Costa alleged in the Italian courts that the nationalisation legislation was a measure which contravened the basic principle of art 37, namely that member states were progressively to adjust any state trading monopolies so as to ensure that when the transitional period ended no discrimination regarding supplies or marketing existed between the nationals of member states. The question for the European Court was whether Signor Costa was entitled to rely on art 37, not whether Italy had in fact been in breach. In language parallel with that it had used in relation to art 53, the Court decided that the prohibition expressed in art 37(2) was so direct that it affected individuals and created rights which their national courts were bound to safeguard.

The Treaty contains a number of general provisions which may be

---

11 [1964] ECR 585 at 596.

regarded as lacking the necessary clarity and precision. Thus art 2 of the EEC Treaty provides that the Community has the task of promoting an accelerated raising of the standard of living. This article does not have direct effect because of its general terms and also because it depends on the progressive approximation of economic policies.[12] Although art 9 has been held to be directly effective in conjunction with a number of other articles,[13] it is probably not directly effective in itself. Similarly, art 5 was held not to be directly effective.[14] The fact that an article contains a degree of uncertainty or a moderate discretionary element will not prevent an otherwise clear provision from having direct effect.[15] But the obligation must be unconditional. In *Casati*[16] the defendant in Italian criminal proceedings was charged with violation of Italian exchange control regulations by illegally exporting German bank notes. One of his defences was that the Italian law was contrary to the EEC Treaty, and in particular to art 71, which provides that member states shall endeavour to avoid introducing new exchange control restrictions. The Italian court referred the question (inter alia) whether art 71 had direct effect. The European Court held that it did not because:

> By using the term 'shall endeavour', the wording of that provision departs noticeably from the more imperative forms of wording employed in other similar provisions concerning restrictions on the free movement of goods, persons and services. It is apparent from the wording that, in any event, the first paragraph of Article 71 does not impose on the Member States an unconditional obligation capable of being relied upon by individuals.[17]

This was a case where there was an obligation, but the obligation was not an absolute one, merely an obligation to use 'endeavours'. Perhaps the Court erred in characterising it as 'conditional', and it might have been more appropriate to hold that the obligation was insufficiently precise or left too great a margin of discretion to give individual rights.

Similarly, it has sometimes been doubted whether art 7 (which provides that, 'within the scope of application' of the Treaty, and without prejudice to any special provisions, discrimination on the ground of nationality is prohibited) of itself has direct effect.[18] There

---

12 Case 126/86 *Giménez Zaera v Instituto Nacional de la Seguridad Social* [1987] ECR 3697, [1989] 1 CMLR 827.
13 See eg cases cited at p 54, nn 4–5 and p 55, n 8, post.
14 Case 9/73 *Schlüter v Hauptzollamt Lörrach* [1973] ECR 1135.
15 Case 28/67: *Molkerei-Zentrale Westfalen v Hauptzollamt Paderborn* [1968] ECR 143, [1968] CMLR 187.
16 Case 203/80 [1981] ECR 2595, [1982] 1 CMLR 365.
17 [1981] ECR 2616.
18 See eg *Jensen v Corpn of the Trinity House of Deptford* [1982] 2 Lloyd's Rep 14, CA; *R v Trinity House London Pilotage Committee, ex p Jensen* [1985] 2 CMLR 413.

Direct effect of Treaty provisions 53

is no doubt that, in conjunction with other provisions of the Treaty or of applicable regulations, art 7 can have direct effect.[19] But this does not mean that art 7 is not itself capable of being directly effective, despite its very general character. It can of course be directly effective in conjunction with other provisions, but it is also clear that it can be directly effective in itself.[20]

Precision and partial direct effect. In a number of cases art 119, which imposes the obligation on member states to ensure and maintain the principle of 'equal pay for equal work' for men and women, has been held to be directly effective but only in relation to discrimination which may be identified solely with the aid of the criteria of equal work and equal pay without national or Community measures being required to define them with greater precision in order to permit of their application.[1] It follows that in this and other areas Treaty provisions may be directly effective only in so far as their *application* is clear and precise, but that the fact that there is a penumbra of uncertainty or imprecision in their application will not prevent them being directly effective.

(iii) The provision must be unconditional and unqualified and not subject to any further measures on the part of member states or of the Community

These qualifications appear from a number of decisions. In the *Van Gend en Loos* case[2] it was emphasised, in holding art 12 to be directly effective, that it did not require legislative intervention by the states in order for it to be carried out. Indeed, the prohibition in art 12 was imposed without any power in the states to subordinate its application to a positive act of internal law. Similar pronouncements were made in *Costa v ENEL*, where it was said that art 53:

> is neither subject to any conditions, nor, as regards its execution or effect, to the adoption of any measure either by the states or by the Commission

---

19 See eg Case 1/78 *Kenny v National Insurance Comr* [1978] ECR 1489, [1978] 3 CMLR 651.
20 Case 24/86 *Blaizot v University of Liège* [1989] 1 CMLR 57. See also Case 186/87 *Cowan v Le Trésor Public* (1989) Times, 13 February.
1 See eg Case 43/75 *Defrenne v Sabena* [1976] ECR 455, [1976] 2 CMLR 98; Case 129/79 *Macarthys Ltd v Smith* [1980] ECR 1275, [1980] 2 CMLR 205; Case 69/80 *Worringham and Humphreys v Lloyds Bank Ltd* [1981] ECR 767 at 802–3, [1981] 2 CMLR 1 at 12, per Warner AG; Case 96/80 *Jenkins v Kingsgate (Clothing Productions) Ltd* [1981] ECR 911, [1981] 2 CMLR 24; cf Case 52/79 *Procureur du Roi v Debauve* [1980] ECR 833 at 874, [1981] 2 CMLR 362 at 384, per Warner AG. See also *Leverton v Clwyd County Council* [1989] IRLR 239; affd [1989] AC 706, [1989] 1 All ER 78, HL.
2 Case 26/62 [1963] ECR 1, [1963] CMLR 105.

and that

> Article 37(2) contains an absolute prohibition: not an obligation to do something but an obligation to refrain from doing something. This obligation is not accompanied by any reservation which might make its implementation subject to any positive act of national law. This prohibition is essentially one which is capable of producing direct effects on the legal relations between member states and their nationals.[3]

In *Diamantarbeiders v Brachfeld*[4] the European Court held that arts 9 and 12 taken together created direct rights for individuals under Community law. By a Belgian law of 1960, there was instituted in Belgium a social fund for diamond workers. In 1962 a further law provided that contributions were to be based on the value of the imported diamonds. In actions by the social fund for payment of arrears of contributions the diamond importers alleged (inter alia) that the contribution was equivalent to a customs duty and so prohibited by arts 9 and 12. In a reference under art 177 by the Antwerp Court for an interpretation of the Treaty, the European Court held that arts 9 and 12 could be relied upon by the diamond importers. It said:

> The provisions of the Treaty laying down the abovementioned prohibitions impose precise and clearly-defined obligations on member states which do not require any subsequent intervention by Community or national authorities for their implementation. For this reason, these provisions directly confer rights on individuals concerned.

But the requirement that the provision must be unconditional and unqualified must be read in the light of a number of cases which indicate that an obligation which is originally conditional or qualified may become unconditional or unqualified by lapse of time or on the happening of an event.

Eunomia di Porro v Ministry of Education[5] was a case which arose from the alleged failure of the Italian authorities to comply with their obligations under the EEC Treaty. In 1968 the Commission brought proceedings against Italy under art 169 of the Treaty, alleging that the Italian export tax on articles of artistic or historical interest should have been abolished, at the latest, by the end of the first stage of the transitional period (that is, 1 January 1962), pursuant to art 16 of the Treaty, which required export taxes to be abolished by that time. In those proceedings by the Commission, the Court held that Italy, by continuing to levy the export tax, had failed to fulfil its obligations under art 16 of the EEC Treaty.[6]

---

3 Case 6/64 [1964] ECR 585 at 597, [1964] CMLR 425 at 458–9.
4 Cases 2–3/69 [1969] ECR 211 at 223, [1969] CMLR 335 at 351.
5 Case 18/71 [1971] ECR 811, [1972] CMLR 4.
6 Case 7/68 [1968] ECR 423, [1969] CMLR 1; see also Case 48/71 *Commission v Italy* [1972] ECR 527, [1972] CMLR 699.

Although legislation had been introduced in Italy during 1967 to exempt exports to member states from the export tax, this lapsed in 1968 on the dissolution of the Italian parliament. In 1970 Eunomia di Porro, an Italian company, exported a painting to Germany. An export tax was levied pursuant to the Italian law. The company brought proceedings for recovery of the sums paid. The Turin court asked the European Court whether art 16 constituted a directly effective rule from the end of the first stage, namely, 1 January 1962. The Court held that the combined effect of arts 9 and 16 was a clear and precise prohibition on export duties from the end of the first stage, which prohibition was not dependent for its implementation on any act of internal law or on any intervention by institutions of the Community. It therefore was capable of direct effect in the member states.

The reasoning of the Court had been similar in the *Lütticke* case,[7] where it was held that art 95 came into effect as regards taxes in existence when the Treaty entered into force only as from the beginning of the second stage in January 1962. Once the time limit had expired, the obligation was unconditional and not subject to intervention by member states or the Community.

SACE v Italian Ministry for Finance[8] concerned art 13(2), which contemplated the gradual abolition of taxes having an equivalent effect to customs duties on imports. In November 1970 the European Court had held, in proceedings brought by the Commission against Italy, that the continued operation of an Italian law of 1950 (which provided for the collection of an administrative fee based on the value of imported goods) put the Italian Government in breach of its obligation under art 13 to abolish customs duties or taxes of equivalent effect by at latest 1 July 1968 in accordance with the directives of the Commission.[9]

The Italian law was also challenged in proceedings brought by SACE in which it sought an order in the Brescia court for a refund of the duties which it alleged had been improperly imposed on it by the Italian state. The Brescia court asked the European Court under art 177 whether the provisions of art 13(2) were directly effective following the issue of the Commission directive whereby a timetable for the abolition of duties having equivalent effect to customs duties had been laid down (and had expired).

---

7 Case 57/65 [1966] ECR 205, [1971] CMLR 674. See also Case 59/75 *Pubblico Ministero v Manghera* [1976] ECR 91, [1976] 1 CMLR 557; Case 45/75 *Rewe v Hauptzollamt Landau* [1976] ECR 181, [1976] 2 CMLR 1.
8 Case 33/70 [1970] ECR 1213, [1971] CMLR 123. See also Case 77/72 *Capalongo v Maya* [1973] ECR 611, [1974] 1 CMLR 230; Case 2/74 *Reyners v Belgium* [1974] ECR 631, [1974] 2 CMLR 305.
9 Case 8/70 *Commission v Italy* [1970] ECR 961.

Like the provision in the *Lütticke* case, art 13(2) could not have had immediate direct effect on the entry into force of the Treaty, because it contemplated only the *gradual* abolition of taxes having an equivalent effect to customs duties on imports. The Commission was charged under art 13(2) with the power to determine by means of directives the timetable for abolition. In any event, they were to be abolished by the end of the transitional period. The Court held that the combined effect of arts 9 and 13(2) was that from the end of the transitional period these articles generated for individuals rights which they could enforce before national courts. The Commission's directive imposing a final date for abolition was held to involve legal consequences which could be invoked by individuals. The Court appears to be saying, not that the directive itself creates individual rights, but that the Treaty provisions conferring individual rights must be read in the light of the directive.[10]

(iv) The provision must not leave substantial discretion to member states or to the Commission

This requirement, suggested in several decisions, is clearly linked with, and clearly overlaps with those previously discussed, particularly (iii), but it is treated separately sufficiently often to justify a separate treatment here.

In *Salgoil v Italian Ministry for Foreign Trade*[11] the European Court developed further the distinction drawn in previous decisions between those provisions which require no further action for their implementation, on the one hand, and those which, on the other hand, leave a latitude to the member states. The former are capable of being directly effective, but the latter are not. The litigation concerned (inter alia) the Treaty provisions concerning the 'Elimination of Quantitative Restrictions as between Member States' and in particular arts 30 to 33 of the EEC Treaty.[12] The plaintiff was an Italian company which had contracted to import products into Italy. It brought an action for damages against the Italian Foreign Trade Ministry, claiming compensation for damage allegedly suffered because of the Ministry's refusal to permit the importation. The plaintiff alleged that the importation had been made subject to a licence (which had been refused) only after the contract for the purchase of the products had been concluded. It claimed that the action by the Ministry constituted an infringement of the EEC Treaty and in particular of arts 31 and 33. The Court of Appeal of Rome

---

10 Cf Case 10/71 *Ministère Public Luxembourgeois v Müller* [1971] ECR 723.
11 Case 13/68 [1968] ECR 453, [1969] CMLR 181. Cf p 85, post.
12 Providing for the prohibition of new quantitative restrictions or equivalent measures; any increase in quotas; and the progressive abolition of quotas.

referred to the European Court the question whether the provisions of arts 30 et seq, especially art 31, produced effects in the relations between a member state and its nationals.

The Court narrowed the question down to the direct effects of arts 30, 31, 32(1) (last sentence), 33(1) and 33(2) (first paragraph). It held that art 30 itself only stated the general rule and was subject to the succeeding articles; and it was not necessary to decide what its effects might be after the end of the transitional period.[13] As regards the other articles concerned, the Court drew a distinction between arts 31 and 32(1), on the one hand, and arts 32(2) (last sentence) and 33(1) and (2), on the other. The former laid down a prohibition which was not subject to any reservation requiring intervention by Community institutions or member states to give it effect. Therefore, they were, in line with the case law of the Court, to be given direct effect in national courts. The manner in which they were to be given effect was a matter for the national authorities.[14]

But the position was different with regard to the latter provisions. The Court asked itself 'whether the member states may in performing them exercise any discretion such as to exclude' direct effects wholly or in part. The answer which it gave itself was that the member states had a discretion in their obligation to transform bilateral quotas into global quotas under art 33; they also had a discretion derived from the vagueness of the concepts of 'total value' and 'national production' in the same article. Because the Treaty did not specify on what basis the concepts were to be applied, several solutions were open to the states. Therefore the obligation under arts 32 and 33 to abolish existing quotas progressively could not be applied with sufficient accuracy for direct effect to be given to the obligation in national courts. It appears that the Court was mindful of the German experience in relation to the *Lütticke* case[15] of multiplicity of actions in cases where a provision was less than absolutely clear.

A similar problem arose in the *Molkerei* cases,[16] in which the Court held that art 97 did not confer individual rights for the following reasons:

> Since this provision gives the member states a discretion of which they may or may not avail themselves to have recourse to average rates, it implies, in the case of states which have used this power properly, the interposition between the rule of Community law and its implementation of legal acts implying a discretion; this means that, in the present state of Community law, such discretion excludes their choice and its consequences from any

---

13 In Case 74/76 *Ianelli v Meroni* [1977] ECR 557, [1977] 2 CMLR 688, art 30 was held to be directly effective from the end of the transitional period.
14 See pp 62–67, ante.
15 Case 57/65 [1966] ECR 205, [1971] CMLR 674.
16 Case 28/67 [1968] ECR 143, [1968] CMLR 187.

possibility of the direct applicability of the relevant provisions of article 97. On the other hand both the fixing of groups of products and the establishment of average rates remain, in the absence of any Community provision on the method of calculating them, at the discretion of the member states, exercised under the Commission's supervision, and preclude the direct applicability of article 97. . . It is therefore apparent from the general scheme of article 97 that, where a member state operating the cumulative multi-stage tax system has elected to have recourse to the procedure of establishing average rates, the article does not create individual rights which national courts must protect.[17]

To put it another way, the distinctive attributes of art 97 were that (a) member states had a discretion under it, (b) it contemplated further action by member states (the establishment of average rates), and (c) the exercise of the discretion of member states was subject to specific control by the Commission.

It is not entirely clear what degree of discretion will prevent a provision from being directly effective. A provision which fell on the right side of effectiveness was art 95(2). In *Fink-Frucht v Hauptzollamt München*[18] the Court said:

Although this provision involves the evaluation of economic factors, this does not exclude the right and duty of national courts to ensure that the rules of the Treaty are observed whenever they can ascertain . . . that conditions necessary for the application of the article are fulfilled. The answer to this question, therefore, must be that the provision in question is capable of producing direct effects and creating individual rights which national courts must protect.

In *Ministère Public Luxembourgeois v Müller*,[19] however, the Court was concerned with the possible direct effects of the Community competition rules and in particular of art 90, which relates to public undertakings and provides broadly, subject to important limitations, that in relation to public undertakings member states shall not enact or maintain legislation which is inconsistent with the basic rules of the Treaty (arts 85 to 94) designed to promote competition. Article 90(2) applies the competition rules to public undertakings if 'the application of such rules does not obstruct the performance, in law or in fact, of the particular tasks assigned to them'. The Court held that art 90(2) was not of such a nature as to create in favour of individuals rights which national courts were under a duty to protect. It said:

Article 90(2) does not lay down an unconditional rule. Its application involves an appraisal of the requirements, on the one hand, of the particular task entrusted to the undertaking concerned and, on the other hand,

---

17 [1968] ECR 143 at 156, [1968] CMLR 187 at 220–1.
18 Case 27/67 [1968] ECR 223 at 232, [1968] CMLR 228 at 230.
19 Case 10/71 [1971] ECR 723 at 730.

the protection of the interests of the Community. This appraisal depends on the objectives of general economic policy pursued by the states under the supervision of the Commission.

If a provision is subject to a consultative procedure before the Commission, this may be sufficient to negative its direct effect. The Court seems so to have held in relation to arts 93 and 102 in *Costa v ENEL*,[20] where it was emphasised that the procedure under art 93 was elaborate and negatived any intention on the part of member states to give rights to individuals. It has been held that art 92(1) is not directly effective until put into concrete form by acts of a general character under art 94 or decisions under art 93(2).[1]

(v) Alternative remedies for breach of the provision are irrelevant to direct effectiveness

It is well established that the availability to other member states and to Community institutions of alternative remedies for breach of a Treaty provision will not negative direct effectiveness. The most striking examples are the two cases involving Italy, *SACE*[2] and *Eunomia di Porro*[3], where the Commission had itself brought proceedings against Italy.

In the *Van Gend en Loos* case, in which the Governments of Belgium, Germany and the Netherlands had argued that the sanctions available to the Commission and member states under arts 169 and 170 negatived the existence of individual rights, the Court said:

> A restriction of the guarantees against an infringement of article 12 by member states to the procedures under articles 169 and 170 would remove all direct legal protection of the individual rights of their nationals. There is the risk that recourse to the procedure under these articles would be ineffective if it were to occur after the implementation of a national decision taken contrary to the provisions of the Treaty. The vigilance of individuals concerned to protect their rights amounts to an effective supervision in addition to the supervision entrusted by articles 169 and 170 to the diligence of the Commission and of the member states.[4]

Similarly, in the *Molkerei* case[5] the Court held that the existence of remedies available to the Community's institutions did not exclude the possibility of individual remedies in national courts. The Court differentiated between the purposes of the relevant remedies: the purpose of an action brought by an individual was to protect his

---

20 Case 6/64 [1964] ECR 585, [1964] CMLR 425.
1 Case 77/72 *Capolongo v Maya* [1973] ECR 611, [1974] 1 CMLR 230.
2 Case 33/70 [1970] ECR 1213, [1971] CMLR 123.
3 Case 18/71 [1971] ECR 811, [1972] CMLR 4.
4 Case 26/62 [1963] ECR 1 at 13, [1963] CMLR 105 at 130.
5 Case 28/67 [1968] ECR 143, [1968] CMLR 187.

individual rights in a particular case, whereas intervention by a Community institution was intended to ensure general and uniform observance of Community law. The principle is not limited to the availability of general remedies under the Treaty such as art 169. *Ministère Public Luxembourgeois v Müller*[6] suggests that even if the article in question (in that case art 90) contemplates enforcement by the Commission that does not of itself negative direct effect and reliance on the provision by individuals in national courts.

Temporal effect

In *Defrenne v Sabena (No 2)*[7] Miss Defrenne, an air hostess employed by Sabena, claimed in the Belgian court for damage suffered as a result of discrimination in terms of pay as compared with male colleagues doing the same work. The Belgian court referred to the European Court the question (inter alia) whether art 119 of the EEC Treaty, which lays down the principle that men and women should receive equal pay, was directly effective. In observations to the Court, the Governments of the United Kingdom and the Republic of Ireland supported their argument that art 119 was not directly effective by pointing to the financial consequences for their economies of such a holding: it 'could throw the social and economic situation in the United Kingdom into confusion' and 'impose a burden on the Irish economy which it is not in a position to support'.[8] The Court's solution was not to hold that art 119 was not directly effective, but to hold that its direct effect was to be limited to the future; accordingly the direct effect of art 119 could not be relied on in order to support claims concerning pay for periods prior to the date of the judgment, except as regards those workers who had already brought legal proceedings or made an equivalent claim.

This holding was exceptional, as the Court itself recognised, and turned not only on the economic consequences of which the United Kingdom and the Republic of Ireland had warned, but also on the failure of the Commission to take action against the member states concerned; that failure had led to the consolidation of the mistaken impression, especially on the part of private employers, that art 119 did not require complete abolition of pay discrimination. For these reasons it will not be often that such a limitation on the direct effect of Treaty provisions will be countenanced. Accordingly, when Lloyds Bank sought to limit the scope of the ruling that employers' contributions to pension schemes were 'pay' within art 119, it failed because

---

6 Case 10/71 [1971] ECR 723.
7 Case 43/75 [1976] ECR 455, [1976] 2 CMLR 98.
8 [1976] ECR 455 at 460, 465.

it could not point either to a reasonable misapprehension of the law or to widespread adverse financial consequences.⁹

In 1985 the European Court held that fees charged by Belgian vocational schools to French students were unlawful because they discriminated against non-Belgian nationals: *Gravier v City of Liège*.¹⁰ After that judgment French students sought in the Belgian courts to reclaim fees which had been unlawfully levied. In *Barra v Belgium and City of Liège*¹¹ the plaintiffs were French students who had followed courses in the gunsmithing section of a technical college in Liège; in *Blaizot v University of Liège*¹² the plaintiffs were French students who had followed courses in veterinary medicine at various Belgian universities. Belgian legislation barred claims for repayment of fees charged up to December 1984 unless a claim had been brought before February 1985, when the European Court ruled in *Gravier* that the fees were unlawful. The Belgian government argued that the Court should rule that the effect of the *Gravier* case should be limited in time to the period from and after 1985 when it was decided. But the Court refused to do so, because the time for the European Court to limit the effect was in 1985 when the *Gravier* case was decided, and not in 1988 when the Court was asked to rule on whether Belgian legislation could limit the claims.

But in *Blaizot* the Court felt itself able to limit the right of the students to a refund. In the first place, *Blaizot* was a case involving access to *university* education, and not vocational training, and it was therefore the first occasion on which it was decided that the prohibition against non-discrimination applied to university studies in veterinary medicine because they amounted to 'vocational training' within the scope of the judgment in *Gravier*. In the second place, the Commission might have led the Belgian authorities to consider that the Belgian legislation was in conformity with Community law: after the *Gravier* case, the Commission informally expressed the view to the Belgian Education Ministries that it considered that the enrolment fees were contrary to Community law, but shortly afterwards it stated that it had not yet completed its review of the matter. The Court concluded that 'pressing considerations of legal certainty preclude any re-opening of the operation of past legal relationships where that would retroactively throw the financing of university education into confusion and might have unforeseeable consequences for the proper functioning of universities.'¹³

---

9 Case 69/80 *Worringham and Humphreys v Lloyds Bank Ltd* [1981] ECR 767, [1981] 2 CMLR 1.
10 Case 293/83 [1985] ECR 593, [1985] 3 CMLR 1.
11 Case 309/85 [1988] 2 CMLR 409.
12 Case 24/86 [1989] 1 CMLR 57.
13 At 69. Cf Case 41/84 *Pinna v CAFS* [1986] ECR 1, [1988] 1 CMLR 350.

In a number of cases the question has arisen in the European Court whether, in order to prevent injustice, the temporal effect of its judgments should be limited where it was held that a tax has been unlawfully levied. The point arises in this way: a tax or customs duty is levied on an importer; the importer includes the cost of the tax in his price to a purchaser; some time later the tax or duty is held to be contrary to art 13 or 95 of the EEC Treaty; the importer seeks to recover the charge from the customs or tax authorities; since he has already recouped its cost from his purchaser he will obtain double payment and be unjustly enriched. In these cases the European Court has held that the solution is not to limit the temporal effect of its judgment, but to make it clear that where a charge is unlawful the national courts may apply national rules, eg of limitation, and may take account of the fact that the charge has been recouped in the price, to avoid an unjust enrichment of the importer.[14] But where a series of regulations fixing a system of calculation of monetary compensatory amounts was held to be invalid, the Court, in order to avoid further distortion in competition, declared that the charging or payment of monetary compensatory amounts by national authorities on the basis of the invalid regulations could not be challenged as regards the period prior to the date of its judgment.[15]

Remedies

It will be apparent from the preceding discussion that the concept of direct effect as developed and applied by the European Court entails that the national courts have a duty to ensure the protection of directly effective rights. This duty derives from art 5 of the EEC Treaty, according to which member states are under a duty to take all appropriate measures to ensure fulfilment of the obligations arising out of the Treaty. Directly effective treaty provisions are obligations within

---

14 Case 61/79 *Amministrazione delle Finanze v Denkavit Italiana Srl* [1980] ECR 1205, [1981] 3 CMLR 394; Cases 66, 127 and 128/79 *Amministrazione delle Finanze dello Stato v Salumi Meridionale Industria Srl* [1980] ECR 1237, [1981] 1 CMLR 1; Case 811/79 *Amministrazione delle Finanze dello Stato v Ariete SpA* [1980] ECR 2545, [1981] 1 CMLR 316; Cases 142 and 143/80 *Amministrazione delle Finanze dello Stato v Essevi SpA and Salengo* [1981] ECR 1413. Cf Case 222/82 *Apple and Pear Development Council v Lewis* [1983] ECR 4083, [1984] 3 CMLR 733.
15 Case 4/79 *Société Coopérative Providence Agricole de la Champagne v ONIC* [1980] ECR 2823; Case 112/83 *Société des Produits de Maïs SA v Administration des Douanes* [1985] ECR 719, [1988] 1 CMLR 459. These decisions were applied by the French Cour de Cassation, but the Conseil d'Etat refused to apply them to the decisions of the French administrative courts: see Hartley *Foundations of European Community Law* (2nd edn 1988) pp 232–235, and for the criticism by the Commission, OJ C No 220, 1 September 1988, p 28. See also Waelbroeck (1981) 1 EL Rev 115.

the scope of art 5, and the duty under art 5 'to take all appropriate measures, whether general or particular, to ensure the fulfilment of that obligation, is binding upon all the authorities of Member States, including, for matters within their jurisdiction, the courts.'[16] That was said in two cases which were concerned, not with directly effective treaty provisions, but with a specific obligation under art 6 of the Equal Treatment Directive. That article obliged member states to introduce such measures as were necessary to enable all persons who considered themselves wronged by discrimination 'to pursue their claims by judicial process'. But the principle is the same in the case of directly effective treaty provisions. There must be a guarantee of real and effective judicial protection.

But it has long been established that the manner of the protection depends on national procedural and substantive law.[17] The leading cases are the 1976 decisions in *Rewe* and *Comet*.[18] In each of these cases importers or exporters had paid levies which were, or were held to be, equivalent to customs charges in contravention of the directly effective provisions of arts 13 and 16 of the EEC Treaty. In each case the national authorities who collected the levies resisted repayment on the ground that the applicants had not made claims for repayment within the time limits required by the applicable German or Dutch laws. The national courts asked the European Court whether it was legitimate for them to apply national limitation rules. The European Court held that arts 13 and 16 had a direct effect which conferred on individuals rights which national courts were required to protect. But, in the absence of Community rules on the subject, it was for the domestic legal system of each member state to designate the courts which had jurisdiction and to determine the procedural conditions governing actions at law intended to ensure the protection of the

---

16 Case 14/83 *Von Colson v Land Nordrhein-Westfalen* [1984] ECR 1891 at 1909, [1986] 2 CMLR 430 at 453; Case 79/83 *Harz v Deutsche Tradax* [1984] ECR 1921 at 1942; Case 60/75 *Russo v AIMA* [1976] ECR 45 at 62, per Reischl AG.
17 For early examples see Case 28/67 *Molkerei-Zentrale Westfalen v Hauptzollamt Paderborn* [1968] ECR 143, [1968] CMLR 187; Case 13/68 *Salgoil SpA v Italian Ministry for Foreign Trade* [1968] ECR 453, [1969] CMLR 181; cf Case 6/60 *Humblet v Belgium* [1960] ECR 559; Case 179/84 *Bozzetti v Invernizzi SpA* [1985] ECR 2301.
18 Case 33/76 *Rewe v Landwirtschaftskammer Saarland* [1976] ECR 1989, [1977] 1 CMLR 533; Case 45/76 *Comet v Produktschap voor Siergewassen* [1976] ECR 2043, [1977] 1 CMLR 533. See also Case 61/79 *Amministrazione delle Finanze dello Stato v Denkavit Italiana Srl* [1980] ECR 1205, [1981] 3 CMLR 394; Cases 66, 127 and 128/79 *Amministrazione delle Finanze dello Stato v Meridionale Industria Salumi Srl* [1980] ECR 1237, [1981] 1 CMLR 1; Case 811/79 *Amministrazione delle Finanze dello Stato v Ariete SpA* [1980] ECR 2545, [1981] 1 CMLR 316; Cases 142 and 143/80 *Amministrazione delle Finanze dello Stato v Essevi SpA* [1981] ECR 1413; Case 386/87 *Société Bessin et Salson v Administration des Douanes* 9 November 1989.

rights which derived from the direct effect of Community law. But those conditions should not be less favourable than those relating to similar actions of a domestic nature. It was permissible for national law to lay down time-limits, but not if they made it impossible in practice to obtain relief:

> The position would be different only if the conditions and time-limits made it impossible in practice to exercise the rights which the national courts are obliged to protect. This is not the case where reasonable periods of limitation of actions are fixed. The laying-down of such time-limits with regard to actions of a fiscal nature is an application of the fundamental principle of legal certainty protecting both the tax-payer and the administration concerned.[19]

Thus it is clear that under no circumstances is it permissible for national law to exclude or make excessively difficult the exercise of the rights which national courts are bound to protect.[20] The requirement of non-discrimination cannot justify national legislation which renders repayment of charges levied contrary to Community law virtually impossible, even if the same treatment was extended to taxpayers who had similar claims arising from an infringement of national tax law.[1]

In 1985 the European Court held that a French vehicle tax was a discriminatory measure contrary to art 95.[2] The French tax was a lump sum tax on cars rated at more than 16 hp. It was discriminatory because no French cars were rated above that power and there was no objective justification for the scale of the tax difference between cars above 16 hp (eg the Mercedes involved in the case) and those with less power. Following that decision the French legislature adopted a law to abolish the fixed tax and substitute a differential tax based on power rating. The legislation also enabled taxpayers to obtain a refund of the difference between the old fixed tax and the new differential tax, but applied a two-year time limit for refunds, which ran from the time when the tax was paid. Mr Deville paid the special tax on his Italian car when he bought it in 1982 and the French tax administration dismissed his claim for a refund on the ground that it should have been brought by December 1984, which was several months before the

---

19 [1976] ECR at 1998, [1977] 1 CMLR at 551.
20 Case 61/79 *Amministrazione delle Finanze dello Stato v Denkavit Italiana Srl* [1980] ECR 1205, [1981] 3 CMLR 394.
1 Case 199/82 *Amministrazione delle Finanze dello Stato v San Giorgio SpA* [1983] ECR 3595, [1985] 2 CMLR 658.
2 Case 112/84 *Humblot v Directeur des Services Fiscaux* [1985] ECR 1367, [1986] 2 CMLR 338. On recovery of unlawful state aids see Cases 205–215/82 *Deutsche Milchkontor GmbH v Germany* [1983] ECR 2633; Case 94/87 *Commission v Germany* [1989] 2 CMLR 425.

European Court gave judgment declaring the tax unlawful. The European Court, while emphasising that it was for the French court to decide whether the true effect of the legislation was to deprive Mr Deville of his claim, held that national legislation may not, subsequent to a judgment of the European Court the effect of which is that certain national legislation is incompatible with the Treaty, adopt a procedural rule which reduces the possibility of bringing proceedings for recovery of taxes which were illegally levied.[3] The effect of the ruling was that national law could not impose a time-limit which would have expired before the date of the judgment.

This is also the effect of the judgment in *Barra v Belgium*,[4] which, by contrast with most of the decisions, did not involve an unlawful tax, but discriminatory enrolment fees paid by French students to Belgian technical colleges. In 1985 the European Court held that the charging of fees to nationals of other member states (which were not charged to Belgian students) as a condition of access to vocational training constituted unlawful discrimination on the ground of nationality contrary to art 7 of the EEC Treaty.[5] After that judgment, Belgian legislation abolished the discriminatory fees but limited the opportunity to claim refunds to those students who had brought proceedings before the date of the Court's judgment in 1985. In *Barra* the Court held that the earlier judgment applied to fees paid before 1985 as well as after,[6] and that legislation which limited repayment to students who instituted proceedings before the 1985 judgment 'simply deprives individuals who do not fulfil this condition of the right to obtain a refund of the sums improperly paid.'[7] Accordingly, the Belgian legislation rendered impossible the exercise of rights conferred by art 7 and the Belgian court was under an obligation not to apply the time-limit.

When taxes are improperly levied on importers and exporters, the importers and exporters frequently pass on the cost of the taxes to their customers. If they were able to obtain repayment of the tax in those circumstances, and did not then reimburse their own customers, they would obtain a double benefit. In *Hans Just v Danish Ministry for Fiscal Affairs*[8] the question which arose was whether taxpayers who had passed on to their customers the burden of discriminatory taxes could nevertheless recover them from the national authorities. The Court held that national law could prevent the unjust

---

3 Case 240/87 *Deville v Administration des Impôts* [1989] 3 CMLR 611.
4 Case 309/85 [1988] 2 CMLR 409.
5 Case 293/83 [1985] ECR 593, [1985] 3 CMLR 1.
6 See Case 24/86 *Blaizot v University of Liège* [1989] 1 CMLR 57 for a different result in relation to university fees. See p 61, ante.
7 At 418–419.
8 Case 68/79 [1980] ECR 501.

enrichment of an importer which such a recovery might entail. The Court said:[9]

> ... the protection of rights guaranteed in the matter by Community law does not require an order for the recovery of charges improperly made to be granted in conditions which would involve the unjust enrichment of those entitled. There is nothing therefore, from the point of view of Community law, to prevent national courts from taking account in accordance with their national law of the fact that it has been possible for charges unduly levied to be incorporated in the prices of the undertaking liable for the charge and to be passed on to the purchasers. It is equally compatible with the principles of Community law for courts before which claims for recovery of repayments are brought to take into consideration, in accordance with their national law, the damage which an importer may have suffered because the effect of discriminatory or protective tax provisions was to restrict the volume of imports from other Member States.

But the European Court[10] has also held that a national law imposing a burden of proof on the exporter or importer which has the effect of making it virtually impossible or excessively difficult to secure the repayment of unlawful charges is incompatible with Community law; that is particularly so in the case of presumptions or rules of evidence intended to place on the taxpayer the burden of establishing that the charges were not passed on to customers, or which restrict the form of evidence, eg by excluding any evidence other than documentary evidence. Thus the European Court held that a French law which placed on the claimant the burden of proof that charges had been passed on to a customer was incompatible with Community law. The result was the same if the law was framed as placing the burden on the taxpayer of proving that the charge had been borne by the taxpayer. Nor could it be generally assumed that, because indirect taxes were usuallypassed on to the final consumer, that was so in every case. The question whether an indirect tax had been passed on was a question of fact to be determined in each case.[11]

It remains to consider the scope of the obligation on national courts to give remedies to enforce individual rights which are by Community law directly effective. For example, are there circumstances in which the national law must give a right to damages, or to an injunction? The

---

9 At 523.
10 Case 199/82 *Amministrazione delle Finanze dello Stato v San Giorgio SpA* [1983] ECR 3595, [1985] 2 CMLR 658 (a case involving charges made contrary to EEC regulations); applied in Case 104/86 *Commission v Italy* [1989] 3 CMLR 25.
11 Cases 331, 376, 378/85 *Les Fils de Jules Bianco SA v Directeur Général des Douanes* [1989] 3 CMLR 36.

answer is that national law must provide real and effective protection, but there is probably no obligation to provide any particular remedy. In the *Von Colson* and *Harz* cases[12] the special obligation imposed by the Equal Treatment Directive to provide judicial remedies was held not to require any specific sanction such as damages; but if a member state chose to penalise breach of the equal treatment provision by the award of damages, the compensation must be adequate and not merely nominal. In *Russo v AIMA* it was said, in the context of an individual producer who had been damaged by unlawful intervention by a member state: 'If such damage has been caused through an infringement of Community law, the State is liable to the injured party for the consequences in the context of the provisions of national law on the liability of the State.'[13] The Commission has accordingly expressed the view that art 5 of the EEC Treaty and the general principles of Community law oblige the member states to provide for a system of compensation for private individuals in cases where those member states were responsible for damage caused to them in violation of Community law.[14] But in 1989[15] the Commission indicated that not all member states (including the United Kingdom) had a complete system of compensation. It is suggested that the Commission's view that there is a right to damages is only correct where damages is the only remedy which can provide adequate protection of the right involved. Some very difficult questions have been raised in England on the availability of the damages remedy, and the relationship between the right to damages and the possibility of obtaining interim relief pending the determination of cases in which directly effective rights are claimed has not yet been definitely established.[16]

2 Direct effect of other treaties

The European Court has extended the concept of direct effect to cover not only certain provisions of the EEC Treaty but also free trade and association agreements entered into between the Community and third states. The legal basis for this extension was most

---

12 N 16, supra. See Curtin (1985) 22 CML Rev 505.
13 Case 60/75 [1976] ECR at 56. See also Case 52/76 *Benedetti v Munari* [1977] ECR 163 at 192, per Reischl AG; Case 106/77 *Amministrazione delle Finanze dello Stato v Simmenthal SpA* [1978] ECR 629 at 656, [1978] 3 CMLR 263 at 279, per Reischl AG. Case 158/80 *Rewe v Hauptzollamt Kiel* [1981] ECR 1805 at 1851, [1982] 1 CMLR 449 at 468, where Capotorti AG accepted that the right to damages depended on national law.
14 OJ C No 303, 28 November 1988, p 2.
15 OJ C No 276, 30 October 1989, p 24.
16 Pp 107–110, infra.

fully articulated in the *Kupferberg* case,[17] which involved the question of the direct effects of the free trade agreement between the EEC and Portugal, which had been raised, but not decided, in the reference from the English Court of Appeal in the *Polydor* case.[18] In the *Kupferberg* case the German customs applied a duty to port wines imported into Germany from Portugal. The importer claimed that the duty was contrary to the provision of the EEC–Portuguese free trade agreement prohibiting discriminatory taxation in a manner substantially similar to art 95 of the EEC Treaty. The German court asked the European Court to rule on whether the provision of the EEC–Portuguese Agreement was directly effective. The European Court held, contrary to the contentions of several Governments (including the United Kingdom), that the provision did have direct effect. The reasoning was this: the responsibility for entering into an association or free trade agreement with a third state was that of the Community rather than that of the member states; agreements of that nature required compliance by member states; the effect of provisions in these agreements must not be allowed to vary between different member states; it did not matter that the agreement contained its own institutional machinery for securing compliance or variation; accordingly, since the provision was sufficiently unconditional and precise, it was capable of conferring individual rights which national courts must protect. On the other hand, it has been held by the European Court that the freedom of movement provisions in the Association Agreement between the EEC and Turkey were not directly effective, and consequently the wife of a Turkish worker in Germany could not rely on them to contest the refusal of the German authorities to allow her to stay;[19] and the English court has held that a Turkish national could not rely on the Association Agreement to contest the decision of the Home Secretary to deport him.[20]

Thus far the direct effect of other treaties has been limited to multilateral association agreements and bilateral free trade agreements. It has been held that provisions of the General Agreement on

---

17 Case 104/81 *Hauptzollamt Mainz v CA Kupferberg & Cie KG* [1982] ECR 3641, [1983] 1 CMLR 1. For earlier examples see Case 87/75 *Bresciani v Amministrazione Italiana delle Finanze* [1976] ECR 129, [1976] 2 CMLR 62 (Yaoundé Convention); Case 17/81 *Pabst and Richarz KG v Hauptzollamt Oldenburg* [1982] ECR 1331, [1983] 3 CMLR 11 (EEC–Greece Association Agreement). See White (1976) 1 EL Rev 402; Schermers (1982) 19 CML Rev 563; Bebr (1983) 20 CMLR Rev 35; Hartley (1983) 8 EL Rev 383.
18 Case 270/80 *Polydor Ltd v Harlequin Record Shops Ltd and Simons Records Ltd* [1982] ECR 329, [1982] 1 CMLR 677.
19 Case 12/86 *Demirel v Stadt Schwäbisch Gmünd* [1989] 1 CMLR 421.
20 *R v Home Secretary, ex p Narin* (1989) *Independent*, 18 December.

Tariffs and Trade (GATT) are not directly effective;[1] and that Spanish fishermen could not use art 234 of the EEC Treaty (which safeguards treaties entered into between member states and third states before the EEC Treaty) in order to rely on a multilateral agreement to which Spain and Ireland were parties so as to avoid the application of Irish fishing regulations.[2]

3 Direct applicability and effect of regulations, decisions and directives

(i) Regulations

If one main area caught by the provisions of s 2(1) of the European Communities Act 1972 is that of the directly effective provisions of the Treaties, then another must be the regulations of the Council and the Commission. The pertinent parts of art 189 are as follows:

> In order to carry out their task the Council and the Commission shall, in accordance with the provisions of this Treaty, make regulations . . . A regulation shall have general application. It shall be binding in its entirety and directly applicable in all member states.

The general application and the direct applicability of regulations is fundamental to the scheme of the Common Market.

Council and Commission regulations fall squarely within the scope of s 2(1) of the European Communities Act 1972: (1) they are liable to create rights, powers, liabilities, obligations and restrictions (2) which arise under the Treaty, and (3) which in accordance with the Treaties (that is, art 189) are *without further legal enactment* to be given legal effect in the United Kingdom. As a result of s 2(1), art 189 will be effective in the United Kingdom to incorporate Community regulations into United Kingdom law.

It follows that under Community law regulations:

> not only by their entry into force render automatically inapplicable any conflicting provision of current national law but—in so far as they are an integral part of and take precedence in the legal order applicable in the territory of each of the member states—also preclude the valid adoption of new national legislative measures to the extent to which they would be incompatible with Community provisions.[3]

---

1 See eg Case 266/81 *Società Italiana per l'Oleodotto Transalpino v Ministero delle Finanze* [1983] ECR 731, [1984] 2 CMLR 231; Cases 267–269/81 *Amministrazione delle Finanze dello Stato v Società Petrolifera Italiana SpA* [1983] ECR 801, [1984] 1 CMLR 354.
2 Case 812/79 *A-G v Burgoa* [1980] ECR 2787, [1981] 2 CMLR 193; Case 181/80 *Procureur Général v Arbelaiz-Emazabel* [1981] ECR 2961.
3 Case 106/77 *Amministrazione delle Finanze dello Stato v Simmenthal SpA* [1978] ECR 629 at 643, [1978] 3 CMLR 263 at 283. See also Case 43/71 *Politi v Ministero delle Finanze* [1971] ECR 1039, [1973] CMLR 60.

Direct applicability of regulations and the constitutions of member states.
The direct applicability of regulations[4] has given rise to grave constitutional problems in Germany and a serious conflict between Community law and German law. In some early decisions German courts refused to give effect to art 189 because it was incompatible with the constitution of the Federal Republic; but other decisions gave effect to the overriding nature of regulations.[5] The conflict became more serious when the European Court ruled that regulations must take precedence over rights protected by the constitutions of the member states. The litigation arose out of Regulations 102/64, 120/67 and 473/67, which provided for the forfeiture of certain deposits in the event that full use was not made of certain export licences. As a matter of German constitutional law, the German courts took the view that such a type of deposit regulation was unconstitutional because (a) it infringed the reasonable freedom of the individual to carry on business and (b) it contravened the fundamental principle of German legal theory that the compulsory payment of money cannot be imposed in the absence of fault on the part of the individual concerned.

In December 1970 the European Court decided four cases which concerned, in a greater or lesser measure, the validity of the regulations dealing with deposits for exports.[6] The Court thought that the protection of human rights was expressly protected by the Treaty in that the general principles of Community law protected basic personal rights.[7] On the facts, however, the Court held that the deposit system did not constitute a particularly serious encroachment on personal rights. The Frankfurt court had taken the view that the principle of proportionality resulted from the articles of the Basic Law of the Federal Republic of Germany and that Community acts should not violate these constitutional provisions. It thought that by ratifying the EEC Treaty the Federal Republic of Germany had not renounced its power, by means of the German constitution, to protect elementary constitutional rights within the framework of a European Community. From the point of view of the German court, the basic principle was that constitutional amendment could not be effected merely through the device of a directly applicable Community law.

The European Court was quick to reassert the supremacy of

---

4 See eg decisions at [1964] CMLR 130.
5 See eg decisions at [1964] CMLR 285, 295, 300, 304, 310.
6 Case 11/70 *Internationale Handelsgesellschaft v Einfuhr- und Vorratsstelle für Getreide* [1970] ECR 1125, [1972] CMLR 255; and associated cases [1970] ECR 1161, 1183, 1197.
7 See also Case 29/69 *Stauder v City of Ulm* [1969] ECR 419, [1970] CMLR 112.

Community law over national law. In a most important statement of principle, the Court said:[8]

> According to the evaluation of the [Frankfurt Court], the system of deposits is contrary to certain structural principles of national constitutional law which must be protected within the framework of Community law, with the result that the primacy of supranational law must yield before the principles of the German Basic Law . . . Recourse to the legal rules or concepts of national law in order to judge the validity of measures adopted by the institutions of the Community would have an adverse effect on the uniformity and efficacy of Community law. The validity of such measures can only be judged in the light of Community law. In fact, the law stemming from the Treaty, an independent source of law, cannot because of its very nature be overridden by rules of national law, however framed, without being deprived of its character as Community law and without the legal basis of the Community itself being called in question. Therefore the validity of a Community measure or its effect within a member state cannot be affected by allegations that it runs counter to either fundamental rights as formulated by the constitution of that state or the principles of a national constitutional structure.

From the point of view of the European Court it was clearly intolerable for national law to have precedence over the clear wording and intention of the Treaty. The holding of the Court is a clear and unequivocal statement of that effect. The Court went on to hold that the Regulations did not infringe the guarantees granted by Community law:

> However, an examination should be made as to whether or not any analogous guarantee inherent in Community law has been disregarded. In fact, respect for fundamental rights forms an integral part of the general principles of law protected by the Court of Justice. The protection of such rights, whilst inspired by the constitutional traditions common to the member states, must be ensured within the framework of the structure and objectives of the Community.

On the facts, the Court held that there has been no violation of the fundamental rights protected by Community law.

The result reached by the Court to the effect that the secondary legislation enacted by Community institutions took precedence even over constitutional rights protected by the laws of member states was clearly not an easy one for the German courts (bound as they were by the German Constitution) to accept. When the case came before the Frankfurt court again, it would not accept that the result of ratification of the EEC Treaty by Germany was such that, as a matter of German law, Germany could have transferred to the Community

---

8 [1970] ECR 1125 at 1133–4, [1972] CMLR 255 at 282–3. For the proceedings in Germany see [1972] CMLR 17, and see also [1972] CMLR 733.

greater legislative powers than it had under its own constitution. Accordingly, the German court refused to apply the decision of the European Court; it still considered the Regulations to be contrary to the German constitution. The court held that under German law Community law could be tested against the fundamental principles of the constitution. The court therefore referred the case to the German Federal Constitutional Court for a ruling as to whether the deposit system was compatible with the German constitution. The Constitutional Court held that it had the power to rule on the question whether EEC regulations were compatible with the German Constitution, at least until such time as the European Parliament became a genuine law-making body which enacted legislation on individual rights which were similar to those set out in the German constitution. The Court held that any German court had the right and duty to refer a matter to the Constitutional Court whenever it felt that an EEC regulation amounted to an infringement of individual constitutional rights, even after a preliminary ruling had been obtained from the European Court. On the facts, however, the Court held that the Regulations were not contrary to the German constitution.[9] The decision of the Constitutional Court was regarded by the Commission as a 'dangerous threat to the unity of Community law' and the Commission informed the German Government of its 'grave concern' at the development.[10]

The Constitutional Court recognised in that decision that the concept of fundamental rights existed in European law[11] but considered that this was not a sufficient substitute for the protection afforded by the German constitution. Subsequently the Constitutional Court in 1979 indicated, without actually holding, that this decision might require reconsideration in view of 'political and legal developments' which had occurred in the European sphere since the 1974 decision;[12] this was an obvious reference to the very considerable developments which had taken place in the sphere of fundamental rights. A few months later the European Court, referring to the moves for the accession of the European Communities to the European Convention on Human Rights, reaffirmed its ruling that the application of EEC regulations could not be made subject to national constitutional standards.[13] Finally, in 1986 the Federal Constitutional Court decided[14]

---

9 [1974] 2 CMLR 540. See also *Re Intervention Buying* [1978] 2 CMLR 644.
10 Eighth General Report on the Activities of the European Communities (1974) p 270.
11 See ch 1, pp 8–13.
12 *Steinike und Weinlig v Bundesamt für Ernährung und Forstwirtschaft* [1980] 2 CMLR 531. The question was raised, but not decided, in a decision in February 1983, NJW 1983, p 1258.
13 Case 44/79 *Hauer v Land Rheinland-Pfalz* [1979] ECR 3727, [1980] 3 CMLR 42. See also Case 234/85 *Staatsanwalt Freiburg v Keller* [1986] ECR 2897, [1987] 1 CMLR 875.
14 *Re Application of Wünsche* [1987] 3 CMLR 225, on which see p 11, ante.

that the development of the standards of fundamental rights in European law had developed to a point that they generally ensured the effective protection of fundamental rights as against the sovereign powers of the Communities, and that protection was substantially similar to the protection of fundamental rights required by the German constitution. The Federal Constitutional Court would therefore no longer exercise its jurisdiction to review secondary Community legislation by the standards of the fundamental rights contained in the Constitution.

One lesson to be drawn in the United Kingdom is that the European Court will go far in holding that any national legislation or case law which cuts down the scope of directly applicable secondary legislation will, as regards Community law, be ineffective, and as regards the state concerned, be likely to place it in breach of its Treaty obligations. In relation to the United Kingdom specifically, three points should be made. First, the problem in the form which it took in Germany will of course not arise in the United Kingdom, because the United Kingdom has no written constitution. Secondly, the problem should be avoided while s 2 of the European Communities Act is in force because (a) by s 2(1) Community regulations will become part of the law of the United Kingdom and (b) any subordinate legislation enacted under s 2(2) will be subject to the overriding effects of Community law and will be ultra vires if it restricts the operation of Community law. Thirdly, the problem will arise in a similar form if a statute subsequent to the European Communities Act is inconsistent with a Community regulation.[15]

Direct effect of regulations. It is now accepted widely that, although by art 189 regulations are directly applicable in the sense that national legislation is not required to implement them, they are not necessarily directly effective in the sense that they in all cases confer direct rights on individuals. As Advocate General Warner has put it:[16]

> Unquestionably every provision of every regulation is directly applicable, but not every provision of every regulation has direct effect, in the sense of conferring on private persons rights enforceable by them in national courts. One can point to numerous examples of provisions of regulations that confer no direct rights on private persons.

The European Court has recognised that regulations are not necessarily directly effective in its frequent use of the formula that 'by

---

15 As to inconsistent legislation see chapter 1, pp 28–39.
16 Case 131/79 *R v Secretary of State for Home Affairs, ex p Santillo* [1980] ECR 1585 at 1608, [1980] 2 CMLR 308 at 317; see also Case 31/74 *Galli* [1975] ECR 47 at 70, [1975] 1 CMLR 211 at 219; Case 74/76 *Iannelli v Meroni* [1977] ECR 557 at 583, [1977] 2 CMLR 688 at 700; cf Case 87/82 *Rogers v Darthenay* [1983] ECR 1579, [1984] 1 CMLR 135.

virtue of article 189 regulations are directly applicable and consequently, may by their very nature have direct effect'.[17]

The operation of regulations in national law—limits on the scope of national implementing legislation and administration. The European Court has established in several important decisions that member states are prohibited from altering the scope of Community regulations in applying their provisions. The precise effect of these rulings on the United Kingdom will be discussed below.

In the leading case,[18] the German Bundesfinanzhof (Supreme Tax Court) referred a question on the interpretation of Council and Commission regulations to the European Court under art 177. The question was whether national authorities had power to categorise doubtful products by interpreting them as being in one of two groups under the agricultural Regulations in question.

In the proceedings before the European Court the German Government took the view that, to the extent that a regulation itself interpreted and defined the designations of products, the member states were no longer able to do so; but where a reference to products in a regulation was not sufficient to achieve an exact classification, additional rules for the interpretation and definition of products had to be issued by member states; the member states were empowered and required to issue rules designed to clarify and differentiate the designations of products subject to the levy. The importing company and the Commission took a different view: they regarded the regulation as overriding and subject only to Community law in its interpretation; therefore the national authorities could not be left the freedom to apply their own criteria in deciding on the classification of any particular product.

The European Court again asserted the supremacy of Community law. The first question was whether the article of the Regulation which obliged member states to take all necessary measures to adapt their legislative and administrative provisions so that the Regulation could be applied effectively was to be interpreted as meaning that the member states were entitled and obliged, by means of national provisions, to explain and differentiate from one another the categories of products which were subject to the levy. The Court thought not. It held:[19]

---

17 Case 41/74 *Van Duyn v Home Office* [1974] ECR 1337 at 1348, [1975] 1 CMLR 1 at 15 and several other cases, eg Case 8/81 *Becker v Finanzamt Münster-Innenstadt* [1982] ECR 53 at 70, [1982] 1 CMLR 499 at 512. See also *Cunningham v Milk Marketing Board for Northern Ireland* [1988] 3 CMLR 815.
18 Case 40/69 *Hauptzollamt Hamburg v Bollmann* [1970] ECR 69, [1970] CMLR 141.
19 [1970] ECR 69 at 79, [1970] CMLR 141 at 153. For a recent example see Case 255/86 *Commission v Belgium* [1989] 3 CMLR 91.

Since [the Regulation], in conformity with the second paragraph of article 189 of the Treaty, is directly applicable in all member states, the latter, unless otherwise expressly provided, are precluded from taking steps, for the purposes of applying the regulation, which are intended to alter its scope or supplement its provisions. To the extent to which member states have transferred legislative powers in tariff matters with the object of ensuring the satisfactory operation of a common market in agriculture they no longer have the powers to adopt legislative provisions in this field.

As a result, the article was interpreted to mean that the member states were obliged to do all that was necessary to eliminate any obstacles to the application of the Regulation. It did not permit member states to make internal provisions affecting the scope of the Regulation itself. The second question was whether the terms describing the products could be interpreted by national legislation. Again, the Court held that interpretation was for Community institutions and not for national authorities.

In a second group of cases[20] the questions before the Court concerned the interpretation and application of Council Regulation 19. The importers into Germany of a certain type of flour claimed that the criteria laid down (a) by the Minister of Finance, of 55% starch maximum content, and (b) by the explanatory notes, of 40% starch maximum content, were arbitrary and invalid. The Court held that it was the Community interpretation of the type of flour in question that was relevant and not the view of domestic authorities. It recognised that the governing criterion was indeed the starch content percentage and 'in order to ensure the functioning of the Common Market and, in particular, the organisations of the agricultural markets this level must be fixed in a uniform manner for the whole Community'.[1]

In *Variola v Italian Ministry of Finance*[2] the Court held that a regulation has immediate effect and that member states are under an obligation not to introduce any measure which might affect the jurisdiction of the Court to pronounce on any question involving the interpretation of Community law or the validity of an act of the institutions. No procedure is permissible whereby the Community nature of a legal rule is concealed from those subject to it. In particular

---

20 Cases 72 and 74/69 *Hauptzollamt Bremen v Bremer Handelsgesellschaft* and *Hauptzollamt Bremen v Krohn* [1970] ECR 427 and 451, [1970] CMLR 466 and 486.
1 [1970] ECR 427 at 435, [1970] CMLR 466 at 484. See also Case 49/71 *Hagen v Einfuhr- und Vorratsstelle für Getreide* [1972] ECR 23, [1973] CMLR 35; Case 18/72 *Granaria v PVV* [1972] ECR 1163, [1973] CMLR 596; Case 93/71 *Leonesio v Italian Ministry of Agriculture* [1972] ECR 287, [1973] CMLR 343.
2 Case 34/73 [1973] ECR 981. See also Case 50/76 *Amsterdam Bulb v Produktschap voor Siergewassen* [1977] ECR 137, [1977] 2 CMLR 218; Case 94/77 *Zerbone v Amministrazione delle Finanze dello Stato* [1978] ECR 99.

the jurisdiction of the Court under art 177 is unaffected by any provisions of national legislation which purport to convert a rule of Community law into national law.

The basis for these principles is that Community regulations must be uniformly applied in all the member states and have, so far as possible, the same effect throughout the Community.[3] But this does not mean that member states have no power at all to adapt regulations to their administrative and procedural principles. Thus they may issue administrative regulations, but not such as to alter the effect of Community rules or to take away Community rights;[4] they may apply national regulations to customs declaration so as to prevent illegal exchange control transactions;[5] they may charge fees for inspections carried out pursuant to regulations relating to aid for skimmed milk, but only if the charges represent the normal cost of the inspection and are not such as to deter the activities which the aid for skimmed milk is intended to encourage.[6] Where there is no provision in the Community rules for sanctions to be imposed on individuals for failure to observe Community regulations, member states may adopt such sanctions as are appropriate.[7]

It is clear that in the absence of specific provision in Community legislation, the remedies for repayment of charges or other payments improperly made depend on national law. Provided that there is an effective and non-discriminatory remedy, the following matters will depend on national law: whether the claim is statute-barred,[8] whether the claimant is entitled to interest,[9] whether a person required to make a refund may set-off the claim against amounts to it,[10] whether the claimant may be refused a refund if he has recovered it from his

---

3 Case 819/79 *Germany v Commission* [1981] ECR 21 at 35.
4 Case 6/71 *Rheinmühlen v Einfuhr- und Vorratsstelle für Getreide* [1971] ECR 823, [1972] CMLR 401; Case 94/71 *Schlüter v Hauptzollamt Hamburg* [1972] ECR 307, [1973] CMLR 113; Case 131/73 *Grosoli* [1973] ECR 1555, [1974] 2 CMLR 40; Case 118/76 *Balkan-Import-Export v Hauptzollamt Berlin-Packhof* [1977] ECR 1177; Case 31/78 *Bussone v Italian Ministry for Agriculture* [1978] ECR 2429, [1979] 3 CMLR 18; Cases 146 and 192–193/81 *Bay-Wa AG v BALM* [1982] ECR 1503.
5 Case 65/79 *Procureur de la République v Chatain Laboratories Sandoz* [1980] ECR 1345, [1981] 3 CMLR 418.
6 Case 233/81 *Denkavit Futtermittel GmbH v Germany* [1982] ECR 2933.
7 Case 50/76 *Amsterdam Bulb* [1977] ECR 137, [1977] 2 CMLR 218.
8 See cases at p 63, ante.
9 Case 26/74 *Société Roquette Frères v Commission* [1976] ECR 677; Case 130/79 *Express Dairy Foods Ltd v Intervention Board for Agricultural Produce* [1980] ECR 1887, [1981] 1 CMLR 451; cf Case 54/81 *Fromme v BALM* [1982] ECR 1449.
10 Case 177/78 *Pigs and Bacon Commission v McCarren* [1979] ECR 2161, [1979] 3 CMLR 389.

own customer,[11] or whether a recipient who has wrongly received a premium in good faith must return it.[12]

These decisions show how in practice Community law views the primacy and direct applicability of Community regulations. The conclusions to be drawn from these decisions in the United Kingdom context are these:

1. Subsequent legislation which is inconsistent with Community regulations will involve the United Kingdom in a breach of its treaty obligations.
2. Subordinate legislation which is inconsistent with Community regulations will be ultra vires so long as s 2 of the European Communities Act 1972 remains in force.
3. United Kingdom authorities will not be able, by subordinate legislation or administrative measure or otherwise, to issue binding interpretations of Community regulations or to modify their scope or add to their provisions.
4. In practice it will in many cases not be necessary, because of s 2(1) of the 1972 Act, for there to be implementing legislation in the United Kingdom to give effect to regulations.[13]

(ii) Decisions

Decisions may be addressed by the Council or the Commission to one or more member states or to individuals. In the case of decisions directed to member states, in the normal case the member state would, if necessary, rely on national legislation to bring them into direct effect within the national state. This section will be concerned only with the effect of decisions in national law. The extent to which they (and regulations) can be challenged within the institutions of the Community raises problems of a different scope which will be discussed in Chapter 4.

Decisions addressed to member states. The Treaties contain many references to the powers of the Council and the Commission to issue binding decisions.[14] The general power is conferred by art 189 which provides in pertinent part that 'in order to carry out their task . . . in accordance with the provisions of this Treaty' the Council and the

---

11 Case 199/82 *Amministrazione delle Finanze dello Stato v San Giorgio SpA* [1983] ECR 3595, [1985] 2 CMLR 658.
12 Case 265/78 *Ferwerda BA v Produktschap voor Vee en Vlees* [1980] ECR 617, [1980] 3 CMLR 737.
13 See p 122, post.
14 See, among many examples, EEC Treaty, arts 33(2), 43(2), 89(2), 90(3); ECSC Treaty, art 64.

Commission shall (inter alia) take decisions.[15] By paragraph 4 of the same article:

> A decision shall be binding in its entirety upon those to whom it is addressed;

and by art 191 decisions are to be notified to those to whom they are directed and shall take effect upon such notification. By art 152 of the Treaty of Accession the new member states have bound themselves to:

> put into effect the measures necessary for them to comply from the date of accession with the provisions of directives and decisions within the meaning of article 189 of the EEC Treaty

and with the corresponding provisions of the other Treaties, subject to certain exceptions contemplated by the Treaty of Accession.

In three important judgments of October 1970[16] the European Court held that in principle decisions could be invoked by individuals even if they were addressed to member states. The reasoning was very similar to that in the cases establishing the direct effect of provisions of the Treaties: decisions (and directives) could be directly effective if they were unconditional and sufficiently clear and precise to be capable of creating direct effects in the legal relations between the member states. The plaintiffs were all long distance road hauliers who alleged the incompatibility of the German Statute on Taxation of Road Freight Traffic with Community rules. By that law there was introduced into Germany a tax on the transportation of goods. Before the tax was introduced the Commission made a recommendation to the Federal Republic asking that the tax not be imposed, and declaring that such taxes were incompatible with the common transport policy. There was no question but that that recommendation was not directly effective, because art 189 of the Treaty expressly provides that recommendations are not to have binding force. Therefore the plaintiffs had to seek protection by another route and this they found primarily in the relevant secondary Community legislation enacted by the Council.

By decisions of the Council of 1965 it was provided, broadly, that as soon as a common turnover tax system had been determined by the

---

15 ECSC Treaty, art 14(1) provides: 'In order to carry out the tasks assigned to it the High Authority shall, in accordance with the provisions of this Treaty, take decisions, make recommendations or deliver opinions.' Art 14(2) provides: 'Decisions shall be binding in their entirety' and where addressed to individuals they become binding upon notification (art 15(2)).
16 Case 9/70 *Grad v Finanzamt Traunstein* [1970] ECR 825, [1971] CMLR 1. The other cases were Case 20/70 *Lesage v Hauptzollamt Freiburg* [1970] ECR 861, [1971] CMLR 1, and Case 23/70 *Haselhorst v Finanzamt Düsseldorf* [1970] ECR 881, [1971] CMLR 1.

Council and brought into force in the member states they were to apply it to (inter alia) road freight haulage. The common turnover tax system was to replace the specific taxes imposed on road freight haulage. The First Council Directive on Turnover Tax of 1967 provided for the introduction of the value added tax system (described in that Directive) in member states not later than 1 January 1970 (which was subsequently extended to 1 January 1972 by a Directive of 1969). The value added tax was introduced in the Federal Republic of Germany with effect from 1 January 1968. The plaintiffs argued that since Germany had introduced the value added tax system in relation to road transport it was required to exclude the operation of other specific taxes from road transport, notwithstanding that the value added tax system had not yet been introduced in all member states and did not become mandatory until the beginning of 1972. The main thrust of the argument was based on the direct effect of the Council Decision of 1965 as implemented by the Directive of 1967, although the plaintiffs relied also on a number of provisions of the Treaty as being directly effective.[17]

The important question was thus raised of the direct effect of decisions of Community institutions, and whether they could create individual rights which national courts had an obligation to protect. The German Government intervened in the proceedings to argue that decisions did not have direct effect. The Commission took the view in these proceedings that there was no compelling argument for denying direct effect. The arguments against direct effect, according to the Commission, were four-fold:

(a) By virtue of art 189 of the EEC Treaty, decisions addressed to member states were binding only for the states to which the decisions were directed; their effect on the individual would only be indirect and direct effect could be achieved only through an implementing act of national law. Such an argument would be supported by the fact that art 189 expressly attributed direct applicability only to regulations.

(b) The Treaty established a distinction between secondary legislation that was directly applicable on the one hand—the regulations—and secondary legislation that was not—decisions and directives—and the distinction would be broken down, causing legal uncertainty, if some provisions of a decision addressed to member states were given direct effect.

(c) In certain areas the Treaty left a choice of legal acts to Community institutions but in others specified only the use of

---

17 In particular (i) arts 5(2) and 74, (ii) art 80(1) and (iii) art 92. The Court did not rule on any of these provisions. The opinion of Roemer AG contains an interesting discussion of the extent to which they are capable of being directly effective.

directives (eg, in the right of establishment and the approximation of laws); this suggested that the member states did not wish to confer direct legislative powers in the latter cases.

(d) The fact that the Treaty did not require publication of decisions meant that it would be a matter of chance whether an individual could know enough in order to rely on a decision addressed to a member state; this fact would produce inequality before the law.

These arguments against direct effect were adopted by the German Government in its submissions, but the Commission produced a number of arguments in favour of direct effect:

(a) As in the cases where Treaty provisions prohibiting states from doing certain things had been held directly effective, the fact that the addressees of decisions were states was not in point; that only art 189 expressly gave direct effect was not in any way conclusive.

(b) Legal uncertainty was not likely to arise in practice; problems would only arise if decisions were not acted on by member states; since to have direct effect the provisions must be clear and unconditional, the question of direct effect should not arise except in a small number of cases.

(c) The fact that certain provisions contained in decisions addressed to member states had direct effect did not mean that the system of Community secondary legislation established in art 189 was abandoned; direct effect would, on the contrary, increase the legal protection of the rights of individuals.

(d) It was in fact customary for decisions to be published in the Official Journal for information purposes and therefore the argument based on the absence of an obligation to publish had little weight in practice.

(e) There were suggestions in earlier judgments of the European Court that decisions might have direct effect.[18]

The Advocate General's opinion supported the arguments in favour of direct effect which he described as a problem of 'great and fundamental importance'. However, on the facts, the prohibition on the reintroduction of specific taxes was not effective before 1 January 1972 and the Council Decision could not therefore give rise to direct

---

18 In Case 38/69 *Commission v Italy* [1970] ECR 47, [1970] CMLR 77, the Court had talked of decisions taking effect in the Common Market and of having immediate effect in member states. The Advocate General also referred in his opinion in *Grad* to cases on art 173 where decisions were said to be directly applicable (see [1970] ECR at 846) but the point on art 173 is a different one; see chapter 4, post. Other authorities supporting direct effect were decisions of German courts. But there were German decisions in the opposite sense; see eg [1971] CMLR 733, and cases cited at 738, and [1974] 1 CMLR 251.

Direct applicability and effect of regulations, decisions and directives

effects until that date. The Court accepted these submissions. It said:[19]

> The question concerns the combined effect of provisions contained in a decision and a directive. According to article 189 of the EEC Treaty a decision is binding in its entirety upon those to whom it is addressed. Furthermore, according to this article a directive is binding, as to the result to be achieved, upon each member state to which it is addressed, but leaves to the national authorities the choice of form and methods. The German Government in its observations defends the view that by distinguishing between the effects of regulations on the one hand and of decisions and directives on the other, article 189 precludes the possibility of decisions and directives producing the effects mentioned in the question, which are reserved to regulations. However, although it is true that by virtue of article 189, regulations are directly applicable and therefore by virtue of their nature capable of producing direct effects, it does not follow from this that other categories of legal measures mentioned in that article can never produce similar effects. In particular, the provision according to which decisions are binding in their entirety on those to whom they are addressed enables the question to be put whether the obligation created by the decision can only be invoked by the Community institutions against the addressee or whether such a right may possibly be exercised by all those who have an interest in the fulfilment of this obligation. It would be incompatible with the binding effect attributed to decisions by article 189 to exclude in principle the possibility that persons affected may invoke the obligation imposed by a decision. Particularly in cases where, for example, the Community authorities by means of a decision have imposed an obligation on a member state or all the member states to act in a certain way, the effectiveness ('l'effet utile') of such a measure would be weakened if the nationals of that state could not invoke it in the courts and the national courts could not take it into consideration as part of Community law. Although the effects of a decision may not be identical with those of a provision contained in a regulation, this difference does not exclude the possibility that the end result, namely the right of the individual to invoke the measure before the courts, may be the same as that of a directly applicable provision of a regulation.

It was necessary, the Court said, to examine in each particular case whether the provision in question, by its legal nature, background and wording, was capable of creating direct effects in the legal relationship between the state concerned and those subject to its jurisdiction. The obligation under the decision not to introduce or reintroduce taxes in addition to value added tax was by its nature binding and general, although it left open the determination of the date on which it was to become effective. But the obligation was:

> unconditional and sufficiently clear and precise to be capable of producing direct effects in the legal relationships between the member states and those subject to their jurisdiction

---

19 [1970] ECR 825 at 836–7.

and the date on which the obligation became effective was laid down by the directives of the Council, namely, 1 January 1970, subsequently extended to 1 January 1972. The fact that the date was determined by a directive did not deprive the directly effective provision of the decision of any of its binding force. The result was that the prohibition laid down in the decision could not come into effect until the beginning of 1972.

This was a bold decision of the European Court,[20] and marked an increase in the effectiveness of the Treaty system at the possible expense of the wording of the Treaty and the intentions of its authors. It was the precursor of the decisions on the direct effect of directives,[1] which have had an even more profound effect.

Decisions authorised by regulation. If by art 189 regulations are directly applicable within member states, does this mean that if a regulation authorises a Community institution to take decisions then those decisions *ipso facto* have direct effect? In *Toepfer v Commission*[2] the European Court was concerned with an application to annul a Commission decision. The decision had been taken by virtue of the provisions of Council Regulation 19. A provision of the Council Regulation stated that the Commission could take certain decisions and that those decisions were to take effect immediately, and the Court concluded that consequently a decision under the regulation was directly applicable. The decision in that case was addressed to a member state and the question for the Court was not whether it was directly applicable but whether it affected individuals in such a way as to give them the requisite standing under art 173. In such cases, the Court takes a much broader view than it would if the question in fact concerned the direct effect of a provision in national law. The dictum in this case must therefore be treated with some reserve.

Decisions addressed to individuals. A decision addressed to an individual, even more than a decision addressed to a member state, has the characteristic of an administrative rather than a legislative or quasi-legislative act. By art 189(4) it is 'binding in its entirety upon those to whom it is addressed' and takes effect (by virtue of art 191) on notification to the person to whom it is directed.

---

20 See also Case 130/78 *Salumificio di Cornuda SpA v Amministrazione delle Finanze dello Stato* [1979] ECR 867, [1979] 3 CMLR 561, where it seems to have taken more than 8 years of litigation for an Italian importer to be told he had, by virtue of a Commission Decision addressed to Italy, the right to import Argentine beef free of an Italian customs levy.
1 See pp 83–92, infra.
2 Cases 106–7/63 [1965] ECR 405, [1966] CMLR 111.

(iii) Directives

It remains, finally, to consider the direct effect of directives.[3] It is by means of directives that member states can be given general directions by Community institutions. Article 189(3) of the EEC Treaty provides:

> A directive shall be binding, as to the result to be achieved, upon each member state to which it is directed, but shall leave to the national authorities the choice of form and methods.[4]

A directive is not directly applicable in the sense that a regulation is. A directive requires a member state to alter its law, but it is left to the state to implement it by appropriate national legislation. It must be implemented by national law, and not merely by changes in administrative practice.[5] *A fortiori* it cannot rely on the fact that a directive may have direct effect to excuse its failure to implement it.[6] The European Court has indicated that exceptionally a change in national law may not be necessary where the existence of general principles of constitutional law or administrative law may render implementation of specific legislation superfluous, provided:

> ... that those principles guarantee that the national authorities will in fact apply the directive fully and that, where the directive is intended to create rights for individuals, the legal position arising from those principles is sufficiently precise and clear and the persons concerned are made fully aware of their rights and, where appropriate, afforded the possibility of relying on them before the national courts. That last condition is of particular importance where the directive is intended to accord rights to nationals of other Member States because those nationals are not normally aware of such principles.[7]

---

3 See Easson (1981) 1 Yb Eur L 1; Wyatt (1983) 8 EL Rev 268.
4 The corresponding provision in the ECSC Treaty is art 14(3) which provides: 'Recommendations shall be binding as to the aims to be pursued but shall leave the choice of the appropriate methods for achieving these aims to those to whom the recommendations are addressed.'
5 Case 102/79 *Commission v Belgium* [1980] ECR 1473, [1981] 1 CMLR 282; Case 96/81 *Commission v Netherlands* [1982] ECR 1791; Case 97/81 *Commission v Netherlands* [1982] ECR 1819; Case 145/82 *Commission v Italy* [1983] ECR 711, [1984] 1 CMLR 148; Case 300/81 *Commission v Italy* [1983] ECR 449, [1984] 2 CMLR 430; Case 116/86 *Commission v Italy* 3 March 1988. But the requirements of a directive may be satisfied if there are already in place national legislative or administrative rules of a general nature which have received sufficient publicity: Case 301/81 *Commission v Belgium* [1983] ECR 467, [1984] 2 CMLR 430.
6 Case 102/79 *Commission v Belgium* [1980] ECR 1473, [1981] 1 CMLR 282; Case 160/82 *Commission v Netherlands* [1982] ECR 4637, [1984] 1 CMLR 230; Case 168/85 *Commission v Italy* [1986] ECR 2945; Case 74/86 *Commission v Germany* 26 April 1988.
7 Case 29/84 *Commission v Germany* [1985] ECR 1661 at 1673, [1986] 3 CMLR 579 at 590. Cf Case 262/85 *Commission v Italy* [1987] ECR 3073 (faithful transposition of directive on conservation of wild birds especially important where management of common heritage entrusted to member states).

But normally a directive will be given effect by legislation. The terms of the legislation are a matter for the member state. It is not necessary that the provisions of the directive be enacted in precisely the same words, provided that the full application of the directive is ensured in a sufficiently clear and precise manner.[8] Thus in implementing the Equal Pay Directive and the provisions applicable to workers who were not members of unions and worked in small or medium-sized businesses:

> . . . the principles of legal certainty and the protection of individuals require an unequivocal wording which would give the persons concerned a clear and precise understanding of their rights and obligations and would enable the courts to ensure that those rights and obligations are observed.[9]

There can be no doubt that the United Kingdom Government has caused much unnecessary litigation and the expenditure of much unnecessary cost by taking the position that implementation of the Equal Pay and Equal Treatment Directives required only the continuation of, or minor amendments to, the Equal Pay Act 1970 and the Sex Discrimination Act 1975, rather than new laws based specifically on the directives.[10]

Once the national legislation has been enacted to implement a directive, then the national courts are under a duty to interpret the legislation to achieve the result required by the directive. This follows from the obligation of the member states under art 189(3) to achieve that result and from their duty under art 5 of the EEC Treaty to take all appropriate measures, whether general or particular, to ensure the fulfilment of that obligation. The duties are binding on all the authorities of the member states, including their courts, and it follows that 'national courts are required to interpret their national law in the light of the wording and the purpose of the directive in order to achieve the result referred to in art 189(3)'.[11]

The unmistakable trend[12] towards holding directives to be capable of being directly effective was confirmed in the decision of the Court in

---

8 A member state cannot impose additional requirements under its law in relation to harmonised technical requirements: Case 60/86 *Commission v UK* [1988] 3 CMLR 437; cf *R v London Boroughs Transport Committee, ex p Freight Transport Association Ltd* [1990] 1 CMLR 229.
9 Case 143/83 *Commission v Denmark* [1985] ECR 427 at 435, [1986] 1 CMLR 44 at 50.
10 See especially *Pickstone v Freemans plc* [1989] AC 66, [1988] 2 All ER 803, HL.
11 Case 14/83 *Von Colson v Land Nordrhein-Westfalen* [1984] ECR 1891 at 1909, [1986] 2 CMLR 430 at 453. See also Case 222/84 *Johnston v Chief Constable of Royal Ulster Constabulary* [1987] QB 129 at 153, [1986] ECR 1651 at 1690, [1986] 3 CMLR 240 at 269; Case 80/86 *Officier van Justitie v Kolpinghuis Nijmegen BV* [1987] ECR 3969, [1989] 2 CMLR 18; Case 31/87 *Gebr Beentjes BV v Netherlands*, 20 September 1988.
12 See Case 9/70 *Grad v Finanzamt Traunstein* [1970] ECR 825, [1971] CMLR 1; Case 33/70 *SACE v Italian Ministry of Finance* [1970] ECR 1213, [1971] CMLR 123.

Van Duyn v Home Office.[13] One of the questions referred was whether a Council directive, co-ordinating special measures concerning the movement and residence of foreign nationals on the grounds of public policy, public security or public health, was directly effective so as to confer upon individuals rights enforceable by them in the courts of a member state. The United Kingdom Government argued in the proceedings before the European Court that because art 189 distinguished between the effects ascribed to regulations and directives, it must be presumed that the Council, in issuing a directive rather than making a regulation, must have intended that the directive should have an effect other than that of a regulation. The Court held, however, that it would be incompatible with the binding effect attributed to a directive by art 189 to exclude, in principle, the possibility that the obligation which it imposed might be invoked by those concerned; the useful effect of the directive would be weakened if individuals were prevented from relying upon it before national courts and if those courts were prevented from taking it into consideration as an element of Community law. The directive was intended to limit the discretionary power which national laws generally confer on the authorities responsible for the entry and expulsion of foreign nationals. Since the provision in question laid down an obligation which was not subject to any exception or condition and which, by its very nature, did not require the intervention on the part either of the institutions of the Community or of member states, the directive was regarded by the Court as directly effective, with the result that it conferred upon individuals rights which were enforceable by them in the national courts and which those courts must protect.

It does not follow from this decision, and those which succeeded it, that the tests for the direct effect of provisions in directives are precisely the same as those for treaty provisions. The test for the direct effect of treaty provisions is the 'clear, unconditional, non-discretionary' requirement, but it is not possible to apply the 'non-discretionary' requirement without qualification in relation to directives, because art 189 makes it plain that member states have a discretion in the implementation of directives, and this makes it difficult, as Advocate General Warner has pointed out,[14] to apply to directives this requirement. In general the decisions of the European Court on the direct effect of directives do not demand this requirement to be fulfilled. The cases suggest that where a member state has a discretion under a

---

13 Case 41/74 [1974] ECR 1337, [1975] 1 CMLR 1; see also Case 131/79 *R v Secretary of State for Home Affairs, ex p Santillo* [1980] ECR 1585, [1980] 2 CMLR 308. See House of Lords Select Committee on the European Communities (1974–5), 10th Report, on the consequence of the *Van Duyn* decision for the UK Government.
14 Case 131/79 *R v Secretary of State for Home Affairs, ex p Santillo* (see n 13 above) at 1610, and 318, [1981] QB 778. See Easson (1981) 1 Yb Eur L 1, 36–37.

directive, but has not exercised it at all, then the provisions of the directive may have direct effect if they are sufficiently clear and unconditional, but that if the discretion has been exercised properly by the implementation of the directive in national law, then the directive will not have direct effect.[15] But once the date by which the member state should have implemented the directive has passed (and only then)[16] its provisions are capable of having direct effect if it has not been implemented.

Thus one case[17] concerned the claim in the Dutch courts by a company which had claimed a deduction of VAT on a printing machine. The Dutch authorities had treated the machine as a 'business asset' on which the company was entitled only to a partial deduction. The Dutch Supreme Court referred to the European Court the question whether art 17 of the Council Directive of 11 April 1967 on VAT had direct effect. That article allowed member states to exclude, in whole or in part, 'capital goods' from the deduction system. The Court recognised that the expression 'capital goods' was not capable of precise definition and therefore member states had a margin of discretion as regards the requirements of durability and value. When the matter in dispute depended on a provision which left the member state a margin of discretion, the exercise of the discretion was not subject to legal review, but the national court did have a duty to determine whether the national legislation fell outside the margin of discretion, and, if it did, to give effect to the individual's claim.

The impact of member states' discretion is illustrated by two decisions relating to the same Council Directive on foodstuff additives. The directives left a large measure of freedom to member states as to whether or not to authorise the use in foodstuffs of certain preservatives or antioxidants. In the first case[18] it was held that a total ban by a member state on the preservatives and antioxidants in question was contrary to the Directive and that consequently its provisions had direct effect and could be relied on before national courts. The prohibition was 'unconditional and sufficiently precise'.[19] In the second case[20] it was held that because the member state had not

---

15 See also Usher (1980) 5 EL Rev 470, Akehurst (1978) 49 BYIL 325.
16 Case 148/78 *Pubblico Ministero v Ratti* [1979] ECR 1629, [1980] 1 CMLR 96; Case 270/81 *Felicitas Rickmers-Linie KG & Co v Finanzamt Hamburg* [1982] ECR 2771 at 2792, [1982] 3 CMLR 447 at 455, per Slynn AG.
17 Cases 51-76 *Verbond van Nederlandse Ondernemingen v Inspecteur der Invoerrechten en Accijnzen* [1977] ECR 113, [1977] 1 CMLR 413.
18 Case 88/79 *Ministère Public v Grunert* [1980] ECR 1827.
19 It does not cease to be 'unconditional' merely because a member state is able to lay down 'conditions' for the application of the directive: Case 8/81 *Becker v Finanzamt Münster-Innenstadt* [1982] ECR 53, [1982] 1 CMLR 499.
20 Case 108/80 *Ministère Public v Kugelmann* [1981] ECR 433. Cf Cases 372-374/85 *Ministère Public v Traen* [1987] ECR 2141, [1988] 3 CMLR 511.

totally prohibited the substance in question (sorbic acid) its regulation was within its discretion under the Directive and consequently the individual could not rely on it before the national court. These cases suggest that where a member state has a discretion pursuant to a directive, the directive is not directly effective where the member state acts within the scope of the discretion, but is directly effective if the member state refuses to exercise its discretion, or abdicates it.

Thus directives have been held to have direct effect in the areas of freedom of movement and establishment,[1] labelling of solvents,[2] foodstuff additives,[3] VAT,[4] customs duties,[5] harmonisation of medicinal product regulations[6] and co-ordination of award procedures for public works contracts.[7] A neat illustration is provided by a case involving a Council Directive on international transport. The Directive, on authorisations for road passenger transport operators, allowed member states to determine the provisions relating to good repute to be satisfied by applicants; but it also provided that where applicants were already authorised by 1 January 1978 to engage in the occupation of road passenger transport operator they would be exempt from the requirement to furnish proof of good repute. Mr Delkvist had several convictions for theft and burglary and he was refused a renewal of his licence by the Danish bus authority on the ground that this record gave reason to believe that there was an imminent danger of misuse of his position. But prior to the introduction of checks on criminal records he had held a valid licence, and he argued (inter alia) that because of the provision of the Directive he was exempt from the requirement to furnish proof of good repute in view of the fact that he had held a licence prior to 1 January 1978. The Danish court asked the European Court (inter alia) whether the Directive was directly binding on Danish courts. The Court held that the Directive did have direct effect and therefore the national

---

1 Case 41/74 *Van Duyn v Home Office* n 13, supra; Case 131/79 *R v Secretary of State for Home Affairs, ex p Santillo* n 13, supra; Case 271/82 *Auer v Ministère Public (No 2)* [1983] ECR 2727, [1985] 1 CMLR 123.
2 Case 148/78 *Pubblico Ministero v Ratti* [1979] ECR 1629, [1980] 1 CMLR 96.
3 Cases cited nn 18 and 20, supra.
4 Case cited supra n 17 and Case 8/81 *Becker v Finanzamt Münster-Innenstadt* [1982] ECR 53, [1982] 1 CMLR 499; Case 255/81 *Grendel GmbH v Finanzamt für körpershaften, Hamburg* [1982] ECR 2301, [1983] 1 CMLR 379; Case 70/83 *Kloppenburg v Finanzamt Leer* [1984] ECR 1075, [1985] 1 CMLR 205; Case 5/84 *Direct Cosmetics Ltd v Customs and Excise Comrs* [1985] ECR 617, [1985] 2 CMLR 145; Case 50/88 *Kühne v Finanzamt München* (1989) Times, 2 August; Case 207/87 *Weissgerber v Finanzamt Neustadt* 14 July 1988; Cases 231/87 and 129/88 *UDIDFA v Comune di Carpaneto Piacentino* 17 October 1989 (public authorities may rely on directive as against tax authorities).
5 Case 158/80 *Rewe v Hauptzollamt Kiel* [1981] ECR 1805, [1982] 1 CMLR 449.
6 Case 301/82 *Clin-Midy SA v Belgium* [1984] ECR 251, [1985] 1 CMLR 443.
7 Case 31/87 *Gebr Beentjes BV v Netherlands* 20 September 1988.

authorities could not require an applicant to furnish proof of 'good repute' if he was authorised to be a road transport operator prior to 1 January 1978.[8] But the Court dealt a blow to Mr Delkvist's somewhat unmeritorious point by holding that, although an applicant could not be required to furnish proof of good repute, nevertheless the national authorities remained competent to verify in each case that the requirement of good repute was fulfilled.

The juridical basis of the direct effect of directives is to be found in the principle that 'a Member State which has not adopted the implementing measures required by the directive in the prescribed periods may not rely, as against individuals, on its own failure to perform the obligations which the directive entails'.[9] Only where the member state has failed to take the implementing measures required or has adopted measures which do not conform to a directive does the Court 'recognise the right of persons affected thereby to rely in law on a directive as against a defaulting State'.[10] This, as Judge Pescatore and others[11] have recognised, is the language of estoppel: a member state cannot be heard to rely on its own law as against an individual if reliance on its own law is contrary to an obligation imposed on it by a directive.

Horizontal effect. If this is the basis of the direct effect of directives it suggests a negative answer to the question whether they can have 'horizontal effect', ie impose obligations on individuals as well as confer rights. It would certainly be odd if individuals could not rely on their own national laws and were directly bound by a directive as from the date it should have been, but was not, implemented. The United Kingdom was strongly of the view that directives cannot have this effect,[12] and the preponderance of opinion supported that view.[13] It has now been authoritatively decided by the European Court in cases on the Equal Treatment Directive[14] that directives do not have a horizontal direct effect, and that they therefore cannot be relied upon by individuals against other private parties.

---

8 Case 21/78 *Delkvist v Anklagemyndigheden* [1978] ECR 2327, [1979] 1 CMLR 372. See also Case 38/77 *Enka v Inspecteur der Invoerrechten en Accijnzen* [1977] ECR 2203, [1978] 2 CMLR 212; Case 126/82 *Smit Transport BV v Commissie Grensoverschrijdend Beroepsgoederenvervoer* [1983] ECR 73, [1983] 3 CMLR 106.
9 Case 148/78 *Pubblico Ministero v Ratti* [1979] ECR 1629 at 1642, [1980] 1 CMLR 96 at 110.
10 Case 102/79 *Commission v Belgium* [1980] ECR 1473 at 1487, [1981] 1 CMLR 282 at 294.
11 Pescatore (1983) 8 EL Rev 155, 169; Easson (1981) 1 Yb Eur L 1, 38.
12 Case 19/81 *Burton v British Railways Board* [1982] ECR 555 at 568; see also Case 69/80 *Worringham and Humphreys v Lloyds Bank Ltd* [1981] ECR 767, [1981] 2 CMLR 1.
13 See eg Pescatore and Easson n 11, supra; Green (1984) 9 EL Rev 295. It had so been held in *Hugh-Jones v St John's College, Cambridge* [1979] ICR 848, EAT.
14 76/207.

Miss Marshall was a senior dietician with the Southampton and South West Hampshire Health Authority. The Health Authority had a policy of compulsorily retiring women at age 60 and men at age 65. She was dismissed at the age of 62, for the sole reason that she had passed the normal retirement age for women. The Sex Discrimination Act 1975 excluded from the ambit of its prohibition on discrimination by an employer on the ground of sex 'provision in relation to death or retirement'. The Industrial Tribunal held that the dismissal of Miss Marshall violated the principle of equal treatment, but the Employment Appeal Tribunal held that violation of the directive could not be relied on in proceedings before the European Court; the Court of Appeal referred to the European Court the questions (in substance) whether the dismissal was an act of unlawful discrimination, and whether the directive had direct effect. The European Court answered both questions in the affirmative. On the direct effect of the directive, the Court confirmed that the relevant provisions were unconditional and sufficiently precise, and could be relied upon by an individual against the State where the State failed to implement the directive.

But under art 189 of the EEC Treaty the obligation to implement the directive was binding on the member states. The Court went on:[15]

> It follows that a directive may not of itself impose obligations on an individual and that a provision of a directive may not be relied upon as such against such a person. It must therefore be examined whether, in this case, the respondent must be regarded as having acted as an individual. In that respect it must be pointed out that where a person involved in legal proceedings is able to rely on a directive as against the State he may do so regardless of the capacity in which the latter is acting, whether as employer or public authority. In either case it is necessary to prevent the State from taking advantage of its own failure to comply with Community law.

Consequently Miss Marshall succeeded because the Health Authority was conceded to be a public authority.[16]

In *Johnston v Chief Constable of the Royal Ulster Constabulary*[17] the background was the terrorist campaign in Northern Ireland. The plaintiff had been a full-time member of the Royal Ulster Constabulary reserve. She was dismissed because of a new policy of arming police officers in Northern Ireland, following which women members were confined to jobs which, it was considered, only women could

---

15 Case 152/84 *Marshall v Southampton and South West Hampshire Area Health Authority* [1986] QB 401 at 422, [1986] ECR 723 at 749, [1986] 1 CMLR 688 at 711. See also Case 71/85 *Netherlands v FNV* [1986] ECR 3855, [1987] 3 CMLR 767; Case 286/85 *McDermott and Cotter v Minister for Social Welfare and A-G* [1987] ECR 1453, [1987] 2 CMLR 607.
16 For further proceedings see [1989] 3 CMLR 771, EAT.
17 Case 222/84 [1986] ECR 1651, [1986] 3 CMLR 240.

perform, and women employed in other areas of work did not have their contracts renewed. The Northern Ireland regulations against discrimination contained an exception for acts done for the purpose of safeguarding security or of protecting public safety or public order. The European Court held that, although the principles of the Equal Treatment Directive were not subject to any such general reservation, the special derogation allowed in the directive for work in which the sex of the worker constituted a determining factor might (if the Northern Ireland industrial tribunal so decided on the facts) justify restricting particular policing tasks to men.

As for the direct effect of the directive, the Court pointed out that the direct effect of the general principle of equal treatment was irrelevant since it was established that the general principle had been properly implemented in Northern Ireland. The real question was whether an individual could rely on the directive as against a derogation laid down by a national legislature which went beyond what was permitted by the directive. The answer to that question was in the affirmative. Although the constitutional position of the police in the United Kingdom is a complex one,[18] the Court had little difficulty in finding that a public authority responsible for the direction of the police is an emanation of the state, in relation to which the directive had direct effect. Thus in each of these cases the European Court held that directives did not have horizontal effect, ie they could not as such impose obligations on individuals, but that in each the defendant, while not the state itself, was a public body which was an emanation of the state.

When a Dutch restaurant mixed tap water and carbon dioxide and sold it as 'mineral water', and was prosecuted for violation of Dutch law and of a directive on the exploitation and marketing of mineral waters, the European Court held that the Dutch prosecuting authorities could not rely on the directive, which had not been implemented in the Netherlands, because, applying *Marshall*, the directive could not of itself impose obligations on an individual.[19]

That was a case in which the state sought to rely on the directive to impose obligations upon an individual, but the essence of the decision in *Marshall* is that the direct effect of directives (by contrast with that of EEC Treaty provisions)[20] has no role to play in private litigation.

---

18 See eg *R v Metropolitan Police Comr, ex p Blackburn* [1968] 2 QB 118, [1968] 1 All ER 763, CA; Wade *Administrative Law* (6th edn 1988) pp 141–152.
19 Case 80/86 *Officier van Justitie v Kolpinghuis Nijmegen BV* [1987] ECR 3969, [1989] 2 CMLR 18; and see also Case 14/86 *Pretore di Salò v X* [1987] ECR 2545, [1989] 1 CMLR 71; Cases 372-374/85 *Ministère Public v Traen* [1987] ECR 2141, [1988] 3 CMLR 511. For this principle in England see *National Smokeless Fuels Ltd v IRC* [1986] 3 CMLR 227, [1986] STC 300 (Warner J); *Azo-Maschinenfabrik Adolf Zimmermann GmbH v Customs and Excise Comrs* [1987] 3 CMLR 462, VAT Tribunal.
20 P 48, supra.

Thus in *Duke v GEC Reliance Ltd*[1] the House of Lords accepted that Mrs Duke could not claim damages for her dismissal, although (like Miss Marshall) she had been required to retire at the age of 60 when men were required to retire at 65, and although the United Kingdom had been held in *Marshall* to be in breach of its obligation to implement the Equal Treatment Directive by allowing differential compulsory retirement ages. That was because Mrs Duke had been working for a private employer.

The concept of what is 'an emanation of the State' is to be determined by Community law, although whether the body fulfils the criterion of Community law will depend on national law (but not on whether national law itself regards the body as an emanation of the state). If national law regards the body as a public authority, that will no doubt mean that the directive may be relied on as against the body; but the fact that national law does not so regard it will not be conclusive.[2] The question has arisen in the English cases involving state-owned companies. In *Rolls-Royce plc v Doughty*[3] Mrs Doughty was a clerk who was compulsorily retired at the age of 60 by Rolls-Royce (before it was privatised). In the Employment Appeal Tribunal Garland J pointed out that in a number of English cases the expression 'emanation' as applied to the Crown had been severely criticised,[4] and preferred a test whether the body was an organ or agent of the state carrying out a state function. Rolls-Royce was not such a body, but merely a commercial trading company. In *Foster v British Gas plc*[5] the Court of Appeal held that six women who had been compulsorily retired at the age of 60 could not rely on the directive, because British Gas (which had not, at the relevant time, yet been privatised), although it was in English law a public authority, was not a department of government. Lord Donaldson MR thought that *Marshall* and *Johnston* established that emanation of the state meant an independent public authority charged by the state with the performance of any of the classic duties of the state, such as defence or maintenance of law and order, and whether British Gas fell within this category depended on English law. It is likely that the Court of Appeal adopted an overly national view of what is the state for the purpose of the direct effect of directives.[6]

---

1 [1988] AC 618, [1988] 1 All ER 626, discussed pp 35–36, ante. See also *Secretary of State for Employment v Levy* [1989] IRLR 469, EAT.
2 Cf the concept of civil or commercial matters in the Brussels Convention of 1968 on jurisdiction and the enforcement of judgments in civil and commercial matters, on which see Collins *Civil Jurisdiction and Judgments Act 1982* (1983) pp 17–21.
3 [1988] 1 CMLR 569, EAT.
4 See, eg *BBC v Johns (Inspector of Taxes)* [1965] Ch 32, [1964] 1 All ER 923, CA.
5 [1988] 2 CMLR 697, CA.
6 The House of Lords has referred the question to the European Court: Case 188/89 (pending). See also *R v London Boroughs Transport Committee, ex p Freight Transport Association Ltd* [1990] 1 CMLR 229.

Remedies. It has already been seen[7] that, in the context of directly effective treaty provisions, the European Court has held that national law must provide real and effective protection, but there is probably no obligation to provide any particular remedy, provided the remedy is not less favourable than the remedy in a similar action of a domestic nature.

Unless the directive expressly so provides, a member state is not obliged to introduce new remedies. Thus in the *Butter Boats* case[8] a trader complained in the German courts that he was prejudiced by the failure of the German authorities to charge duty on goods bought on the 'butter-buying cruises'; these cruises were designed to take advantage of customs duty and VAT exemptions in Council regulations and a directive for travellers' personal luggage. The exemptions were only available to passengers coming from non-member states. The butter-buying cruises originated from Germany and only made token calls at Danish ports (at the time before Denmark acceded). The European Court held that the customs duty exemption did not apply to travellers who only made such token visits and were not in the non-member state for an appreciable time. In answer to the German court's question whether the plaintiffs, wholesale and retail traders, could institute proceedings against the German authorities to compel compliance with the regulations and the directive, the European Court answered that the EEC Treaty was not intended to create new remedies in the national courts to ensure the application of Community law other than those already laid down by national law, but 'it must be possible for every type of action provided for by national law to be available for the purpose of ensuring observance of Community provisions having direct effect, on the same conditions concerning the admissibility and procedure as would apply were it a question of ensuring observance of national law'.[9]

Article 6 of the Equal Treatment Directive[10] requires member states to introduce into their national legal systems such measures as are necessary to enable all persons who consider themselves wronged by discrimination 'to pursue their claims by judicial process'. In the *Von Colson* and *Harz* cases[11] women sought remedies in the German courts for unlawful discrimination: in the first case they were social workers with better qualifications than men who were engaged by a German prison; in the second, the plaintiff was an economist who was not recruited for a training programme with a commercial company.

---

7 Pp 62–67, supra.
8 Case 158/80 *Rewe v Hauptzollamt Kiel* [1981] ECR 1085, [1982] 1 CMLR 449.
9 [1981] ECR at 1822.
10 76/207.
11 Case 14/83 *Von Colson v Land Nordrhein-Westfalen* [1984] ECR 1891, [1986] 2 CMLR 430; Case 79/83 *Harz v Deutsche Tradax GmbH* [1984] ECR 1921.

In each of the cases the plaintiffs sought an order in the German courts that they be compulsorily engaged by the defendants, or alternatively be awarded substantial damages in lieu of salary. But under German law the sole remedy was damages incurred in reliance on the expectation that there would be no discrimination. In these cases the damages were trivial amounts expended in travel to the interviews, some 7 DM in the first case and 2 DM in the second one. The German courts asked the European Court whether the directive required a sanction of compulsory engagement or an award of substantial damages. The European Court answered that no specific sanction was required, but that there must be an *effective* sanction. The Court said:[12]

> ... Member States are required to adopt measures which are sufficiently effective to achieve the objective of the directive and to ensure that those measures may in fact be relied on before the national courts by the persons concerned. Such measures may include, for example, provisions requiring the employer to offer a post to the candidate discriminated against or giving the candidate adequate financial compensation, backed up where necessary by a system of fines. However the directive does not prescribe a specific sanction; it leaves Member States free to choose between the different solutions suitable for achieving its objective.

The Court was also asked whether art 6 of the directive had direct effect. The Court held that it did not include any unconditional and sufficiently precise obligation as regards sanctions, and accordingly individuals could not rely on it to obtain specific compensation where national law did not provide for it. But the directive did require that, if a member state chose to penalise breaches by the award of compensation, that compensation must be adequate in relation to the damage sustained and must amount to more than purely nominal compensation.[13] It was for the national court to interpret and apply the legislation adopted to implement the directive in conformity with the requirements of Community law, in so far as it was given discretion to do so under national law.

But in *Johnston v Chief Constable of the Royal Ulster Constabulary*[14] the Court held that art 6 of the directive did have direct effect as regards the obligation to provide a judicial remedy. In that case the Northern Ireland regulations implementing the Equal Treatment Directive provided that nothing in them would render unlawful an act done for the purpose of safeguarding national security or of protecting public safety or public order, and also provided that a certificate by

---
12 [1984] ECR at 1907, [1986] 2 CMLR at 452.
13 See the application of this principle in *Marshall v Southampton and South West Hampshire Health Authority (No 2)* [1988] 3 CMLR 389, revsd in part [1989] 3 CMLR 771, EAT, p 97, post.
14 Case 222/84 [1987] QB 129, [1986] ECR 1651, [1986] 3 CMLR 240. See pp 89–90, above.

the Secretary of State for Northern Ireland would be conclusive as to the existence of those conditions. The position taken by the United Kingdom Government was that art 6 of the directive did not require the member states to submit to judicial review every question which might arise in the application of the directive, even where national security and public safety were involved. The Court rejected this point, and relying on general principles of law, and on the European Convention on Human Rights, held that the conclusive evidence provision allowed the member state to deprive the individual of the possibility of asserting by judicial process the rights conferred by the directive, and was therefore contrary to the principle of effective judicial control required by the directive. The Court confirmed its rulings in the *Von Colson* and *Harz* cases that art 6 did not contain any unconditional or sufficiently precise obligation with regard to specific sanctions upon which individuals could rely, but in *Johnston* the Court held that:

> . . . in so far as it follows from that article, construed in the light of a general principle which it expresses, that all persons who consider themselves wronged by sex discrimination must have an effective judicial remedy, that provision is sufficiently precise and unconditional to be capable of being relied upon as against a Member State which has not ensured that it is fully implemented in its internal legal order.[15]

The national reaction. Some national courts reacted strongly against the attribution by the European Court of direct effects to directives. When Daniel Cohn-Bendit, famous for his activities in the events of 1968, tried to return to France he was refused entry. He sought to rely on the directive on freedom of movement which had been held to be directly effective in the *Van Duyn* case, but the Conseil d'Etat, in a much criticised judgment, refused to refer to the European Court under art 177 and held that directives could not be invoked by individuals against administrative acts of the government, thereby flying in the face of the jurisprudence of the European Court.[16] In 1986 the Conseil d'Etat again failed to apply a decision of the European Court that a directive had direct effect, in a case involving the Sixth VAT Directive.[17]

---

15 [1986] ECR at 1692, [1988] 3 CMLR at 271.
16 *Minister of the Interior v Daniel Cohn-Bendit* [1980] 1 CMLR 543, Simon & Dowrick (1979) 95 LQR 376. But the ordinary French courts accept the concept of the direct effect of directives: see eg the references in the *Grunert* and *Kugelmann* cases p 86, nn 18 and 20, supra.
17 *Cabinet Mantout SARL* 16 June 1986; not applying Case 70/83 *Kloppenburg v Finanzamt Leer* [1984] ECR 1075, [1985] 1 CMLR 205. See also *Assn Club Chasse du Vert Galant* 2 March 1988, summarised in EC Commission *Sixth Annual Report to the European Parliament on Commission Monitoring of Community Law* 1989 (not yet published). But in *Compagnie Alitalia* [1990] 1 CMLR 248 the Conseil d'Etat held that the government's decision not to revoke or repeal a prior decree inconsistent with the Sixth VAT directive was invalid.

Two and a half years after the *Cohn-Bendit* decision, the German Federal Fiscal Court adopted the decision of the Conseil d'Etat and held that the Sixth VAT Directive did not have direct effect.[18] Within a few months the European Court twice re-affirmed that the provisions of the Sixth VAT Directive could be relied on by individuals in national courts.[19] In a subsequent case the German Fiscal Court again refused to give direct effect to the Sixth VAT Directive, notwithstanding that a lower court had referred the question of direct effect to the European Court and received an affirmative answer.[20] In 1987 the German Federal Constitutional Court held that the Federal Fiscal Court had been wrong; the Fiscal Court should either have accepted the ruling of the European Court or made a further reference to it; and that the power of the European Court to hold that directives had direct effect did not offend against German sovereignty or the German constitution.[1]

In the United Kingdom the courts have substantially accepted the principle of the direct effect of directives.[2] In some cases the United Kingdom courts and tribunals have applied the principle to give[3] or refuse[4] direct effect without a reference to the European Court. In other cases they have made references to the European Court on the question of whether particular directives had direct effect, and applied the answer in the United Kingdom proceedings.[5] Two examples will suffice.

In *R v Secretary of State for the Home Department, ex p Santillo*[6] the

---

18 [1982] 1 CMLR 527.
19 Cases 8/81 *Becker v Finanzamt Münster-Innenstadt* [1982] ECR 53, [1982] 1 CMLR 499; Cases 255/81 *Grendel GmbH v Finanzamt Hamburg* [1982] ECR 2301, [1983] 1 CMLR 379.
20 Case 70/83 *Kloppenburg v Finanzamt Leer* [1984] ECR 1075, [1985] 1 CMLR 205.
1 *Re Application of Kloppenburg* [1988] 3 CMLR 1. See also *Re Value Added Tax Exemption* [1989] 1 CMLR 113.
2 Cf *Shields v E Coomes (Holdings) Ltd* [1979] 1 All ER 456, [1978] 1 WLR 1408, CA, but contrast *R v Home Secretary, ex p Muhammad Ayub* [1983] 3 CMLR 140 (Forbes J); *O'Brien v Sim-Chem Ltd* [1980] 2 All ER 307, [1980] 1 WLR 734, CA; revsd [1980] 3 All ER 132, [1980] 1 WLR 1011, HL.
3 *Yoga for Health Foundation v Customs and Excise Comrs* [1985] 1 CMLR 340, and several decisions by VAT Tribunals.
4 *National Smokeless Fuels Ltd v IRC* [1986] 3 CMLR 227, [1986] STC 300 (Crown cannot rely on direct effect); *Duke v GEC Reliance Ltd* p 91, n 1, supra, and other cases applying the principle that the direct effect of directives is not horizontal p 91 supra.
5 See Case 131/79 *R v Secretary of State for the Home Department, ex p Santillo* [1981] QB 778, [1980] ECR 1585, [1980] 2 CMLR 308; Case 5/84 *Direct Cosmetics Ltd v Customs and Excise Comrs* [1985] ECR 617, [1985] 2 CMLR 145; Case 152/84 *Marshall v Southampton and South West Hampshire Area Health Authority* [1986] QB 401, [1986] ECR 723, [1986] 1 CMLR 688; Case 222/84 *Johnston v Chief Constable of the Royal Ulster Constabulary* [1987] QB 129, [1986] ECR 1651, [1986] 3 CMLR 240. There are other cases in which the question of direct effect was referred, but not answered by the European Court: see cases at p 88, n 12.
6 Case 131/79 [1981] QB 778, [1980] ECR 1585, [1980] 2 CMLR 308.

defendant was an Italian national who was convicted in England of very serious sexual offences; he was sentenced to eight years' imprisonment and recommended for deportation. After he had spent more than four years in prison the Home Secretary ordered him to be deported. He sought to have the order quashed on the ground that it infringed the requirement in the 1964 Council Directive on movement and residence of foreign nationals that the administrative authorities of a member state must obtain the 'opinion' of an independent 'competent authority' before deporting a national of another member state. The United Kingdom authorities had not introduced legislation to give effect to the Directive because they thought at the time of United Kingdom accession in 1972 that the United Kingdom's existing laws complied with the Directive. The Divisional Court referred to the European Court the question whether the relevant provision of the Directive had direct effect, and a series of questions designed to elicit whether the recommendation of deportation by the trial judge could be regarded as the opinion of the competent authority. The European Court held that the provision did have direct effect; that the recommendation for deportation made by the criminal court at the time of conviction was capable of constituting an opinion of a competent authority; and that the opinion of the competent authority must be sufficiently proximate in time to the decision ordering expulsion to ensure that there are no new factors to be taken into consideration. When the case went back to the Divisional Court, and, on appeal, to the Court of Appeal, it was held that, notwithstanding the four-year period between the recommendation for deportation and the expulsion order, the recommendation was sufficiently proximate in time to constitute a valid opinion. This result may have been in accordance with the letter of the European Court's judgment, but it was probably against its spirit. Some indication of the Court of Appeal's anxiety to uphold the Home Secretary's decision to deport a man who, on any view, was a potential danger to the public in England (and who would also be a danger in Italy, once he had been deported) comes from the judgment of Templeman LJ, who said:[7]

> ... the Divisional Court was obliged to turn its back on reality and to propound certain questions to the European Court of Justice. Immersed in the cloudy generality of its functions under article 177 of the EEC Treaty, the European Court was also obliged to ignore reality but furnished replies which enable this court now to approach the moment of truth.

It has already been seen[8] that when Miss Marshall sought to obtain redress for what she perceived as unfair discrimination in compul-

---

7 [1981] QB 778 at 797, [1981] 2 All ER 897 at 921, CA.
8 P 89, supra.

sory retirement at the age of 60, the European Court held that discriminatory compulsory retirement for women at age 60 was contrary to the directive, and that the directive had direct effect as against the health authority which employed her. The reason for the reference to the European Court was that the Sex Discrimination Act 1975, s 6(4) excluded from the prohibition of discrimination by an employer on the ground of sex 'provision in relation to . . . retirement'. The Industrial Tribunal and the Employment Appeal Tribunal had dismissed her claim for that reason, and the Court of Appeal referred the questions whether her dismissal was an act of discrimination, and, if so, whether the directive could be relied on in the English court notwithstanding the inconsistency (if any) between the directive and the Sex Discrimination Act 1975.

The consequence of the European Court's ruling was that Miss Marshall's dismissal was unlawful, and that the directive could be relied upon by her in the English courts because the Health Authority was a public authority and therefore to be regarded as an emanation of the United Kingdom government. When the case was remitted to the Industrial Tribunal, the Health Authority argued that her claim was limited to the then maximum figure of £6,250 under the Sex Discrimination Act 1975. The Industrial Tribunal, following the *Von Colson* case,[9] held that the statutory limit was a wholly inadequate remedy and awarded her an additional £11,500 in damages, and some £7,500 interest.[10] The Health Authority appealed to the Employment Appeal Tribunal. But it did not appeal on the award of the additional damages, although it is clear from the judgment of the Employment Appeal Tribunal that there was a serious question as to whether the Industrial Tribunal, with limited statutory powers, had jurisdiction to award more than the statutory maximum. The appeal was on the award of interest. It was held that the Industrial Tribunal had no power to award interest, and that the *Von Colson* case did not require the tribunal to award interest, because the essence of that decision was that the courts must give a remedy where national law provided no judicial remedy or gave a remedy which was *de minimis*. United Kingdom law gave a judicial remedy before the Industrial Tribunal and the High Court, and gave a right to statutory damages. There was therefore no room for an argument that Community law required the additional remedy of interest.[11]

---

9 P 92, supra.
10 *Marshall v Southampton and South-West Hampshire Area Health Authority (No 2)* [1988] 3 CMLR 389.
11 [1989] 3 CMLR 771, EAT.

98 *Community law as part of United Kingdom law*

But the European Court had also held that the directive did *not* have horizontal direct effect, ie it could not be relied upon as against private employers. After the decision the Sex Discrimination Act 1986 was enacted, which amended the Equal Pay Act 1970 and the Sex Discrimination Act 1975 and made discriminatory retirement ages unlawful. But it was not retrospective. Finally, in *Duke v GEC Reliance Ltd*[12] the House of Lords held that Mrs Duke, who was dismissed at the age of 60 before 1986, could not claim compensation because (a) her employer was a private employer against whom the directive did not have direct effect, and (b) because it was not possible to construe the Sex Discrimination Act 1975 in such a way as to be consistent with the directive.[13]

It remains to underline the clear authority in the European Court that:

> ... the Member States' obligation arising from a directive to achieve the result envisaged by the directive and their duty under Article 5 of the Treaty to take all appropriate measures, whether general or particular, to ensure the fulfilment of that obligation, is binding on all the authorities of Member States including, for matters within their jurisdiction, the courts. It follows that, in applying the national law specifically introduced in order to implement [the Directive in question], national courts are required to interpret their national law in the light of the wording and the purpose of the directive in order to achieve the result referred to in Article 189(3).[14]

In the United Kingdom this principle is part of, or related to, the principle that United Kingdom legislation must be interpreted, where possible, so as to be in conformity with Community law, which is discussed in the next chapter.[15] For present purposes it is sufficient to point out that, after some initial hesitation, the House of Lords has fully accepted the principle enunciated in the *Von Colson* case. Thus in *Duke v GEC Reliance Ltd*[16] Lord Templeman said that the *Von Colson* case was 'no authority for the proposition that a court of a member state must distort the meaning of a domestic statute so as to conform with Community law which is not directly applicable.' A year later Lord Templeman cited *Von Colson* for the proposition that 'the courts of the United Kingdom are under a duty to follow the practice of the European Court of Justice by giving a purposive

---

12 [1988] AC 618, [1988] 1 All ER 626.
13 See also cases at p 91, above.
14 Case 14/83 *Von Colson v Land Nordrhein-Westfalen* [1984] ECR 1891 at 1909, [1986] 2 CMLR 430 at 453, and other cases cited above, p 84, n 11.
15 Pp 137–142.
16 *Duke v GEC Reliance Ltd* [1988] AC 618 at 641, [1988] 1 All ER 626 at 637, HL.

construction to Directives and to Regulations issued for the purpose of complying with Directives.'[17]

4 Directly applicable or effective Community law—its operation in the United Kingdom

(1) By virtue of s 2(1) of the European Communities Act 1972 all rights and liabilities which are in accordance with the Treaties to be given legal effect in the United Kingdom are to be recognised and available in the United Kingdom.

(2) The rights and liabilities contemplated by s 2(1) are all those rights and liabilities which by Community law have direct effect in member states and give rise to individual rights which must be protected by national courts.

(3) According to the Treaties and the case law of the European Court the following may have direct applicability or effect in member states:
   (i) certain provisions of the Treaties and associated treaties;
   (ii) regulations;
   (iii) certain provisions of Community decisions;
   (iv) certain provisions of Community directives.

(4) The circumstances in which a Community rule may be invoked in the United Kingdom courts will vary and it is for the United Kingdom court to decide in what way it will discharge its obligation to give effect to a Community rule.

(5) For a Treaty provision to be directly effective it must be (a) clear and precise, (b) unconditional and unqualified and (c) free from any substantial latitude or discretion in member states as to application. A provision originally conditional may become unconditional in this sense by (a) lapse of time, or (b) a Community decision or directive, or (c) the happening of an event. Similar, but not identical, principles may make provisions of regulations, decisions and directives directly effective.

(6) It is irrelevant whether there are other remedies available to other member states or to Community institutions.

(7) Regulations are directly applicable by virtue of art 189 of the Treaty and constitute an overriding source of law. While s 2 of the European Communities Act 1972 remains in force United Kingdom authorities will not be able to modify, extend, or issue binding interpretations of, Community regulations.

---

17 *Litster v Forth Dry Dock and Engineering Co Ltd* [1989] 2 WLR 634 at 640, [1989] 1 All ER 1134 at 1139, HL.

It is not possible to anticipate the many different contexts in which the question of direct applicability or effect will arise in United Kingdom courts, but a few general points will indicate the approach to be adopted:

(a) In so far as a Treaty provision is recognised (by its terms or as a result of a decision of the European Court) as having direct effect, s 2(1) of the European Communities Act 1972 provides that it is to be 'recognised and available in law, and be enforced, allowed and followed accordingly'.

(b) Additionally, s 2(2)(b) authorises delegated legislation for the purpose of dealing with the operation from time to time of s 2(1), which must include the operation and availability of directly enforceable rights.

(c) If the issue before the United Kingdom courts depends on a statute or statutory instrument existing prior to the European Communities Act and not specifically affected by it, the question will turn on whether the prior legislation has been impliedly repealed as a result of the effect of section 2 of the European Communities Act 1972.

(d) If the issue depends on the validity of contractual arrangements, then the Community law can be readily applied. Thus, for example, one party to a contract may resist enforcement on the ground that it is null and void under art 85. The United Kingdom court will merely apply art 85, provided at any rate that the validity of the contract is not at issue before the Commission.[18]

(e) In matters of administrative discretion or other matters involving the Crown or public body an application for judicial review or an action for a declaration[19] will most often be the appropriate remedy. Thus, for example, if the Department of Trade refuses to authorise a foreign insurance company under the Insurance Companies Act 1982 and the decision is challenged on the ground that a refusal is justified neither by the EEC Treaty nor the directives on insurance business, the aggrieved company could challenge the refusal in the High Court.

(f) If there is a real question as to whether a provision is directly effective, then the appropriate course would be for the United Kingdom court to refer the question under art 177 to the European Court. Whether a provision is directly effective is a

---

18 Cf *Garden Cottage Foods Ltd v Milk Marketing Board* [1984] AC 130, [1983] 2 All ER 770, HL.
19 On the relationship between judicial review and private law remedies in the context of EEC law see *An Bord Bainne Co-operative Ltd (Irish Dairy Board) v Milk Marketing Board* [1984] 2 CMLR 519.

Directly applicable or effective Community law 101

question of interpretation which in doubtful cases may be, and in some cases should be, referred to the European Court.

In practice the application of the concepts of direct applicability and effect have given rise to few difficulties in the English courts. In *Shields v E Coomes (Holdings) Ltd*[20] Lord Denning MR warned English lawyers against looking at the Treaty provisions and concluding that they imposed obligations only on member states; he emphasised the importance of the development of direct applicability not only of treaty provisions, but also of directives, by the European Court to overcome evasion by member states of their treaty obligations. It has been seen above[1] that English courts have dealt with directives by referring the question whether they had direct effect to the European Court and then applying the answer, and there have been several cases, particularly in the area of equal pay under art 119, where they have referred the question whether treaty provisions had direct effect.[2] In applying directly effective treaty provisions, United Kingdom courts have accepted that a conviction for a crime such as illegal importation would have to be set aside if the importation could not be prohibited under the EEC Treaty;[3] this is because a criminal conviction is contrary to Community law where criminal proceedings are brought by virtue of national legislation which is contrary to Community law.[4]

In this way directly effective Community law is part of the corpus juris of the United Kingdom law.[5] Thus in *Re Westinghouse Uranium Contract*[6] the English courts were asked to give effect to letters rogatory issued by a United States court by ordering (inter alia) production of documents held in England by Rio Tinto Zinc ('RTZ'). The evidence was required for United States proceedings in which Westinghouse was being sued by various power companies for breach of a contract to supply uranium; Westinghouse alleged that the contracts had been frustrated because of price rises in uranium allegedly caused by an international cartel of which RTZ was said to be a part.

RTZ resisted production of the documents on the ground, inter

---

20 [1979] 1 All ER 456 at 460, [1978] 1 WLR 1408 at 1414.
1 See above p 95, Case 41/74 *Van Duyn v Home Office* [1974] ECR 1337, [1975] 1 CMLR 1; Case 131/79 *R v Secretary of State for Home Affairs, ex p Santillo* [1980] ECR 1585, [1980] 2 CMLR 208.
2 See eg cases at p 88, n 12, supra.
3 See eg *Henn and Darby v DPP* [1981] AC 850, [1980] 2 All ER 166, HL; *R v Goldstein* [1983] 1 All ER 434, [1983] 1 WLR 151, HL.
4 Case 269/80 *R v Tymen* [1981] ECR 3079, [1982] 2 CMLR 111.
5 *Jensen v Corpn of the Trinity House of Deptford* [1982] 2 Lloyd's Rep 14, 26, per Kerr LJ.
6 *Rio Tinto Zinc Corpn v Westinghouse Electric Corpn* [1978] AC 547, [1978] 1 All ER 434.

alia, that they were privileged from production because of the rule against self-incrimination; it was argued that if the allegations of Westinghouse were well-founded there would be a breach of art 85 of the EEC Treaty because the alleged conspiracy affected not only trade with the United States but also within the Common Market; and that a breach of art 85 exposed the parties to penalties under reg 17. Section 14 of the Civil Evidence Act 1968 retained the privilege against self-incrimination as regards criminal offences under the law of any part of the United Kingdom and 'penalties provided for by such law'. Were the penalties under reg 17 provided for by the law of any part of the United Kingdom? The Court of Appeal and the House of Lords held that RTZ could claim the privilege because art 85 was:[7]

> directly applicable in the member states; it forms part of the law of England; so does Regulation 17 . . . [A] fine imposed by the Commission under the regulation is a 'penalty' for the purposes of section 14 of the Civil Evidence Act 1968, and . . . it is enforced by proceedings for recovery of a penalty under the European Communities (Enforcement of Community Judgments) Order 1972.

It is also clear that directly effective Community law must be applied by all courts in the United Kingdom and by all administrative bodies. As regards the jurisdiction of courts to apply Community law, a point which originally gave rise to difficulty was the extent to which tribunals with a statutory jurisdiction, such as industrial tribunals, could enforce directly effective Community law. The difficulty arose in the case of industrial tribunals because, it was thought, they could apply only the equal pay provisions of the Sex Discrimination Act 1975, and not art 119 of the Treaty,[8] but in *Shields v E Coomes (Holdings) Ltd*[9] Lord Denning said:

> . . . when the Parliament of the United Kingdom sets up a tribunal to carry out its Treaty obligations, the tribunal has jurisdiction to apply Community law, and should apply it, in the confident expectation that this is what Parliament intended . . . I think that Community law applies not only in the High Court, but also in the industrial tribunal and the Employment Appeal Tribunal.

It has been seen above[10] that as a matter of Community law rights which are directly effective *must* be protected by the courts, but that the method of protection is a matter for domestic law, subject to two

---

7 [1978] AC 547 at 636, [1978] 1 All ER 434 at 464, per Lord Diplock.
8 See eg *Snoxell and Davies v Vauxhall Motors Ltd* [1978] QB 11, [1977] 3 All ER 770.
9 [1979] 1 All ER 456 at 461–2, [1978] 1 WLR 1408, at 1415. But it does not follow that an industrial tribunal can, as a result, become a court of general jurisdiction: cf *Southampton and South-West Hampshire Area Health Authority v Marshall (No 2)* [1989] 3 CMLR 771, EAT.
10 Pp 62–63, supra.

important conditions: first, the remedy must not be discriminatory in the sense of being less favourable than the remedy relating to a similar action of a domestic nature; secondly, the remedy must not be such that it is virtually impossible or excessively difficult for the right to be exercised.

It is not practicable to deal exhaustively with the range of substantive rights and procedural remedies which might be deployed. They will include contractual and tortious causes of action, and the remedies of damages, declaration, injunction, and decree of specific performance, as well as the public law remedies which may result from an application for judicial review of governmental or administrative action. Where there is a special judicial or administrative remedy, the plaintiff cannot disregard it and bring an ordinary action merely because he relies on directly effective Community law,[11] provided that the remedy is effective.

The House of Lords in *Garden Cottage Foods Ltd v Milk Marketing Board*[12] considered, but did not finally decide, the question of what national remedies would be available in England to the victim of an abuse of dominant position under art 86 by an undertaking. The plaintiffs were engaged in the purchase and sale of bulk butter for export; they complained that the Milk Marketing Board had abused its dominant position by wrongfully refusing to sell them butter and had instead appointed four independent distributors to handle the sales of its bulk butter for export. The plaintiffs sought to obtain an interlocutory injunction; this was refused by the judge at first instance but it was granted by the Court of Appeal on the ground that damages could not be said to be an adequate remedy because it was doubtful whether there was a cause of action in damages for abuse of a dominant position under art 86. The House of Lords (Lord Wilberforce dissenting) reversed the decision of the Court of Appeal. Lord Diplock recognised that art 86 had been held by the European Court to produce direct effects in relations between individuals and to create direct rights in respect of the individuals concerned which the national courts must protect.[13] Consequently the rights which art 86 conferred on citizens in the United Kingdom fell within s 2(1) of the European Communities Act 1972 and were to be given legal effect in the United Kingdom and enforced accordingly. He went on:[14]

---

11 *Jensen v Corpn of the Trinity House of Deptford* [1982] 2 Lloyd's Rep 14, CA. Contrast *R v Trinity House London Pilotage Committee, ex p Jensen and Leu* [1985] 2 CMLR 413.
12 [1984] AC 130, [1983] 2 All ER 770, HL.
13 Case 127/73 *Belgische Radio en Televisie v SV SABAM and NV Fonior* [1974] ECR 51, [1974] 2 CMLR 238.
14 [1984] AC at 141–144, [1983] 2 All ER at 775–7, discussing dicta of Lord Denning in *Application des Gaz SA v Falks Veritas Ltd* [1974] Ch 381 at 396, [1974] 3 All ER 51 at 58, CA, and Roskill LJ in *Valor International Ltd v Application des Gaz SA* [1978] 3 CMLR 87 at 100, CA. See also *Camera Care Ltd v Hasselblad* [1986] 1 FTLR 348, CA.

A breach of the duty imposed by article 86 not to abuse a dominant position in the Common Market or in a substantial part of it, can thus be categorised in English law as a breach of a statutory duty that is imposed not only for the purpose of promoting the general economic prosperity of the Common Market but also for the benefit of private individuals to whom loss or damage is caused by a breach of that duty . . . I, for my own part, find it difficult to see how it can ultimately successfully be argued, as [the board] will seek to do, that a contravention of article 86 which causes damages to an individual citizen does not give rise to a cause of action in English law of the nature of a cause of action for breach of statutory duty.

This case does not of course mean that an injunction will never be granted in a case involving an alleged infringement of arts 85 and 86. All that the case decided is that it was not an adequate *sole* ground for an injunction that damages was not an available remedy, and interim injunctions have been granted[15] (or refused)[16] to restrain breaches of arts 85 and 86 for a variety of other reasons. The question whether there might be circumstances in which the United Kingdom court will be *bound* to grant an interim injunction where there is no adequate remedy in damages has arisen in the *Factortame* case mentioned later.[17]

An important procedural vehicle for the protection of individuals against the failure to apply Community law is the public law remedy of judicial review. For example, in 1984 the Department of Health and Social Security introduced regulations for the reimbursement of chemists for the cost of prescriptions dispensed under the National Health Service. The object of the regulations was to prevent chemists making profits out of discounts obtained when purchasing parallel imports. The applicants were importers who alleged that the effect of the regulations was to hinder imports because the scale paid to chemists under the new regulations for domestic products was more advantageous. The applicants therefore succeeded in their application for judicial review and obtained a declaration that the regulations were invalid.[18]

It is clear that, if judicial review is the only possible remedy, the courts will endeavour to ensure that it is an effective remedy. Thus

---

15 *Cutsforth v Mansfield Inns Ltd* [1986] 1 All ER 577, [1986] 1 WLR 558; *Holleran v Daniel Thwaites plc* [1989] 2 CMLR 917.
16 *Argyll Group plc v Distillers Co Ltd* [1986] 1 CMLR 764.
17 P 108, post.
18 *R v Secretary of State for Social Security, ex p Bomore Medical Supplies Ltd* [1986] 1 CMLR 228, CA. See also *R v Minister of Agriculture, Fisheries and Food, ex p Bell Lines Ltd* [1984] 2 CMLR 502; *R v Secretary of State for Social Services, ex p Clarke* [1988] 1 CMLR 279. For the separate remedies in tax law see *Customs and Excise Comrs v Fine Art Developments plc* [1989] AC 914, [1989] 1 All ER 502, HL.

ICI successfully challenged the assessment by the Revenue of petroleum revenue tax on a gas production plant operated by BP. ICI's complaint was that the tax assessment on BP gave an unfair advantage to BP over ICI's competing plant and was an unlawful state aid contrary to arts 92 and 93 of the EEC Treaty. The Revenue argued that ICI had no standing to challenge an assessment on BP. Lord Oliver, speaking for the Court of Appeal, noted that art 93(3) had direct effect, that enforcement was properly a matter for the national court, but that any procedural or substantive limitations of domestic law must not be such as to render enforcement of the right practically impossible. He went on to hold that the Revenue's argument:

> ... necessarily involves the conclusion that the substantive law ... has precisely the effect which the EEC cases establish is impermissible—it renders the enforcement of a directly effective provision of the Treaty practically impossible and I do not, for my part, think that it is an answer to say that ICI could, instead of invoking as they were entitled to do, the jurisdiction of the national court, have approached the Commission of the EEC and complained in the hope that the Commission would intervene.[19]

It has been seen above[20] that it is a matter of some controversy whether Community law requires, in some circumstances, that individuals have a remedy in damages against national authorities. The position in the United Kingdom law remains unsettled. In *Bourgoin SA v Ministry of Agriculture, Fisheries and Food*[1] the plaintiffs were French turkey producers. In 1981 the Ministry restricted imports of turkey into the United Kingdom, ostensibly for health reasons, to importers from countries where a disease to which turkeys were prone was controlled by vaccination rather than by slaughter. In 1982 the European Court held that the import restriction was in breach of art 30 of the EEC Treaty because the object of the restriction was to block the import of poultry from other EEC member states, especially France, for economic reasons rather than health reasons.[2]

The French producers sued the Ministry for damages for the large losses caused to them by the restrictions on imports for the period up to the time the Ministry granted licences in order to comply with the

---

19 *R v A-G, ex p ICI plc* [1987] 1 CMLR 72 at 103, CA. See also *R v Minister of Agriculture, Fisheries and Food, ex p Bell Lines Ltd* [1984] 2 CMLR 502 for the willingness of the court to engage in fact-finding in a judicial review case involving Community law.
20 P 67, supra. For a discussion of the problem in England and other countries (especially the Netherlands and France) see Barav, in *Non-Contractual Liability of the European Communities* (ed Schermers et al) (1988) p 149. The Dutch administrative courts have awarded damages against the state for breach of Community law in several cases.
1 [1986] QB 716, [1985] 3 All ER 585, CA. See Cripps [1986] CLJ 165; Green and Barav (1986) 6 Yb Eur L 55; Steiner (1987) 12 EL Rev 102; Oliver (1987) 50 MLR 881.
2 Case 40/82 *Commission v UK* [1982] ECR 2793, [1982] 3 CMLR 497.

judgment of the European Court. They argued that the breach of art 30 was equivalent to a breach of statutory duty, or that the Ministry was guilty of misfeasance by knowingly withdrawing licences for an improper purpose, namely to protect British producers. On the hearing of a preliminary issue as to whether the statement of claim disclosed a cause of action, Mann J held that there was an arguable cause of action in misfeasance, and his decision was affirmed by a unanimous Court of Appeal. The basis for this part of the decision was that the tort of misfeasance in public office was not limited to cases where the public officer had been guilty of malice, but also included cases where the officer knew both that he had no power to do what he had done, and that his act would injure the plaintiff. If therefore the plaintiffs' licences had been revoked with knowledge that the revocation constituted a breach of the United Kingdom's obligations under art 30 and would injure the plaintiffs' trade, the tort would have been committed. But on the question whether there was a cause of action for damages for breach of the directly effective prohibition on import restrictions in art 30, the judges were divided. Mann J held that there was a remedy in damages, but his decision was reversed by a majority of the Court of Appeal (Parker and Nourse LJJ, Oliver LJ dissenting). All were agreed that Community law required that there should be a judicial remedy, and the difference between them was what that remedy should be. Parker and Nourse LJJ decided that the remedy was limited to judicial review of the Ministry's revocation of licences.

For Mann J and Oliver LJ the essential question was the form of protection which would comply with the requirement of Community law that there should be effective judicial protection. Mann J's reasoning was that the form of protection must be a form available on the same conditions as that which is available for a right of a similar character conferred by domestic law, and which dissuades breaches of the right conferred by art 30; the decision of the House of Lords in the *Garden Cottage* case[3] strongly supported the conclusion that breach of art 86 gave a cause of action for breach of statutory duty, and there was no sensible distinction between art 86 and art 30. Accordingly, a contravention of art 30 which caused damage to a person gave that person an action for damages for breach of statutory duty; the duty was imposed by art 30, as interpreted by the European Court, and by s 2(1) of the European Communities Act 1972. Thus Mann J's decision was based essentially on the point that because the directly effective provisions imposed *statutory* duties they gave private law rights which were enforceable in the same way as any other private law right, including an action for damages for breach of statutory duty.

---

3 N 12, supra.

Oliver LJ agreed, but went much further, and based his decision not only on the ground that it would be discriminatory to withhold the private law remedy of breach of statutory duty from a claimant who sought redress for breach of directly effective Community law, but also on the principle of effectiveness. To put it differently, there is much in Oliver LJ's judgment to support the view that Community law *requires* a remedy in damages, not only because the right infringed is a private law right, which must be protected by private law remedies, but also because to withhold those remedies would remove the right of effective protection. The jurisprudence of the European Court recognised that 'in principle the "protection" of the individual rights under Community law involves, subject to the procedural requirements of the national forum, the payment of compensation in respect of the period between the commission of the wrong and its rectification . . .'[4]

The majority in the Court of Appeal agreed that directly effective rights must be effectively protected, but decided that the appropriate remedy was judicial review, and a declaration as to invalidity of the measure constituting the breach, and (perhaps) an order directing the officials to permit the loading of the goods. Accordingly to Parker LJ a breach of art 30 by the United Kingdom government was to be regarded as the making of an invalid order or a simple excess of power, which did not sound in damages, and not in the nature of a breach of statutory duty. The right given by art 30 was closely akin to the right of an individual not to be subjected to an invalid order.

Leave was given to appeal to the House of Lords, but the case was settled before the appeal was heard. It is, perhaps, because the government feared that the House of Lords would agree with Mann J and Oliver LJ, or because they feared that the factual allegations of misfeasance would be made out that the settlement was a substantial payment to the plaintiffs.[5]

The reason why the plaintiffs in *Bourgoin* did not have an effective public law remedy was that they clearly took the view that they could not obtain immediate and effective relief when their licences were revoked in 1981. They could have sought judicial review, but they could not have obtained an interim declaration, and the case would not have been so clear that they could have expected immediate relief from proceedings for judicial review, which might have involved a reference to the European Court and the delay which that would have entailed. It is the inability to obtain effective interim relief which is at

---

4 [1986] QB at 771, [1985] 3 All ER at 619.
5 [1987] 1 CMLR 169. See also *An Bord Bainne Co-operative Ltd v Milk Marketing Board* [1988] 1 CMLR 605, where the Court of Appeal applied *Bourgoin* in a case involving alleged breach of a regulation, and also gave leave to appeal. But the appeal was not proceeded with.

the heart of the reference by the House of Lords in the *Factortame* case.[6] The commercial background to the case was the issue of 'quota hopping', where ships beneficially owned by Spanish interests were registered under the British flag in order to fish for the quotas allocated to the United Kingdom under the common fisheries policy.[7] The applicants were English companies which operated deep-sea fishing vessels. Although the companies were English they were substantially owned by Spanish interests. Under the Merchant Shipping Act 1988, and regulations made under it, the ships lost their previous qualification for registration because the Act introduced British citizenship requirements and also United Kingdom residence and domicile requirements. The owners sought to challenge the legality of the legislation on the ground that it contravened Community law, and in particular that it infringed rights given by the EEC Treaty, by the Spanish Accession Treaty, and by regulations relating to the common fisheries policy. In the House of Lords it was accepted by both sides that the case was one in which the courts below had correctly exercised the discretion to seek a preliminary ruling on the difficult issues of Community law raised by the application, but it was estimated that the preliminary ruling on the substance of the case might not be given by the European Court for about two years.

The question for the House of Lords was whether the applicants were entitled to interim relief pending final determination of the proceedings after the decision of the European Court. They argued that, unless they were protected by an injunction which would have the effect of enabling them to continue to operate their vessels as if they were duly registered British vessels, they would suffer irreparable damage. The vessels could not fish against the Spanish quota, and the applicants would have to sell their interests at disastrously low prices, and many of the individual operators would lose their livelihood. In the light of the *Bourgoin* case, if it were not overruled by the House of Lords, they would have no remedy in damages. On the other hand, if an injunction were granted, and the ruling of the European Court were ultimately in favour of the British government, then for a substantial period the policy behind the 1988 Act (to ensure that the United Kingdom quota should be fully available to those engaged in the British fishing industry) would be frustrated.

The House of Lords held that the English court had no power under national law to make an order postponing the coming into force of a statute pending a reference to the European Court. There was a presumption that an Act of Parliament was compatible with Com-

---

6 *Factortame Ltd v Secretary of State for Transport* [1989] 2 WLR 997, [1989] 2 All ER 692, HL.
7 See Churchill (1989) 14 EL Rev 470.

munity law unless and until declared to be incompatible. Nor was there power to grant an interim injunction against the Crown in judicial review proceedings: the Crown Proceedings Act 1947 forbade injunctions against the Crown. But it was also argued on behalf of the applicants that there was an overriding principle of Community law which imposed an obligation on the national court to secure effective interim protection of rights having direct effect under Community law where a seriously arguable claim was advanced to be entitled to such rights, and where the rights claimed would in substance be nugatory or irremediably impaired if not effectively protected during any interim period pending final determination of the existence of the rights.

Lord Bridge, with whom all the other members of the House agreed, indicated that at one point in the argument he was convinced by the argument that, if English law as it stood could provide no effective remedy to secure the interim protection, it was the duty of the court under Community law to devise such a remedy. But the Solicitor General had shown that the relevant decisions of the European Court on the duty to secure effective protection were all made by reference to rights which the European Court was itself affirming or which had been established. Accordingly, the House of Lords referred to the European Court the question whether Community law obliged the court, or gave it the power, to grant interim relief to protect rights which were claimed by the applicants and which (if established) would have direct effect in national law.

After the reference was made, the Commission brought proceedings against the United Kingdom Government in the European Court in relation to the nationality requirements in the Merchant Shipping Act 1988 and also applied to the European Court for interim suspension of the statutory requirements pending trial of the proceedings. The President of the Court held that there was a *prima facie* case that the statutory requirements were in breach of the nationality discrimination principles in the EEC Treaty; and the President granted the interim order sought by the Commission because, among other reasons, under English law the losses suffered by the shipowners could not be recovered against the British authorities, and they would suffer irrecoverable damage if the injunctions were not granted.[8] Following this order, the British Government suspended the British citizenship requirements (but *not* the United Kingdom residence[9] and domicile requirements) of the 1988 Act in so far as they related to fishing vessels which were fishing under the British flag up

---

8 Case 246/89R *Commission v UK* [1989] 3 CMLR 601.
9 See Cases C3/87 *R v Minister of Agriculture, Fisheries and Food, ex p Agegate Ltd*; C216/87 *R v Minister of Agriculture, Fisheries and Food, ex p Jaderow Ltd* (1990) *Times*, 19 January.

to 31 March 1989 and were owned by nationals of member states.[10] The ruling of the European Court on the reference by the House of Lords is awaited, but it should be noted that the reference, and much of the argument, would have been unnecessary if the law of the United Kingdom allowed injunctions against the Crown or gave a right to damages for governmental acts in breach of Community law. In Ireland the Supreme Court granted an interim injunction against the Minister in very similar circumstances. The injunction restrained him from enforcing a condition in a fishing licence requiring Irish nationality pursuant to Irish legislation which was alleged to be unconstitutional and contrary to Community law. Finlay CJ said:[11]

> It is . . . the duty of the courts to protect persons against the invasion of their constitutional rights and against unconstitutional action. It would seem wholly inconsistent with that duty if the Court were to be without power in an appropriate case to restrain by injunction an action against a person which found its authority in a statutory provision which might eventually be held to be invalid having regard to the Constitution. In particular, it seems to me that this power must exist in an appropriate case where the form of the action is under a penal section and involves conviction of and the imposition of a penalty for the commission of a criminal offence.

If *Bourgoin* had gone the other way, or been reversed, there would have been an effective remedy for the applicants. Perhaps the remedy would not have been perfect (for some of the applicants would have suffered irremediable loss awaiting the answer) but it would not have been illusory. It does seem that there must be an effective remedy, but it is not likely that the effect of the European Court's ruling will be to require interim relief in all such cases.

But the concept of direct effect cannot be taken further than EEC law itself allows, and two attempts by Lord Denning MR to use EEC law in order to change English law have been rejected firmly by the House of Lords. It was a long-standing, though heavily criticised, rule of English law that judgment could only be given for sterling, and the rate of exchange to be applied was that prevailing at the date the debt became due. In *Schorsch Meier v Hennin*[12] German plaintiffs appealed to the Court of Appeal from the refusal of a county court judge to give them judgment in German Marks and to refer to the European Court the question whether the English rule that an English court could give judgment only in sterling was compatible with art 106. By art 106 each member state undertook to authorise, in the currency of the

---

10 SI 1989/2006.
11 *Pesca Valentia Ltd v Minister for Fisheries* [1985] IR 193, 201. See also *Bearra Fisheries and Shipping Ltd v Minister for the Marine Ireland* [1989] 1 CMLR 840.
12 [1975] QB 416, [1975] 1 All ER 152.

creditor, payments connected with the movement of (inter alia) goods to the extent that the movement of goods had been liberalised pursuant to the EEC Treaty. The majority of the Court of Appeal held that the English rule was in any event obsolete, regardless of the provisions of the EEC Treaty. But the Court also unanimously held, in relation to judgments in favour of residents in countries belonging to the EEC, that art 106 had as one of its purposes to ensure that the creditor should receive payment for his goods in his own currency without any impediment or restriction by reason of changes in the rate of exchange. Lord Denning said that the English courts would be acting contrary to the spirit and intent of the EEC Treaty if they made a German creditor accept payment in depreciated sterling; in order to comply with the Treaty they should give judgment that the defendant do pay the stated sum in Marks or its sterling equivalent at the time of payment.[13] The defendants were not represented in this case, and the House of Lords did not therefore have an opportunity of considering the point. In *Miliangos v George Frank (Textiles) Ltd*[14] the House of Lords, in a case not involving money due to an EEC national, did confirm that henceforth English courts could give judgment in foreign currency, but Lord Wilberforce took the opportunity of criticising the use which had been made of art 106 in *Schorsch Meier v Hennin*. He said:[15]

> ... I entertain the strongest reservations concerning the use made by the Court of Appeal of article 106 in the present context, and I cannot believe that, if the court had heard argument on the other side ... very weighty arguments would not have been brought forward concerning such questions as the direct applicability of this article, its bearing on any question of the currency in which claims may be made in the courts of member states or its relevance at all to the ascertainment of the date of conversion of such claims, which arguments seem to have been unappreciated. Any other court in which such issues may arise would be well advised to refer them to the European Court.

In *The Siskina*[16] Lord Denning had relied on art 3(h) of the EEC Treaty, which provides that the activities of the Community shall include approximation of laws, and on art 220, which provides that member states shall enter into negotiations for the reciprocal recognition and enforcement of judgments, and on the 1968 EEC Convention on Jurisdiction and Judgments (which the United Kingdom had neither signed nor ratified at that time) to support the conclusion that

---

13 See also Lawton LJ [1975] QB 416 at 465, [1975] 1 All ER 152 at 161.
14 [1976] AC 443, [1975] 3 All ER 801.
15 [1976] AC 443 at 465, [1975] 3 All ER 801 at 810.
16 [1979] AC 210, [1977] 3 All ER 803. See also *Trendtex Trading Corpn v Central Bank of Nigeria* [1977] QB 529 at 558, [1977] 1 All ER 881 at 892.

the English courts had jurisdiction to grant interlocutory injunctions[17] to restrain defendants from removing assets from the jurisdiction even if the English court did not have substantive jurisdiction in the case. Both the conclusion and reasoning based on EEC law were rejected by the House of Lords. Lord Diplock pointed out that the machinery for harmonisation was to be found in art 100 of the EEC Treaty, and that harmonisation was not to be effected by individual member states but pursuant to directives issued by a unanimous decision of the Council on a proposal from the Commission; Lord Hailsham observed that where, under the terms of the Treaties, Community law applied directly there was no question of harmonisation, since:

> it is the duty of the courts here and in other member states to give effect to community law as they interpret it in preference to the municipal law of their own country over which ex hypothesi community law prevails.[18]

But where, as in the present case, there was no relevant directly applicable Community law it was not for the courts to anticipate the work of diplomats and legislators. Since this decision, the diplomats and legislators have acted and the United Kingdom has acceded to the 1968 EEC Convention and has enacted legislation giving effect (inter alia) to the provision of the Convention allowing provisional measures to be granted in the United Kingdom even though the main proceedings are pending abroad.[19]

II. THE EUROPEAN COMMUNITIES ACT 1972, SECTION 2(2)

Section 2(2) of the European Communities Act 1972 deals comprehensively with two aspects of Community law. In the first place, it provides for the enactment of subordinate legislation to put into effect those Treaty and other Community obligations which are not directly applicable or effective. In the second place, it provides for the enactment of subordinate legislation to put into effect within the context and confines of United Kingdom law those Treaty and other Community obligations which are directly applicable or effective.

Section 2(2) of the Act provides:

> (2) Subject to Schedule 2 to this Act, at any time after its passing Her Majesty may by Order in Council, and any designated Minister or department may by regulations, make provision—
> (a) for the purpose of implementing any Community obligation of the United Kingdom, or enabling any such obligation to be imple-

---

17 'Mareva' injunctions, after *Mareva Compania Naviera SA v International Bulkcarriers SA* [1975] 2 Lloyd's Rep 509.
18 [1979] AC 210 at 262, [1977] 3 All ER 803 at 829–30.
19 See Collins *Civil Jurisdiction and Judgments Act 1982* (1983) pp 98–102.

mented, or of enabling any rights enjoyed or to be enjoyed by the United Kingdom under or by virtue of the Treaties to be exercised; or
(b) for the purpose of dealing with matters arising out of or related to any such obligation or rights or the coming into force, or the operation from time to time, of subsection (1) above;

and in the exercise of any statutory power or duty, including any power to give directions or to legislate by means of orders, rules, regulations or other subordinate instrument, the person entrusted with the power or duty may have regard to the objects of the Communities and to any such obligation or rights as aforesaid.

In this subsection 'designated Minister or Department' means such Minister of the Crown or government department as may from time to time be designated by Order in Council in relation to any matter or for any purpose, but subject to such restrictions or conditions (if any) as may be specified by the Order in Council.

Summarised, the main general provisions of the Act[20] authorising subordinate legislation are as follows:

(1) Subordinate legislation may be enacted[1] in order to implement any Community obligation of the United Kingdom or to enable any Community right of the United Kingdom to be enjoyed.
(2) It may also be enacted to deal with matters arising out of any such Community obligation or right.
(3) Further, it may be enacted to deal with matters arising out of those Community rules which are directly effective in the United Kingdom by virtue of s 2(1) of the Act.
(4) The subordinate legislation may make provision for any matters for which provision could have been made by Act of Parliament, except that:
   (i) it may not provide for the imposition or increase of taxation;
   (ii) it may not be retrospective;
   (iii) it may not confer the power to enact sub-delegated legislation; and
   (iv) it may not create any new criminal offence punishable with more than specified penalties (European Communities Act 1972, Sch 2).
(5) The subordinate legislation is subject to annulment in pursuance of a resolution of either House of Parliament (Sch 2).

The essential aim behind the section is to incorporate into the law of the United Kingdom not only those Community rights and obligations which are *not* directly applicable or effective by virtue of s 2(1) but also to fill out and make specific provisions for those rights and obligations which *are* directly applicable or effective. The European

---

20 For the text of Sch 2, see Appendix.
1 This word is not used here in any technical sense.

Court has said on several occasions[2] that if a provision of Community law is directly effective it is for the national courts (and presumably other national authorities) to decide in what way the provision is to be given effect.

1 Subordinate legislation and the implementation of Community law

The following are the principal sources under which a member state such as the United Kingdom may have EEC rights and obligations:

(i) Provisions of the Treaties and associated Treaties;
(ii) Regulations of the Council and Commission;
(iii) Directives of the Council and Commission;
(iv) Decisions of the Council and Commission;
(v) Binding Judgments of the European Court.

Article 5 of the EEC Treaty obliges member states to 'take all appropriate measures, whether general or particular, to ensure the carrying out of the obligations arising out of this Treaty or resulting from measures taken by the institutions of the Community', and there are several other provisions requiring member states to introduce or modify their own laws.[3]

The width of the powers conferred by s 2 to enact subordinate legislation can be readily demonstrated by the juxtaposition of four provisions, two of which have already been mentioned:

(1) By s 2(2)(b) of the Act, delegated legislation is authorised 'for the purpose of dealing with matters arising out of or related to' any obligation or rights of the United Kingdom under the Treaties.
(2) One of the obligations which must be included within the scope of s 2(2) of the act is the obligation in art 5 of the EEC Treaty to 'facilitate the achievement of the Community's tasks'.
(3) The EEC Treaty provides in art 2:

> The Community shall have as its task, by establishing a common market and progressively approximating the economic policies of member states, to promote throughout the Community a harmonious development of economic activities, a continuous and balanced expansion, an increase in stability, an accelerated raising of the standard of living and closer relations between the states belonging to it.

(4) By art 235 of the EEC Treaty:

> If action by the Community should prove necessary to attain, in the course of the operation of the common market, one of the objectives of

---

2 See cases at p 63, n 18, ante.
3 See eg EEC Treaty, arts 11, 27, 100 and 101.

the Community and this Treaty has not provided the necessary powers, the Council shall, acting unanimously on a proposal from the Commission and after consulting the Assembly, take the appropriate measures.

Thus the powers conferred by s 2 are extremely wide. They encompass 'matters arising out of or relating to' any obligation of the United Kingdom; one of those obligations is to facilitate the task of the Community; the task is set out in extremely broad terms; and in any event gaps in the Treaty can be filled by the Council under art 235, thus extending the scope of the obligations of member states.

The definition of Treaties in s 1(2)[4] of the Act is very wide, and includes not only the Treaties establishing the European Communities, the Accession Treaties, and the Single European Act, but also 'any other treaty entered into by any of the Communities, with or without any of the member states, or entered into, as a treaty ancillary to any of the Treaties, by the United Kingdom'. It may be declared conclusively that a Treaty is to be regarded as a Community Treaty, subject to approval, in the case of Treaties entered into by the United Kingdom after 22 January 1972 by resolution of each House of Parliament.[5] In *R v HM Treasury, ex p Smedley*[6] the Court of Appeal held that the Government could legitimately regard the undertaking made by representatives of the member states, to make payments to the Community to finance a supplementary budget, as a 'treaty ancillary' to the named Treaties, but the point was put beyond doubt by what is now the European Communities (Finance) Act 1988, which includes in the definition of treaties the equivalent undertaking given in 1988.

The Minister or Department legislating by means of subordinate instruments may have regard to the objects of the Communities and to any rights or obligations of the United Kingdom under the Treaties. It may be that the right to have regard to the objects, rights and obligations is designed to avoid the difficulties inherent in those decisions which cast doubt on the ability of administrative organs entrusted with discretions to have regard to general policies.[7] Those objects are set out in very general terms in art 2 of the EEC Treaty and of the ECSC Treaty and more particularly in art 3 of the EEC Treaty.

In the succeeding sections of the Treaty those obligations are repeated in the opening articles of the relevant sections. To take just a few examples, art 9 states that the Community shall be based on a

---

4 As amended by (a) the European Communities (Greek Accession) Act 1979; (b) the European Communities (Spanish and Portuguese Accession) Act 1985; (c) the European Communities (Amendment) Act 1986; and (d) the European Communities (Finance) Act 1988. See Appendix for the full text.
5 Section 1(3).
6 [1985] QB 657, [1985] 1 All ER 589, CA.
7 As to which see Wade *Administrative Law* (6th edn 1988) pp 370–375.

customs union which shall cover all trade in goods and which shall involve the prohibition of customs duties and the adoption of a common customs tariff; art 39 sets out the objectives of the common agricultural policy; and arts 103 and 110 articulate the economic and commercial policies of the member states.

(i) Procedural aspects

The power to make provisions by subordinate legislation is delegated to (a) the Crown in Council and (b) any Minister of the Crown or government department who or which has been designated by Order in Council (s 2(2) of the Act).[8]

The Orders in Council and regulations contemplated are, by Sch 2, para 2(1) to the Act, to be exercisable by statutory instrument. By para 2(2) of the same Schedule any statutory instrument containing an Order in Council or regulations made by a Minister of the Crown or government department, if made without a draft having been approved by resolution of each House of Parliament, shall be subject to annulment in pursuance of a resolution of either House.

Sections 5 and 6 of the Act also confer power to make provisions by statutory instrument in relation to customs and the common agricultural policy respectively.

(ii) Limits on power

The powers conferred by s 2(2) of the Act are subject to the exceptions specified in Sch 2 to the Act, which excludes the powers to enact subordinate legislation in four important areas. The powers, according to Sch 2, para 1(2), do not include power:

> '(a) *to make any provision imposing or increasing taxation.*'

This is an important exception because significant provisions of the EEC Treaty deal with taxation. For example, by art 99 (as substituted by the Single European Act):

> The Council shall, acting unanimously on a proposal from the Commission and after consulting the European Parliament, adopt provisions for the harmonisation of legislation concerning turnover taxes, excise duties and other forms of indirect taxation to the extent that such harmonisation is necessary to ensure the establishment and the functioning of the internal market within the time-limit laid down in Article 8A.

Removing such an area from the scope of delegated legislation preserves the powers of Parliament in at least one important area.[9]

---

8 See Halsbury's *Statutes* vol 17, p 34, for orders designating the relevant Ministers and Departments.
9 For the different senses in which the word 'taxation' is used see eg Stroud *Judicial Dictionary* (4th edn) vol 5, p 2719.

'(b) *to make any provision taking effect from a date earlier than that of the making of the instrument containing the provisions.*'

This reaffirms the fundamental repugnance of legal policy to retroactive legislation.[10]

'(c) *to confer any power to legislate by means of orders, rules, regulations or other subordinate instrument, other than rules of procedure for any court or tribunal.*'

There is in general a presumption against construing a grant of delegated legislative powers as empowering the delegate to sub-delegate the law-making power.[11] That is made explicit in this Act and does not require further discussion.

This restriction does not of itself extend to powers to legislate conferred otherwise that under s 2(2); in addition, a power to give directions as to matters of administration is not to be regarded as a power to legislate within the meaning of Sch 2, para (c).[12]

'(d) *to create any new criminal offence punishable with imprisonment for more than two years or punishable on summary conviction with imprisonment for more than three months or with a fine of more than level 5 on the standard scale (if not calculated on a daily basis) or with a fine of more than £100 a day.*'

It should be noted at this point that pecuniary penalties laid down in Community regulations may be enforceable in the United Kingdom under the European Communities (Enforcement of Community Judgments) Order 1972.[13]

(iii) Interpretation of and challenge to delegated legislation

It will be seen[14] that the House of Lords has held that the United Kingdom courts are under a duty to follow the practice of the European Court by giving a purposive construction to Community instruments and to regulations issued under the European Communities Act 1972 for the purpose of giving effect to Community law. This is not always an easy task for the English courts. Thus Kerr LJ, when attempting to construe regulations made under s 2(2) of the 1972 Act to comply with a Council directive on harmonisation of insurance laws, said that the classification introduced by the directive

---

10 For a reaffirmation of the 'strong feeling' against retrospective legislation see Lord Reid in *R v Miah* [1974] 2 All ER 377 at 379, [1974] 1 WLR 683 at 694.
11 Wade *Administrative Law* (6th edn 1988) pp 366–368.
12 Sch 2, para 1(2).
13 SI 1972/1590. See RSC Ord 71, rr 15–24.
14 Pp 118, 137–142, post.

bore a considerable resemblance to the existing United Kingdom law but:

> unfortunately differs in a number of crucial respects which accord badly with insurance law and practice in this country, and – as many in the market would no doubt say – even with common sense.[15]

In each of the leading cases the House of Lords implied words in regulations made under the 1972 Act to give effect to the relevant directives. *Pickstone v Freemans plc*[16] was concerned with the interpretation of amendments made to the Equal Pay Act 1970 by a statutory instrument made under s 2(2) of the European Communities Act 1972 in order to comply with a judgment of the European Court.[17] The House of Lords held that where draft regulations were presented to Parliament as giving full effect to the judgment of the European Court, and were not subject to the parliamentary process of consideration and amendment in committee (as a Bill would have been), it was legitimate in ascertaining the intention of Parliament to take into account the terms in which it was presented to Parliament by the responsible Minister and which formed the basis of its acceptance. As a result the House of Lords was able to depart from a strict and literal interpretation, and to construe the amendment as bearing a meaning which would comply with the directive as interpreted by the European Court.

Litster v Forth Dry Dock and Engineering Co Ltd[18] was also concerned with regulations made under s 2(2), in this case to implement a directive on protection of employment on the transfer of businesses from one employer to another. The House of Lords held that it was legitimate to imply additional words into the regulation in order to ensure that it complied with the obligation in the directive (as interpreted by the European Court) that it should apply not only to employees who were employed in the business immediately before the transfer, but also to employees who would have been so employed if they had not been unfairly dismissed in contemplation of the transfer.

The law-maker under s 2(2) of the Act is entitled to have regard to the objects of the Communities but the Act has not swept aside the common law, whose guardians the judges will continue to be. Schedule 2 has in a sense given statutory authority and binding force to what are at common law only presumptions, namely (i) that express words are necessary to empower the raising of money from the

---

15 *Phoenix General Insurance Co of Greece SA v Halvanon Insurance Co Ltd* [1988] QB 216 at 255, [1987] 2 All ER 152 at 161.
16 [1989] AC 66, [1988] 2 All ER 803, HL.
17 Case 61/81 *Commission v UK* [1982] ECR 2601, [1982] 3 CMLR 284.
18 [1989] 2 WLR 634, [1989] 1 All ER 1134, HL.

subject;[19] (ii) that express words are required to warrant retroactive effect;[20] (iii) that a power is to be exercised only by the person entrusted with it and is not to be sub-delegated;[1] and (iv) that, in the absence of express words or necessary intendment, statutes are not to be interpreted so as to authorise interference with the liberty of the person.[2]

These presumptions are species of a generic presumption to the effect that Parliament does not intend to deprive the subject of his common law rights except by express words or necessary intendment. The other species are that in the absence of express words or necessary intendment statutes are not to be interpreted so as (i) to deprive property rights of the subject without compensation, (ii) restrict the subject's right of access to the ordinary courts, and (iii) abrogate existing contractual rights. It is not likely that these common law presumptions could operate so as to *invalidate* delegated legislation,[3] but they may continue to have a role to play in the *interpretation* of delegated legislation.

It is probably only on the ground of ultra vires that any subordinate legislation is likely to be challenged. Possible reasons for the suggestion that any statutory instrument would be ultra vires would be:

(i) that the subordinate legislation in question goes beyond or significantly differs from the 'Community obligation' or rights to which it is intended to relate;[4] or
(ii) that the 'Community obligation' to which the subordinate legislation purports to give effect is not an obligation at all for one reason or another; or
(iii) that there is bad faith on the part of the Minister or designated department[5] or that the legislation is being enacted for an unauthorised purpose.

The procedure for testing the scope and validity of Community law will be considered in chapter 3 but it should be mentioned at this point that if a question on Community law arises as it would in cases (ii) and (iii) above, the United Kingdom court would be entitled (and in some cases bound) to refer the question of the validity or scope of a Community obligation to the European Court. As to the procedures

---

19 See eg *A-G v Wilts United Dairies* (1922) 127 LT 822.
20 Cf *Howell v Falmouth Boat Construction* [1951] AC 837, [1951] 2 All ER 278.
1 Cf *King-Emperor v Benoari Lal Sarma* [1945] AC 14 at 24, [1945] 1 All ER 210 at 213.
2 See eg *R v Halliday, ex p Zadig* [1917] AC 260 at 274.
3 A different view was expressed in previous editions of this book.
4 Cf *Hayward v Cammell Laird Shipbuilders Ltd* [1988] AC 894 at 903, [1988] 2 All ER 257 at 262, HL.
5 Bad faith cannot, it would appear, be imputed to the Crown in Council: see Australian cases cited in Wade, p. 871.

for testing the validity of subordinate legislation, reference may be made to the standard works on administrative law and it is only necessary to point out that the validity of a statutory instrument may arise in collateral proceedings to enforce its terms[6] or its validity may be sought to be impugned by means of an application for judicial review.[7]

(iv) Scrutiny of European legislation

The Select Committee of the House of Lords on the European Communities and the Select Committee of the House of Commons on European Legislation consider Community proposals, in draft or otherwise, and report to the respective Houses whether they raise questions of policy or principle. The terms of reference of the House of Commons Scrutiny Committee include the consideration of draft proposals by the Commission for legislation and other documents published for submission to the Council, and the reporting of their opinion as to whether they raise questions of legal or political importance, and the making of recommendations for their further consideration by the House of Commons. The terms of reference of the House of Lords Select Committee are to consider Community proposals, to obtain all necessary information about them, and to make reports on those which raise important questions of policy or principle, and on other questions to which the Committee consider that the special attention of the House of Lords should be drawn. In 1980 the House of Commons resolved that, in the opinion of the House, no Minister of the Crown should agree in the Council of Ministers to any proposal for European legislation which had been recommended by the Scrutiny Committee for consideration before the House had given it that consideration, unless the Committee had indicated that agreement need not be withheld or the Minister concerned decides that for special reasons agreement need not be withheld. A similar undertaking has been given to the House of Lords.[8]

The House of Lords Select Committee has a distinguished legal sub-committee, one of whose tasks is to consider whether Community regulations impliedly repeal or amend United Kingdom legislation. Since 1975 the two Select Committees have had power to confer and meet concurrently with each other.

The work of the House of Lords Select Committee has been especially valuable. It recommends whether primary or delegated legislation

---

6 See eg *Customs and Excise Comrs v Cure & Deeley Ltd* [1962] 1 QB 340, [1961] 3 All ER 641.
7 RSC, Ord, 53. But no injunction can be granted against the Crown: Crown Proceedings Act 1947, s 21(1); *Factortame Ltd v Secretary of State for Transport Ltd* [1989] 2 WLR 997, [1989] 2 All ER 692, HL, p 109, ante.
8 See Lord Fraser, *In Memoriam JDB Mitchell* (ed Bates et al) (1983) p 29, at 31–32.

should be adopted to give effect to Community law in the United Kingdom; it reports on the effects of developments in European law, eg the consequences of the adoption of the concept of direct effect by the European Court;[9] its criticisms of the width of the proposals put forward under art 100 of the EEC Treaty to harmonise laws;[10] on proposals for accession of the Communities to the European Convention on Human Rights;[11] on the Commission's powers of investigation and inspection;[12] the external competence of the Community;[13] on the proposals for a European Court of First Instance;[14] and on merger control.[15]

2 Subordinate legislation in practice

No clear distinction can be drawn for the purposes of s 2(2) of the European Communities Act 1972 between directly applicable or effective Community law and Community law which is not directly applicable or effective. The scheme of s 2 is broadly as follows:

(i) By s 2(1) directly applicable and effective Community law becomes part of the law of the United Kingdom.
(ii) By s 2(2)(a) provision is made for the implementation in United Kingdom law of the Community rights and obligations of the United Kingdom.
(iii) By s 2(2)(b) provision is made (inter alia) for the further implementation of directly applicable or effective law.

There is an overlap because, in the first place, as shown above, Community *obligations* of the United Kingdom may be directly effective Community law and so part of the law of the United Kingdom and yet special provision is made in s 2(2)(a) for their incorporation and, secondly, specific provision is made in s 2(2)(b) for the implementation of Community law which is already directly effective by virtue of s 2(1). When orders are made under this section, it is not the practice for the order to distinguish between s 2(2)(a) and s 2(2)(b); they are stated as having been made under s 2(2).

In practice the number of orders made under s 2 of the 1972 Act has not been enormous. The reasons for this derive partly from United Kingdom law and partly from Community law. First, orders have been made to implement Community obligations not under the 1972 Act, but under other legislation: thus in 1989 orders were made under

---

9 (1974–75) 10th and 15th Reports.
10 (1977–78) 22nd Report.
11 (1979–80) 71st Report.
12 (1983–84) 18th Report.
13 (1984–85) 16th Report.
14 (1987–88) 5th Report.
15 (1988–89) 6th Report.

the Agricultural Act 1970, the Fisheries Act 1981, and the Food Act 1984. Secondly, by Community law national authorities may not modify a provision, such as a regulation, which is directly applicable: the European Court has established that to the extent that the member states have assigned legislative powers in particular matters to the Community they no longer have the power to make legislative provisions in that field; the member states were not entitled to issue binding interpretations of Community law, for otherwise the policy of uniform interpretation within the community would be jeopardised.[16] Thirdly, the European Court has established the principle that the Community origin of legislation must not be hidden.[17]

As a result, most of the more important orders made under the 1972 Act deal with directives. In 1988 and 1989 they included orders giving effect to Council directives on measuring instruments and methods of metereological control,[18] and on the environment.[19]

Because under art 189 of the Treaty regulations are directly applicable, the effect of s 2(1) is to dispense with the need for national legislation to give them effect, except to the extent that member states may issue administrative regulations supplementing Community regulations, eg by providing sanctions and laying down procedural rules. The number of orders implementing Community regulations has, as a result, been small and they have been concerned to a large extent with matters relating to enforcement and procedure. For example in 1989 orders were made to give effect to EEC Regulations on the European Economic Interest Groupings;[20] and to provide for the enforcement of regulations concerning fishing by vessels of non-member Scandinavian countries.[1] The former was necessary because certain provisions were left to national law by the Council regulation, including, in particular, matters relating to winding up and insolvency.

III. DIRECTLY EFFECTIVE PROVISIONS OF THE EEC TREATY[2]—A SUMMARY

PART ONE: PRINCIPLES

ARTICLE
1 & 4   By their nature not capable of conferring individual rights: cf *Sacchi* [1974] ECR 409 at 435, per Reischl AG.

---

16 See pp 74–75, ante.
17 Case 34/73 *Variola SpA v Amministrazione Italiana delle Finanze* [1973] ECR 981.
18 SI 1988/186.
19 SI 1989/167; SI 1989/424.
20 SI 1989/638.
1 SI 1989/217.
2 As amended by the Single European Act.

2	Held, not directly effective: *Gimenez Zaera* [1989] 1 CMLR 827.
3	Not directly effective: cf *Leclerc* [1985] ECR 1.
5	Held, not directly effective: *Schlüter* [1973] ECR 1135; 44/84 *Hurd v Jones* [1986] ECR 29.
7(1)	Held, directly effective in conjunction with other provisions: *Kenny* [1978] ECR 1489; cf *Wilhelm* [1969] ECR 1 at 28, per Roemer AG; cf *Jensen v Corpn of the Trinity House of Deptford* [1982] 2 Lloyd's Rep 14; Kon (1981) 6 EL Rev 75.

PART TWO: FOUNDATIONS OF THE COMMUNITY

TITLE I—FREE MOVEMENT OF GOODS

9	Held, directly effective in conjunction with other articles (12, 13(2), 16): *Diamantarbeiders* [1969] 211; *SACE* [1970] ECR 1213; *Eunomia di Porro* [1971] ECR 811; *Denkavit* [1979] ECR 3369.
10(1)	Probably directly effective.
10(2)	By its nature not capable of conferring individual rights.
11	Not directly effective—insufficiently precise.

Chapter 1—The Customs Union

12	Held, directly effective: *Van Gend en Loos* [1963] ECR 1; *Diamantarbeiders*, supra; *Da Costa* [1963] ECR 31.
13 & 14	Held, as to 13(2) directly effective: *SACE*, supra; *Capalongo* [1973] ECR 611; *IGAV* [1975] ECR 699; *Bresciani* [1976] ECR 129; *Rewe* [1976] ECR 1989; *Ariete* [1980] ECR 2545; *Denkavit*, supra. The other articles are probably directly effective, despite complexities. See also arts 32, 35 and 36 of Act of Accession.
15 & 17	Not of themselves capable of conferring individual rights. See also arts 34 and 38 of Act of Accession.
16	Held, directly effective: *Eunomia di Porro*, supra; *Commission v Italy* [1972] ECR 527; *Comet* [1976] ECR 2043. See also art 37 of Act of Accession.
18	Not directly effective: insufficiently precise.
19	Not directly effective: insufficiently clear and subject to adjustment under arts 21(2) and 28. See also art 39 of Act of Accession.
20–22	By their nature not capable of conferring individual rights.
23	Probably directly effective: cf arts 32(2) and 33.
24–29	Not capable of conferring individual rights.

Chapter 2—Elimination of Quantitative Restrictions between Member States

30	Held, directly effective: *Iannelli* [1977] ECR 557; *Pigs Marketing Board* [1978] ECR 2347; *Waterkeyn* [1982] ECR 4337; *Denkavit*, supra; *Commission v Ireland* [1987] ECR 1369; *R v Goldstein* [1983] 1 All ER 434, HL; *Wychaven*

	District Council v Midland Enterprises (Special Event) Ltd [1988] 1 CMLR 397; *Bourgoin SA v Ministry of Agriculture, Fisheries and Food* [1986] QB 716, CA.
31	Held, directly effective: *Salgoil* [1968] ECR 453. See also art 42 of Act of Accession.
32(1)	Held, directly effective: *Salgoil*, supra.
32(2)	First sentence directly effective, but last sentence not directly effective: *Salgoil*, supra.
33	Held, not directly effective: *Salgoil*, supra.
34	Held, directly effective: *Pigs Marketing Board*, supra.
35	By its nature not capable of conferring individual rights.
36	Last sentence directly effective: cf *Deutsche Grammophon* [1971] ECR 681; *Hag* [1974] ECR 731.
37(1)	Held, directly effective: *Manghera* [1976] ECR 91; *Rewe* [1976] ECR 181; *Hansen* [1979] ECR 935.
37(2)	Held, directly effective: *Costa v ENEL* [1964] ECR 585; *Hansen*, supra.

TITLE II—AGRICULTURE

38–47	Not capable of conferring individual rights. See also arts 50–63 of Act of Accession.

TITLE III—FREE MOVEMENT OF PERSONS, SERVICE AND CAPITAL

Chapters 1, 2 & 3—Workers, Right of Establishment, Services

NOTE: In *Watson and Belmann* [1976] ECR 1185 at 1200 it was said that arts 48 to 66 were directly effective as a whole. It is difficult to see how certain of these provisions can be directly effective, such as arts 51 (as to which see *Warry* [1977] ECR 2085 at 2101, per Warner AG), 54, 57, 61, 63 and 64.

48	Held, directly effective: *Commission v France* [1974] ECR 359; *Van Duyn* [1974] ECR 1337; *Royer* [1976] ECR 497; *Dona v Mantero* [1976] ECR 1333; *Commission v Italy* [1986] ECR 2945. But cf Joint Declaration appended to Treaty of Accession, Cmnd 4862—I, p 117.
52	Held, directly effective: *Reyners v Belgium* [1974] ECR 631; *Royer*, supra; *Patrick* [1977] ECR 1199; *Commission v Italy* [1979] ECR 3247; *Steinhauser* [1985] ECR 1819; *Commission v Italy* [1986] ECR 2945.
53	Held, directly effective: *Costa v ENEL*, supra.
59(1)	Held, directly effective: *Van Binsbergen* [1974] ECR 1299; *Walrave* [1974] ECR 1405; *Dona v Mantero*, supra; *Royer*, supra; *Van Wesemael* [1979] ECR 35; *Webb* [1981] ECR 3305. See also on arts 59 and 60 *Commission v Germany* [1986] ECR 3755 (and related cases on insurance services). Held, not directly effective in transport sector: *Parliament v Council* [1985] ECR 1513; *Commission v Italy* [1986] ECR 2945.
59(2)	Not directly effective: *Debauve* [1980] ECR 833 at 873, per Warner AG.
60(3)	Held, directly effective: *Van Binsbergen*, supra; *Dona v Mantero*, supra.

Chapter 4—Capital

67	Probably not directly effective: *Casati* [1981] ECR at 2624, per Capotorti AG; cf *Luisi and Carbone* [1984] ECR 377.
68 & 71	Not directly effective: art 68 too imprecise: *Lütticke* [1966] ECR 205 at 215, per Gand AG. Art 71 conditional: *Casati* [1981] ECR 2595.
69–70 & 72–73	By their nature not capable of conferring individual rights.

TITLE IV—TRANSPORT

74–84	Not directly effective, except perhaps art 76: cf *Grad* [1970] ECR 825; *Lesage* [1970] ECR 861.

PART THREE: POLICY OF THE COMMUNITY

TITLE I—COMMON RULES

Chapter 1—Rules on Competition

85 & 86	Held, directly effective: *BRT v SABAM* [1974] ECR 313; *Sacchi* [1974] ECR 409; *Marty v Lauder* [1980] ECR 2481; *Garden Cottage v Milk Marketing Board* [1984] AC 130, HL.
87–89	By their nature not capable of conferring individual rights.
90(1)	Held, directly effective in conjunction with art 86: *Sacchi* [1974] ECR 409.
90(2)	Held, not directly effective; *Ministère Public Luxembourgeois* [1971] ECR 723; *Syndicat National* [1983] ECR 555.
91(1)	By its nature not capable of conferring individual rights.
91(2)	Probably not directly effective.
92(1)	Held, not directly effective: *Capalongo* [1973] ECR 611; *Iannelli* [1977] ECR 557; cf *Steinike* [1977] ECR 595.
93	Held, not directly effective (*Costa v ENEL*, supra) except last sentence of art 93(3) (held, directly effective: ibid, and *Lorenz* [1973] ECR 1471; *Heineken* [1984] ECR 3435; *R v AG, ex p ICI plc* [1987] 1 CMLR 72, CA).
94	By its nature not capable of conferring individual rights.

Chapter 2—Tax Provisions

95	Held, directly effective: *Molkerei* [1968] ECR 143; *Lütticke* [1966] ECR 205; *Rewe* [1976] ECR 181; *Iannelli* [1977] ECR 557; *Essevi* [1981] ECR 1413; *Pabst and Richarz KG* [1982] ECR 1331; *Schul* [1982] ECR 1409.
96 & 98	Probably directly effective.
97	Held, not directly effective: *Molkerei*, supra.
99	By its nature not capable of conferring individual rights.

Chapter 3—Approximation of Laws

100–101	By their nature not capable of conferring individual rights.
102	Held, not directly effective: *Costa v ENEL*, supra.

TITLE II—ECONOMIC POLICY

Chapter 1—Cooperation in Economic and Monetary Policy

102A	By its nature not capable of conferring individual rights.

Chapter 2—Conjunctural Policy

103 By its nature not capable of conferring individual rights.

Chapter 3—Balance of Payments

104–109 In general not capable of conferring individual rights (art 107 held not directly effective: Schlüter [1973] ECR 1135), except perhaps art 106, on which see *Schorsch Meier v Hennin* [1975] QB 416 and *Miliangos v George Frank (Textiles) Ltd* [1976] AC 443, p 111, ante; cf *Boussac* [1980] ECR 342).

Chapter 4—Commercial Policy

110–116 In general not capable of conferring individual rights.

TITLE III—SOCIAL POLICY

Chapter 1—Social Provisions

117–122 In general not capable of conferring individual rights. Arts 117–118 held not directly effective: *Defrenne* [1978] ECR 1365; see also *Triches* [1976] ECR 1243 at 1257; *Gimenez Zaera* [1989] 1 CMLR 827. Art 119 held directly effective: *Defrenne* [1976] ECR 455; *Macarthys* [1980] ECR 1275; *Worringham* [1981] ECR 767; *Jenkins* [1981] ECR 911; *Garland* [1982] ECR 359; *Murphy* [1988] 1 CMLR 879.

Chapter 2—The European Social Fund

123–128 Not capable of conferring individual rights.

TITLES IV, V, VI, AND VII—THE EUROPEAN INVESTMENT BANK, ECONOMIC AND SOCIAL COHESION, RESEARCH AND TECHNOLOGICAL DEVELOPMENT, ENVIRONMENT

129–130T Not capable of conferring individual rights.

PART FOUR: ASSOCIATION OF THE OVERSEAS COUNTRIES AND TERRITORIES

131–136A Not capable of conferring individual rights.

PART FIVE: THE INSTITUTIONS OF THE COMMUNITIES

137–238 The institutional provisions do not require the concept of direct effectiveness to make them effective. Arts 177 and 192 may be directly effective: cf *Van Gend en Loos* [1963] ECR 1 at 20, per Roemer AG. Arts 220 (*Ministère Public v Mutsch* [1985] ECR 2681) and 234 (*AG v Burgoa* [1980] ECR 2787) held not directly effective.

Chapter 3

The national court and the European Court

It has been seen in the previous chapters that within the United Kingdom context questions of Community law lead initially to the relevant United Kingdom legislation and ultimately through that route to Community law itself. In particular, under the law of the United Kingdom, except in the most unusual circumstances, treaties cannot affect private rights—that can only be done by legislation. The principle was authoritatively reiterated by Diplock LJ in *Salomon v Customs and Excise Comrs*[1] when he said:

> Where, by a treaty, Her Majesty's Government undertakes either to introduce domestic legislation to achieve a specified result in the United Kingdom or to secure a specified result which can only be achieved by legislation, the treaty, since in English law is not self-operating, remains irrelevant to any issue in the English courts until Her Majesty's Government has taken steps by way of legislation to fulfil its treaty obligations.

It has recently been reaffirmed by the House of Lords in the cases involving the International Tin Council. Lord Oliver said:[2]

> Quite simply, a treaty is not part of English law unless and until it has been incorporated into the law by legislation. So far as individuals are concerned, it is res inter alios acta from which they cannot derive rights and by which they cannot be deprived of rights or subjected to obligations; and it is outside the purview of the court not only because it is made in the conduct of foreign relations, which are a prerogative of the Crown, but also because, as a source of rights and obligations, it is irrelevant.

The first question, therefore, is what legislative provisions have been enacted to deal with questions of interpretation, and, where they have not been enacted, what principles apply.

---

1 [1967] 2 QB 116 at 143, [1966] 3 All ER 871 at 875, CA. See also chapter 1, pp 23–26.
2 *J H Rayner (Mincing Lane) Ltd v Department of Trade and Industry* [1989] 3 WLR 969 at 1002, [1989] 3 All ER 523 at 544–5, HL.

I. THE 1972 ACT: THE STATUS OF COMMUNITY LAW

It will be shown below that where domestic legislation is intended to give effect to the treaty obligations of the United Kingdom, the treaty (or other international) obligations may be looked at for certain purposes. As is apparent on the face of the European Communities Act 1972, it is a piece of legislation which is intended to give effect to treaty obligations. The long title, and ss 1, 2 and 3 each make that abundantly clear.

In relation to questions of interpretation and application the following provisions are relevant:

1. By s 2(1), already extensively discussed in chapter 2, directly applicable or effective Community law is to be recognised and available in the United Kingdom.
2. By s 2(2)(a) power is granted to the executive to give effect by subordinate legislation to Community law which is *not* directly applicable or effective.
3. By s 2(2)(b) power is granted to the executive to make regulations to deal with matters arising out of or related to directly applicable Community law.
4. By s 2(4):

   any enactment passed or to be passed, other than one contained in this Part of this Act, shall be construed and have effect subject to the foregoing provisions of this section . . .

   As submitted above,[3] this means that, subject to clear provision to the contrary, subsequent enactments are to be read subject to the rule that directly applicable or effective Community law is to be given effect in the United Kingdom.
5. Section 3(1) provides:

   For the purposes of all legal proceedings any question as to the meaning or effect of any of the Treaties, or as to the validity, meaning or effect of any Community instrument, shall be treated as a question of law (and, if not referred to the European Court, be for determination as such in accordance with the principles laid down by and any relevant decision of the European Court or any court attached thereto[4])

   and by s 3(2) judicial notice is to be taken of the Treaties, the Official Journal of the Communities and any decision of, or expression or opinion by, the European Court. Section 3 makes explicit what as a result of s 2 must be implicit, namely that

---

3 See p 28, ante.
4 This phrase was added by the European Communities (Amendment) Act 1986 in order to include the proposed Court of First Instance, which was established in 1989.

Community law is to be treated in the United Kingdom as law and not, like foreign law,[5] as fact.

In *R v Goldstein*,[6] the defendant had been convicted of the fraudulent importation of 'citizen's band' radio sets from Belgium. At trial it was submitted that the prohibition on importation imposed by the relevant statutory instrument was contrary to art 30 of the EEC Treaty as being a quantitative restriction on imports or a measure having equivalent effect. The prosecution argued that the prohibition was allowed by art 36 because it was justified on grounds of public policy, public security and the protection of health and life of humans. Expert evidence was called by the prosecution in the absence of the jury to show what adverse effects the abolition of the prohibition of importation of the apparatus into the United Kingdom would have. Following this evidence, the judge ruled that the statutory instruments prohibiting the importation were not affected by the EEC Treaty. On appeal, the defendant argued that the evidence should have been given in the presence of the jury, and that it was the function of the jury alone to determine whether the evidence established beyond reasonable doubt the validity under art 36 of the prohibition in so far as it imposed a ban on the import of the apparatus into the United Kingdom from Belgium. The House of Lords held that the issue whether the prohibition of importation contained in the statutory instrument was ineffective by virtue of arts 30 and 36 of the EEC Treaty was a question of law falling 'fairly and squarely' within s 3(1) of the European Communities Act 1972, and therefore was for the purposes of all legal proceedings to be treated as a question of law and thus, in a criminal trial, as a question for the judge and not a question for the jury. Where Community law is relevant to the determination of a case in the United Kingdom, it is the duty of counsel to draw the court's attention to it.[7]

Section 3 contemplates references to the European Court in appropriate cases and at this point it is sufficient to refer to art 177 of the EEC Treaty which provides for references to the Court on (inter alia) points of interpretation and to indicate that the principles of interpretation of Community law are not identical with the principles of interpretation normally applied by United Kingdom courts, and this will be the principal subject of this chapter. A question may arise as to whether in an individual case it is the Community law principles of interpretation or the United Kingdom principles which apply and as

---

5 See Dicey & Morris *Conflict of Laws* (11th edn, 1987), pp 217 et seq.
6 [1983] 1 All ER 434, [1983] 1 WLR 151.
7 Cf *Garland v British Rail Engineering Ltd* [1983] 2 AC 751 at 770, [1982] 2 All ER 402 at 414.

to the extent of the power of the United Kingdom court to look to Community law in interpreting a domestic enactment.

The following consequences, it is suggested, flow from the 1972 Act:

1. If a norm of Community law (be it a Treaty provision, directive, regulation or decision) is directly applicable or effective the combined effect of s 2(1) and s 3(1) is that Community principles of interpretation apply.
2. If a norm of Community law is directly applicable or effective but has also been implemented or supplemented under s 2(2)(b) by subordinate legislation then the subordinate legislation will be interpreted in accordance with Community principles, as a result of ss 2(1), 2(4) and 3(1). If the subordinate legislation differs from or is in conflict with Community law, then to that extent it may be ultra vires and void as a result of s 2(4).
3. But if Community law which is not directly applicable or effective is in question more difficult problems arise. Thus legislation (subordinate or otherwise) giving effect to a directive or a Treaty provision which is not directly effective—even the European Communities Act 1972 itself—is in a special position. This type of legislation must be construed, if it is reasonably capable of bearing such a meaning, as intended to carry out that objective, even if the construction involves a departure from the strict and literal interpretation of the legislation.[8]

In the next section of this chapter the general principles of interpretation of Community law will be discussed, with a view to showing the problems which may arise in the context of the enactment of legislation in the United Kingdom designed to give effect to Community law, and to set the stage for the discussion of references to the European Court by United Kingdom courts.

II. INTERPRETATION OF COMMUNITY LAW AND THE EUROPEAN COURT

Although a detailed account would be outside the scope of this book,[9] it may be helpful if some indications were given of the techniques of interpretation used by the European Court. The first point to note is that it is difficult to establish general principles of interpretation which will, of necessity, be followed in future cases. This is so for two reasons: first, because the methods of interpretation are very fluid

---

8 See pp 137–142, post.
9 For a good general account see Brown & Jacobs *The Court of Justice of the European Communities* (3rd edn 1989) pp 268–292.

when compared with traditional common law methods, and, secondly, because of the lack of a system of precedent and the consequent willingness to depart from previous decisions. As in all systems, in Community law the techniques of interpretation are only methods to achieve a result. It would not be appropriate to talk of *rules*. One technique can be used to justify one result, another technique to justify another result.

Too much perhaps has been made of the differences between the civil law and common law approaches to interpretation. The wording of the text must in all cases be the starting point. Lord Mackenzie Stuart has emphasised that 'it is the text—including of course its expressed objectives—which dictates the approach of the Court'.[10] The nature of the Treaty, and the dynamic role of the Court has meant that the 'teleological' or 'purposive' approach to interpretation has become dominant. As the European Court put it, 'every provision of Community law must be placed in its context and interpreted in the light of the provisions of Community law as a whole, regard being had to the objectives thereof and to its state of evolution at the date on which the provision in question is to be applied'.[11]

That this approach is less precise than the approach to textual interpretation in the United Kingdom is obvious, and is now fully recognised by the courts in the United Kingdom. To take two examples, Lord Diplock said in *Henn and Darby v DPP*:[12]

> The European Court, in contrast to English courts, applies teleological rather than historical methods to the interpretation of the Treaties and other Community legislation. It seeks to give effect to what it conceives to be the spirit rather than the letter of the Treaties; sometimes, indeed, to an English judge, it may seem to the exclusion of the letter. It views the Communities as living and expanding organisms and the interpretation of the provisions of the Treaties as changing to match their growth.

and in *Customs and Excise Comrs v ApS Samex*[13] Bingham J added:

> The interpretation of Community instruments involves very often not the process familiar to common lawyers of laboriously extracting the meaning

---

10 *The European Communities and the Rule of Law* (1977), p 77.
11 Case 283/81 *CILFIT Srl v Ministry of Health* [1982] ECR 3415 at 3430, [1983] 1 CMLR 472 at 491.
12 [1981] AC 850 at 905, [1980] 2 All ER 166 at 196. For the enthusiastic acceptance of this approach by Lord Denning MR see *Bulmer v Bollinger* [1974] Ch 401 at 425, [1974] 2 All ER 1226 at 1232; *Application des Gaz v Falks Veritas* [1974] Ch 381 at 394, [1974] 3 All ER 51 at 56; *Schorsch Meier v Hennin* [1975] QB 416 at 426, [1975] 1 All ER 152 at 157; *James Buchanan & Co v Babco Forwarding and Shipping (UK) Ltd* [1977] QB 208 at 213–14, [1977] 1 All ER 518 at 522–3; affirmed on different grounds [1978] AC 141, [1977] 3 All ER 1048. Cf *Lawlor v Minister for Agriculture* [1988] 3 CMLR 22 (Irish High Court).
13 [1983] 1 All ER 1042 at 1056.

from words used, but the more creative process of supplying flesh to a spare and loosely constructed skeleton. The choice between alternative submissions may turn not on purely legal considerations but on a broader view of what the orderly development of the Community requires.

The European Court is not one which fully articulates its reasoning, but it is possible to see at least two underlying principles. The first is that the Court adopts a restrictive interpretation when an exception to a general Community rule is involved. The second is that the outstanding characteristic of the Court's method of interpretation is that it has regard to the principles and objectives of the Treaties even where no ambiguity is involved. The Court sees its role as essentially a dynamic one, to contribute to the development of the Communities.

It may be helpful to see these principles at work in the cases which have been referred under art 177 by United Kingdom courts. The first principle, that exceptions to general Community rules are to be interpreted strictly, is illustrated by *Van Duyn v Home Office*[14] and *R v Bouchereau*.[15] Each case involved the interpretation of the concept of public policy in the context of art s 48 of the EEC Treaty, which spells out the basic principles of freedom of movement 'subject to limitations justified on the grounds of public policy, public security or public health'. Miss Van Duyn was refused entry into the United Kingdom because of her association with Scientology and M. Bouchereau was liable to deportation because of previous convictions. In the first case the Court held that the United Kingdom authorities could take into account Miss Van Duyn's association with an organisation thought to be socially harmful, and in the second case that to justify deportation there must be a genuine and serious threat affecting one of the fundamental interests of society. In reaching its conclusion in the *Van Duyn* case the Court said:[16]

> It should be emphasised that the concept of public policy in the context of the Community and where, in particular, it is used as a justification for derogating from the fundamental principle of freedom of movement for workers must be interpreted strictly, so that its scope cannot be determined unilaterally by each member state without being subject to control by the institutions of the Community.

The second principle, of interpretation by reference to the purposes and objectives of the Treaties, has of course been applied in cases too numerous to mention. In *R v Thompson*[17] the defendants were accused of illegal importation into the United Kingdom of Krugerrand gold

---

14 Case 41/74 [1974] ECR 1337, [1975] 1 CMLR 1.
15 Case 30/77 [1977] ECR 1999, [1977] 2 CMLR 800.
16 [1974] ECR 1337 at 1350, [1975] 1 CMLR 1 at 17. See also Case 30/77 *R v Bouchereau* [1977] ECR 1999 at 2013, [1977] 2 CMLR 800 at 824.
17 Case 7/78 [1978] ECR 2247, [1979] 1 CMLR 47.

coins and importation and exportation of silver alloy coins. The defendants submitted at their trial that the ban on the import and export of coins was invalid because of the principle of free movement of goods within the common market. The Court of Appeal (Criminal Division) referred to the European Court the question (as reformulated by the European Court) whether the gold coins were goods to which arts 30 to 37 applied. The Court held that they were not goods, and in reaching this conclusion indicated that the 'questions must be considered in the context of the general system of the Treaty',[18] and then went on to analyse the aims of the Treaty with regard to movement of capital to infer that under the system of the Treaty means of payment were not to be regarded as goods falling within the purview of arts 30 to 37 of the Treaty. In cases from United Kingdom courts on the interpretation of regulations, the European Court has interpreted the regulations in the light of their objective and the objective of the Treaty provision under which they were made. Thus in *Brack v Insurance Officer*[19] it was said that the regulation 'must be interpreted above all in the light of the spirit and the objectives of the Treaty'.

The Community system is multilingual. All of the languages (except Irish) are working languages and Community legislation is published in all the working languages, which are equally authentic. As a result,

> . . . it must be borne in mind that Community legislation is drafted in several languages and that the different language versions are all equally authentic. An interpretation of a provision of Community law thus involves a comparison of the different language versions.[20]

Thus Warner J (formerly Advocate General at the European Court) said that he had learned from experience that it was in general unwise to look at the text of an EEC instrument in one language only.[1]

It follows that when such a comparison has to be made the multinational European Court is better equipped to make it than a national judge.[2] The European Court has made it clear that the different language versions of a Community text must be given a uniform

---

18 [1978] ECR 2247 at 2273. See also Case 34/79 *R v Henn and Darby* [1979] ECR 3795, [1980] 1 CMLR 246, [1981] AC 850; Case 231/78 *Commission v United Kingdom* [1979] ECR 1447, [1979] 2 CMLR 427.
19 Case 17/76 [1976] ECR 1429 at 1451, [1976] 2 CMLR 592 at 616. See also Case 41/77 *R v Warry* [1977] ECR 2085 at 2095, [1977] 2 CMLR 783 at 794.
20 Case 283/81 *CILFIT Srl v Ministry of Health*, ante, n 11.
1 *National Smokeless Fuels Ltd v IRC* [1986] 3 CMLR 227.
2 *Customs and Excise Comrs v ApS Samex* [1983] 1 All ER 1042 at 1055, per Bingham J. Cf *Henn and Darby v DPP* [1981] AC 850 at 906, [1980] 2 All ER 166 at 197.

interpretation and that in the case of a divergence between the versions the provision in question must be interpreted by reference to the purpose and general scheme of the rules of which it forms a part.[3] Each text should be interpreted in the light of the other versions,[4] with a view to not giving preference to any one of the texts involved.[5] But if one of the language versions is clear (and the others are not) the clear text will be adopted if it is consistent with the purpose of the provision and its context.[6]

An illustration of these principles is the *Anglo-Polish Fishing* case,[7] where the question for the European Court was whether the United Kingdom was bound to charge customs duties on the importation of fish which had been fished by British and Polish trawlers in collaboration in Polish fishery limits. The catch was landed at British ports by British trawlers, but had to be treated as Polish imports if the fish had been 'taken from the sea' ('extraits de la mer') by Polish vessels. What happened in practice was that the British trawlers cast their nets, and the Polish trawlers then took the lines and trawled the nets; the Polish trawlers handed the lines back to the British vessels, which then hauled the nets, and the catch, on board. The United Kingdom government argued that the catch was therefore 'taken from the sea' by the British vessels and that it was not therefore required to levy customs duties as if the catch were Polish. The European Court held that the different language versions were divergent and that it was necessary to interpret the regulation by reference to the purpose of the rules. The intention was to determine the origin of the fish on the basis of the nationality of the vessel which caught them; where there was a joint fishing operation, the origin of the fish depended on the nationality of the vessels which performed the essential part of the operation; and the vessel which located the fish and netted them performed the essential part; consequently the fish were Polish imports and the United Kingdom had failed to fulfil its obligation to levy duties.

---

3 Case 30/77 *R v Bouchereau* [1977] ECR 1999, [1977] 2 CMLR 800, applied in *Cunningham v Milk Marketing Board for Northern Ireland* [1988] 3 CMLR 815, where the Northern Ireland court undertook a very detailed consideration of different language versions, dictionaries and expert evidence in order to decide whether 'processing' of milk included pasteurisation.
4 Case 19/67 *Sociale Verzekeringsbank v Van der Vecht* [1967] ECR 345, [1968] CMLR 151; Case 26/69 *Stauder v City of Ulm* [1969] ECR 419, [1970] CMLR 112; Case 9/79 *Wörsdorfer née Koschniske v Raad van Arbeid* [1979] ECR 2717, [1980] 1 CMLR 87.
5 Case 80/76 *North Kerry Milk Products Ltd v Minister for Agriculture and Fisheries* [1977] ECR 425, [1977] 2 CMLR 769.
6 Case 90/83 *Paterson v Weddell & Co Ltd* [1984] ECR 1567, [1984] 2 CMLR 540.
7 Case 100/84 *Commission v UK* [1985] ECR 1169, [1985] 2 CMLR 199.

III. INTERPRETATION OF UNITED KINGDOM LEGISLATION GIVING EFFECT TO COMMUNITY LAW WHICH IS NOT DIRECTLY APPLICABLE

1 Statutes and treaties

The basic question is whether, and, if so, to what extent, a treaty or other international instrument (such as a Community act) can be taken into account in interpreting the domestic legislation which is designed to give it effect.[8] The judgment in Diplock LJ in the *Salomon* case is a convenient starting point for the basic principle, namely, that 'if the terms of the legislation are clear and unambiguous they must be given effect to'.[9] That is so whether or not the legislation in fact carries out the treaty obligations. The technical reason for this principle is the overriding rule that in the law of the United Kingdom everything yields to statute law. So much so that in a case where a statute referred to an international convention and a schedule to the statute incorporated it, the House of Lords refused to look to the convention to cast doubt on the clarity of a section of the statute.[10] That was an unusual case and would probably not be followed today.[11] But the principle is not in doubt. As Ungoed-Thomas J put it in *Cheney v Conn*:[12]

> First, international law is part of the law of the land, but it yields to statute. That is made clear by *IRC v Collco Dealings Ltd* where Lord Simonds quoted with approval, and in accordance with the decision of the House of Lords in that case, Maxwell on the Interpretation of Statutes. I quote 10th edn (1953) at p 148: 'But if the statute is unambiguous, its provisions must be followed even if they are contrary to international law.'

If, however, the legislation is ambiguous or unclear, then it is well established that the text of the treaty may be resorted to in order to clarify the legislation or resolve the ambiguity. It has already been seen that in the *International Tin Council* cases the House of Lords has vigorously re-affirmed that, so far as private parties are concerned, a treaty is *res inter alios acta* from which they cannot derive rights or be subjected to obligations. But the House of Lords also re-affirmed that this did not:

---

8 On which, see eg Mann *Studies in International Law* (1973) pp 614 et seq, (1983) 99 LQR 376, *Foreign Affairs in English Courts* (1986) Ch 5, and Sinclair (1963) 12 ICLQ 508 at 528 et seq.
9 [1967] 2 QB 166 at 143, [1966] 3 All ER 871 at 875.
10 *Ellerman Lines v Murray* [1931] AC 126.
11 See *James Buchanan & Co Ltd v Babco Forwarding and Shipping (UK) Ltd* [1978] AC 141 at 152, [1977] 3 All ER 1048 at 1053, per Lord Wilberforce.
12 [1968] 1 WLR 242 at 245, [1968] 1 All ER 779 at 780. See also *IRC v Collco Dealings* [1962] AC 1, [1961] 1 All ER 762; *R v Home Secretary, ex p Bhajan Singh* [1976] QB 198, [1975] 2 All ER 1081.

... involve as a corollary that the court must never look at or construe a treaty. Where, for instance, a treaty is directly incorporated into English law by Act of the legislature, its terms become subject to the interpretative jurisdiction of the court in the same way as any other Act of the legislature ... Again, it is well established that where a statute is enacted in order to give effect to the United Kingdom's obligations under the treaty, the terms of the treaty may have to be considered and, if necessary, construed in order to resolve any ambiguity or obscurity as to the meaning or scope of the statute.[13]

It is sometimes not apparent that the statute is on its face unclear or ambiguous. Sometimes an ambiguity in the statute does not appear until the treaty is looked at. At one time it was said that, before the convention could be looked at, there had to be an ambiguity on the face of the legislation.[14] But today 'there is no need to impose a preliminary test of ambiguity',[15] and even Lord Diplock, once a proponent of the 'ambiguity' test, seems to have abandoned it. In *Garland v British Rail Engineering Ltd*[16] he said:

... it is a principle of construction of United Kingdom statutes, now too well established to call for citation of authority, that the words of a statute passed after the treaty has been signed and dealing with the subject matter of the international obligation of the United Kingdom are to be construed, if they are reasonably capable of bearing such a meaning, as intended to carry out the obligation and not to be inconsistent with it.

Many of the recent cases show that the courts will adopt a liberal approach in deciding whether or not to look at the treaty or convention. They will not require strict proof of the fact that a piece of domestic legislation was enacted to give effect to a treaty or convention. As Diplock LJ said in *Salomon v Comrs of Customs and Excise*[17] a treaty is a public act of state of Her Majesty's Government of which the judiciary must take notice if relevant; in the same case he suggested that if there were intrinsic evidence that the enactment was intended to give effect to an international obligation the treaty or convention could be looked at.

Once the court resorts to the international agreement, both the

---

13 *J H Rayner (Mincing Lane) Ltd v Department of Trade and Industry* [1989] 3 WLR 969 at 1002, [1989] 3 All ER 523 at 545, per Lord Oliver.
14 See, eg *Salomon v Customs and Excise Comrs* [1967] 2 QB 116 at 143–4, [1966] 3 All ER 871 at 875–6, per Diplock LJ. See also Law Commission, Interpretation of Statutes, 1969 (Law Com No 21), pp 8 et seq.
15 *James Buchanan & Co Ltd v Babco Forwarding and Shipping (UK) Ltd* [1978] AC 141 at 152, [1977] 3 All ER 1048 at 1052, per Lord Wilberforce. See also *Salomon v Customs and Excise Comrs* [1967] QB 116 at 141, [1966] 3 All ER 871 at 874, per Lord Denning MR.
16 [1983] 2 AC 751 at 771, [1982] 2 All ER 402 at 415. But cf *Fothergill v Monarch Airlines Ltd* [1981] AC 251 at 299, [1980] 2 All ER 696 at 719, HL per Lord Roskill.
17 [1967] 2 QB 116 at 143, [1966] 3 All ER 871 at 875.

agreement and the legislation giving effect to it should be interpreted free from technicalities of English rules. As Lord Wilberforce put it:[18]

> ... the current approach is to interpret the English text, which after all is to be used by many others than British businessmen, in a normal manner, appropriate for the interpretation of an international convention, unconstrained by technical rules of English law, or by English legal precedent, but on broad principles of general acceptance.

Thus, in order to interpret the international agreement, the court may resort to the French text even if only the English text is scheduled to the legislation;[19] it should look at the relevant provision in the context of the whole agreement;[20] but travaux préparatoires may only be looked at if the material involved is public and accessible and where it clearly and indisputably points to a definite legislative intention.[1]

2 Statutes and Community law

These principles apply when the United Kingdom court is concerned with the relationship between statute and obligations assumed by the United Kingdom under Community law, but their application is subject to some modification because of the special status of Community law. Thus, after restating the general principle that the words of a statute should be construed, if they are reasonably capable of bearing such a meaning, as intended to carry out the treaty obligation, Lord Diplock said:

> *a fortiori* is this the case where the treaty obligation arises under one of the Community treaties to which s 2 of the European Communities Act 1972 applies.[2]

Among the reasons the obligations under Community law are in a special position, as compared with obligations under other international treaties, are, first, that in the United Kingdom for the purposes of all legal proceedings any question as to the meaning or effect of the EEC Treaties or of any Community instrument must be determined in accordance with the principles laid down by, and any

---

18 *James Buchanan & Co Ltd v Babco Forwarding and Shipping (UK) Ltd* [1978] AC 141 at 152, [1977] 3 All ER 1048 at 1052.
19 *James Buchanan & Co Ltd v Babco Forwarding and Shipping (UK) Ltd*, supra; *Corocraft v Pan American Airways* [1969] 1 QB 616, [1969] 1 All ER 82.
20 *Wilson, Smithett & Cope Ltd v Terruzzi* [1976] QB 683, [1975] 2 All ER 649.
1 *Fothergill v Monarch Airlines Ltd*; see n 16 supra. Cf *Open University v Customs and Excise Comrs* [1982] 2 CMLR 572 (VAT Tribunal).
2 *Garland v British Rail Engineering Ltd* [1983] 2 AC 751 at 771, [1982] 2 All ER 402 at 415. See also *Apple and Pear Development Council v Customs and Excise Comrs* [1987] 2 CMLR 634 at 654, per Lord Brightman; *Rainey v Greater Glasgow Health Board* [1987] AC 224, [1987] 1 All ER 65, HL.

relevant decision of, the European Court;[3] second, one of the principles laid down by the European Court is that:

> it is for the national court to interpret and apply the legislation adopted for the implementation of the directive in conformity with the requirements of Community law, in so far as it is given discretion to do so under national law.[4]

As has been seen in the preceding section, it is sometimes said that the United Kingdom legislation must be 'ambiguous' before resort may be had to the international instrument for the purpose of interpretation. Although this formula has also been used in the context of statutes to be interpreted in the light of Community law,[5] there is no doubt that the correct starting point is to consider whether the words of the statute are 'reasonably capable' of bearing a meaning which complies with the obligations imposed by Community law. Moreover, the court may not be restricted merely to a process of 'interpretation' of the words. If the legislation does not give full effect to the Community obligation, the court may, under the guise of interpretation, depart from the strict and literal construction of the statute and may also fill in gaps in the legislation.[6]

In *Pickstone v Freemans plc*[7] the House of Lords held that the Equal Pay Act 1970, as amended by statutory instrument in 1983, allowed a woman to claim equal pay with a man doing another job of equal value for the same employer but earning more, even if there was another man doing the same work as her for the same pay. The problem of construction arose because the United Kingdom had legislated in a very complex way in order to comply with the Equal Pay Directive as interpreted by the European Court.[8] Lord Oliver said:

> ... a construction which permits the section to operate as a proper fulfilment of the United Kingdom's obligation under the Treaty involves not so much doing violence to the language of the section as filling a gap by an implication which arises, not from the words used, but from the manifest purpose of the Act and the mischief it was intended to remedy.

---

3 European Communities Act 1972, s 3(1).
4 Case 14/83 *Von Colson v Land Nordrhein-Westfalen* [1984] ECR 1891 at 1909, [1986] 2 CMLR 430 at 455. See p 84, above.
5 See *Bell Concord Educational Trust Ltd v Customs and Excise Comrs* [1989] 1 CMLR 845 at 851, CA.
6 But it has been seen that a directive cannot of itself impose criminal liability on private parties without implementing national legislation (p 90, ante) and in Cases 206 etc/88 *Vessoso and Zanetti* (not yet decided) Jacobs AG expressed the view that Community Law did not require national courts to interpret domestic legislation in order to conform with a directive where the result would be to impose criminal liability which would not otherwise arise.
7 [1989] AC 66, [1988] 2 All ER 803.
8 Case 61/81 *Commission v UK* [1982] ECR 2601, [1982] 3 CMLR 284.

The question is whether that can be justified by the necessity—indeed the obligation—to apply a purposive construction which will implement the United Kingdom's obligations under the Treaty.[9]

In that case the result was achieved by a process of what could fairly be described as interpretation, but in *Litster v Forth Dry Dock and Engineering Co Ltd*[10] the House of Lords went further in order to conform with a directive regulations which had been introduced to implement it. The Business Transfer Directive (77/187) provided that upon the transfer of a business from one employer to another, the benefit and burden of a contract of employment between the transferer and a worker should devolve on the new owner, and the European Court[11] held that workers whose employment had been terminated by reason of the proposed transfer should still be considered as employed as at the date of transfer. The United Kingdom regulations gave that protection to workers who were employed 'immediately before the transfer'. In *Litster* the workers were dismissed by their old employers one hour before the transfer of the business to the new owners. The House of Lords held that they were entitled to the benefit of the regulations because it was proper to imply into them a phrase adding to the protected group those who *would* have been employed immediately before the transfer if they had not been dismissed beforehand for a reason connected with the transfer. Lord Oliver said:[12]

> If the legislation can reasonably be construed so as to conform with [the obligations under the directive]—obligations which are to be ascertained not only from the wording of the relevant Directive but from the interpretation placed upon it by the European Court of Justice at Luxembourg—such a purposive construction will be applied even though, perhaps, it may involve some departure from the strict and literal application of the words which the legislature has elected to use

and

> the greater flexibility available to the court in applying a purposive construction to legislation designed to give effect to the United Kingdom's Treaty obligations to the Community enables the court, where necessary, to supply by implication words appropriate to comply with those obligations.

These decisions also illustrate the point that it is the meaning of the directive as interpreted by the European Court which the United Kingdom court must take into account. In those cases the European Court had already pronounced on the meaning of the directive, but

---

9 [1989] AC at 125, [1988] 2 All ER at 817.
10 [1989] 2 WLR 634, [1989] 1 All ER 1134.
11 Case 101/87 *Bork International A/S v Foreningen af Arbejdsledere i Danmark* [1989] IRLR 41.
12 [1989] 2 WLR at 641, 658, [1989] 1 All ER at 1140, 1153.

where it has not so pronounced, and there is some doubt as to the meaning of the directive, a reference to the European Court would be appropriate.[13]

The general principle that the court should construe legislation so as to be in conformity with Community law has been applied in many cases, particularly in relation to directives,[14] by tribunals from the VAT Tribunal to the House of Lords. Where legislation to give effect to a directive re-enacts legislation existing prior to the directive, the court may resort to the directive to interpret the legislation just as if it had been enacted afresh to implement the directive.[15] Once resort is made to the directive, it is appropriate for the court to look not only at the English language version, but also at the versions in other languages, especially if the English text is ambiguous or capable of bearing more than one meaning.[16]

In *Phonogram Ltd v Lane*[17] the question for the Court of Appeal was the meaning of s 9(2) of the European Communities Act 1972[18] which was designed to give effect to the First Company Law Directive and which imposed personal liability on a person who contracts for a company at a time 'when the company has not been formed'. The defendant, relying on the French text of the directive, sought to narrow this expression to mean that he was only liable if the contract was made at a time when the company had already started to be formed. Lord Denning MR rejected this argument on the basis that the French text was drafted with regard to a different system of company law and that the English court should go by s 9(2) of the 1972 Act: under art 189 the directive was only binding in so far as the spirit and intent was concerned, and the section was in accordance with the spirit and intent. It is suggested that this is too narrow an approach and that the same result in the case could have been reached by a more balanced look at the section in the light of the directive. In *International Sales and Agencies Ltd v Marcus*,[19] decided a few weeks

---

13 As in *Apple and Pear Development Council v Customs and Excise Comrs* [1987] 2 CMLR 634.
14 In addition to the cases cited in the preceding notes in this section see also, especially, *Hayward v Cammell Laird Shipbuilders Ltd* [1988] AC 894, [1988] 2 All ER 257; *Leverton v Clwyd County Council* [1989] AC 706, [1989] 1 All ER 78 (equal pay); *J Rothschild Holdings PLC v IRC* [1989] 2 CMLR 621, CA (transfer of business); *Barkworth v Customs & Excise Comrs* [1988] 3 CMLR 759; *Osman v Customs and Excise Comrs* [1989] STC 596 (VAT).
15 *Bell Concord Educational Trust Ltd v Customs and Excise Comrs* [1989] 1 CMLR 845, CA; *Barkworth v Customs and Excise Comrs* [1988] 3 CMLR 759.
16 *Bell Concord Educational Trust Ltd v Customs and Excise Comrs*, supra; *National Smokeless Fuels v IRC* [1986] 3 CMLR 227.
17 [1982] QB 938, [1981] 3 All ER 182.
18 See now Companies Act 1985, s 36(4).
19 [1982] 3 All ER 551.

before, Lawson J considered s 9(1) of the 1972 Act,[20] which also gave effect to the First Company Law Directive. The section made a major change to the *ultra vires* doctrine of company law and provided, broadly, that in favour of a person dealing with a company in good faith acts of directors should be deemed to be within the capacity of the company to enter into, despite any limitation of their powers under the memorandum or articles of association. Lawson J had no hesitation in looking at the directive as an aid to interpretation of the section in order to conclude that the section only related to legal obligations vis-à-vis third parties and that lack of good faith included cases where it could be shown that a party could not have been unaware of the lack of *vires*. In *TCB Ltd v Gray*,[1] Browne-Wilkinson V-C considered the purpose of the directive in construing the same section which was considered by Lawson J. It is suggested that the approach of Lawson J and Browne-Wilkinson V-C was sounder than that of Lord Denning MR.

The clear current trend is for the English courts to feel free to resort to the directive, unconstrained by any prior test of ambiguity. But in *Duke v GEC Reliance Ltd*[2] the House of Lords felt unable to give Mrs Duke the protection against compulsory (and discriminatory) retirement at the age of 60, which the European Court had held that the United Kingdom was bound to afford her, and which the United Kingdom had given (but not retrospectively) to women who had the benefit of the Sex Discrimination Act 1986. Lord Templeman confirmed that:[3]

> . . . a British court will always be willing and anxious to conclude that United Kingdom law is consistent with Community law. Where an Act is passed for the purpose of giving effect to an obligation imposed by a directive or other instrument a British court will seldom encounter difficulty in concluding that the language of the Act is effective for the intended purpose.

But the relevant provisions of the Equal Pay Act 1970 and the Sex Discrimination Act 1975 were not enacted to give effect to the Equal Treatment Directive and were intended to preserve discriminatory retirement ages. The European Court's ruling in *Von Colson*[4] that the national court should interpret national legislation adopted to implement a directive so as to be in conformity with Community law did not

---

20 See now Companies Act 1985, ss 35 to 35B (as substituted by Companies Act 1989, s 108).
1 [1986] Ch 621, [1986] 1 All ER 587; affd on other grounds [1987] Ch 458n, [1988] 1 All ER 108, CA.
2 [1988] AC 618, [1988] 1 All ER 626, pp 35–36, ante.
3 [1988] AC at 638, [1988] 1 All ER at 635.
4 See above p 84.

apply because the legislation was not adopted to implement the directive, and, in the words of Lord Templeman, the case

> was no authority for the proposition that a court of a Member State must distort the meaning of a domestic statute so as to conform with Community law which is not directly applicable.[5]

This decision may be no more than an illustration of the point that the rule that legislation should be construed so as to be in conformity with international obligations is regarded exclusively as a rule of construction, whereby the court treats the legislature as having an intention not to involve the executive in a breach of the international obligations of the United Kingdom. But the rule is not really one of construction in the narrow sense, ie a rule designed to elicit the true meaning of legislation. It is really a rule of foreign relations law designed to ensure that, where possible, the legislature and the judiciary do not put the executive in a position where the United Kingdom will avoidably be in breach of its obligations under international law. But once it is regarded as a rule of construction, it follows that the application of a statute prior in time to a Community obligation which is not part of United Kingdom law (either by direct effect or incorporation) may lead to a breach of the Community obligation.[6]

IV. PRELIMINARY RULINGS BY THE EUROPEAN COURT

It was in part to deal with the disparate approaches of national legal systems to what was intended to be a common and harmonious new Community legal system that the European Court was established, and it was for this reason that the Treaties provided for a measure of co-operation between national courts and the European Court.

If a United Kingdom court is presented with a question involving (a) interpretation of the Treaties or (b) the validity or interpretation of measures taken by Community institutions, it may (and in certain circumstances, must), refer the question to the European Court.

Article 177 of the EEC Treaty[7] provides:

---

5 [1988] AC at 641, [1988] 1 All ER at 637. Contrast *Pickstone v Freemans plc* [1989] AC 66 at 123, [1988] 2 All ER 803 at 815, per Lord Templeman. See also *Clymo v Wandsworth London Borough Council* [1989] ICR 250, EAT; cf *Haughton v Olau Line (UK) Ltd* [1986] 2 All ER 47, [1986] 1 WLR 504, CA.
6 Cf Mann *Foreign Affairs in English Courts* (1986) pp 75–77, 110.
7 Cf ECSC Treaty, art 14 and Euratom Treaty, art 150. By the amended art 95 of the Rules of Procedure art 177 references in matters which do not justify a ruling in plenary session may be referred to Chambers of the Court, that is, to a court of three or five members. The proportion of cases decided by Chambers has increased under the new Rules.

The Court of Justice shall have jurisdiction to give preliminary rulings concerning:
  (a) the interpretation of this Treaty;
  (b) the validity and interpretation of acts of the institutions of the Community;
  (c) the interpretation of the statutes of bodies established by an act of the Council, where those statutes so provide.

Where such a question is raised before any court or tribunal of a member state, that court or tribunal may, if it considers that a decision on the question is necessary to enable it to give judgment, request the Court of Justice to give a ruling thereon.

Where any such question is raised in a case pending before a court or tribunal of a member state, against whose decisions there is no judicial remedy under national law, that court or tribunal shall bring the matter before the Court of Justice.

In practice references on questions of interpretation are more frequent than references on validity of acts of the Community. The grounds for invalidity will be dealt with in chapter 4,[8] and the special problems which arise in relation to preliminary rulings on validity will be discussed at the end of this chapter.[9]

Whether it is a question of interpretation or validity in each case the following conditions must be met: (i) a question of interpretation or validity must be raised in a case pending before the national court or tribunal; and (ii) the national court or tribunal must consider that a decision on the question is necessary to enable it to give judgment. It is important to note the distinction between the *power* of national courts to make references under the second paragraph of art 177, on the one hand, and the *duty* of national courts of final resort to make references under the third paragraph. In the former case the national court has a discretion; in the latter it is a matter of duty.

1 The purpose of article 177

From the point of view of the Communities themselves the object of art 177 is uniformity and harmonisation, the policy being to avoid as far as possible decisions of national courts on matters of Community law differing as between themselves and from the European Court. The first reference to the European Court under art 177 was by a Rotterdam court in 1961, and in its judgment of the following year[10] the European Court referred to the purpose of art 177 as being to

---

8 See pp 256–271, post.
9 See pp 211–214, post.
10 Case 13/61 *De Geus v Bosch* [1962] ECR 45 at 51, [1962] CMLR 1 at 27; see also Case 26/62 *Van Gend en Loos v Nederlandse Administratie der Belastingen* [1963] ECR 1 at 12, [1963] CMLR 105 at 129.

harmonise interpretation, and in 1980 it said that 'the duty of the Court of Justice under article 177 of the EEC Treaty is to supply all courts in the Community with the information on the interpretation of Community law which is necessary to enable them to settle genuine disputes which are brought before them'.[11] Where there is an obligation to refer under art 177(3) that obligation 'is based on co-operation, established with a view to ensuring the proper application and uniform interpretation of Community law in all the Member States between national courts, in their capacity as courts responsible for the application of Community law, and the Court of Justice'.[12]

Under art 177 United Kingdom judges have the power, and in some cases the duty, to make use of what Bingham J has described as the advantage enjoyed by the European Court:

> It has a panoramic view of the Community and its institutions, a detailed knowledge of the treaties and of much subordinate legislation made under them, and an intimate familiarity with the functioning of the Community market which no national judge denied the collective experience of the Court of Justice could hope to achieve.[13]

2 The national courts which may refer questions to the European Court

Article 177 refers to the power (and, in some cases, the duty)[14] of a national 'court or tribunal', the French text referring to 'une juridiction'. What is a 'court or tribunal' for the purpose of art 177 is a question to be answered by Community law and by the European Court. It does not matter whether United Kingdom law classifies the tribunal as a court for the purposes eg of contempt of court.[15]

---

11 Case 104/79 *Foglia v Novello (No 1)* [1980] ECR 745 at 760, [1981] 1 CMLR 45 at 58.
12 Case 283/81 *CILFIT Srl v Ministry of Health* [1981] ECR 3415 at 3428, [1983] 1 CMLR 472 at 489.
13 *Customs and Excise Comrs v ApS Samex* [1983] 1 All ER 1042 at 1055.
14 Whether art 177 is one of those Treaty provisions conferring direct rights is largely academic. The question can only arise if a lower court wishes to refer a matter to the European Court but refuses to do so on the ground that there is no procedural rule of United Kingdom law allowing it to do so. It could then be suggested that such a procedural rule is not necessary because of the direct applicability or effect of art 177. This is not likely to arise in practice. Several tribunals (from magistrates' courts to the House of Lords) have made references without express statutory authority. See p 183, post. As will be shown below, the European Court once seised of a case under art 177 does not concern itself with whether the national court had the right under *national law* to refer a question under art 177.
15 See for a recent example *Pickering v Liverpool Daily Post and Echo Newspapers plc* [1990] 1 All ER 335, CA (mental health review tribunal a 'court' for contempt purposes).

The problem has arisen mainly in relation to administrative tribunals, statutory disciplinary tribunals and arbitration tribunals. The principles for determining whether a body is a court or tribunal for the purposes of art 177 may be summarised as follows: first, whether a body is a court or tribunal for this purpose is a question of Community law, and it does not matter that it is not so classified under national law; second, the following factors are relevant: whether its members are appointed, or its rules of procedure are regulated, by the state; whether it has compulsory jurisdiction over disputes; whether it must apply legal principles; and whether parties have the right to be legally represented.

(i) Administrative tribunals

One of the first cases under art 177 was a reference made by the Dutch Tariefcommissie, which is an administrative tribunal. The European Court had no hesitation in dealing with the case on the basis that the tribunal was a court within the meaning of art 177.[16] In the leading decision,[17] the reference was made by the Dutch Arbitration Tribunal of the Mine Employees' Fund, which was hearing a widow's claim to be reinstated as a member of the Fund. The defendant in the case before the tribunal was the Mine Employees' Fund, a Dutch social security organisation of a private nature. In the reference under art 177 the defendant questioned the power of the Arbitration Tribunal to refer to the European Court, on the ground that it was not a court within the meaning of art 177. It was accepted on all sides (including the Dutch Government and the Commission in their observations) that the question was not whether Dutch law classified the body as a tribunal but whether it had such a character from the standpoint of Community law. In finding that the tribunal was a court within the meaning of art 177, the European Court emphasised (a) that the power to nominate the members of the tribunal and lay down rules of procedure was in the hands of a Government Minister, (b) that the tribunal was a permanent body which was charged with the settlement of disputes[18] and followed a procedure in which full argument was given on both sides similar to that used by ordinary

---

16 Case 26/62 *Van Gend en Loos v Nederlandse Administratie der Belastingen* [1963] ECR 1 at 10, [1963] CMLR 105 at 128.
17 Case 61/65 *Vaassen v Beambtenfonds Mijnbedrijf* [1966] ECR 261, [1966] CMLR 508.
18 Case 318/85 *Greis Unterweger* [1986] ECR 955 (reference by 'Consultative Commission' charged with delivering reasoned opinions to Italian Treasury on sanctions for exchange control violations; inadmissible because function of Commission was not to resolve disputes but to submit opinions in administrative proceedings).

courts of law, and (c) that it was bound to apply rules of law of a public law character.[19]

For the United Kingdom the implications of this decision were far-reaching because of the very large number of administrative tribunals daily at work in the United Kingdom. As a result any such tribunal with powers and procedure of a judicial character may in theory refer a question of Community law to the Court. A glance at any of the leading textbooks on administrative law[20] will reveal the complexity and the diversity of the appeals procedure, the vastness of the case law on which bodies have a duty to act judicially and other similar problems. The case law on which bodies in the United Kingdom are under a duty to act judicially is derived from a diversity of sources: the prerogative orders of certiorari and prohibition issued to such bodies; privilege pertains to judicial acts and words spoken in judicial proceedings; and there are many others.[1] The tests include the consideration of whether the body issues an order which has conclusive effect; whether it observes rules of procedure rather like ordinary courts. But from the point of view of the European Court it is likely that any public body, which has any of the characteristics of what in the United Kingdom would be regarded as an administrative tribunal bound to apply rules of law, will have the power to refer questions to the Court under art 177. The first such body to make a reference to the European Court was the National Insurance Commissioner (now the Social Security Commissioner) who acts as an administrative tribunal and is legally qualified and equivalent in rank to a circuit judge,[2] and he has since made several references.[3] Other tribunals

---

19 See also, on the Dutch Council of State, Case 36/73 *Nederlandse Spoorwegen v Minister Verkeer en Waterstaat* [1973] ECR 1299 at 1317–20, [1974] 2 CMLR 148 at 154–8. There are decisions of the Court in cases involving unusual procedures which were held or assumed to be within art 177: see eg Case 32/74 *Haaga* [1974] ECR 1201, [1975] 1 CMLR 32 (Germany: objection raised in non-contentious proceedings before Registrar of Companies); Case 70/77 *Simmenthal v Amministrazione delle Finanze dello Stato* [1978] ECR 1453, [1978] 3 CMLR 670 (Italy: one of several cases involving *ex parte* proceedings before the Pretore, on which see Case 104/79 *Foglia v Novello (No 1)* [1980] ECR 745 at 767–8, [1981] 2 CMLR 45 at 54–5, per Warner AG; Case 14/86 *Pretore di Salò v X* [1987] ECR 2545, [1989] 1 CMLR 71; Case 338/85 *Fratelli Pardini SpA v Ministry of Foreign Trade* 21 April 1988; cf Case 199/82 *Amministrazione delle Finanze dello Stato v San Giorgio SpA* [1983] ECR 3595, [1985] 2 CMLR 658).
20 See Wade *Administrative Law* (6th edn 1988) ch 23.
1 Ibid pp 630 et seq.
2 See Case 17/76 *Brack v Insurance Officer* [1976] ECR 1429, [1976] 2 CMLR 592.
3 For recent examples see Case 384/85 *Clarke v Chief Adjudication Officer* [1987] ECR 2865, [1987] 3 CMLR 277; Case 377/85 *Burchell v Adjudication Officer* [1987] ECR 3329, [1987] 3 CMLR 757.

which have made references include the Special Commissioners for Income Tax,[4] the Employment Appeal Tribunal,[5] and the VAT Tribunal.[6]

(ii) Disciplinary tribunals

The power of professional disciplinary bodies to refer under art 177 arose in *Borker*,[7] where the Council of the Bar Association of Paris had been requested to give a ruling by a French lawyer on whether he was entitled to appear, as a matter of right under Community law, before a German court. The Council of the Bar Association referred the question of Community law to the European Court, which held that it had no jurisdiction because the Bar Association was not acting as a tribunal within the meaning of art 177, ie 'a court or tribunal which is called upon to give judgment in proceedings intended to lead to a decision of a judicial nature'. The Council was not handling a lawsuit which it had a statutory function to decide, merely a request for a declaration relating to a dispute between a member of the French bar and the courts of another member state.

In *Broekmeulen v Huisarts Registratie Commissie*[8] the European Court held that it had jurisdiction to give a ruling on a reference from the Dutch Appeal Committee for General Medical Matters. The Committee was established by the Royal Dutch Society for the Promotion of Medicine. A Dutch doctor who had been trained in Belgium was refused registration as a general practitioner in the Netherlands because he had not completed a year's training in general medicine: the registration committee decided that the directives on the mutual recognition of medical qualifications did not apply to the doctor because they applied in the Netherlands only to nationals of other member states, and the doctor was Dutch. He appealed to the Appeal Committee, which referred the question of the applicability of the directives to the European Court. The Court held that it had jurisdiction because of the following factors: first, the membership of

---

4 Case 208/80 *Lord Bruce of Donington v Aspden* [1981] ECR 2205, [1981] 3 CMLR 506; Case 44/84 *Hurd v Jones (Inspector of Taxes)* [1986] ECR 29, [1986] 2 CMLR 1.
5 Case 19/81 *Burton v British Railways Board* [1982] ECR 555, [1982] 2 CMLR 136; Case 96/80 *Jenkins v Kingsgate (Clothing Productions) Ltd* [1981] ECR 911, [1981] 2 CMLR 24; Case 192/85 *Newstead v Department of Transport* [1987] ECR 4753, [1988] 1 CMLR 219.
6 Case 5/84 *Direct Cosmetics Ltd v Customs and Excise Comrs* [1985] ECR 617, [1985] 2 CMLR 145; Cases 138–139/86 *Direct Cosmetics Ltd v Customs and Excise Comrs* [1988] 3 CMLR 333. For reference by Patents Court see Case 238/87 *AB Volvo v Erik Veng (UK) Ltd* [1989] 4 CMLR 122.
7 Case 138/80 [1980] ECR 1975, [1980] 3 CMLR 638. See also decision referred to in Case 65/77 *Razanatsimba* [1977] ECR 2229 at 2242, [1978] 1 CMLR 246 at 250.
8 Case 246/80 [1981] ECR 2311, [1982] 1 CMLR 91.

the Appeal Committee showed considerable involvement by the Dutch public authorities, who nominated one-third of its membership (and also approved its rules of procedure); second, under its rules it made decisions after full argument on both sides, and an appellant was entitled to be legally represented; third, a doctor who wished to practise could not do so without recognition and registration by the Society and accordingly a general practitioner who wished to invoke rights given to him by Community law was obliged to use its appeal procedure; fourth, there was some doubt whether the ordinary Dutch courts had the power to review a decision of the Appeal Committee. Although under Dutch law the Appeal Committee was not a judicial body, it followed that[9]

> in the absence, in practice, of any right of appeal to the ordinary courts, the Appeals Committee, which operates with the consent of the public authorities and with their co-operation, and which, after an adversarial procedure, delivers decisions which are in fact recognised as final, must, in a matter involving the application of Community law, be considered as a court or tribunal of a Member State within the meaning of article 177 of the Treaty.

In the United Kingdom there are many professional disciplinary authorities, but many of these, such as the Law Society, would not be entitled to refer, since they lack many of the characteristics which the European Court thought were relevant, including state involvement in their membership or rules, and absence of a right of recourse to the courts.[10]

(iii) Arbitral tribunals

Although the tribunal in the *Vaassen* case was described in the Netherlands as an arbitration tribunal it was really an administrative tribunal, and it was recognised in that case that the European Court was not being asked to decide the power of arbitrators in general to refer. In the United Kingdom, as elsewhere, arbitrators may be appointed by the parties, or by professional associations or arbitral institutions, or by statutory authority.[11] Although those appointed by statute may have the power to refer, it is now clear that private arbitrators appointed pursuant to agreement between the parties (and whether they are appointed by the parties or by some body chosen by the parties for that purpose) do not have the power to refer. In *Nordsee v Reederei Mond*[12] three German shipping groups were parties to a joint venture for the building of factory-ships for fishing; they entered into an agreement to share and receive aid from Community funds; a

---

9 [1981] ECR at 2328, [1982] 1 CMLR at 113.
10 On these tribunals see Wade *Administrative Law* (6th edn 1988) p 647.
11 See, eg *R v National Joint Council for the Craft of Dental Technicians, ex p Neate* [1953] 1 QB 704, [1953] 1 All ER 327.
12 Case 102/81 [1982] ECR 1095. See Bebr (1985) 22 CML Rev 489.

dispute arose as to whether the sharing agreement was lawful; the agreement contained an arbitration clause, and the dispute was referred to an arbitrator appointed by the Bremen Chamber of Commerce. The arbitrator referred to the European Court for guidance, not only on the Community law relating to the aids in question, but also on whether he was entitled to refer to the European Court under art 177, as an arbitrator bound to decide according to law and whose decision was as binding on the parties as a judgment of a court. In deciding that it had no jurisdiction to give a ruling the European Court relied on the following factors: first, the parties had voluntarily agreed to their disputes being settled by arbitration, and there was no obligation on them to go to arbitration; second, the German public authorities were not involved in the arbitral process. Therefore 'the link between the arbitration procedure in this instance and the organisation of legal remedies through the courts in the Member State in question is not sufficiently close for the arbitration to be considered as a "court or tribunal" within the meaning of Article 177'.[13] But the Court emphasised that if a question of Community law arose in an arbitration the ordinary courts might be called upon to examine them either in the context of collaboration with arbitration tribunals, eg in order to interpret the relevant law or in the course of a review of the award on an appeal or an application to set aside. In such cases the national court (but not the arbitrator) would have to consider whether or not to make a reference under art 177.

In England the power of the courts to review decisions of arbitrators is now regulated by the Arbitration Act 1979.[14] Unless the parties have validly excluded the power of the court to grant leave to appeal from the award of an arbitrator, the court may grant leave to appeal if a question of law arises which could substantially affect the rights of one of the parties, and the House of Lords has held that normally the court should not grant leave unless there is a strong prima facie case that the arbitrator has come to a wrong conclusion.[15] But in *Bulk Oil (Zug) AG v Sun International Ltd*[16] the Court of Appeal recognised that the strict application of the test laid down by the House of Lords on an application to the High Court for leave to appeal against a decision of an arbitrator on a point of Community law might result in a situation where the English court could not adequately comply with the direction of the European Court in *Nordsee*, that it should, as supervisor of arbitration proceedings, ensure the observance of Community law. In this case Sun International had agreed to sell North Sea crude oil to

---

13 [1982] ECR at 1110–11.
14 On which see Mustill & Boyd *Commercial Arbitration* (2nd edn 1989) pp 600–611.
15 *Pioneer Shipping Ltd v BTP Tioxide Ltd* [1982] AC 724, [1981] 2 All ER 1030.
16 [1984] 1 All ER 386, [1984] 1 WLR 147, CA.

Bulk Oil. On loading it appeared that the destination of the oil was Israel and the sellers refused to load the oil, relying on a contractual term that the destination had to be 'in line with exporting country's government policy', on the basis that the United Kingdom government policy precluded the export of North Sea crude oil to Israel. The buyers contended that the United Kingdom policy was void under EEC law. The arbitrator held in favour of the sellers. The question before the Court of Appeal was whether leave should be granted to appeal against the award of the arbitrator under the Arbitration Act 1979. It held that Bingham J was right to exercise his discretion to grant leave to appeal, as a prelude to the Commercial Court making a reference under art 177,[17] on the basis that the point of Community law involved was 'capable of serious argument'.

Finally, it should be noted that provided the tribunal is one which may refer under art 177, the European Court will not question whether it was properly constituted or whether it observed its own rules of procedure.[18]

3 The national courts which must make references under article 177

Article 177(3) provides that where the question is raised before a court or tribunal 'against whose decisions there is no judicial remedy under national law' that court *shall* bring the matter before the European Court. Three major questions have arisen on the effect and scope of this obligation. The first relates to the identification of the tribunal of last resort; the second relates to whether the obligation applies in all cases, or only where the court of last resort is giving a final decision; and the third question is whether the obligation applies even if the point of Community law raised is clear, the question of 'acte clair'.

(i) *Identification of the final court*

The identification of the final court is initially a matter of national law, but ultimately it is for Community law to determine the principles on which the identification must be made. An initial question is whether it means the court or courts in the national legal system against whose decisions there is *never* a right of recourse, or the court from whose decisions there is no right of recourse in the particular case. Although the wording of art 177(3) may favour the former view, it is the latter view which is more consistent with common sense and with the policy of ensuring uniform interpretation of Community law. The point

---

17 Which was subsequently done: [1984] 1 Lloyd's Rep 531, [1984] 2 CMLR 91; Case 174/84 [1986] ECR 559, [1986] 2 CMLR 732, [1986] 2 All ER 774.
18 Case 65/81 *Reina v Landeskreditbank Baden-Württemberg* [1982] ECR 33, [1982] CMLR 744.

arises most obviously in cases where the right of appeal is subject to the permission of a higher court, or where the right of appeal from inferior courts is limited or excluded. The case law of the European Court suggests strongly that the relevant court for the purpose of art 177(3) is the highest court in the case, rather than the highest court in the country. In *Costa v ENEL*[19] the reference was by an Italian magistrate in a case involving less than £2, and under Italian law there was no right of appeal from a decision of the magistrate because the amount in issue was so small. The European Court indicated that 'the present case' was one under art 177(3), ie that the magistrate was a tribunal 'against whose decisions [in such a case] there is no judicial remedy under national law'. The cases which show that art 177(3) does not apply to interlocutory decisions, even of the highest courts, to be discussed below[20] are only explicable on the basis that the relevant court is the final court *in the case*.

In England non-appealable decisions may arise both at interlocutory stages, and after trial. If a plaintiff seeks and obtains an interlocutory injunction pending trial and the action proceeds to trial, non-appealable decisions may arise at the following stages:

(a) on the hearing of the injunction by the Court of Appeal if it refuses leave to appeal to the House of Lords and the House of Lords Appeal Committee subsequently refuses leave to appeal;
(b) on the hearing of the striking out application by the judge if he refuses leave to appeal and the Court of Appeal subsequently also refuses leave to appeal;
(c) after the hearing of the final trial, by the Court of Appeal if it refuses leave to appeal and the House of Lords Appeal Committee subsequently also refuses leave to appeal.

The question arises how the court of last resort is to be identified when there is a system by which an appeal court may be asked for (and may grant or refuse) leave to appeal. Let it be assumed that at the final trial of the action, the judge decides a question of interpretation of the Treaty without referring to the European Court; there is an automatic right of appeal to the Court of Appeal of which the losing party takes advantage; the Court of Appeal affirms the judgment of the trial judge, but gives leave to appeal to the House of Lords. Clearly, in these circumstances it is the House of Lords which is the final appellate court. But if the Court of Appeal refuses leave to appeal, what then? No practical problem arises if the House of Lords itself gives leave to appeal and hears the appeal, because it thereby becomes the final court of appeal. But what if the House of Lords refuses leave to

---

19 Case 6/64 [1964] ECR 585, [1964] CMLR 425.
20 See pp 189–194, post.

appeal? So far as the House of Lords is concerned, it cannot refer the case to the European Court, because it has refused to hear the case and it is not empowered by the law of the United Kingdom merely to refer cases to the European Court without the appeal actually taking place,[1] but the Court of Appeal has placed it out of its hands to refer the case to the European Court because it has delivered a final judgment. One practical way to deal with this problem is to treat the final court for the purposes of art 177(3) as being that court from which there is no appeal as of right. Alternatively, the highest court, the House of Lords, could in theory be treated as the highest court for the purpose of art 177(3) but there could be a rule of practice whereby the court from which there was no appeal as of right would always make any necessary reference under art 177.

The view appears to have become established in England that the relevant court for the purpose of art 177(3) is the court which, in theory, is the court of last resort, even if leave to appeal to that court is required. In *Bulmer v Bollinger*[2] Lord Denning MR clearly thought that it was the House of Lords, and only the House of Lords, which was the final court within the meaning of art 177(3) and his judgment implies that in most cases *only* the House of Lords should refer cases to the European Court. He did not advert to the problem raised by the necessity for leave to appeal. All Stephenson LJ added was that the Court of Appeal did not have to decide whether the absence of any right of appeal from the Court of Appeal without leave would ever bring it within art 177(3). In *Hagen v Fratelli D and G Moretti SNC*[3] Buckley LJ indicated, obiter, that the ultimate court for the purposes of art 177(3) was, in England, the Court of Appeal if leave to appeal to the House of Lords 'was not obtainable', or the House of Lords. But this cannot be regarded as a concluded view, since the actual decision involved the question whether pleadings could be amended. This is an interlocutory matter, and in such a case the leave of the judge or the Court of Appeal is needed to bring the matter even before the Court of Appeal. Since under English law some interlocutory proceedings may involve what is in effect a final determination of an issue (eg an application to strike out a claim or part of a pleading) the logical conclusion of Buckley LJ's suggestion would be that where the decision is an interlocutory one by English procedural notions then it is the decision of the judge at first instance which is the final decision for the purposes

---

1 Thus in *Henn and Darby v DPP* [1981] AC 850, [1981] 2 All ER 166, the House of Lords gave leave to appeal and made a reference to the European Court under art 177. See also discussion after judgment in *Re Healey's Habeas Corpus Application* [1984] 3 CMLR 575 at 584–585.
2 [1974] Ch 401 at 420, [1974] 2 All ER 1226 at 1233. See, for criticism, 8th General Report on the Activities of the European Communities (1974) p 274.
3 [1980] 3 CMLR 253 at 255.

of art 177(3). Nevertheless the thought which underlies Buckley LJ's approach is preferable to the notion that the House of Lords is the only tribunal under art 177(3), which is plainly wrong.

In *R v Pharmaceutical Society of Great Britain ex p Association of Pharmaceutical Importers*[4] Kerr LJ (with whose judgment Ralph Gibson and Russell LJJ agreed) said that the case fell within art 177(2). It was not 'a case pending before a court . . . against whose decisions there is no judicial remedy' because:

> . . . there is a judicial remedy against a decision of this Court by applying for leave to appeal to the House of Lords, first to this court and then to the House of Lords itself if necessary. A court or tribunal below the House of Lords can only fall within the last paragraph where there is no possibility of further appeal from it.

But this view can lead to odd results. In *Magnavision NV v General Optical Council*[5] the Divisional Court held that the prohibition on spectacles being sold otherwise than through a doctor or optician was not contrary to art 30 of the EEC Treaty, and dismissed an appeal against conviction under the Opticians Act 1958. The court refused to refer the matter to the European Court because the question raised was clear and a decision from the European Court was not necessary to enable the court to give judgment. Appeal lies from a decision of the Divisional Court in criminal matters only if it certifies points for consideration by the House of Lords, and there is no appeal from the refusal to certify a point of law for consideration by the House of Lords. After judgment in the case, the appellants applied for certification, and when it was refused, the appellants argued that, having in effect refused leave to appeal, the Divisional Court had become the final court for the purposes of art 177(3) and was bound to make a reference. The Divisional Court refused the application.[6] The *ex tempore* judgment is by no means free from obscurity, but the main thrust of the reasoning was that the court was *functus officio*, since 'the issues in this case have been resolved and final judgment given'.[7] It is plain that both members of the court were confident that no injustice had been done, because both thought that there was no point of interpretation for the European Court that was not acte clair.

In practice, no doubt, an intermediate court which refuses in its

---

4 [1987] 3 CMLR 951 at 969. Cf *Pickstone v Freemans plc* [1989] AC 66 at 96, [1987] 3 All ER 756 at 776, per Purchas LJ.
5 [1987] 1 CMLR 887.
6 (*No 2*) [1987] 2 CMLR 262.
7 At p 266, per Watkins LJ. The Commission has expressed the view that the court denied the plaintiff the opportunity of having the question of Community law examined by a court of final instance which was bound by art 177(3): OJ C No 310, 5 December 1988, p 44.

discretion to refer a question which may be necessary for the decision in the case, and which is not acte clair, would give leave.

In the case of other courts and tribunals, the problem may not be a purely procedural one. The legal system of the United Kingdom is replete with a myriad of different courts, and the appellate system is entirely lacking in uniformity. It will therefore be necessary in relevant cases to look very closely at the remedies by way of appeal which are open. The expression 'judicial remedy' in art 177(3) must be interpreted by Community law, and whether United Kingdom law characterises a process as an appeal is irrelevant. For example, in English law the jurisdiction of the High Court to quash a decision of an administrative tribunal on an application for certiorari by way of judicial review under Order 53 is not an appeal.[8] But the distinction between an appeal and an application for judicial review is not a distinction which the draftsman of an instrument such as the EEC Treaty could possibly have had in mind. It is possible that for the purposes of art 177 an application for judicial review should be treated as if it were an application for leave to appeal. This would mean that if there were no statutory right of appeal *stricto sensu* then the administrative tribunal might itself have to be treated as the court of last resort.[9] Particularly since the Tribunals and Inquiries Acts of 1958 and 1971, there is often a right of appeal from administrative tribunals to higher courts.[10] Although these appeals are usually limited to questions of law, it is not likely that there will be any difficulty in establishing that all of the matters provided for in art 177 are substantially matters of law and that factual questions may only arise incidentally.

It has already been shown[11] that there may be some difficulty in deciding whether a body is a court or tribunal for the purposes of art 177. Similar difficulties may arise in determining whether there is a right of appeal. For example, it may be alleged that the refusal to grant a licence is contrary to the right of freedom of establishment guaranteed by the EEC Treaty. In *Jeffrey v Evans*[12] justices granting licences were held to be a magistrates' court for the purpose of stating cases on questions for the opinion of the High Court under what is now the Magistrates' Courts Act 1980; but there is also an appeal to the Crown Court, whose decision is final.

---

8 On the distinction between appeal and review see Wade *Administrative Law* (6th edn, 1988), pp 36–38.
9 In *Re a Holiday in Italy* [1975] 1 CMLR 184, Mr J G Monroe, sitting as a national insurance commissioner, treated the availability of the writ of certiorari as indicating that the tribunal was not one against whose decisions there was no judicial remedy. See Jacobs (1977) 2 EL Rev 119.
10 See Wade *Administrative Law* pp 906 et seq.
11 See pp 144–150, ante.
12 [1964] 1 All ER 536, [1964] 1 WLR 505.

(ii) Final courts and interlocutory appeals

Two questions of general importance arise in relation to art 177 references and interlocutory proceedings in national courts for interim relief. The first is whether references can be made in such cases, since they may not involve a final determination of the merits of the case; the second question is whether a national court from which no appeal could be taken is to be regarded, in relation to a decision of an application for summary relief, as a final court within the meaning of art 177(3), and so bound to refer any question of interpretation of EEC law to the European Court. Both of these issues arose in *Hoffman-La Roche AG v Centrafarm*.[13] The European Court held, in line with its previous practice, that references could be made in interlocutory proceedings, but that there was no obligation to refer imposed even on a court of last resort where the order for interim relief was not final and could be re-opened in the subsequent proceedings on the merits. But the Court made it clear that its ruling applied only where each of the parties was entitled to institute proceedings on the substance of the case and where during such proceedings the question provisionally decided in the summary proceedings could be re-examined and made the subject of a reference to the European Court. This applies even where the court which decides on the substance may be different, as in the Netherlands in some cases, from the court which grants interim relief.[14]

In England the current practice, since *American Cyanamid v Ethicon*,[15] is that in deciding whether or not to grant interim relief the court should not normally decide, even provisionally, the merits of the case. Once the plaintiff has shown that there is a serious issue to be tried on the merits, the only questions for the court in deciding whether to grant an interlocutory injunction are whether damages, rather than injunctive relief, would be an adequate remedy, and, if not, whether the balance of convenience favours the grant of an injunction. Only at trial will the court decide the underlying merits. When a judge exercises his discretion to grant or refuse an interlocutory injunction there is an appeal as of right to the Court of Appeal, and (with leave of the Court of Appeal or the House of Lords) to the House of Lords, but it will only be rarely that the appellate court will be entitled to interfere with the exercise of the judge's discretion.[16] It

---

13 Case 107/76 [1977] ECR 957, [1977] 2 CMLR 334.
14 Cases 35 and 36/82 *Morson and Jhanjan v Netherlands* [1982] ECR 3723, [1983] 2 CMLR 221.
15 [1975] AC 396, [1975] 1 All ER 504. For exceptions to the *American Cyanamid* rule see eg *Cayne v Global Natural Resources plc* [1984] 1 All ER 225, CA; *Lawrence David Ltd v Ashton* [1989] ICR 123, CA.
16 *Hadmor Productions Ltd v Hamilton* [1983] 1 AC 191, [1982] 1 All ER 1042.

follows, therefore, from the decision in *Hoffman-La Roche AG v Centrafarm* that when the House of Lords decides an appeal on an application for an interlocutory injunction involving a question of Community law, it is not bound to make a reference under art 177 even if the question of Community law is a difficult one. This is because the question of Community law does not arise for decision at that stage. Thus in *Garden Cottage Foods Ltd v Milk Marketing Board*[17] the judge at first instance, Parker J, refused to grant an injunction to restrain what was alleged to be an abuse of a dominant position under art 86 of the EEC Treaty. He thought that damages would be an adequate remedy; and that the balance of convenience was against the grant of injunction. The Court of Appeal reversed this decision on the ground that there was some doubt whether there was a cause of action in damages for breach of art 86. The House of Lords restored the order of Parker J on the ground that it was likely, without deciding the point, that there was a cause of action in damages. The House of Lords clearly recognised that the case involved a number of difficult questions on the effect of art 86 in the case, but that it was impossible at that stage, 'and probably at any stage until after a reference under art 177'[18] to the European Court, to decide these questions.

(iii) Acte clair

In this context the principle of acte clair is that a court of final resort which would otherwise be obliged to make a reference under art 177(3) is not bound to do so when the point of European law sought to be referred by a party is clear or free from doubt. The expression acte clair derives from French law. Its origin lies in the principle that the ordinary courts must seek a ruling from the Ministry of Foreign Affairs where a question of treaty interpretation arises; but the courts have held that this principle, derived from separation of powers requirements, does not apply where the point of treaty interpretation is clear. It is not surprising, therefore, that it was the French Conseil d'Etat and the Cour de Cassation, Criminal Chamber, which were the first courts in Europe to adopt a similar principle with regard to references under art 177(3).

In *Re Shell-Berre*[19] the Conseil d'Etat was concerned with an application brought by a number of oil companies for the annulment of a ministerial decree which affected the establishment of garages selling petrol. It was suggested by the oil companies that (inter alia) the law on which the decrees were based had been affected by the EEC Treaty, in particular by art 37 which provides for the progressive

---

17 [1984] AC 130, [1983] 2 All ER 770.
18 [1984] AC at 142, [1983] 2 All ER at 776.
19 [1964] CMLR 462.

adjustment of state trading monopolies so as to remove discrimination. They argued that the French court should refer the matter under art 177 to the European Court. The Conseil d'Etat rejected the suggestion. It said:[20]

> ... it follows from the very terms of [art 177] that a national court from the decisions of which there is no possibility of appeal under domestic law, such as the Conseil d'Etat acting in its judicial capacity, is only required to stay proceedings in a case pending before it and to seise the Court of Justice of the EEC if a 'question' relating to the interpretation of the Treaty is 'raised' in that case. That could only happen in a case in which there is a doubt as to the meaning or scope of one or several clauses of the Treaty applicable to the main action and if the issue of the action depends on the settlement of this difficulty.

A similar approach was adopted by German courts. For example, they held that where the wording of art 85 was clear and its treatment by the European Court was clear, there was no need to refer to the European Court for a preliminary ruling under art 177.[1]

The European Court accepted that a national court of last resort is not under a duty to make a reference under art 177(3) if (a) the provision in question has already been interpreted by the European Court or (b) the correct application of European law is so obvious as to leave no scope for any reasonable doubt. In the *Da Costa* case[2] a Dutch administrative court had referred to the European Court under art 177 the question whether art 12 of the EEC Treaty had direct effect in national law and created individual rights which national courts were under a duty to protect. The same question had been referred to the Court in the *Van Gend en Loos*[3] litigation and had been answered in the affirmative by a judgment delivered in February 1963, which was subsequent to the reference in the *Da Costa* case. Therefore in the latter case the Court was content to refer the Dutch administrative court to its previous decision in the *Van Gend en Loos* case, and to indicate that if the Court had already

---

20 [1964] CMLR 462 at 481. Cf Cour de Cassation, Criminal Chamber, in *Re Riff* [1985] CMLR 29. See also *State v Cornet* [1967] CMLR 351 (Cour de Cassation, Criminal Chamber); *Lapeyre v Administration des Douanes* [1967] CMLR 362 at 368 (Cour de Cassation, Criminal Chamber); *Re Syndicat National des Importateurs Français en Produits Laitiers et Agricoles* [1968] CMLR 81 at 84–6 (Conseil d'Etat).
1 *Re Yoga Fruit Juices* [1969] CMLR 123 (Bundesgerichtshof). Cf *Re French Widow's Pension Settlement* [1971] CMLR 530 (Bundessozialgericht); *Re Taxation of Foreign Workers* [1977] 1 CMLR 659 (Federal Supreme Fiscal Court). For Italy see *Schiavello v Nesci* [1975] 2 CMLR 198 (Court of Cassation).
2 Cases 28–30/62 [1963] ECR 31, [1963] CMLR 224, and especially Lagrange AG [1963] ECR at 45, 1963, CMLR at 234.
3 Case 26/62 [1963] ECR 1, [1963] CMLR 105.

pronounced on a question of interpretation it might have an effect on the obligation of the national court to refer because 'the authority of an interpretation under article 177 already given by the Court may deprive the obligation of its purpose and thus empty it of its substance'.[4]

This applies not only where the question raised is 'materially identical with a question which has already been the subject of a preliminary ruling in a similar case' (the phrase in the *Da Costa* case), but also where previous decisions of the European Court have already dealt with the point of law in question, irrespective of the nature of the proceedings, even though the questions at issue are not strictly identical. This qualification was added in *CILFIT Srl v Ministry of Health*,[5] where the Italian Court of Cassation asked the European Court whether, in a case to which art 177(3) might otherwise apply because the national court concerned was a court of last resort, the obligation to refer under art 177(3) was conditional on there being some reasonable doubt about the interpretation of the Community instrument involved.

The European Court in *CILFIT* has in substance accepted the principle of acte clair. It emphasised that the purpose of art 177 in general was to ensure the proper application and uniform interpretation of Community law in all the member states and, of art 177(3) in particular, to prevent divergencies in national judicial decisions. The Court, noting the phrase in art 177(3) 'where any such question is raised', indicated that the mere fact that a party contended that the dispute gave rise to a question of interpretation of Community law did not mean that the national court was compelled to consider that a question had been raised; nor was a national court obliged to refer where a decision on the question of Community law was not 'necessary' to enable it to give judgment, ie the problem of Community law was not strictly relevant. But once the national court thought that the question of Community law was necessary then the obligation under art 177(3) arose. There were two cases in which the obligation might not arise. The Court, citing *Da Costa*, indicated that the first was where the question involved was materially identical with a question which had already been the subject of a ruling by the European Court or the point of law in question had already been answered; even in such cases national courts were entirely free to refer the question to

---

4 [1963] ECR 31 at 38, [1963] CMLR 224 at 237. See also Case 166/73 *Rheinmühlen-Düsseldorf v Einfuhr- und Vorratsstelle für Getreide* [1974] ECR 33 at 39, [1974] 1 CMLR 523 at 578.
5 Case 283/81 [1982] ECR 3415, [1983] 1 CMLR 472.

the European Court.⁶ The second case was very close to acte clair. The Court said:⁷

> ... the correct application of Community law may be so obvious as to leave no scope for any reasonable doubt as to the manner in which the question raised is to be resolved. Before it comes to the conclusion that such is the case, the national court or tribunal must be convinced that the matter is equally obvious to the courts of the other Member States and to the Court of Justice. Only if those conditions are satisfied may the national court or tribunal refrain from submitting the question to the Court of Justice and take upon itself the responsibility for resolving it.

But the Court warned that a national court, before deciding that there is no reasonable doubt, must bear the following factors in mind: (a) Community legislation is drafted in several language versions, all of which are equally authentic; the process of interpretation therefore involves a comparison of the different versions; (b) even where the different language versions are in accord, Community law uses terminology which is peculiar to it, and legal concepts do not necessarily have the same meaning in Community law as in the law of the member states; (c) every provision of Community law must be placed in its context and interpreted in the light of the provisions of Community law as a whole.

The House of Lords has adopted what is, in essence, a very similar approach to that which the European Court has recommended in the *CILFIT* case. In *Henn and Darby v DPP*⁸ the defendants had been convicted of conspiring to import pornographic material from Denmark. Their defence was that the ban on such material amounted to a quantitative restriction on imports or a measure having equivalent effect, contrary to art 30 of the EEC Treaty. The Court of Appeal, Criminal Division, dismissed their appeal against conviction on the ground (inter alia) that a total ban was not a 'quantitative' restriction, and refused to refer to the European Court. Although the decision was justified on the alternative ground that imports could be restricted on the basis of public morality under art 36, the holding that a total ban was not a quantitative restriction was contrary to the case law of the European Court. As a result the House of Lords referred to the

---

6 For such a case see Case 255/81 *Grendel GmbH v Finanzamt Hamburg* [1982] ECR 2301, where the German court persisted in its request for a ruling on a question already resolved in Case 8/81 *Becker v Finanzamt Münster-Innenstadt* [1982] ECR 53. The German Federal Constitutional Court has held that a national court cannot adopt its own view of acte clair to avoid applying a decision of the European Court: in such a case it must make a further reference setting out the considerations which lead it to doubt the European Court's view: *Re Value Added Tax Exemption* [1989] 1 CMLR 113.
7 [1982] ECR at 3430, [1983] 1 CMLR at 491.
8 [1981] AC 850, [1980] 2 All ER 166.

European Court questions designed to determine whether a total ban on pornographic articles was a measure having equivalent effect to a quantitative restriction within the meaning of art 30, and whether, if so, the ban could be justified under art 36 on the ground of public morality. After the European Court had answered in such a way that the House of Lords could determine that the ban was within art 30 but could be justified under art 36, the House of Lords delivered a sharp warning to lower courts not to be too eager to treat a question of interpretation as clear, and also indicated that it would not itself necessarily refrain from referring to the European Court even if the answer to the question seemed clear. Lord Diplock said:[9]

> in the light of this established case law of the European Court, it appeared to me to be so free from any doubt that an absolute prohibition of importation of goods of a particular description from other member states fell within article 30 that I should not have been disposed to regard the instance case as involving any matter of interpretation of that article that was open to question. But the strong inclination expressed by the Court of Appeal to adopt the contrary view shows that there is involved a question of interpretation on which judicial minds can differ. It serves as a timely warning to English judges not to be too ready to hold that because the meaning of the English text (which is one of six of equal authority) seems plain to them no question of interpretation can be involved. It was for this reason that your Lordships thought it proper to submit to the European Court for a preliminary ruling the question as to the interpretation of article 30 which is set out hereafter: it was not through any doubts upon your Lordships' part as to the answer that would be received.

In *Garland v British Rail Engineering Ltd*[10] Lord Diplock indicated that the reference to the European Court on the equal pay obligations in relation to free travel facilities after retirement had been made by the House of Lords not because any of the members of the House 'had any serious doubt what answer would be given to that question by the European Court' but because there was not in existence at the date when the reference was made

> so considerable and consistent a line of case law of the European Court of Justice on the interpretation and direct applicability of article 119, as would make the answer too obvious and inevitable to be capable of giving rise to what could properly be regarded as a 'question' within the meaning of article 177.

---

9 [1981] AC 850 at 906.
10 [1983] 2 AC 751, [1982] 2 All ER 402.

As a result, Lord Diplock said, 'It thus became mandatory on this House, as a court from whose decisions there is no possibility of appeal under internal law, to refer to the European Court . . .'[11]

There are of course inherent dangers in the acte clair doctrine. If misused it can lead to the misapplication or non-application of Community law by national courts, and it involves the danger that its effect is 'to deprive the third paragraph of article 177 of any meaning'.[12] In the *Cohn-Bendit*[13] case the French Conseil d'Etat not only held, contrary to several decisions of the European Court, that a directive could not have direct effect but also refused to refer the question whether it had direct effect to the European Court. As a result the Commission's view is that where a national court is in breach of its obligation to refer under art 177, the member state may itself be in breach of its obligations under the treaty and therefore subject to a complaint by the Commission under art 169. In 1987 the German Federal Constitutional Court said that:

> . . . the breach of the obligation under Community law to seek a ruling may give rise to the danger of the German Federal Republic incurring liability under the law of treaties. Although not every erroneous disregard by a German court of the obligation to seek a ruling will amount to a breach of the EEC Treaty by the German Federal Republic, in the case of a fundamental misconception or deliberate disregard of a duty to seek a ruling arising in a particular case such a danger cannot be dismissed out of hand.[14]

But the Commission has made it clear that it would only contemplate such action where a court of last instance of a member state has shown that it is systematically and deliberately unprepared to comply with art 177.[15] The Commission's view is that the procedure under art 169 is not likely to enhance the co-operation between the national courts and the European Court. For that reason, the Commission endeavours to induce the member states to ensure, by the enactment of legislation or by administrative means, that Community law is respected.[16]

In its 1989 report to the European Parliament on its monitoring of the application of Community law, the Commission indicated that it had commenced infringement proceedings against France in connection with a 1986 decision in which the Cour de Cassation had

---

11 [1983] 2 AC at 771–2, 1982 2 All ER at 415.
12 [1982] ECR at 3437, per Capotorti AG.
13 See p 94, ante, and see Bebr (1983) 20 CML Rev 439.
14 *Re Patented Feedingstuffs* [1989] 2 CMLR 902 at 909.
15 OJ C No 268, 6 October 1983, p 25.
16 Eg OJ C No 310, 5 December 1988, pp 43–44, where two decisions in 1987 of the French Conseil d'Etat are also criticised for undue application of the acte clair doctrine.

misapplied customs regulations and refused to make a reference to the European Court.[17]

4 The questions which may be referred

Article 177 lists the questions on which preliminary rulings may be given (only the first two of which are likely to be of substantial practical importance):

'(a) the interpretation of this Treaty;
 (b) the validity and interpretation of acts of the institutions of the Community;
 (c) the interpretation of the statutes of bodies established by an act of the Council, where those statutes so provide.'

The expression 'acts of the institutions of the Community' primarily includes regulations, decisions[18] and directives but it also includes treaties entered into by the Community or treaties concluded by member states to which it has succeeded.[19] But not all agreements concluded under the auspices of the Community are subject to the jurisdiction of art 177. Thus in *Hurd v Jones*[20] the questions referred by the Special Commissioners of Income Tax related to whether the United Kingdom could tax the English headmaster of the European School in England on a European Supplement paid by the School out of general funds provided by the Commission. The European Court held that it had jurisdiction to decide whether the member state could tax the European Supplement; but that it did not have jurisdiction to interpret the constituent documents of the European School and of its Board of Governors, because the European Schools were set up, not on the basis of the treaties establishing the Communities or on the basis of measures adopted by the Community institutions, but on the basis of international agreements concluded by the member states. The mere fact that the agreements were linked to the Community and to the functioning of its institutions did not mean that they were to be

---

17 *Sixth Annual Report*, not yet published.
18 But not decisions of the European Court: see Case 69/85 *Wünsche v Germany* [1986] ECR 947, p 210, post.
19 Case 181/73 *Haegeman Sprl v Belgium* [1974] ECR 449, [1975] 1 CMLR 515; Case 87/75 *Bresciani v Amministrazione Italiana delle Finanze* [1976] ECR 129, [1976] 2 CMLR 62; Case 104/81 *Hauptzollamt Mainz v CA Kupferberg & Cie KG* [1982] ECR 3641, [1983] 1 CMLR 1; Cases 21 to 24/72 *International Fruit Co NV v Produktschap voor Groenten en Fruit* [1972] ECR 1219, [1975] 2 CMLR 1; Case 266/81 *Soc Italiana per l'Oleodotto Transalpino v Ministero delle Finanze* [1983] ECR 731 at 788, [1984] 2 CMLR 231 at 241 per Reischl AG; Cases 267–269/81 *Amministrazione delle Finanze dello Stato v Società Petrolifera Italiana SpA* [1983] ECR 801, [1984] 1 CMLR 354; Case 12/86 *Demirel v Stadt Schwäbisch Gmünd* [1989] 1 CMLR 421. See also pp 67–69, ante.
20 Case 44/84 [1986] ECR 29, [1986] 2 CMLR 1.

regarded as an integral part of Community law, the uniform interpretation of which fell within the jurisdiction of the European Court. Nor could the Court rule on the interpretation of the uniform agreement concluded by the national bureaux of motor vehicle insurers (the green card scheme), which was entered into to comply with a Council directive on motor vehicle licence laws. The agreement was a measure adopted by a private association and was not an act of a Community institution, since no Community institution took part in its conclusion. This result was not affected by the fact that the agreement was a precondition of the entry into force of the Council directive, or that one of the relevant agreements was annexed to a Commission decision and published in the Official Journal.[1]

The question of what may be referred to the European Court is a question of Community law, and the Court has laid down rules in relation to the application of art 177 which have a dual function: in the first place, they are a self-imposed restraint on the scope of preliminary rulings; in the second place, they are capable of being used as guidelines for national courts in the formulation of the questions for the European Court. These rules are as follows:

1. The European Court will normally accept the national court's determination that the question of interpretation which has been referred is relevant to the outcome of the national proceedings.
2. The European Court will interpret the provisions of the Treaty but will not apply its interpretation to the facts of the case.
3. The European Court will not interpret national law nor rule on its compatibility with Community law.

In practice, the general nature of these rules is such as to make their specific application a matter of some difficulty. But they play an important role in the context of the co-operation between the European Court and the national courts which is the basis of art 177. So important are they that the Court has reasserted them in many references from national courts under art 177.

(i) *Relevance*

In one of the first references under art 177, *Van Gend en Loos*,[2] which concerned the direct effect of art 12 of the EEC Treaty in relation to a Dutch customs duty, the governments which submitted observations argued that the European Court did not have jurisdiction to receive the reference because any answer it could give to the question would

---

1 Case 152/83 *Demouche v Fonds de Garantie Automobile* [1987] ECR 3833.
2 Case 26/62 [1963] ECR 1, [1963] CMLR 105.

not be relevant to the disposition of the action before the Dutch court. The European Court rejected the argument by pointing out:[3]

> in order to confer jurisdiction on the Court in the present case, it is necessary only that the question posed should clearly be concerned with the interpretation of the Treaty. The considerations which may have led a national court or tribunal to its choice of questions as well as the relevance which it attributes to such questions in the context of a case before it are excluded from review by the Court of Justice.

What this means in practice is that a finding by a national court that 'it considers that a decision on the question is necessary to enable it to give judgment' is not reviewable by the European Court except in the case of manifest error, and the Court will not criticise a national court for making a reference.[4] Thus in one case the Court refused to accept the arguments of the parties that the question of Community law referred by the national court bore no relation to the dispute and should not be answered. The request should only be rejected 'if it is quite obvious that the interpretation of Community law . . . sought by [the national] court bears no relation to the actual nature of the case or to the subject matter of the main action'.[5] In one recent case an Italian court referred some questions in proceedings brought by doctors whose contracts had been terminated by the Italian health service. In those proceedings the doctors alleged that they had been dismissed because of the excessive number of doctors qualifying in Italy, and that the oversupply was caused by the absence of a *numerus clausus* limiting the number of medical students. The Italian court asked the European Court whether the absence of the *numerus clausus* was contrary to Community law. The European Court found it impossible to determine either from the documents or the facts what use the questions had for the purpose of the national proceedings, but nevertheless the Court decided that it should deal with the questions and respect the assessment by the national court that the answers were necessary.[6] But where a Belgian court had based its request for a preliminary ruling on an obvious misapprehension of a French social

---

3 [1963] ECR at 11.
4 Case 13/68 *Salgoil SpA v Italy* [1968] ECR 453, [1969] CMLR 181. See also Case 106/77 *Amministrazione delle Finanze dello Stato v Simmenthal SpA* [1978] ECR 629, [1978] 3 CMLR 263; among many other examples see also Case 6/64 *Costa v ENEL* [1964] ECR 585, [1964] CMLR 425; Case 43/71 *Politi SAS v Ministero delle Finanze* [1971] ECR 1039, [1973] CMLR 60; Case 53/79 *Office National des Pensions pour Travailleurs Salariés v Damiani* [1980] ECR 273, [1981] 1 CMLR 548; Case 180/83 *Moser v Land Baden-Württemberg* [1984] ECR 2539, [1984] 3 CMLR 720; Case 126/86 *Giménez Zaera v Instituto Nacional de la Seguridad Social* [1987] ECR 3697, [1989] 1 CMLR 827.
5 Case 126/80 *Salonia v Podomani and Giglio* [1981] ECR 1563 at 1576–7, [1982] 1 CMLR 64 at 76.
6 Cases 98 etc/85 *Bertini v Regione Lazio* [1986] ECR 1885, [1987] 1 CMLR 774.

security decision, the European Court held that the question lacked any purpose and that no reply need be given to it.[7]

(ii) *Interpretation and application*

In each of the cases in the famous early trilogy of references under art 177 the European Court emphasised that its duty was to interpret the relevant Community law, and not to apply it to the facts. In *De Geus v Bosch*[8] the Court made it clear that it would not engage in fact finding in art 177 references, and was therefore unable to decide whether the export prohibitions imposed in that case by the German manufacturer on its buyers were agreements prohibited by the restrictive practices provisions of art 85 and in particular whether they were liable to affect trade between member states.

The Court, however, has been extremely liberal in its treatment of references under art 177 and if a question has prima facie appeared to be a question of fact the Court has in most cases rephrased it so as to raise a question of interpretation. Thus the second question in the *Van Gend en Loos* case was whether the duty imposed by the Dutch authorities was an increase or merely a modification in customs duties. If the question were put in this way, the Court said:[9]

> The question clearly does not call for an interpretation of the Treaty but concerns the application of Netherlands customs legislation to the classification of aminoplasts, which is outside the jurisdiction conferred upon the Court of Justice of the European Communities by subparagraph (a) of the first paragraph of article 177. The Court has therefore no jurisdiction to consider the reference made by the Tariefcommissie.

But the Court was anxious not to weaken its power to interpret Community law and it therefore rephrased the question by going on to hold:

> However, the real meaning of the question put by the Tariefcommissie is whether, in law, an effective increase in customs duties charged on a given product as a result not of an increase in the rate but of a new classification of the product arising from a change of its tariff description contravenes the prohibition in article 12 of the Treaty. Viewed in this way the question put is concerned with an interpretation of this provision of the Treaty and more particularly of the meaning which should be given to the concept of duties applied before the Treaty entered into force. Therefore the Court has jurisdiction to give a ruling on this question.

In *Costa v ENEL*[10] the Court re-emphasised that art 177:

---

7 Case 132/81 *Rijksdienst voor Werknemerspensionen v Vlaeminck* [1982] ECR 2953.
8 Case 13/61 [1962] ECR 45, [1962] CMLR 1.
9 [1963] ECR 1 at 14.
10 Case 6/64 [1964] ECR 585 at 592–3, [1964] CMLR 425 at 454–5.

gives the Court no jurisdiction either to apply the Treaty to a specific case or to decide upon the validity of a provision of domestic law in relation to the Treaty, as it would be possible for it to do under article 169. Nevertheless, the Court has power to extract from a question imperfectly formulated by the national court those questions which alone pertain to the interpretation of the Treaty.

These decisions have been applied in many subsequent cases. An example will show the principle in operation. In the *Perfume* cases[11] the French court submitted exclusive dealing agreements entered into by the perfume companies so that the European Court could decide whether they were entitled to exemption under art 85(3). The Court pointed out that it could not apply Community law to the case but was prepared to extract from the file the main point of Community law involved, namely the effect of 'comfort letters' sent by the Commission indicating that they would take no further action under art 85.

But the distinction between interpretation and application is an elusive one, and there are many answers on preliminary rulings which look very much like an application of Community law to the facts. Where a question of Community law is phrased very specifically, the national court may have little to do except mechanically apply the answer. For example the questions put to the European Court by English courts on equal pay were generally phrased with great precision, so that it would be obvious what the outcome of the case would be once the answer was given. In *Macarthys Ltd v Smith*[12] the European Court held that art 119 was not confined to cases where male and female employees worked contemporaneously and this effectively decided the case;[13] in *Garland v British Rail Engineering Ltd*[14] the question put by the House of Lords was whether an employer who provided special travel facilities for former employees which discriminate against female employees acted contrary to Community law: the European Court answered that this constituted discrimination under art 119.

(iii) Compatibility of national law with Community law

It has been well established since *Costa v ENEL* that the European Court may not, in art 177 references (by contrast with proceedings under art 169) decide upon the compatibility of national legislation

---

11 Cases 253/78 and 1–3/79 *Procureur de la République v Giry and Guerlain SA* [1980] ECR 2327, [1981] 2 CMLR 99. See also Cases 36 and 71/80 *Irish Creamery Milk Suppliers Association v Ireland* [1981] ECR 735, [1981] 2 CMLR 455; Case 188/86 *Ministère Public v Lefèvre* [1987] ECR 2963.
12 Case 129/79 [1980] ECR 1275, [1980] 2 CMLR 205.
13 See *Macarthys Ltd v Smith (No 2)* [1981] 1 All ER 111 at 120.
14 Case 12/81 [1982] ECR 359, [1982] 1 CMLR 696.

with Community law, and there are many cases which reaffirm this principle. This is because there has been a strong tendency for national courts to ask specifically whether a piece of legislation offends against Community law. The reaction of the European Court has usually been to rephrase the question in a more abstract fashion. Thus in *Boussac Saint-Frères SA v Gerstenmeier*[15] a German court asked whether a rule of German procedure, that summary relief was not available for claims against German residents in foreign currency, was contrary to art 7 as discriminating against foreign creditors of German residents. The European Court said that it could not express an opinion on the validity of the German rule but was able to extract from the question the aspects of Community law which were relevant for the purposes of interpretation: it ruled that art 7 did not preclude a rule of procedure whereby summary relief was not available in such cases.

By contrast, more recently an Italian magistrate asked the European Court whether the Italian law on protection of waters from pollution was consistent with the principles and objectives of a Council directive on the quality of fresh waters. The European Court referred to the fact that it had consistently held that, in art 177 references, it could not rule on the compatibility of national measures with Community law; it repeated that it could extract from the questions formulated by the national court the aspects of Community law which required interpretation, but in that case, in view of the generality of the question and the absence of any specific elements which would make it possible to identify the doubts entertained by the national court, it was not possible to reply to the question.[16]

It is clear that the distinction between interpretation of Community law and ruling on the validity of national law is as elusive as the distinction between interpretation and application. Two examples relating to the compatibility of United Kingdom law with Community law will make the point clear. In *R v Henn and Darby*[17] the House of Lords asked (inter alia) whether a law which prohibited the import of pornographic articles was a measure having equivalent effect to a quantitative restriction on imports prohibited by art 30 of the EEC Treaty. The Court answered in the affirmative, although it also held that a member state could, under art 36, lawfully impose restrictions on pornography. The difference between this holding and a holding that the United Kingdom legislation was compatible with EEC law is entirely academic. In *Union Laitière Normande v French Dairy*

---

15 Case 22/80 [1980] ECR 3427, [1982] 1 CMLR 202.
16 Case 14/86 *Pretore di Salò v X* [1987] ECR 2545, [1989] 1 CMLR 71; see also Cases 91 and 127/83 *Heineken Brouwerijen BV v Inspecteur der Vennootschapsbelasting* [1984] ECR 3435, [1985] 1 CMLR 389; Case 98/86 *Ministère Public v Mathot* [1987] ECR 809, [1988] 1 CMLR 411.
17 Case 34/79 [1979] ECR 3795, [1980] 1 CMLR 246.

Farmers Ltd[18] a French agricultural co-operative consigned UHT milk to its English subsidiary in one-litre packages; the United Kingdom authorities refused their importation because the packages were not fractions or multiples of a pint, and the French parent sued its English subsidiary in a *French* court in order to test the compatibility of the United Kingdom import licence regulations with the EEC Treaty. The French court referred questions to the European Court designed to help it determine this question. In particular, it asked whether United Kingdom weights and measures legislation which required UHT milk to be packed in fractions or multiples of a pint constituted a means of arbitrary discrimination or disguised restriction on trade prohibited by art 36. The Court, in accordance with its usual practice, did not answer the question directly, but ruled expressly that, until the time for implementation of a Council Directive on weights and measures had expired, the maintenance in force of the Weights and Measures Act 1963 in relation to the imports in question was not prohibited by Community law. It is not easy to see how such a ruling is consistent with the principle that the Court will not rule in art 177 references on the validity of national law.

A question which was not considered in the *Union Laitière* case was whether a national court could rule on the validity under Community law of the legislation of another member state. In that case the dispute had, no doubt, been artificially constructed[19] so that it could be decided in a French court: the natural forum was clearly the English court, where the English subsidiary could have contested the refusal of the import licence. One of the questions which arose in *Foglia v Novello (No 2)* was whether a national court (in the case, the Italian court) which was considering the compatibility of the legislation of another member state (France) with Community law should order the joinder of the other member state in the national proceedings. The European Court held that whether this was possible was a matter for the lex fori but that the principles of public international law must also be taken into account. No doubt, like Advocate General Slynn, the Court had in mind considerations of sovereign immunity, and perhaps also the principle that the courts of one state may not sit in judgment on the compatibility of the legislation of another state with international law.[20] But the Court also added that it must be particularly vigilant when, in connection with an action between private individuals, a question is referred to it which is intended to give the national court an opinion on whether the legislation of another member state is compatible with Community law. But this did not

---

18 Case 244/78 [1979] ECR 2663, [1980] 1 CMLR 314. The effect of Case 63/83 *R v Kirk* [1984] ECR 2689, [1985] 1 All ER 453, was that UK law was invalid.
19 See p 170, post.
20 Cf *Buttes Gas and Oil Co v Hammer (Nos 2 and 3)* [1982] AC 888, [1981] 3 All ER 616.

prevent the European Court, in a reference from a German court, from giving an answer relating to Belgian margarine packaging laws which would have led the German court to find that the Belgian law was contrary to art 30 of the Treaty.[1]

5 Refusal of the European Court to give preliminary rulings

In recent years there have been signs that the European Court will refuse to give preliminary rulings where it is satisfied that the art 177 procedure is being misused or abused. In some cases the national court making the reference misunderstands the purpose of art 177 and attempts to obtain an answer to a question which is not one of Community law but of national law. The European Court has no power to answer such questions and will hold that it has no jurisdiction in the case.[2] An extreme example of this case is represented by two attempts by an acting judge in France: first he asked, in a case involving a traffic accident, what protection the EEC Treaty afforded with regard to the observance of the fundamental principle of the independence of the judiciary; next, in a case involving the eviction of tenants, he asked whether an action for damages against a judge for denial of justice was compatible with Community law. In each case the European Court declared, within a few weeks of the reference being received, that it had no jurisdiction because the questions did not relate to the interpretation of the Treaty or the validity or interpretation of an act of a Community institution.[3]

There is a further limit to the exercise of the jurisdiction under art 177, and that limit has its foundation in the notion of justiciability. In *Mattheus v Doego*[4] the parties had entered into a contract whose continuation was expressed to be conditional on the practicability of the accession of Spain, Portugal and Greece to the Communities. The German court asked the European Court to rule on whether the provisions of art 237 of the EEC Treaty (which lays down the procedure for accession) contained substantive legal limits on the accession and whether, as a result, the accession of Spain, Portugal and Greece was not possible in law in the foreseeable future. The European Court held that it had no jurisdiction to rule on the matter, because the conditions of accession depended on an agreement between existing member states and the applicant, and accordingly 'the legal conditions for such accession remain to be defined in the

---

1 Case 261/81 *Rau v de Smedt* [1982] ECR 3961, [1983] 2 CMLR 496.
2 See Case 93/75 *Alderblum v Caisse National d'Assurance Vieillesse des Travailleurs Salariés de Paris* [1975] ECR 2147, [1976] 1 CMLR 236; Case 101/78 *Granaria BV v Hoofdproduktschap voor Akkerbouwprodukten* [1979] ECR 623, [1978] 3 CMLR 124; Case 74/79 *OCE v Samavins* [1980] ECR 239.
3 Case 105/79 [1979] ECR 2257; Case 68/80 [1980] ECR 771.
4 Case 93/78 [1978] ECR 2203, [1979] 1 CMLR 551.

context of that procedure without its being possible to determine the content judicially in advance.' In effect, therefore, the Court held that it was presented with a non-justiciable and political question, to which a legal answer could not be given.

Foglia v Novello[5]

This litigation resulted in two rulings from the European Court which imposed considerable limits on the well-established principle that the relevance of the question of Community law is for the national judge and that, accordingly, it was not for the European Court to criticise the reasons which led the national court to make a reference.[6] Although the Court had previously indicated that it had jurisdiction to give preliminary rulings only in the case where a national tribunal was seised of a dispute,[7] it had given many rulings in the course of national ex parte applications of a kind which could not be said to be disputed cases,[8] and even in some cases which had, no doubt, been artificially contrived.[9]

But in the *Foglia v Novello* cases the Court held that the art 177 procedure could not be abused by allowing artificially constructed law suits to be used as a vehicle for deciding points of Community law. In fact what was involved was an attempt by Italian wine growers to have the European Court give a ruling the effect of which would have been to hold that a French tax was discriminatory and contrary to the EEC Treaty. Mrs Novello ordered some cases of Italian wine from Foglia, an Italian wine grower, for despatch to France. The contract provided that Mrs Novello would not be liable for any French or Italian taxes which were contrary to the free movement of goods between the two countries. The despatch of the goods was the responsibility of an Italian company, Danzas, and the contract between Danzas and Foglia contained a corresponding provision about taxes. On importation into France, the French customs authorities levied a charge based on the alcoholic content of the wine. Foglia reimbursed Danzas for the charge it had paid to the French authorities and sought to recover it from Mrs Novello in the Italian courts. Mrs Novello said the charge was unlawful under art 95 of the EEC Treaty, and she was therefore not under an obligation to pay it by virtue of the contractual clause; Foglia sought to join Danzas in the Italian proceedings, on the basis that if the charge were unlawful (and therefore Mrs Novello did

---

5 (No 1) Case 104/79 [1980] ECR 745, [1981] 1 CMLR 45; (No 2) Case 244/80 [1981] ECR 3045, [1982] 1 CMLR 585.
6 See pp 163–165, supra.
7 Case 138/80 *Borker*, p 147, n 7, supra.
8 See, eg cases cited in p 146, n 19, supra.
9 See especially the *Union Laitière* case, n 18, supra.

not have to pay) then Danzas should bear their cost. The Italian judge refused the joinder of Danzas, and referred the question to the European Court whether the French tax was compatible with the Treaty. The European Court, following the lead of Advocate General Warner, held that it had no jurisdiction to give a ruling because there was no genuine dispute between the parties, and the litigation was an artificial device by the Italian parties to obtain a ruling from the European Court that the French legislation was invalid. The Court emphasised the following features of the case: first, both parties were agreed that the French law was incompatible with Community law; second, Foglia was acting on behalf of a group of Italian wine growers; third, the clause in the contract had been inserted in the contract to induce the Italian court to give a ruling on the point; fourth, the forwarding agent, Danzas, had not challenged the French tax in the French courts although it had the right to do so. Accordingly, a situation in which the Court was obliged by the expedience of such arrangements to give rulings would jeopardise the whole system of legal remedies available to private individuals to enable them to protect themselves against tax provisions which were contrary to the Treaty.

There was then a further reference by the Italian judge. The Italian judge correctly pointed out that the first decision marked a departure by the European Court from the case law which had consistently held that evaluation of the necessity for a reference was a matter for the national court; he also thought he had the power and duty to decide the Italian action for a declaration, and accordingly addressed a series of further questions to the European Court designed, in part, to further elucidate the relationship between the national courts and the European Court. The European Court, contrary to the view of Advocate General Slynn, adhered to its earlier decision not to answer the question on the discriminatory nature of the French law. It held that the role of the European Court under art 177 was not to give abstract advisory opinions[10] but to contribute to the actual decisions of cases and it did not, therefore, have jurisdiction to answer questions submitted as a part of a device to procure holdings on Community law which were not necessary for the decision. In several subsequent cases a doubt was raised as to whether the reference was a genuine one, but in

---

10 In Case 149/82 *Robards v Insurance Officer* [1983] ECR 171, [1983] 2 CMLR 37, the Court again emphasised that it was not its task to deliver opinions on general or hypothetical questions, but to assist in the administration of justice in the member states. Accordingly, although it would answer the question which arose in that case, ie entitlement to family allowances where the beneficiaries were the children of divorced parents residing in different member states, it would be for the Community institutions to take the necessary measures to enable other analogous cases to be satisfactorily resolved.

each case the European Court thought that the doubt was unfounded.[11]

Although these decisions have been criticised,[12] the better view is that in order to preserve its judicial integrity the Court must have power to refuse to hear cases which are not genuine and are an abuse of its process.[13] The problem is unlikely to arise in references from United Kingdom courts. In England a declaratory judgment can only be given after proper argument and cannot be made on the basis of admissions by the parties.[14]

V. THE EXERCISE OF THE NATIONAL COURT'S DISCRETION TO REFER

1 The European Court's guidelines

Although the exercise of the discretion to refer under art 177 is for the national court, the limits of the discretion are a matter of Community law. The relations between the national court and the European Court 'are governed exclusively by the provisions of Community law'.[15] In recent years the Court has begun to lay down what it has itself described as 'guidelines'[16] for the manner of the exercise of the discretion, both as to the basis on which the reference is made and the stage at which it is made. It has stressed the need for the national court to define the legal context in which the reference is made[17] and to explain the reasons, unless they are clear beyond doubt from the file, it considers that a reply to its question is necessary for the decision in the case.[18]

Although the decision at what stage in the national proceedings it is appropriate to make a reference under art 177 is a matter for the

---

11 Case 140/79 *Chemial Farmaceutici SpA v DAF SpA* [1981] ECR 1, [1981] 3 CMLR 350; Case 46/80 *Vinal SpA v Orbat SpA* [1981] ECR 77, [1981] 3 CMLR 524; Case 261/81 *Rau Lebensmittelwerke v De Smedt PvbA* [1982] ECR 3961, [1983] 2 CMLR 496; cf Case 203/80 *Casati* [1981] ECR 2595, [1982] 1 CMLR 365; Case 180/83 *Moser v Land Baden-Württemberg* [1984] ECR 2539, [1984] 3 CMLR 720; Cases 98 etc/85 *Bertini v Regione Lazio* [1986] ECR 1885, [1987] 1 CMLR 774; Cases 209–213/84 *Ministère Public v Asjes* [1986] ECR 1425, [1986] 3 CMLR 173. See Wyatt (1981) 6 EL Rev 447, Freeman (1981) 1 Yb Eur L 408.
12 See especially Barav (1980) 5 EL Rev 443; Bebr (1980) 17 CML Rev 525, (1982) 19 CML Rev 428.
13 Cf Wyatt (1982) 7 EL Rev 186; Gray (1983) 8 EL Rev 24.
14 See eg *Metzger v DHSS* [1977] 3 All ER 444, [1978] 1 WLR 1046.
15 Case 244/80 *Foglia v Novello (No 2)* [1981] ECR 3045 at 3062, [1982] 1 CMLR 585 at 608.
16 Cases 141 to 143/81 *Holdijk* [1982] ECR 1299 at 1311, [1983] 2 CMLR 635 at 647.
17 Case 244/78 *Union Laitière* [1979] ECR 2663, [1980] 1 CMLR 314; Cases 36 and 71/80 *Irish Creamery Milk Suppliers Association v Ireland* [1981] ECR 735, [1981] 2 CMLR 455; Case 14/86 *Pretore di Salo v X* [1987] ECR 2545, [1989] 1 CMLR 71.
18 *Foglia v Novello (No 2)*; see n 5, supra.

discretion of the national court[19] the European Court has suggested that, in order for the legal context of the question to be clear, 'it might be convenient, in certain circumstances, for the facts in the case to be established and for questions of purely national law to be settled at the time the reference is made to the Court of Justice so as to enable the latter to take cognizance of all the features of fact and of law which may be relevant to the interpretation of Community law which it is called upon to give.'

But, the Court continued:

> However, those considerations do not in any way restrict the discretion of the national court, which alone has a direct knowledge of the facts of the case and of the arguments of the parties, which will have to take responsibility for giving judgment in the case and which is therefore in the best position to appreciate at what stage in the proceedings it requires a preliminary ruling from the Court of Justice. Hence it is clear that the national court's decision when to make a reference under article 177 must be dictated by considerations of procedural organization and efficiency to be weighed by that court.[20]

Nevertheless these guidelines do not prevent the Court from grappling with questions from national courts which do not comply with them. Thus in an important case on the right of a member state to expel nationals of another state, a Belgian court submitted a list of no less than 29 questions which had been prepared by the plaintiff's counsel: Advocate General Capotorti criticised the national court for failing to make a careful selection of relevant questions and to take direct responsibility for their formulation, but the Court did in substance answer the questions without criticism of the Belgian judge.[1] French courts have asked whether French aviation law[2] or French town planning legislation[3] was compatible with Community law, without specifying what aspect of Community law they thought was relevant. Not only did the French courts disregard the consistent position of the European Court that it was not its role to consider the compatibility of national law with Community law, but also they failed to comply with the Court's guidelines, by failing to define the

---

19 *Irish Creamery Milk* case; see n 17, supra.
20 [1981] ECR at 748, [1981] 2 CMLR at 473; Case 72/83 *Campus Oil Ltd v Minister for Industry and Energy* [1984] ECR 2727, [1984] 3 CMLR 544. See also *Holdijk*, supra n 16, on the relationship between these guidelines and the effective use of the power of member states and Community institutions to submit observations to the Court.
1 Cases 115 and 116/81 *Adoui and Cornuaille v Belgium* [1982] ECR 1665, [1982] 3 CMLR 631.
2 Cases 209–213/84 *Ministère Public v Asjes* [1986] ECR 1425, [1986] 3 CMLR 173.
3 Case 204/87 *Bakaert v Procureur de la République, Rennes* [1988] 2 CMLR 655; Case 20/87 *Ministère Public v Gauchard* [1987] ECR 4879. See also Case 251/83 *Haug-Adrion v Frankfurter Versicherungs-AG* [1984] ECR 4277.

legal context and the reasons the reply to the question was necessary. But in these cases the European Court deduced from the files what the underlying questions were (competition law in the first case, and freedom of establishment in the others) and answered them.

2 The role of article 177 before lower courts

This section and the succeeding sections will be concerned with the stage at which a national judge *may* refer a question to the European Court under art 177(2) but is not bound to refer it under art 177(3). They will therefore be concerned with the lower courts and also with appellate courts whose decision is not final under art 177(3) in the sense to be discussed below. Since such courts will not be bound to refer, the question relates to the desirability or propriety of such courts making references under art 177 to the Court.

In some respects the practical problem is not unlike that which is posed by having preliminary points of law tried as preliminary issues prior to the main action. In the long term they may reduce the costs of the action and reduce[4] the length of the proceedings but in the short term they may increase the costs of the action and may proliferate the proceedings.[5]

The initial question is the extent to which judges of first instance from whom there is the possibility of appeal (or appellate courts from which there is a further appeal) should make references under art 177 in the course of the proceedings on the merits or as a specific preliminary to those proceedings. This involves the further question of what is the most expeditious and procedurally appropriate method of making references to the European Court so as to save time, expense and the unnecessary adjournment of a trial.

The points in favour of references under art 177 by courts which are not courts of last resort are these:

1. Such references would support the policy of art 177 to ensure uniformity of interpretation.
2. Many cases do not go to appeal and it is in the public interest that litigation be settled or determined at the earliest possible stage (subject to the overall policy of the availability of appellate courts to correct error).
3. An early reference might save costs if it removed a significant area of controversy from a particular piece of litigation which

---

4 Any reduction in the length of the proceedings is now purely theoretical so far as references to the European Court are concerned, because of the very long delays (an *average* of eighteen months) involved in the reference.
5 See RSC Ord 33, r 3. Cf Stephenson LJ in *Bulmer v Bollinger* [1974] Ch 401 at 429, [1979] 2 All ER 1226 at 1240.

would otherwise take up much time before each court in which the litigation was conducted.
4. An early reference might isolate the relevant areas of fact so that the judge would not have to make findings of fact on irrelevant areas.

The points against references under art 177 by courts which are not courts of last resort are these:

1. The European Court is already seriously overburdened with references, and such references exacerbate the problem.
2. Early references would be unnecessarily costly if the questions raised were not in fact ultimately found to be material.
3. Early references cause unnecessary delay, particularly in current circumstances, where references can take more than two years to be decided.

There is no easy answer to the problem and the courts will have to take a flexible view of their powers. In some cases one policy will outweigh another, but some criteria could in practice be deduced. Thus, the costs element will be very significant if the point arises before a court or tribunal where the costs are not normally high. A reference by an administrative tribunal, or a county court or magistrates' court would add enormously to the cost of the proceedings if the parties were minded (as they probably would be) to submit written and oral observations to the European Court. In these circumstances, it is suggested that courts on the lower level in cases in which the costs would normally be modest should exercise their power to refer very sparingly and in only the most exceptional circumstances. On the other hand, the judge in a very heavy and lengthy commercial case may feel that the cost of a reference would be made up for by the isolation of relevant issues. It is ultimately a question of balancing the costs and convenience with the proper administration of justice. Quite often, as in appeals to the House of Lords, the public interest will outweigh the interests of one or more parties. For example, in revenue cases (especially those involving small amounts) the Revenue is sometimes given leave by the Court of Appeal to appeal to the House of Lords on special terms as to costs, such as that the costs of the appeal will be borne entirely by the Revenue and that the order as to costs of the courts below will not be disturbed.

A very important element is the potential relevance of the question to be referred. No judge (or lawyer) can make a confident prediction as to the relevance of any particular issue in the ultimate legal analysis; but there are certainly cases in which certain questions loom large and other questions are obviously peripheral and likely to be relevant only if a particular (and unlikely) view of the facts turns out to be the correct one. Also to be taken into account is the difficulty and general importance of the point of law. The point involved may have important repercussions on administrative practice, which may have to be altered or abolished, and the administrative authorities may wish to have the practical position resolved as soon as possible. The litigation itself may be important, in the sense that large sums of money or some major principle may be at stake or in the sense that it is a test case, on the result of which other and numerous cases depend.

3 When a decision is necessary and Lord Denning's guidelines—*Bulmer v Bollinger*

Bulmer v Bollinger[6] was in effect a passing off action by the French producers of champagne against English producers of champagne cider and champagne perry to prevent the use of the expression 'champagne' in connection with any beverage other than wine produced in the Champagne district of France. The French producers amended their pleadings in 1973, after the United Kingdom joined the Common Market, to add claims that on the true construction of Regulations 816/70 and 817/70 the use of the word 'champagne' in connection with any beverage other than champagne would contravene Community law.

The French producers asked that two points of Community law should be referred to the European Court under art 177, namely, (a) whether the use of the word 'champagne' in connection with any beverage other than champagne was a contravention of Community law and (b) whether a national court of a member state should refer to the European Court such a question as was raised by question (a).

The proceedings had not yet reached the stage of trial and Whitford J refused to refer either of the questions before trial. The Court of Appeal was asked to review the judge's exercise of discretion. The intention of its decision was to discourage judges of first instance, and particularly before trial, from making references to the European Court. Before this decision, it is possible that a broader view was being taken. As Graham J put it in *Löwenbräu München v Grunhalle Lager International*:[7]

> As I read the Treaty, references are not to be made unnecessarily, but on the other hand the power to refer is not confined only to courts whose decisions are final, or to any particular stage of a case. It seems to me therefore that if I felt in this case in need of guidance upon the interpreta-

---

6 [1974] Ch 401, [1974] 2 All ER 1226. See Jacobs (1974) 90 LQR 486; Freeman (1975) 28 Curr Legal Prob 176; Mitchell (1974) 11 CML Rev 351; Bebr (1974) 11 CML Rev 408.
7 [1974] 1 CMLR 1 at 9, approved by Pennycuick V-C in *Van Duyn v Home Office* [1974] 3 All ER 178, [1974] 1 WLR 1107.

tion of any article of the Treaty and that such guidance was necessary for my decision I have unfettered power to refer the matter to the EEC Court. Such appears to me to be the clear intention of the Treaty from its wording.

The Court of Appeal, however, took a stricter view of what attitude lower courts ought to take to the expression 'necessary' in the context of the phrase 'if it considers that a decision on the question is necessary' under art 177.

Lord Denning MR began by pointing out that it was a condition precedent to the exercise of the power to refer that the English judge should consider that a decision on the question was necessary. He continued by explaining, quite rightly, that the European Court could not interfere (positively or negatively) with the exercise of the judge's power. If he made a reference, the European Court would not question the grounds on which he made it; if he did not, the litigants could not appeal to the European Court.

When was a decision 'necessary'? Lord Denning MR sought to lay down guidelines. By way of preface, however, it should be pointed out that there may be some confusion in the judgment of Lord Denning MR (though not in that of Stephenson LJ) as to the matter which must be 'necessary'. Lord Denning MR suggests that what must be considered 'necessary' by the judge is a *reference* to the European Court. But what art 177 says is that the judge must refer under art 177 if he considers that a *decision* on the question of Community law is necessary. In other words, it is not the *decision* by the *European Court* which must be necessary, but a decision by the *national judge*. As a result Lord Denning MR goes on, in enumerating the factors to be taken into account in considering whether a decision is necessary, to include factors which more properly relate to the existence of a 'question' or to the discretion of the judge.

The four 'guidelines' given by Lord Denning as to whether a decision is necessary are as follows:

1. The point must be conclusive

Lord Denning put it thus:[8]

> The English court has to consider whether 'a decision on the question is *necessary* to enable it to give *judgment*'. That means judgment in the very case which is before the court. The judge must have got to the stage when he says to himself: 'This clause of the Treaty is capable of two or more meanings. If it means *this*, I give judgment for the plaintiff. If it means *that*, I give judgment for the defendant.' In short, the point must be such that, whichever way the point is decided, it is conclusive of the case. Nothing more remains but to give judgment.

---

8 [1974] Ch 401 at 422, [1974] 3 All ER 1226 at 1234.

This is a very narrow formulation. It is suggested, with respect, that it reintroduces into the context of art 177 an error which Lord Denning himself pointed out had crept into the practice relating to preliminary points of law. In *Carl-Zeiss-Stiftung v Herbert Smith & Co*[9] Lord Denning said:

> I know that it has been said on one or two occasions that a preliminary issue should be ordered only when, *whichever way it is decided*, it is conclusive of the whole matter. That was said by Lord Evershed MR in *Windsor Refrigerator Co Ltd v Branch Nominees Ltd*; and Harman LJ in *Yeoman Credit Ltd v Latter*. I do not think that that is correct. The true rule was stated by Romer LJ in *Everett v Ribbands*:
>
> 'Where you have a point of law which, *if decided in one way*, is going to be decisive of litigation, then advantage ought to be taken of the facilities afforded by the rules of court to have it disposed of at the close of pleadings.'

A decision will of course be necessary if it is on a question which is in every sense conclusive. But judges do often decide questions which are only decisive one way and their power to refer such questions should not be limited by this very strict test.

2. Previous ruling

3. Acte clair

These can be taken together, because as shown above,[10] a point can often be said to be clear if it has been the subject of a previous ruling. Lord Denning put it in this way:[11]

> In some cases, however, it may be found that the same point—or substantially the same point—has already been decided by the European Court in a previous case. In that event it is not necessary for the English Court to decide it. It can follow the previous decision without troubling the European Court. But, as I have said, the European Court is *not* bound by its previous decisions. So if the English court thinks that a previous decision of the European Court may have been wrong—or if there are new factors which ought to be brought to the notice of the European Court— the English Court may consider it *necessary* to re-submit the point to the European Court. In that event, the European Court will consider the point again . . . In other cases the English court may consider the point is reasonably clear and free from doubt. In that event there is no need to interpret the Treaty but only to apply it: and that is the task of the English court.

---

9 [1969] 1 Ch 93 at 98, [1968] 2 All ER 1002 at 1004.
10 See p 158, ante.
11 [1974] Ch 401 at 422–3, [1974] 3 All ER 1226 at 1235.

In each case, however, it is suggested that there is a confusion between the points whether the *decision* on the question is necessary and whether the *reference* is necessary. If the point is abundantly clear, there may be no 'question' of interpretation to be decided. But if there is a question it may still be necessary to decide it even though the process may be simple. This is not to suggest that Lord Denning is wrong in saying that these factors militate against reference. But it is submitted they are factors for the discretion of the judge rather than conditions precedent to the exercise of his discretion.

4. Decide the facts first

It was Lord Denning's view that it will not in effect be possible to know whether a decision on a point is necessary until the facts are decided. He said:[12]

> It is to be noticed, too, that the word is 'necessary'. This is much stronger than 'desirable' or 'convenient'. There are some cases where the point, if decided one way, would shorten the trial greatly. But, if decided the other way, it would mean that the trial would have to go its full length. In such a case it might be 'convenient' or 'desirable' to take it as a preliminary point because it might save much time and expense. But it would not be 'necessary' at that stage. When the facts were investigated, it might turn out to have been quite unnecessary. The case would be determined on another ground altogether. As a rule you cannot tell whether it is necessary to decide a point until all the facts are ascertained. So in general it is best to decide the facts first.

Although Stephenson LJ explained that a decision on the question must be 'necessary' and not merely convenient or expedient, he did not try to lay down guidelines. He did point out that:

> all experience in our courts of attempts to take short cuts by obtaining preliminary decisions on points of law shows how difficult it is to isolate an issue and the relevant facts and to avoid going back to the beginning and taking the ordinary route.[13]

The only practical result of any confusion between what is properly to be regarded as a condition precedent to the exercise of the judge's discretion and what is properly to be regarded as a factor in the exercise of the discretion is that the former is more susceptible of appeal to the Court of Appeal. If the judge has a discretion the Court of Appeal will not interfere with its exercise merely because it would have come to a different conclusion. But if there is, as a matter of law, a condition precedent to the exercise of the discretion the Court of Appeal may, and must, consider whether that condition was satisfied.

---

12 Ibid.
13 Ibid, at 429 and 1240.

As for the factors which could be taken into account in the exercise of the discretion, Lord Denning MR mentioned the following:

(i) the time it took to get a ruling from the European Court—a stay of the English proceedings might have unfortunate results;
(ii) the importance of not overloading the European Court—it had to sit in plenary session and so national judges should 'not put too much on them';[14]
(iii) the need to formulate the question clearly—this was another reason for finding the facts first;
(iv) the difficulty and importance of the point, as to which he said:

> Unless the point is really difficult and important, it would seem better for the English judge to decide himself. For in so doing, much delay and expense will be saved. So far, the English judges have not shirked their responsibilities. They have decided several points of interpretation on the Treaty to the satisfaction, I hope, of the parties. At any rate, there has been no appeal from them . . .

(v) the expense of getting a ruling;
(vi) the wishes of the parties—they should not be given undue weight, but the English court should hesitate before making a reference against the wishes of the parties, in view of the expense and delay which it involved.

Stephenson LJ (in whose judgment Stamp LJ concurred) thought that the guidelines should be few and firmly related to the basic requirement that the decision on the question raised must be necessary at the time the reference is requested to enable the national court to give judgment at the end of the case; the national judge should bear in mind that the object of art 177 is to safeguard the uniform judicial interpretation of Community law; he should exercise his right to refer sparingly and in cases of serious doubt or difficulty only and should also bear in mind the other considerations set out by Lord Denning.

Lord Denning's 'guidelines' have been said to be contrary to the principle that a national court cannot be restrained by national law from making a reference under art 177.[15] But they are only guidelines, and there is no evidence that English judges have regarded themselves as bound to apply them mechanically. Indeed, the evidence is to the contrary: in *Lord Bethell v Sabena*[16] Parker J emphasised that they were only guidelines and that the discretion of the judge at first

---

14 But see p 142, n 7, ante, for the use of Chambers.
15 Case 166/73 *Rheinmühlen-Düsseldorf v Einfuhr- und Vorratsstelle für Getreide* [1974] ECR 139, [1974] 1 CMLR 523 is usually cited in this connection, but it deals with a different question. In Ireland Barrington J refused to follow Lord Denning's guidelines in the *Irish Creamery* case: (1972) 7 EL Rev 337.
16 [1983] 3 CMLR 1.

instance could not be fettered. There are really two issues: the first is the extent to which the guidelines step over the matters which are reserved to national law, and the second is whether, to the extent that they deal with matters of Community law, they are inconsistent with it. So far as the first question is concerned, it seems clear that it is for national law to determine the circumstances in which a point of Community law is conclusive of the national proceedings, and it should follow from this that guidelines concerning deciding questions of fact and of national law are legitimate matters for a national court of appeal to lay down, particularly when they are entirely consistent with the European Court's own guidelines. Similarly, it is a matter of common sense that the national court should take into account the delay involved in a reference and the wishes of the parties, provided that these matters are not in any sense conclusive.

Some of the strain on the list of the Court has been alleviated by the increase in the use of Chambers of the Court to give opinions in references under art 177, but this ceased to be effective with the huge increase in the workload of the Court. A reference for a preliminary ruling interrupts, and delays the conclusion of, national proceedings, and yet the *average* time for a preliminary ruling from the European Court has now become the wholly unacceptable one of eighteen months, and in several cases from the United Kingdom a delay of two and a half to three years has not been uncommon. Thus the reference by the Employment Appeal Tribunal in *Newstead v Department of Transport*[17] was given in June 1985, and the preliminary ruling was not given until December 1987, after the case had been transferred from the fifth chamber to the full Court; and the reference by the House of Lords in *Allen & Hanbury's Ltd v Generics (UK) Ltd*[18] was made in December 1985, and the opinion of the European Court rendered in March 1988. The problem has been alleviated, but not solved, by the creation of the Court of First Instance in October 1989, which hears cases brought against the Community by officials, competition and anti-dumping cases, and certain cases under the ECSC Treaty.

The main difficulty with Lord Denning's guidelines lies in his exhortation to English judges not to refer where they consider a point is reasonably clear and free from doubt, and that 'unless the point is really difficult and important' it would seem better for the English judge to decide it himself. It was the latter question which caused misgivings for Bingham J in *Customs and Excise Comrs v ApS Samex*.[19]

---

17 Case 192/85 [1987] ECR 4753, [1988] 1 CMLR 219.
18 Case 434/85 [1988] 2 All ER 454, [1989] 1 WLR 414. For another recent example see Case C-216/87 *Minister of Agriculture, Fisheries and Food, ex p Jaderow Ltd* C216/87 (1990) Times, 19 January.
19 [1983] 1 All ER 1042.

In that case a question arose as to the power of the Customs and Excise to confiscate goods originating in Korea. That turned on the interpretation of a Council Regulation imposing quotas on imports from Korea and on the powers of the Customs and Excise under Community law to impose implementing rules under it. The importers sought to have four questions referred to the European Court. Bingham J thought that three of them should 'certainly', if it rested with him, be answered in favour of the Customs and Excise, but he did not regard the matter as so free from doubt as to render those points acte clair and he did not regard the fourth point as either reasonably clear or reasonably free from doubt. He went on:[20]

> In endeavouring to follow and respect these guidelines I find myself in some difficulty, because it was submitted by counsel on behalf of the defendant that the issues raised by his client should be resolved by the Court of Justice as the court best fitted to do so, and I find this a consideration which does give me some cause for thought.

He then went on to indicate the advantages enjoyed by the European Court when deciding questions of Community law, which have been quoted above,[1] and continued:

> It does not follow from this that a reference should be made by a national court of first instance, wherever a litigant raises a serious point of Community law and seeks a reference, or wherever he indicates an intention to appeal, even if he announces an intention to appeal, if necessary, to the highest court which is effectively bound to refer the question to the Court of Justice. For example . . . it can rarely be necessary to make a reference until the relevant facts have been found, and unless the points raised are substantially determinative of the action. Or the question raised may admit of only one possible answer, or it may be covered by Community authority precisely in point, although even here some slight caution is necessary since the Court of Justice is not strictly bound by its own decisions. These considerations relate to whether a decision is necessary. Other considerations may affect the exercise of discretion. Sometimes, no doubt, it may appear that the question is raised mischievously, not in the bona fide hope of success but in order to obstruct or delay an almost inevitable adverse judgment, denying the other party his remedy meanwhile.

In 1987 the Court of Appeal was asked to refer to the European Court the question whether art 30 of the EEC Treaty prevented a system whereby chemists could not dispense generic drugs imported from other member states when doctors had prescribed proprietary

---

20 At 1055.
1 See p 144, ante.

brands. In making the reference, Kerr LJ, speaking for a unanimous Court of Appeal, said:[2]

> There can... be no doubt that the case is one of great general importance, not only for this country but for the Community in general, and that the Court of Justice in Luxembourg is in a far better position to reach a decision which is *communautaire* than this Court.

4 The operation of article 177 in United Kingdom practice

Bulmer v Bollinger is still authoritative in England, and it has been applied in many cases.[3] Although no doubt the unarticulated and, therefore, unreported influence of *Bulmer v Bollinger* has had its effect, nevertheless the evidence from reported cases is that United Kingdom courts which have required guidance from the European Court have not hesitated to seek it. There have been some 70 judgments on references to the European Court by United Kingdom courts, of which the vast majority have been by judges at first instance or intermediate courts of appeal. The courts which have made references have included the House of Lords, the Court of Appeal (Civil Division), the Court of Appeal (Criminal Division), the Court of Session, the Queen's Bench Divisional Court, the High Court of Justiciary, first instance judges of the Queen's Bench Division and the Chancery Division, the Patents Court, the Employment Appeal Tribunal, County Courts, Magistrates' Courts, VAT Tribunals, the Social Security Commissioner, and the Special Commissioners for Income Tax. Since the question whether to make a reference under article 177 is a matter of discretion,[4] at least for courts of first instance, the factors which have led one judge to refer or not to refer are not capable of precise calculation, but it is possible to see some general trends.

---

2 *R v Pharmaceutical Society of Great Britain, ex p Association of Pharmaceutical Importers* [1987] 3 CMLR 951, CA (see Cases 266–267/87 [1989] 2 CMLR 751); *R v Intervention Board for Agricultural Produce, ex p Fish Producers' Organisation Ltd* [1988] 2 CMLR 661, CA; *R v Secretary of State for Transport, ex p Factortame Ltd* [1989] 2 CMLR 353 at 369–370, DC (for subsequent proceedings, see ibid p 392, CA, and [1989] 2 WLR 997, [1989] 2 All ER 692, HL).

3 For recent examples see *An Bord Bainne Co-operative Ltd v Milk Marketing Board (No 2)* [1985] 1 CMLR 6; *R v HM Treasury, ex p Daily Mail and General Trust plc* [1987] 2 CMLR 1; *R v Pharmaceutical Society of Great Britain, ex p Association of Pharmaceutical Importers* [1987] 3 CMLR 951, CA; *R v Intervention Board for Agricultural Produce, ex p Fish Producers' Organisation Ltd* [1988] 2 CMLR 661, CA. See also *Prince v Secretary of State for Scotland* 1985 SLT 74. For a survey of English practice see Dashwood and Arnull (1984) 4 Yb Eur L 255; Gormley (1986) 23 CML Rev 287.

4 Where the question is one of application, as opposed to interpretation, of Community law, the United Kingdom judge should not make a reference: see pp 165–166, ante, and *MacMahon v Department of Education and Science* [1983] Ch 227.

Although a decision on the question to be referred must be necessary, the word 'necessary' is not to be construed narrowly.[5] In *EMI Records Ltd v CBS United Kingdom Ltd*,[6] Graham J pointed out, before ordering a reference, that if the defendants succeeded in establishing their argument on EEC law, they would have a complete defence, and conversely if the defendants failed on that argument the plaintiffs would succeed in their action; when *Bulmer v Bollinger* came to the trial stage Whitford J[7] held that it was unnecessary to refer any question of interpretation of Community regulations to the European Court because a declaration in relation to them would be of no material assistance to the defendants, who were relying on them. In *Customs and Excise Comrs v ApS Samex*[8] Bingham J took account, in deciding to make a reference, of the fact that the answer to be given by the European Court would be conclusive in the sense that, if the answers were adverse to the defendant importers, that would admittedly be the end of their case, and if the answers were given in their favour, there might be some short issues to be tried; but there was no doubt that the answer which the European Court would give would be substantially, if not quite totally, determinative of the litigation.

A reference is, of course, not necessary where the result of the case would be the same whatever the answer to the question of Community law. In two decisions the House of Lords has been at pains to emphasise that a reference will not be necessary or required under art 177(3) if the case does not turn on Community law. In *Wellcome Foundation Ltd v Secretary of State for Social Services*[9] the House of Lords held that the Secretary of State, in considering whether or not to grant product licences for parallel imports of medicines, was not entitled to take into account the fact that those medicines might infringe trade mark rights. This conclusion was based purely on a construction of the Medicines Act 1968, but the same conclusion had been reached by the Court of Appeal on the basis of Community law.[10] Lord Ackner pointed out that in the light of the House of Lords' decision on English law:

> it was clearly undesirable to embark upon considerations of Community

---

5 *An Bord Bainne Co-operative Ltd v Milk Marketing Board (No 2)* [1985] 1 CMLR 6; *Polydor Ltd v Harlequin Record Shops Ltd* [1980] 2 CMLR 413, 428; *R v Plymouth Justices, ex p Rogers* [1982] QB 863, 869, [1982] 2 All ER 175, 181.
6 [1975] 1 CMLR 285.
7 [1975] 2 CMLR 479; reversed in part [1977] 2 CMLR 625.
8 [1983] 1 All ER 1042.
9 [1988] 2 All ER 684, [1988] 1 WLR 635, HL.
10 [1987] 2 All ER 1025, [1987] 1 WLR 1166, CA.

law, which might ultimately have necessitated a reference to the European Court of Justice under article 177 of the Treaty.[11]

In *Re Smith Kline and French Laboratories Ltd*,[12] the House of Lords held that the licensing authority under the Medicines Act 1968 was entitled, when considering the grant of product licences to manufacturers of generic drugs, to look at documentation supplied by the patentees of the equivalent proprietary drugs. A Council directive authorised the grant of a product licence, subject to certain particulars being provided 'without prejudice to the law relating to the protection of industrial and commercial property'. The House of Lords held that the only relevant law for this purpose was English law, and English law did not prevent the licensing authority from using confidential information supplied to it by the patentee. No question of Community law arose and a reference under art 177 was therefore not appropriate.

The practice of the courts with regard to Lord Denning's exhortation to lower courts not to refer where the point was reasonably clear and free from doubt and preferably, unless the point was really difficult and important, to decide the question themselves is not, of course, acte clair in the classic sense, ie a limitation upon the obligation of the court of final instance to refer if there is no serious question. Where a point of Community law has seemed to a lower court to be hopeless, then it has not hesitated to refuse to make a reference. Thus, where it was suggested on behalf of a person in relation to whom extradition proceedings were pending that there should be a reference to the European Court on the question whether the power of extradition was affected by the EEC Treaty, the court refused to do so on the ground that it was 'common sense' that the EEC Treaty did not affect extradition.[13] But when the Court of Appeal (Criminal Division) in *Henn and Darby v DPP* refused to refer the problem of the extent to which a ban on the importation of pornography might be compatible with EEC law because they had no doubt at all as to whether they had got the right solution to the problem, the House of Lords warned that English judges should not be too ready to hold that because the meaning of the English text seemed plain to them no question of interpretation could be involved, and submitted to the European Court questions on articles 30 and 36 of the EEC Treaty, even though the House of Lords had little doubt as to the answer that would be received.[14] As indicated above, in *Customs and Excise Comrs v ApS Samex*, Bingham J referred

---

11 [1988] 1 WLR at 643.
12 [1989] 2 WLR 397, [1989] 1 All ER 578, HL.
13 *R v Governor of Pentonville Prison, ex p Budlong* [1980] 1 All ER 701, [1980] 1 WLR 1110, applied in *Re Virdee* [1980] 1 CMLR 709. See also *R v Metropolitan Borough Council of Wirral, ex p Wirral Licensed Taxi Owners Association* [1983] 3 CMLR 150.
14 [1981] AC 850, [1980] 2 All ER 166.

four questions to the European Court, notwithstanding that his view on three of them was that they should be answered in favour of the Customs and Excise, but not so as to make the answer so clear and obvious as to make the matter acte clair; and in *Polydor Ltd v Harlequin Record Shops Ltd*,[15] the Court of Appeal (Civil Division), mindful of the different methods employed for interpretation of the Treaty and English law, made a reference to the European Court notwithstanding that it had formed a firm view on the question in favour of the defendant. But in the event the European Court reached a conclusion which was different from the firm view expressed by the Court of Appeal.[16]

As Kerr LJ has put it:

> Although the doctrine of 'acte clair' is primarily applicable to cases in which the answer to a particular question of EEC law is already covered by a decision of the Court of Justice . . . the principle of 'acte clair' is equally applicable in cases where there can be no doubt about the correct answer . . . The English authorities show that our courts should exercise great caution in relying on the doctrine of 'acte clair' as a ground for declining to make a reference.[17]

Nevertheless in several reported cases English courts have applied the 'acte clair' principle and refused to make references.[18]

Their training naturally leads English judges to the view that facts must be decided before it can properly be seen that a particular question of law arises, whether it is national law or European law. This is what lies behind the reluctance of English courts to order the trial of preliminary issues.[19] In practice the great majority of the references by United Kingdom courts under art 177 have been in cases where the facts were found or were not in substantial dispute. This is so particularly in the many cases from the Social Security Commissioner (and his predecessor the National Insurance Commissioner) and in the case of the references by the Employment Appeal Tribunal, the Court of Appeal and the House of Lords in employment matters, which were made after the facts had been found by the

---

15 [1980] 2 CMLR 413.
16 Case 270/80 [1982] ECR 329, [1982] 1 CMLR 677.
17 *R v Pharmaceutical Society of Great Britain, ex p Association of Pharmaceutical Importers* [1987] 3 CMLR 951 at 969–971, CA.
18 See eg in the Court of Appeal: *R v Secretary of State for Home Affairs, ex p Tombofa* [1988] 2 CMLR 609; *R v Bow Street Metropolitan Stipendiary Magistrate, ex p Noncyp Ltd* [1989] 3 WLR 467; *J Rothschild Holdings plc v IRC* [1989] 2 CMLR 621, CA; *R v Secretary of State for Social Security, ex p Bomore Medical Supplies Ltd* [1986] 1 CMLR 228. See also *Magnavision NV v General Optical Council* [1987] 1 CMLR 887; *(No 2)* [1987] 2 CMLR 262; *Bernstein v Immigration Appeal Tribunal* [1988] 3 CMLR 445, CA; *Barkworth v Customs and Excise Comrs* [1988] 3 CMLR 759; *R v ILEA, ex p Hinde* [1985] 1 CMLR 716.
19 Cf *Bulmer v Bollinger*, per Stephenson LJ, p 179, n 13, supra.

industrial tribunal. In *Church of Scientology of California v Customs and Excise Comrs*[20] Brightman LJ said that as a general rule no question should be submitted to the European Court based on an assumption which did not coincide with the facts which had been found or agreed. This was followed by Parker J in *Lord Bethell v Sabena*[1] who, refusing to make a reference at an early stage in the proceedings, said:

> Until all the facts have been investigated, it is impossible to frame a question which will ensure that the court is provided with real assistance. The only result, as I see it, of trying to frame a question now would be that the matter would go before the European Court some very considerable time later . . . and after the expenditure of much money it appears to me likely that it will then come back before this court in a form which does not enable the matter to be disposed of satisfactorily without asking further questions, and that thus there will be then a repetition of the exercise. It is the common experience of courts that preliminary questions are likely to produce extra expense and extra delay. This is a case in which that appears to me to be the likely result.

It is therefore especially important for the pleadings to be properly formulated so as to raise the essential facts on which the ultimate question may be referred.[2] Where the facts are agreed[3] or where there is no serious triable issue of fact raised, then it is appropriate to order a reference at a preliminary stage. Thus in *Polydor Ltd v Harlequin Record Shops Ltd*, the Court of Appeal thought there was no serious question about whether the imported records originated in Portugal, and therefore it was appropriate, at an interlocutory stage, to ask the European Court whether the Portuguese Association Agreement had the effect of allowing parallel imports from Portugal.

In practice this means, as Parker J recognised in *Lord Bethell v Sabena*, that in the more substantial commercial cases there is a danger that the parties will have to be put to the expense and inconvenience of discovery and a full trial before a reference can be made,

---

20 [1981] 1 All ER 1035.
1 [1983] 3 CMLR 1, 9–10. See also *An Bord Bainne v Milk Marketing Board (No 2)* [1985] 1 CMLR 6; *Potato Marketing Board v Drysdale* [1986] 3 CMLR 331, CA; *Waltham Forest London Borough v Scott Markets Ltd* [1988] 3 CMLR 773; *Prince v Younger* [1984] 1 CMLR 723 (Scotland).
2 See *Hagen v Fratelli D and G Moretti* [1980] 3 CMLR 253. On the pleading of Community law see also *British Leyland Motor Corpn Ltd v TI Silencers Ltd* [1981] 2 CMLR 75, CA; *ICI Ltd v Berk Pharmaceuticals Ltd* [1981] CMLR 91; *Lansing Bagnall Ltd v Buccaneer Lift Parts Ltd* [1984] 1 CMLR 224, CA; *Ransburg-Gema AG v Electrostatic Plant Systems Ltd* [1989] 2 CMLR 712. Cf *British Leyland Motor Corpn Ltd v Armstrong Patents Co Ltd* [1986] AC 577, [1986] 1 All ER 850, HL.
3 *Customs and Excise Comrs v ApS Samex*, n 8, supra; *R v Intervention Board for Agricultural Produce, ex p Fish Producers' Organisation Ltd* [1988] 2 CMLR 661, CA. Cf *R v Fishing Department of the Ministry of Agriculture, Fisheries and Food, ex p Agegate Ltd* [1987] 3 CMLR 939.

but where the question of Community law is obviously limited in scope and crucial to the outcome the judges of the Commercial Court have not hesitated to make references at very early stages of the litigation; this tendency has been particularly marked in cases involving the validity (as opposed to the interpretation) of Community legislation.

In criminal cases before a jury special problems arise, not least because it is inconceivable that a jury trial be interrupted for over a year while a reference is made. As Lord Diplock put it in *Henn and Darby v DPP*[4]

> . . . in a criminal trial upon indictment it can seldom be a proper exercise of the presiding judge's discretion to seek a preliminary ruling before the facts of the alleged offence have been ascertained, with the result that the proceedings will be held up for nine months or more in order that at the end of the trial he may give to the jury an accurate instruction as to the relevant law, if the evidence turns out in the event to be as was anticipated at the time the reference was made—which may not always be the case. It is generally better, as the judge himself put it, that the question be decided by him in the first instance and reviewed thereafter if necessary through the hierarchy of the national courts.

This was the approach of *R v Tymen*[5] where the trial judge refused to make a reference, the trial then proceeded and the appellant was convicted: the Court of Appeal, Criminal Division, referred a series of questions to the European Court on whether a member state had power to adopt and bring into force fishery conservation measures of the kind in connection with which the defendant had been convicted.

Where the hearing is before magistrates and the facts are not in dispute, a reference under art 177 may be appropriate if the guilt of the accused turns decisively on the interpretation or validity of Community law. Thus in *R v Pieck*[6] a Dutch national was charged with remaining in the United Kingdom after the endorsement on his passport 'given leave to enter the United Kingdom for six months' had expired: the Pontypridd Magistrates' Court referred a series of questions to the European Court, and the effect of its answers was that the prosecution could not succeed, and it was subsequently dropped by the Home Office.

In *R v Plymouth Justices, ex p Rogers*[7] the defendant was charged before the Plymouth Magistrates' Court with using fishing nets in

---

4 [1981] AC at 904, [1980] 2 All ER at 197.
5 [1981] 2 CMLR 544; Case 269/80 [1981] ECR 3079, [1982] 2 CMLR 111. See also Case 7/78 *R v Thompson* [1978] ECR 2247, [1979] 1 CMLR 47 for a similar approach.
6 Case 157/79 [1980] ECR 2171, [1980] 3 CMLR 220.
7 [1982] QB 863, [1982] 2 All ER 175; Case 87/82 *Rogers v Darthenay* [1983] ECR 1579, [1984] 1 CMLR 135.

contravention of a Council Regulation contrary to the United Kingdom implementing legislation. The defendant, at the close of the prosecution case, contended before the magistrates that the charge should be dismissed because the regulations on which it was based were invalid as a matter of Community law and that the proceedings should be adjourned to enable a reference to be made to the European Court. There was then an application for judicial review on behalf of the prosecution in which the Divisional Court was asked to review the decision of the magistrates to make the reference. The Divisional Court rejected the argument of the prosecution that no court or tribunal could refer questions to the European Court unless all the facts had been admitted or found because, in the case of a criminal trial, this would mean that it would have no jurisdiction to refer on a submission being made that there was no case to answer unless all the facts had been admitted. It held that the magistrates' court had jurisdiction to refer questions to the European Court at that stage because the validity of the regulations was the substantive issue before the court and this was an exceptional case where they had jurisdiction to refer and it was proper for them to do so. In general, however, the Divisional Court said that it would be highly undesirable for justices to decide to refer until all the evidence had been called and until they could be satisfied there was no question of the respondent being acquitted on the facts; this was the obvious precaution to take to avoid the expense and delay of a reference to the European Court, even if it might involve the justices themselves taking a decision on the issue as to Community law without the advantage of the guidance of the European Court. In the ordinary way the justices should exercise considerable caution before referring even after they had heard all the evidence, since, if they come to a wrong decision on Community law, a higher court could make the reference. Where the issue of Community law affects the sentence following conviction it may be appropriate for the final court to make the reference following conviction and before sentence, so that, for example, it may know whether it has the power to order the deportation of,[8] or impose a residence requirement upon,[9] a convicted person.

5 The role of article 177 in interlocutory proceedings

An important reason for the reluctance of national courts to refer under art 177 at the stage of application for interim relief is that interlocutory proceedings have at least two characteristics which militate against the desirability of references to the European Court being made in the course of them. In the first place, they do not

---

8 Case 30/77 *R v Bouchereau* [1977] ECR 1999, [1977] 2 CMLR 800, [1978] QB 732.
9 Case 175/78 *R v Saunders* [1979] ECR 1129, [1979] 2 CMLR 216.

usually involve final decisions on any disputed points of law, in the sense that at the trial of the action the judge will have to take a firm view on some matters on which only a provisional view was necessary at the interlocutory stage. In the second place, they often take place in a context that requires speedy and informal determination. In the normal case in England an injunction may be granted at a very early stage either on an ex parte application by the plaintiff or at a hearing *inter partes* but before the defendants have had an opportunity to file evidence in reply. If either party raises a question of Community law and requests the national court to refer it to the European Court under art 177 a substantial delay will be unavoidable. In any event, whatever decision is given on the hearing for an injunction it will not be a final one. Moreover, the national court will not have made any relevant factual findings. There is always a danger in having abstract points of law decided without a decision on the facts which will put the points of law into clear focus.

Two points were considered in *Hoffman-La Roche v Centrafarm*.[10] The first was whether references could validly be made under art 177 in interlocutory proceedings for interim relief. The second was whether a national court from which no appeal could be taken was to be regarded as a final court within the meaning of art 177(3)[11] and so *bound* to refer any question of interpretation to the European Court. In its submissions to the European Court, the United Kingdom Government argued that normally it was impracticable to make a reference in interlocutory proceedings for interim relief; it did recognise that there could be cases where such a reference might be appropriate, eg where the parties are prepared to accept the outcome of the interlocutory application as resolving their dispute; but in any event there would not be any *obligation* to make a reference, even by a court of last resort, because no order for interim relief was absolutely final. These submissions were broadly in line with those of the French Government, the Commission, and Advocate General Capotorti, and with the judgment of the Court. The actual decision involved a reference by the Provincial Court of Appeal for Karlsruhe, Germany, on the question whether it was *bound* to refer to the European Court, because no appeal lay from it from decisions on interlocutory injunctions. Nevertheless the European Court did express a view on the question whether national courts had the power to refer under art 177 in interlocutory proceedings. It said:[12]

---

10 Case 107/76 [1977] ECR 957, [1977] 2 CMLR 334.
11 See p 155, ante.
12 [1977] ECR 957 at 973.

... it is necessary to note that there is no doubt that the summary and urgent character of a procedure in the national court does not prevent the Court from regarding itself as validly seised under that paragraph [art 177(2)] whenever a national court or tribunal considers that it is necessary to make use of that paragraph.

This holding that courts could make references under art 177 in interlocutory proceedings was in line with the practice of the Court.[13]

In *Löwenbräu München v Grunhalle Lager International Ltd*[14] the defendants had begun to market a product in England under the name 'Grunhalle Lager'. The plaintiffs moved the English court for an interlocutory injunction to restrain the defendants from passing off their beer as the beer of the plaintiffs. The defendants asked the court to refer a point of Community law to the European Court, namely, whether, broadly, a plaintiff could restrain the importation into one member state of goods which bore a mark capable of being affixed in another member state, whether the plaintiff has expressly or impliedly consented, or cannot in law object, to the use of the trade mark in the latter state. In argument it seems to have been suggested that, as a matter of law, it could never be 'necessary' to have the views of the European Court at the interlocutory stage because no final decision was being given. It was argued on behalf of the plaintiffs that the earliest time at which it could possibly be 'necessary' to know the views of the European Court was when the trial court had found the facts and had come to the conclusion that a final injunction should be granted subject to the Common Market point. Graham J, however, rightly pointed out that although 'references are not to be made unnecessarily', the power to refer is not confined only to courts whose decisions are final or to any particular stage of the case. In the result Graham J did not deal at all with the role of art 177 in interlocutory proceedings, except to hold, quite rightly, that he did have the power to make a reference notwithstanding that the interlocutory proceedings were not of a final character. Instead, he took another and more questionable route, namely, of deciding that no problem of interpretation of the EEC Treaty arose at all.

The same judge was faced in *EMI Records Ltd v CBS United Kingdom Ltd*[15] with another trade mark battle. EMI sought an interlocutory injunction against the English subsidiary of the American company Columbia to restrain the latter from marketing records under

---

13 See cases referred to by Capotorti AG, ibid, at 978–9 and also Case 70/77 *Simmenthal SpA v Amministrazione delle Finanze dello Stato (No. 3)* [1978] ECR 1453, [1978] 3 CMLR 670. See also Collins (1974) 23 ICLQ 840. The point was expressly left open by Stephenson LJ in *Bulmer v Bollinger* [1974] Ch 401 at 430, [1974] 2 All ER 1226 at 1241.
14 [1974] 1 CMLR 1.
15 [1975] 1 CMLR 285.

the market 'Columbia' which CBS was importing from the United States. The defendants sought to resist the application for an interlocutory injunction because of the necessity for a reference to the European Court under art 177 of the question whether Community law allowed EMI as the owner of the trade mark 'Columbia' in England to prevent the importation into the Community of goods bearing the same mark validly affixed in the United States. Graham J held that because the Community law point would dispose of the action it was necessary to have a ruling on the point, not necessarily for the purposes of an interlocutory injunction, but so that he could ultimately be in a position to give a final judgment. Meanwhile, however, there was no reason why an interlocutory injunction should not be granted pending the trial (and the reference to the European Court) to preserve the status quo.

In *Polydor Ltd v Harlequin Record Shops Ltd*[16] the defendants had imported into the United Kingdom from Portugal records which were lawfully made in Portugal with the consent of the Portuguese copyright holders, but without the consent of Polydor, the United Kingdom copyright holders. Polydor sought an interlocutory injunction and were granted one by Megarry V-C; the defendants argued that the EEC-Portuguese Free Trade Agreement had the effect of prohibiting the use of copyright law to prevent parallel imports, but the Vice-Chancellor refused to make a reference because the facts were not found or agreed, and it could not be said that a ruling from the European Court was necessary to enable the trial court to give judgment. This decision was reversed by the Court of Appeal, which refused to allow the interim injunction to stand and made a reference to the European Court because if the view of the Court of Appeal as to the effect of the Portuguese agreement was right (which it was found by the European Court not to be) the action by Polydor was dead and, in the words[17] of Templeman LJ:

> ... what I am not prepared to do is to allow the plaintiffs to have an injunction which to my mind would be a complete breach of Community law on the view I have formed, unless and until the European Court has ruled that some other interpretation is to be placed on article 14.

In *Portsmouth City Council v Richards*[18] the local authority sought an interim injunction to restrain the operation of an unlicensed sex shop. The defendants had persuaded several courts in criminal proceedings or proceedings for judicial review involving other local authorities, to refer questions to the European Court, the ultimate object of which was to determine whether the licensing provisions of the Local

---

16 [1980] 2 CMLR 413.
17 At 426.
18 [1989] 1 CMLR 673, CA.

Government (Miscellaneous Provisions) Act 1982 were compatible with the prohibition on restriction of imports under art 30 of the Treaty. The defendants had been convicted of more than 30 offences in various parts of the country, and had brought 56 applications for judicial review against licence refusals, most of which had been unsuccessful. In the *Portsmouth* case the defendants resisted the application for an injunction on the ground of the pending applications to the European Court. Kerr LJ pointed out that by seeking to rely on art 30 the defendants had succeeded in neutralising the effect of the criminal law. The Court of Appeal held that the local authority was entitled to the exceptional remedy of an interim civil injunction to restrain criminal offences because the activities of the defendants had effectively nullified the criminal law. The fact that references were pending to the European Court did not prevent an injunction being granted. Kerr LJ said:[19]

> It must also be borne in mind that in order to decide whether or not to grant an interim injunction, a reference under Article 177 can rarely be 'necessary to enable [the court] to give judgment' . . . since the grant or refusal of an injunction is not a final judgment. Accordingly there is no necessary correlation . . . between the circumstances that there is a pending reference or that one may be granted on the one hand, and the mandatory refusal of an interlocutory injunction on the other. The two things are not interdependent.

Mann LJ was persuaded that 'the prospect of a reference to Luxembourg makes this one of the exceptional cases where an injunction on an interim basis in aid of the criminal law should issue'.[20]

In the *Factortame* case[1] the House of Lords refused the applicants an interim injunction to restrain the application of the Merchant Shipping Act 1988, because the court had no power to make an order postponing the operation of a statute pending a reference to the European Court, and had no power to grant an interim injunction against the Crown. But the House of Lords referred to the European Court the question whether *under Community law* a national court was under an obligation to provide an effective interlocutory remedy to protect rights which were directly effective.

The cases dealing with injunctions fall in several categories: first, those where Community law was raised, but an injunction was granted or refused without any question of a reference under art 177

---

19 At p 704.
20 At p 711.
1 *Factortame Ltd v Secretary of State for Transport* [1989] 2 WLR 997, [1989] 2 All ER 692, HL, on which see pp 108–110, above.

being raised;[2] second, cases in which a reference was refused, and an injunction was granted[3] or refused;[4] third, cases in which a reference was made, and the injunction was granted[5] or refused.[6]

It is clear that on applications for interlocutory injunctions a reference may be made by a lower court under art 177(2), but that even for the final court under art 177(3) there is no obligation to refer, because no final decision is involved.[7] It is equally clear that only sparing use of the art 177 procedure should be made at this stage of proceedings because:

1. Applications for interim relief do not usually[8] fully dispose of the matters in issue.
2. They are taken at a stage when it is often not clear what the matters in issue will ultimately be.
3. They are taken at a stage when the facts have not been ascertained.
4. In England (although the position is different in other countries) the current practice is that the merits of the underlying action are not crucial to the decision on provisional measures.
5. They require by their nature speedy determination.

6 Appeals from decisions of lower courts to refer

One of the parties may feel aggrieved at a decision by a United Kingdom court making, or refusing to make, a reference, and may wish to appeal to a higher court. Whether it is a referral or a refusal, the question arises as to the extent of the right of appeal under national law. Two additional questions arise in relation to a referral by a lower

---

2 *Lerose Ltd v Hawick Jersey International Ltd* [1973] CMLR 83; *Minnesota Mining and Manufacturing Co v Geerpres Europe Ltd* [1973] CMLR 359; *Esso Petroleum Co Ltd v Kingswood Motors (Addlestone) Ltd* [1974] QB 142, [1973] 3 All ER 1057 (injunctions granted); *Chelmkarm Motors Ltd v Esso Petroleum Co Ltd* [1979] 1 CMLR 73 (injunction refused).
3 *Löwenbrau*, n 14, ante, *Maxims Ltd v Dye* [1978] 2 All ER 55, [1977] 1 WLR 1155; *Portsmouth City Council v Richards* [1988] 1 CMLR 673. Cf *Wychavon District Council v Midland Enterprises (Special Event) Ltd* [1988] 1 CMLR 397 (application for interlocutory injunction treated as trial; final injunction granted, reference refused). See also *The Who Group Ltd v Stage One (Records) Ltd* [1980] 2 CMLR 429.
4 *Sirdar Ltd v Les Fils de Louis Mulliez* [1975] 1 CMLR 378.
5 *EMI v CBS*, n 15, ante.
6 *Polydor v Harlequin*, n 16, ante; *Factortame Ltd v Secretary of State for Transport* [1989] 2 WLR 997, [1989] 2 All ER 692, HL; cf *Rochdale Borough Council v Anders* [1988] 3 CMLR 431 (a decision of doubtful authority).
7 See p 155, ante, and *Garden Cottage Foods Ltd v Milk Marketing Board* [1984] AC 130, [1983] 2 All ER 770, HL.
8 But there are exceptional cases where, for all practical purposes they do: see *NWL Ltd v Woods* [1979] 3 All ER 614 at 625, [1979] 1 WLR 1294 at 1306; *Cayne v Global Natural Resources Plc* [1984] 1 All ER 225, CA.

court: the first is whether any such right of appeal is compatible with Community law; and the second is the effect on the proceedings in the European Court of appeals in the national proceedings against a decision to refer.

Under Ord 114, r 6 of the English Rules of the Supreme Court, an order making a reference is deemed to be a final order, and therefore an appeal against it lies to the Court of Appeal without leave. If, as Lord Denning pointed out in *Bulmer v Bollinger*,[9] a judge refuses an order referring a question to the European Court, leave to appeal (by the judge or the Court of Appeal) is required because it is an interlocutory order. Stephenson LJ said:[10]

> It is curious that new Rules of the Supreme Court RSC Ord 114, rr 1–6, deal with references to the European Court under article 177 (and under articles of two other Treaties) but, perhaps by an oversight, Ord 114, r 6, which deals with appeals, does not deal with refusals to make an order referring to the European Court. By Ord 114, r 6, an appeal lies against an order referring without leave, but that special provision cannot affect the general power of the judge or this court to grant leave against a refusal to make such an order just as against any other interlocutory exercise of judicial discretion. The special provisions cannot give a party dissatisfied with a judge's refusal to refer a corresponding right to appeal, nor can it take away his right to apply for leave to appeal—which the judge appears to have given here. And it cannot alter this court's duty to interfere with an exercise of judicial discretion when and only when the judge's decision 'exceeds the generous ambit within which reasonable disagreement is possible and is, in fact, plainly wrong'.[11]

So far as a refusal by a lower court to refer is concerned, whether that refusal is effectively appealable is likely to depend on the stage of the proceedings at which the refusal takes place. If the refusal is at the trial of the action and is part of the final judgment, the appeal court will have power, as part of the process of review, to refer the question to the European Court. Thus, for example, if at the trial the judge has found for the defendant and has refused to refer a question of Community law to the European Court, the plaintiff will have lost its case and will appeal to the Court of Appeal asking for a complete reversal of the decision. The Court of Appeal will have to make up its own mind on the merits and may decide to refer the question of Community law to the European Court, but it would not remit the question back to the trial judge for him to refer it to the European Court. Similarly, where the decision of a judge is given at an interlocutory stage, although the Court of Appeal will not normally interfere with an exercise of

---

9 [1974] Ch 401 at 421, [1974] 2 All ER 1226 at 1233.
10 Ibid at 430–431, 1241.
11 Citing Asquith LJ in *Bellenden (formerly Satterthwaite) v Satterthwaite* [1948] 1 All ER 343 at 345.

discretion,[12] it may reverse a decision to refer if it is satisfied that the judge's discretion was based on some wrong principle. This may happen at an early stage of the proceedings, such as on an application for a reference or on the summons for directions; or the judge may adjourn a trial for a short time to enable an appeal to be made immediately to the Court of Appeal against a ruling made in the course of the trial.

If there is a decision to refer by a lower court, then, as indicated above, an appeal lies to the Court of Appeal without leave under Ord 114, r 6. If the reference is by the Court of Appeal, then an appeal would only be possible with the leave of the Court of Appeal or of the House of Lords. Ord 114, r 5 provides that where a judge has made an order referring a question under art 177, the Senior Master is not to transmit a copy of the order to the European Court until the time for appealing has expired, or, if an appeal is entered, until the appeal has been determined or disposed of; in either case the court of first instance or the Court of Appeal may order that the reference be transmitted, notwithstanding that the time for appealing has not expired or the appeal has not been determined.

The right of appeal provided by Ord 114, r 6 is probably in conformity with Community law. In the *Rheinmühlen* case[13] Advocate General Warner suggested[14] that rr 5 and 6 of Ord 114 were in conflict with Community law and void, because they fettered the discretion of the national judge. The European Court, however, indicated, although it was not necessary to the decision, that art 177 did not preclude a decision referring a question from remaining subject to the judicial remedies normally available under national law. The Court (in a rather cryptic passage) indicated that decisions referring questions to the Court might be the subject of appeal. It said:[15]

> ... in the case of a court against whose decision there is a judicial remedy under national law, art 177 does not preclude a decision of such a court referring a question to this Court for a preliminary ruling from remaining subject to the remedies normally available under national law. Nevertheless, in the interests of clarity and legal certainty, this Court must abide by the decision to refer, which must have its full effect so long as it has not been revoked.

Thus the Court has removed a reference from its register when the national court held that a body which had made a reference was not a

---

12 For the principles to be applied in the review of a judge's discretion see *Hadmor Productions Ltd v Hamilton* [1983] 1 AC 191, [1982] 1 All ER 1042.
13 Cases 146 and 166/73 [1974] ECR 139 and 33, [1974] 1 CMLR 523.
14 [1974] ECR at 47.
15 [1974] ECR at 147.

'court or tribunal',[16] and in the *Simmenthal* case[17] the Court indicated that it was validly seised of a reference under art 177 'so long as the reference has not been withdrawn by the court from which it emanates or has not been quashed on appeal by a superior court'. It would, therefore, appear that the court will, in an appropriate case, recognise the right to appeal in national law against a decision referring a question to the European Court under art 177. But in *Campus Oil Ltd v Minister for Industry and Energy*[18] the Irish Supreme Court held that it had no power to review the decision of a lower court to make a reference under art 177. This was because as a matter of Irish law art 177 conferred an unfettered discretion on the Irish judge to make a reference under art 177; the absence of a rule giving a right of appeal in Irish law was based on the view that such rules would be in breach of the Treaty. The Supreme Court did not decide whether that view was right as a matter of European law.

Ord 114, r 5, differs from the ordinary procedural law in that, in effect, it puts a compulsory stay on the effect of an order to refer until disposition of any appeal or until the time for appealing expires. Ord 114, r 6 differs from the ordinary law in that it turns what would otherwise be an interlocutory order into a final order and thus removes the need for leave to appeal. These differences, it is suggested, do not take the rules outside the scope of judicial remedies normally available. In the first place, although generally an appeal does not involve any automatic stay of the order appealed from, a stay will be granted in an appropriate case.[19] In the second place, the distinction between interlocutory and final orders is a fine one, which has been a constant source of confusion.[20] For these reasons, although the matter is not free from doubt, it is likely that Ord 114 is intra vires.[1] The question of the compatibility of a right of appeal against an order making a reference with Community law has been considered in Ireland,[2] but there is no reported case in England in which an appellate court has reversed the decision of a lower court to make a reference. In *R v*

---

16 See Case 65/77 *Razanatsimba* [1977] ECR 2229 at 2242, [1978] 1 CMLR 246 at 248.
17 Case 106/77 *Amministrazione delle Finanze delle Stato v Simmenthal SpA* [1978] ECR 629 at 642, [1978] 3 CMLR 263 at 282. See also Case 154/77 *Procureur du Roi v Dechmann* [1978] ECR 1573 at 1587–8, [1979] 2 CMLR 1 at 7, where Mayras AG criticised the delays caused by appeals.
18 [1984] 1 CMLR 479. See O'Keefe (1984) 9 EL Rev 87.
19 See RSC Ord 59, r 13.
20 See now RSC Ord 59, r 1A.
 1 Contra Jacobs and Durand *References to the European Court* (1975) p 172, who rely particularly on the fact that rr 5 and 6 purport to suspend the power of the lower court to make its references, and Usher *European Court Practice* (1983), p 164.
 2 See text at n 18, supra, and cf Cases 36 and 71/80 *Irish Creamery Milk Suppliers v Ireland Association* [1981] ECR 735, [1981] 2 CMLR 455.

Plymouth Justices, ex p Rogers[3] there was an appeal to the Queen's Bench Divisional Court against a decision of the Plymouth Magistrates' Court to make a reference to the European Court. The Divisional Court dismissed the appeal, but it does not seem to have been suggested that the Divisional Court was wrong, as a matter of Community law, to hear an appeal.

The effect of appeals in the national proceedings on the proceedings in the European Court has arisen in several cases. The question arose in the first case to be referred under art 177, *De Geus v Bosch*.[4] In that case (in which the defendants had raised a defence based on art 85) the reference had been made by the Court of Appeal in the Hague and the European Court was notified of the request in July 1961. In September 1961, at a time before the art 177 reference was very far advanced, the plaintiffs in the Dutch litigation appealed to the highest Dutch court for reversal of the order of the Court of Appeal which had referred the question on art 85 under art 177. Oral proceedings on the reference to the European Court were conducted in January 1962 when the plaintiffs in the original litigation (supported by the French Government) argued that the reference was not admissible because the effect of appeal under Dutch law was to deprive the order appealed from of final effect and to suspend execution pending the outcome of the appeal.[5] They argued therefore that the European Court should await the decision of the highest Dutch court. The Court held that in effect the mere request by a court or tribunal within the meaning of art 177 was sufficient to seise the Court under that article, no matter whether the domestic legal system provided otherwise if the request itself was under appeal. Therefore the Court was able in its view to give a preliminary ruling, even though the very request for that preliminary ruling was under appeal and the answer might fall on entirely deaf judicial ears should the appeal be allowed.

Subsequently, the Court refined its approach to the problem of the effect of appeals against referral orders. In *Chanel v Cepha*[6] the plaintiffs were the well-known French perfume producers, who entered into a contract with a Dutch company for the supply of perfume to the Dutch company for export to Indonesia. When Chanel

---

3 [1982] QB 863, [1982] 2 All ER 175.
4 Case 13/61 [1962] ECR 45, [1962] CMLR 1. See also Cases 2–4/82 *Delhaize Frères 'Le Lion' SA v Belgium* [1983] ECR 2973, [1985] 1 CMLR 561.
5 The defendants argued that the effect of art 20 of the Protocol on the Statute of the Court was to suspend the domestic proceedings while the reference was heard by the Court. But it is not likely that the mere reflection in art 20 of the fact that a domestic court normally suspends its proceedings is sufficient to impose a Community obligation on a domestic legal system of so far-reaching a character. Cf Lagrange AG [1962] ECR 45 at 58 and the opinion of the Court at 49–50.
6 Case 31/68 [1970] ECR 403, [1971] CMLR 403. See also Case 152/83 *Demouche v Fonds de Garantie Automobile* [1987] ECR 3833.

sued the Dutch company for breach of contract alleging that, contrary to the terms of the contract, the perfume had been exported to Germany, the Dutch company alleged (inter alia) that Chanel's practice of concluding agreements which implied a prohibition of parallel imports of Chanel products to other EEC members was incompatible with the EEC Treaty. The Rotterdam Court stayed the proceedings and asked for a preliminary ruling from the European Court under art 177. The order of the Rotterdam Court was made in December 1968 and in January 1969 Chanel appealed to the Court of Appeal of the Hague. In May 1969 Advocate General Roemer made his submissions to the European Court in the art 177 reference by the Rotterdam Court, but before the Court of Appeal at the Hague had pronounced on the appeal. He recommended that the reference under art 177 be stayed until a decision was given in the Dutch courts with regard to whether the interpretation requested was necessary. Accordingly, in June 1969 the Court noted that it had been informed by the Rotterdam Court that (i) an appeal had been lodged against its judgment and (ii) the appeal had the consequence of staying execution of the judgment. It held therefore that in the circumstances of the case and as a consequence of the communication, judgment should be suspended. In May 1970 the Court of Appeal at the Hague quashed the order of the Rotterdam Court on the grounds (inter alia) that the Rotterdam Court was wrong in holding that the defence raised a question of interpretation of the EEC Treaty and was essential for rendering judgment. In the following month the Rotterdam Court informed the European Court of the decision of the Court of Appeal and accordingly the European Court decided that the proceedings for interpretation had lost their purpose and that the case should be removed from the Court register.

In *Belgische Radio en Televisie v SABAM*[7] the reference under art 177 was by the first instance court of Brussels. After the reference was notified to the European Court in April 1973 SABAM appealed against the order to the Court of Appeal of Brussels. Later that month the Registrar of the first instance court sent a letter to the European Court in which he stated that the appeal suspended the proceedings before the European Court, but in September the same Registrar, upon reconsideration, informed the European Court that the Brussels court did not wish the European Court to suspend the examination of the preliminary questions. The European Court noted that the Belgian court had intimated that it did not wish the examination of the preliminary questions to be suspended pending the appeal and therefore the judgment of the European Court does not deal with this point.

As a practical matter, the problem is not likely to arise in references

---

7 Case 127/73 [1974] ECR 51, [1974] 2 CMLR 238. See also *Simmenthal*, n 17, ante.

from the United Kingdom if the party appealing from a decision to refer takes care to ask for appropriate directions. In references by the High Court, Ord 114, r 5, if it is valid (as it probably is), ensures that the European Court will not be seised until an appeal has been disposed of.

7 Procedural aspects

This section will deal with procedural aspects of references: the form of the reference; the role of the parties; costs and legal aid.

(i) Order 114—references by the High Court

Order 114 of the Rules of the Supreme Court[8] sets out the procedure for references by the High Court. It is of such practical importance that it may be helpful if it is set out in full:

Interpretation

1. In this Order—
'the Court' means the court by which an order is made and includes the Court of Appeal;
'the European Court' means the Court of Justice of the European Communities; and
'order' means an order referring a question to the European Court for a preliminary ruling under Article 177 of the Treaty establishing the European Economic Community, Article 150 of the Treaty establishing the European Atomic Energy Community or Article 41 of the Treaty establishing the European Coal and Steel Community or for a ruling on the interpretation of the Conventions referred to in section 1(1) of the Civil Jurisdiction and Judgments Act 1982.[9]

---

8 Rules have also been laid down for other tribunals. See Criminal Appeal (References to the European Court) Rules 1972, SI 1972/1786, Crown Court (References to the European Court) Rules 1972, SI 1972/1787 and County Court (Amendment No 2) Rules 1973, SI 1973/847. For Scotland see Act of Sederunt (Rules of Court Amendment No 5) 1972, SI 1972/1981; Act of Adjournal (References to the European Court) 1973, SI 1973/450 as amended by SI 1978/125; Act of Sederunt (Sheriff Court Procedure Amendment No 2) 1973, SI 1973/543. For Northern Ireland see Rules of the Supreme Court (Northern Ireland) (No 5) 1972, SR 1972/317; Criminal Appeal (References to the European Court) (Northern Ireland) Rules 1972, SR 1972/354; County Court (Amendments) No 3 Rules (Northern Ireland) 1972, SR 1972/380. Other courts have made references without express authority: see p 183, ante.
9 References under the 1982 Act (which gives effect to the Brussels Convention on jurisdiction and the enforcement of judgments of 1968) are governed by somewhat different principles and are outside the scope of this book: see Collins *Civil Jurisdiction and Judgments Act 1982* (1983) pp 10–16.

Making of order

2. (1) An order may be made by the Court of its own motion at any stage in a cause or matter, or on application by a party before or at the trial or hearing thereof.
(2) Where an application is made before the trial or hearing, it shall be made by motion.
(3) In the High Court no order shall be made except by a judge in person.

Schedule to order to set out request for ruling

3. An order shall set out in a schedule the request for the preliminary ruling of the European Court, and the Court may give directions as to the manner and form in which the schedule is to be prepared.

Stay of proceedings pending ruling

4. The proceedings in which an order is made shall, unless the Court otherwise orders, be stayed until the European Court has given a preliminary ruling on the question referred to it.

Transmission of order to the European Court

5. When an order has been made, the Senior Master shall send a copy thereof to the Registrar of the European Court; but in the case of an order made by the High Court, he shall not do so, unless the Court otherwise orders, until the time for appealing against the order has expired or, if an appeal is entered within that time, until the appeal has been determined or otherwise disposed of.

Appeals from orders made by High Court

6. An order made by the High Court shall be deemed to be a final decision, and accordingly an appeal against it shall lie to the Court of Appeal without leave; but the period within which a notice of appeal must be served under Ord 59, r 4(1), shall be 14 days.

(ii) The reference and its form

Article 20 of the Protocol on the Statute of the Court of Justice of the EEC merely provides in relation to references under art 177, that:

> the decision of the court or tribunal of a member state which suspends its proceedings and refers a case to the Court shall be notified to the Court by the court or tribunal concerned.

The European Court itself has been very liberal in accepting references from national courts. Although it has stressed the need for the national court to define the legal context of, and explain the reasons for, its references,[10] nevertheless the failure by a national court to observe these guidelines will not normally prevent the Court from dealing with a reference. Not only does it rephrase questions to avoid

---

10 *Foglia v Novello (No 2)*, p 168, ante.

answering questions of fact and questions of national law, but often it has almost to invent the questions which the national court was not able or willing to formulate. *Costa v ENEL*[11] was a case where the national judge merely referred to the Treaty provisions which had been involved and sent the file on the case, without actually formulating the question. Another striking example occurred when a French court did not put the request for interpretation in the form of a precise question, but merely asked 'for a preliminary ruling on the interpretation of article 85'. The European Court nevertheless admitted the reference and extracted from the judgment what it thought the questions ought to be.[12]

In general United Kingdom courts have formulated the questions in a way which the European Court has found satisfactory, although it has sometimes been necessary for the question to be reformulated.[13] There have, however, been exceptions. Thus, in one of the cases involved in the *Isoglucose* litigation, the reference was made by Donaldson J[14] three days after the writ was issued and was in a very laconic form; Advocate General Reischl said that 'the reference falls short of the ideal' and it was necessary for the Court to look at the file to extract the real question.[15] In another case a Northern Ireland magistrate asked a bewildering variety of questions, from which the Court had to extract the real issues.[16]

The following prescribed form has been added to the Supreme Court Practice as Form 109. The Schedule was amended in 1988 to provide for more precise information to be supplied to the European Court.

Order for reference to the European Court (Ord 114, r 2)
[Heading as in cause or matter]
It is ordered that the question[s] set out in the Schedule hereto concerning the interpretation [or validity] of [specific Treaty provision or Community instrument or act concerned] be referred to the Court of Justice of the European Communities for a preliminary ruling in accordance with article 177 of the Treaty establishing the European Economic Community [or

---

11 Case 6/64 [1964] ECR 585, [1964] CMLR 425.
12 Case 1/71 *Cadillon v Höss* [1971] ECR 351, [1971] CMLR 420.
13 See Case 7/78 *R v Thompson* [1978] ECR 2247, [1979] 1 CMLR 47, where the emphasis of the English Court of Appeal (Criminal Division) on whether gold coins were 'capital' was changed by the European Court to whether they were 'goods'; and Case 175/78 *R v Saunders* [1979] ECR 1129, [1979] 2 CMLR 216, where the Crown Court asked the European Court to rule on the validity of its own order; the European Court interpreted the question as being 'in substance' a question of interpretation of the scope of freedom of movement.
14 [1977] 2 CMLR 449.
15 Case 103/77 *Royal Scholten-Honig (Holdings) Ltd v Intervention Board for Agricultural Produce* [1978] ECR 2037, [1979] 1 CMLR 675.
16 Case 83/78 *Pigs Marketing Board v Redmond* [1978] ECR 2347, [1979] 1 CMLR 177.

article 150 of the Treaty establishing the European Atomic Energy Community or article 41 of the Treaty establishing the European Coal and Steel Community or for a ruling under Schedule 2 to the Civil Jurisdiction and Judgments Act 1982, as the case may be].

And it is ordered that all further proceedings in the above-named cause [or matter] be stayed until the said Court of Justice has given its ruling on the said question[s] or until further order.

SCHEDULE
REQUEST FOR PRELIMINARY RULING OF THE COURT OF JUSTICE OF THE EUROPEAN COMMUNITIES

(Here set out a clear and succinct statement of the case giving rise to the request for the ruling of the European Court of Justice in order to enable the European Court of Justice to consider and understand the issues of Community Law raised and to enable Governments of member states and other interested parties to submit observations. The statement of the case should include:

(a) particulars of the parties;
(b) the history of the dispute between the parties;
(c) the history of the proceedings;
(d) the relevant facts as agreed by the parties or found by the Court or, failing such agreement or finding, the contentions of the parties on such facts;
(e) the nature of the issues of law and fact between the parties;
(f) the (English) law, so far as is relevant, and
(g) the Treaty provisions or other Acts, Instruments or Rules of Community Law concerned.

The preliminary ruling of the Court of Justice of the European Communities is accordingly requested on the following questions:

1, 2 etc. (here set out the questions on which the ruling is sought, identifying the Treaty provisions or other Acts, Instruments or Rules of Community Law concerned).

Dated the   day of   19   .

(iii) The role of the parties

It is not the parties but the national court itself which makes the reference to the European Court under art 177. By art 177(2) where a relevant question is raised before 'any court or tribunal' of a member state *that court or tribunal* may request the European Court to give a ruling. By art 177(3) where such a question is raised before a court or tribunal of last resort, *that court or tribunal* shall be bound to bring the matter before the European Court. Under the procedure laid down in art 20 of the Protocol on the Statute of the Court, it is for the national court which suspends proceedings and applies for a preliminary ruling to notify the European Court of its decision. The parties, the Commission and the member states (and in certain cases the Council) then have a right to submit to the Court written statements of case or comments and may subsequently be heard in oral arguments.

Although neither art 177 nor the decisions of the European Court *require* the parties to be heard before the national court makes a reference, the European Court has on several occasions pointed out that 'it may where necessary prove to be in the interests of the proper administration of justice that a question should be referred for a preliminary ruling only after both sides have been heard',[17] and Advocate General Warner in *Foglia v Novello (No 1)*[18] warned of the dangers of references in cases where the defendant was not heard by the national court before the order was made. The European Court held it had no jurisdiction to give a ruling because the parties had resorted to an artificial device to obtain a ruling from the Italian courts that the French tax system was invalid. The duty of the European Court was to national courts and not to parties.[19] Thus where a plaintiff in its written observations asked the European Court to widen the ambit of the question referred by the German court, the European Court refused. The point raised by the plaintiff concerned a regulation different from that which the German court had asked the court to interpret, and neither the facts nor the legal arguments in the order for reference allowed the European Court to conclude that the German court considered a decision on that point necessary in order for it to give judgment. Consequently the point could only be raised if the German court made a further reference.[20] In *CILFIT Srl v Ministry of Health*[1] the Court emphasised that art 177 was not a means of redress available to the parties: the mere fact that a party contended that the dispute gave rise to a question concerning the interpretation of Community law did not mean that the court or tribunal concerned was compelled to consider that a question had been raised;[2] conversely, the national court or tribunal might refer a matter to the European Court of its own motion. The latter was the situation in *Salonia v Poidomani and Giglio*;[3] the Court held that the fact that the parties to the main action had failed to raise a point of Community law before the national court did not preclude the latter from bringing the matter before the court under art 177.

Although Ord 114, r 2 provides that a reference may be made by the High Court, it is unthinkable that a United Kingdom court would

---

17 Case 70/77 *SpA Simmenthal v Amministrazione delle Finanze dello Stato* [1978] ECR 1453 at 1468, [1978] 3 CMLR 670 at 682. See also Case 52/76 *Benedetti v Munari* [1977] ECR 163.
18 Case 104/79 [1980] ECR 745, [1981] 1 CMLR 45.
19 See pp 169–172, ante, and Case 93/78 *Mattheus v Doego* [1978] ECR 2203, [1979] 1 CMLR 551.
20 Case 299/84 *Fa Karl-Heinz Neumann v BALM* [1985] ECR 3663, [1987] 3 CMLR 4.
1 Case 283/81 [1982] ECR 3415, [1983] 1 CMLR 472.
2 Cf Cases 115 and 116/81 *Adoui and Cornuaille v Belgium* [1982] ECR 1665 at 1715, [1982] 3 CMLR 631 at 642, per Capotorti AG.
3 Case 126/80 [1981] ECR 1563, [1982] 1 CMLR 64.

formulate a reference without hearing all parties or that a reference would be made on an ex parte application. The court will normally invite the comments of the parties on the nature and wording of the reference. But it will be its reference and the parties cannot control it, although they may be able to appeal against it.

In *Bulmer v Bollinger*[4] Lord Denning MR suggested that the wishes of the parties were a factor to be taken into account, but the English court 'should not give them undue weight' although it 'should hesitate before making a reference against the wishes of one of the parties, seeing the expense and delay which it involves'. Thus the court may be placed in the position where it feels it has to make a reference even though neither of the parties wishes it[5] or one party cannot afford it.[6] In *Portsmouth City Council v Richards*[7] the Court of Appeal was clearly concerned that references had been made in several cases as to whether restrictions on the importation and sale of articles for use in sex shops contravened art 30 of the EEC Treaty. Kerr LJ said:[8]

> It is very important that the concept of so-called references by consent should not creep into our practice. All references are by the court. The court must itself be satisfied of the need for the reference; that the factual material accompanying the reference is sufficient to provide a proper foundation for it, and that it is of sufficient assistance to the European Court to enable it to reach a decision . . .

But there can be no direct recourse by the parties to the European Court under art 177. In one decision individual parties purported to refer under art 177 a question of the validity of certain decisions of the Commission. The Court in its judgment dismissing the application was quick to remind the private applicants that they had no right under art 177. It said:[9]

> It must be stressed that the Treaty clearly defines the respective jurisdictions of the Court of Justice and of national courts or tribunals. In fact, by virtue of both article 177 and article 20 of the Protocol on the Statute of the Court of Justice of the European Economic Community, the decision to

---

4 [1974] Ch 401 at 425, [1974] 2 All ER 1226 at 1236. See also *R v Tymen* [1981] 2 CMLR 544 at 546; *R v Pharmaceutical Society of Great Britain, ex p Association of Pharmaceutical Importers* [1987] 3 CMLR 951 at 970, CA.
5 Cf *Bulmer v Bollinger (No 2)* [1975] 2 CMLR 479 at 489, and see also *Pigs Marketing Board v Redmond* [1978] 2 CMLR 697, where the Northern Ireland magistrate required to be satisfied of his jurisdiction even though the defendant had pleaded guilty.
6 See *Maxim's Ltd v Dye* [1978] 2 All ER 55, [1977] 1 WLR 1155.
7 [1989] 1 CMLR 673.
8 At p 708. Contrast *Rochdale Borough Council v Anders* [1988] 3 CMLR 431 (probably wrongly decided).
9 Case 31/62 *Wöhrmann v Commission* [1962] ECR 501 at 507, [1963] CMLR 152 at 158. See also Case 44/65 *Hessische Knappschaft v Singer* [1965] ECR 965, [1966] CMLR 82.

suspend proceedings and to refer a case to this Court is one for the national court or tribunal. If the parties to an action pending before a national court or tribunal were entitled to make a direct request to this Court for a preliminary ruling, they could compel the national court to suspend proceedings pending a decision of the Court of Justice. Neither the Treaty nor the Protocol, however, imposes such a limitation on the powers of the national court.

Article 20 of the Protocol on the Statute of the Court provides that, after notification to the European Court of the national court's decision to refer:

> The decision shall then be notified by the Registrar of the Court to the parties, to the member states and to the Commission, and also to the Council if the act the validity or interpretation of which is in dispute originates from the Council. Within two months of this notification, the parties, the member states, the Commission and, where appropriate, the Council, shall be entitled to submit statements of case or written observations to the Court.

Thus the timetable is: (i) decision by the national judge referring a question to the Court; (ii) notification of that decision by the national judge to the Court; (iii) notification by the Court to the parties, all the member states and the Commission (and in certain circumstances to the Council); (iv) submission of written comments; (v) oral proceedings; (vi) preliminary ruling by the Court. The pendency of an appeal in the national courts may affect the timetable if the appeal has not been decided when the proceedings in the Court begin. In the *Chanel* case,[10] where an appeal was pending against the reference, the Court allowed the written submissions to be made and the oral proceedings to take place despite the objections of the plaintiff in the original action. But it did not pronounce judgment before the result of the appeal was known—when the national appellate court quashed the order of the judge making the reference, the Court declared the request to be without object and struck the case off its list.

Article 20 of the Protocol makes provision for the notification to, and the participation in the proceedings by, certain named groups. The Court has held that the list of groups is an exhaustive one and that no other interested persons may make representations. In the *De Cicco* case[11] the defendant in the original German proceedings was a German social security organ. The question posed was whether payments made to an Italian pension fund could be aggregated with those paid to a German fund for the purpose of Regulation 3. In the proceedings before the Court the German social security organ argued that its Italian counterpart should be given an opportunity of making

---

10 Case 31/68 [1970] ECR 403, [1971] CMLR 403.
11 Case 19/68 [1968] ECR 473, [1969] CMLR 67.

its views known to the Court. The Court held that it could not permit the participation in the proceedings of persons or organs other than those mentioned in art 20 of the Statute. Since the Italian social security organ was not a party to the original proceedings, the German social security organ failed in its application for the Italian organ to be joined in the proceedings.[12]

(iv) Costs and legal aid

By art 35 of the Protocol on the Statute, the Court is empowered to adjudicate on costs. The question of costs in art 177 references was raised in the first reference under that article, *De Geus v Bosch*.[13] The Court took a position on costs which it has since consistently followed, and which is now embodied in art 104(3) of its Rules of Procedure, namely that the costs of the parties to the original litigation incurred in respect of the reference to the Court are incidental to the domestic proceedings, and are therefore reserved to, and to be decided by, the national court. When the question of costs comes before the national court it is to be determined by national law.[14] The costs of the governments and Community institutions which submit observations to the Court are not recoverable. If a Government is itself a party to the domestic litigation, then the Court deals with it as if it were a private party for costs purposes and reserves costs to the national court.[15] In one case in which an individual party tried to invoke art 177 directly before the European Court, the application was declared inadmissible and the applicants were ordered to bear the costs of the application.[16]

In the United Kingdom courts, costs will be in the discretion of the court and will normally follow the event. Whether the costs of the reference will be treated separately will probably depend upon whether the national court considers the particular reference to be an integral part of the national proceedings. If the reference is so considered, then the costs of the reference would appropriately be costs in the cause, that is, the costs will depend upon and follow upon the ultimate result in the national proceedings. If the reference is not considered an integral part and one party has unsuccessfully resisted

---

12 The reasoning of Gand AG ([1968] ECR 473 at 484) suggests that the expression 'parties in the case' is not to be interpreted very narrowly as meaning only plaintiffs and defendants, but any person or body which is heard in the domestic proceedings. Thus in relator actions in England, the plaintiff is nominally the Attorney General but the actual conduct of the proceedings is often in the hands of the relator: see Wade *Administrative Law* (6th edn 1988) p 604. In any event it is possible for a third party which has an interest in an action to apply to be joined: see RSC Ord 15, r 6.
13 Case 13/61 [1962] ECR 45, [1962] CMLR 1.
14 Case 62/72 *Bollmann v Hauptzollamt Hamburg-Waltershof* [1973] ECR 269.
15 See eg Case 13/68 *Salgoil v Italy* [1968] ECR 453, [1969] CMLR 181.
16 Cases 31 and 33/62 *Wöhrmann v Commission* [1962] ECR 501, [1963] CMLR 152.

the other party's application for the matter to be referred, then a separate costs order may be appropriate. A difficulty is that in the case of an advisory jurisdiction such as that of the European Court under art 177 it is not always easy to see which side has been successful because it does not result in an order but merely in an opinion. Sometimes it will be clear, such as when one party has argued that a Community act is invalid and the Court rules that a particular measure is valid. In other cases, the divergence of opinion on the interpretation of a Treaty provision (such as whether it creates direct rights) will be clear. But in some cases the reference would be so integral a part of the domestic proceedings that it would only be appropriate to deal with costs at the end of the domestic proceedings in the usual way.

It follows also from the fact that a reference to the European Court is a step in the national proceedings that legal aid is available in United Kingdom references. In *R v Bouchereau*[17] the Marlborough Street magistrate made a reference to the European Court but refused the defendant legal aid to cover legal representation on the reference. The Divisional Court granted a declaration that the existing legal aid certificate covered the European Court reference because, according to the decisions of the European Court, the reference was a step in the national proceedings and costs of the reference were for the national court. In civil proceedings the authority of the general committee is required before a legal aid certificate can extend to proceedings in the European Court.[18]

But these rules may lead to anomalies. In *Burton v British Railways Board*, following the reference to the European Court which had resulted in a finding in favour of the employers,[19] the Employment Appeal Tribunal was unable to award the employers the costs of the reference because under its own rules it was only competent to grant costs where (inter alia) the proceedings were unnecessary, improper or vexatious. It therefore recommended that, because of this anomaly, consideration should be given to making it a term of any reference that the parties should agree how the costs of the reference should be dealt with; otherwise, it might have to be the Court of Appeal which made the reference, since in that court costs follow the event in the ordinary way. The European Court itself may grant legal aid in special circum-

---

17 [1977] 1 WLR 414, [1977] 1 CMLR 269. See also *R v Johnson* [1978] 1 CMLR 390 at 392–3. Cf *Maxims Ltd v Dye* [1978] 2 All ER 55, [1977] 1 WLR 1155 on the problems posed when legal aid is not available.
18 SI 1980/1894, reg 52.
19 In Case 19/81 [1982] ECR 555, [1982] 2 CMLR 136, [1982] QB 1080. The costs decision is reported [1983] 1 All ER 1094.

stances,[20] for example where legal aid is not available in the national court.[1]

8 The effect and authority of a ruling on an article 177 reference

In the proceedings in which a reference has been made, the ruling by the European Court is binding on the national court, both in references on interpretation of Community law and references on validity of acts of Community institutions. As regards references on interpretation, the Court itself put it in this way:[2]

> An interpretation given by the Court of Justice binds the national court in question but it is for the latter to decide whether it is sufficiently enlightened by the preliminary ruling given or whether it is necessary to make a further reference to the Court.

In that case a German court had submitted 12 questions to the European Court which gave a ruling in 1968. The plaintiff applied direct to the European Court to expand on some of the answers and the application was rejected on the ground that it was only for the national court to judge whether it considered a ruling sufficient. The German court then, once again, stayed proceedings and made a further reference to the European Court. On that basis the European Court felt itself able to elaborate on the answers it had given in its previous ruling.

It does not follow that the judgment of the European Court has binding effect for all purposes within the relevant jurisdiction. It merely means that it has res judicata effect within the context of the particular litigation in the course of which the reference was made. In the *Da Costa* case[3] a Dutch court had referred the same question which had been referred in the *Van Gend en Loos* case,[4] although the second reference had in fact been made before a ruling in the first reference had been given. The Commission argued in the *Da Costa* case that the reference should be rejected because the questions on which an interpretation had been requested were decided on identical

---

20 Art 104 of the Rules.
1 Legal aid was granted in Case 152/79 *Lee v Minister of Agriculture* [1980] ECR 1495, [1980] 2 CMLR 682 in a reference from Ireland at a time when legal aid was not available there. It was refused in Case 96/80 *Jenkins v Kingsgate (Clothing Productions) Ltd* [1981] ECR 911, [1981] 2 CMLR 24. See also Case 240/81 *Einberger v Hauptzollamt Freiburg* [1982] ECR 3699, [1983] 2 CMLR 170; Usher *European Court Practice* (1983) pp 328–9.
2 Case 29/68 *Milchkontor v Hauptzollamt Saarbrücken* [1969] ECR 165 at 180, [1969] CMLR 390 at 400. See also Case 52/76 *Benedetti v Munari Fratelli SAS* [1977] ECR 163.
3 Cases 28–30/62 [1963] ECR 31, [1963] CMLR 224. See also Case 283/81 *CILFIT Srl v Ministry of Health* [1982] ECR 3415, [1983] 1 CMLR 472.
4 Case 26/62 [1963] ECR 1, [1963] CMLR 105.

questions in a similar case, *Van Gend en Loos*. The Court, while answering the question merely by referring to its earlier decision, affirmed the right of national courts to resubmit questions already decided. That right was exercised most notably in the *Molkerei-Zentrale* decision[5] when the German courts asked the European Court to reconsider a previous ruling[6] because of the practical difficulties to which it was alleged to have given rise.

A striking example was the attempt by a German company, assisted by the Administrative Court in Frankfurt, to reverse the ruling by the European Court that a provision in a regulation (the effect of which was to require an importer to pay a levy on the import of mushrooms) was valid.[7] When the case was remitted to the Administrative Court it referred further questions to the European Court, including the question whether the prior judgment of the European Court (and not the regulation in question) was invalid because it infringed the general principle of law of *audi alteram partem* in that the importer's arguments were not taken into account, and the European Court undertook enquiries into facts which were a matter for the national court. The European Court held that a preliminary ruling was not susceptible to review for invalidity under art 177, since it was not one of the acts of Community institutions whose validity was open to review. The Court reaffirmed that a preliminary ruling conclusively determined the questions of Community law and was binding on the national court. It was open to a national court to refer again to the European Court when it encountered difficulty in understanding or applying the judgment, or when a new question of law arose, or when new factors were submitted which might lead the European Court to give a different answer. But it was not permissible to use the right to refer further questions as a means of contesting the validity of the earlier judgment.[8]

Sometimes a national court will refer a question which also arises in another case before the European Court. In those circumstances the court whose question has been answered in the other case would normally wish to withdraw its reference.[9] But French and Italian courts have refused to withdraw references in those circumstances, in the case of the French courts because (it seems) French procedural law did not allow it. Advocate General Slynn pointed out that when the same questions posed in a reference are answered in a judgment

---

5 Case 28/67 [1968] ECR 143, [1968] CMLR 187.
6 Case 57/65 *Lütticke GmbH v Hauptzollamt Saarlouis* [1966] ECR 205, [1971] CMLR 674.
7 Case 345/82 *Wünsche Handelsgesellschaft GmbH & Co v Germany* [1984] ECR 1995.
8 Case 69/85 *Wünsche v Germany* [1986] ECR 947. See Bebr (1987) 24 CML Rev 719.
9 As in *R v Minister of Agriculture, Fisheries and Food, ex p FEDESA* [1988] 3 CMLR 207 (Henry J).

which is given after the reference has been made, it is clearly desirable that the reference be withdrawn.[10]

The problem of the effect of a preliminary ruling in litigation other than that in which the reference is made is not likely to cause difficulty in the United Kingdom. This is because s 3(1) of the European Communities Act 1972 makes it clear that Community law must be applied in accordance with the principles laid down by, and in accordance with any relevant decision of, the European Court. Because the European Court has power to reconsider its own previous decisions, the corpus of law involved may be subject to change entirely independent of matters which, at the time the decisions are rendered, are relevant to the United Kingdom. The effect of s 3 is that if a United Kingdom court does not wish to follow a relevant European Court precedent, it should refer a question under art 177. Until then, as Lord Diplock seems to have accepted in *Garland v British Rail Engineering Ltd*,[11] a ruling would be binding on all courts in England, including the House of Lords.

9 Validity rulings: special considerations

United Kingdom courts have made several references to the European Court on the validity of Community acts, principally (but not exclusively) of Commission regulations and decisions.[12] A striking example is *R v Intervention Board for Agricultural Produce, ex p ED & F Man (Sugar) Ltd*.[13] A large British firm of sugar traders made tenders for the export of 30,000 tonnes of sugar. Under the relevant regulation, the exporter had to put up security and undertake to apply for an export licence if the tender was accepted: if the export licence was not made within a four-day period from acceptance, the security was to be forfeit. The exporters' tender was accepted, they put up

---

10 Cases 271–274/84 and 6–7/85 *Procureur de la République v Chiron* [1986] ECR 529, [1988] 1 CMLR 735. See also Case 422/85 *Mattiazzo* [1987] ECR 5413, [1989] 2 CMLR 482.
11 [1983] 2 AC 751 at 771–2, [1982] 2 All ER 402 at 415. Other national courts take a similar view: see *FIVA v Mertens* [1963] CMLR 141 (Amsterdam); *SAFA v Amministrazione delle Finanze dello Stato* [1973] CMLR 152 (Milan Court of Appeal); *Entreprises Garoche v Société Striker Boats (Nederland)* [1974] 1 CMLR 469 (French Cour de Cassation, Criminal Chamber); *Re Brewery Solus Agreement* [1975] 1 CMLR 611 (German Federal Supreme Court, Cartel Division); *Re Deportation of Aliens* [1977] 2 CMLR 255 (German Federal Supreme Administrative Court); *Re Application of Kloppenburg* [1988] 3 CMLR 1 (German Constitutional Court).
12 For recent examples, see Case 141/86 *R v HM Customs and Excise, ex p Imperial Tobacco Ltd* [1988] 2 CMLR 43; Cases 138–139/86 *Direct Cosmetics v Customs and Excise Comrs* [1988] 3 CMLR 333; Case 77/86 *R v HM Customs and Excise Comrs, ex p National Dried Fruit Association* [1988] 2 CMLR 195; Case 162/86 *Livestock Sales Transport Ltd v Intervention Board for Agricultural Produce* [1988] 2 CMLR 186.
13 Case 181/84 [1985] ECR 2889, [1985] 3 CMLR 759.

security, and made an application for a licence. But the licence application was sent at about 4 pm, when under the regulations it should have been received by noon, and the Intervention Board thereupon forfeited the whole of the security. The security which the traders had put up was about £2 million, and represented some three years' profits. The exporters brought proceedings for judicial review of the decision to forfeit the security, claiming that it was grossly unfair and contrary to the principle of proportionality. Glidewell J stayed the proceedings and referred to the European Court the question whether the Commission regulation requiring forfeiture (except in the event of force majeure) in every case when an application for a licence was not received in time was valid. The European Court held that automatic forfeiture of the entire security in the event of an infringement of the obligation to obtain an export licence was too drastic a penalty in relation to the function of the obligation. The Commission was entitled to impose a time-limit, and even to exact a penalty, but the penalty should have been less severe. Consequently the regulation was to that extent invalid, because it contravened the principle of proportionality, ie that the means employed must be appropriate and necessary to attain the objective sought.

The special feature of invalidity rulings is the immediate consequences they may have outside the context of the actual case in which the question of validity is raised. It is this special feature which has given rise to two very important decisions of the European Court. In *SpA International Chemical Corpn v Amministrazione delle Finanze dello Stato*[14] one of the questions was the effect on third parties of various judgments given in 1977 declaring a Council regulation on the compulsory purchase of skimmed milk powder to be invalid. The earlier cases were references by German and Dutch courts and the present case was a claim in the Italian court for the return of security which the plaintiff had provided to secure its performance of an obligation to purchase skimmed milk powder by intervention agencies. The European Court held, on the reference from the Italian court, that where an act had been declared void under art 177 there were 'particularly imperative requirements concerning legal certainty' involved; that once an act had been declared void a national court could not apply the act without creating serious uncertainty as to the Community law applicable; therefore, although a judgment of the European Court under art 177 declaring an act of an institution to be void is directly addressed only to the national court which referred the question:

> ... it is sufficient reason for any other national court to regard that act as void for the purposes of a judgment which it has to give. That assertion does not however mean that national courts are deprived of the power given to them by article 177 of the Treaty and it rests with those courts to decide

---

14 Case 66/80 [1981] ECR 1191, [1983] 2 CMLR 593.

whether there is a need to raise, once again, a question which has already been settled by the Court where the Court has previously declared an act of a Community institution to be void. There may be such a need in particular if questions arise as to the grounds, the scope and possibly the consequences of the invalidity established earlier. If that is not the case, national courts are entirely justified in determining the effect on the cases brought before them of a judgment declaring an act void given by the Court in an action between other parties.[15]

In the very important *Foto-Frost* case[16] the European Court held that while national courts had a discretion whether or not to make a validity reference, they did *not* have power to make a finding of invalidity of an act of the Community institutions. Only the European Court was competent to declare invalid the acts of Community institutions. Before the decision in that case several courts, especially in the Federal Republic of Germany, had taken the view that they had jurisdiction to rule that Community acts were invalid, at any rate if the case was sufficiently clear.[17] In this case the German tax court asked whether it was competent to declare a Commission decision invalid. The European Court held that national courts could *reject* an argument based on invalidity of a Community measure, but they could not declare a measure invalid. The main purpose of art 177 was to ensure that Community law was applied uniformly by the national courts throughout the Community, and uniformity was particularly imperative when the validity of a measure was in question:

> Divergences between courts in the Member States as to the validity of Community acts would be liable to place in jeopardy the very unity of the Community legal order and detract from the fundamental requirement of legal certainty . . . Since Article 173 gives the Court exclusive jurisdiction to declare void an act of a Community institution, the coherence of the system requires that where the validity of a Community act is challenged before a national court the power to declare the act invalid must also be reserved to the Court of Justice.[18]

---

15 [1981] ECR at 1215–16.
16 Case 314/85 *Firma Foto-Frost v Hauptzollamt Lübeck-Ost* [1988] 3 CMLR 57, on which see Bebr (1988) 25 CMLR Rev 667. See generally Harding (1981) 1 Yb Eur L 93.
17 See cases discussed by Mancini AG at pp 64–65. When *R v Intervention Board for Agricultural Produce, ex p E D & F Man (Sugar) Ltd* went back to the Divisional Court, the court dealt not only with the regulation which had been the subject of the reference discussed above, but also with a similar, but not identical regulation, under which another deposit had been forfeited because a clerk had omitted to make a licence application. The Intervention Board, it seems, consented to an order for the return of the deposit, and the court recognised that it could not make an order that the regulation was invalid, since that was a matter for the European Court: [1986] 2 All ER 115.
18 At p 80.

The Court also emphasised that it was in a better position than national courts to decide on the validity of Community acts, since Community institutions whose acts were under challenge were entitled to participate in the reference, and member states and Community institutions who were not participating could be required by the Court to supply all necessary information to the European Court. The Court left open whether there might be exceptions to the rule, such as when the validity of a measure was raised in an interlocutory application in a national court.[19] Advocate General Mancini had suggested that in urgent interlocutory cases, provided it was impossible to have recourse to remedies before the European Court (eg under art 173) a national court did not have to make a reference, if any questions decided at that stage could be re-examined at a later stage of the proceedings, in the course of which a reference would be made under art 177.

Whether or not a private party in national proceedings is able to bring a direct action in the European Court for annulment of a Community measure, the private party may still bring an action in a national court against a national authority to challenge a measure adopted to implement the Community measure. In these proceedings, the private party may require the national court to adjudicate on the legality of the Community measure, if necessary after making a reference to the European Court.[20]

The *Foto-Frost* decision was applied in a case in which a federation of producers of animal health products sought to challenge the validity of a statutory instrument on the ground that it was made to implement a directive which, it was alleged, was invalid.[1] Henry J accepted that it was an appropriate case for a reference. Plainly the case turned on the validity of the directive, and the discretion should be exercised in favour of a reference under art 177 because, as the European Court had held in the *Foto-Frost* case, only the European Court could declare a Community act void, and therefore unless a reference were made, the applicants would be denied the chance of success in their motion. The reference was made notwithstanding that the European Court was already seised of the question in proceedings brought by the United Kingdom against the Community. In those proceedings the directive was annulled because of procedural defects in its adoption,[2] and the reference to Henry J was therefore not proceeded with.

---

19 In an interlocutory matter the national court, even of final instance, has no obligation to make a reference under art 177: p 155, ante.
20 The *'Berlin Butter'* cases: Case 97/85 *Union Deutsche Lebensmittelwerke v Commission* [1987] ECR 2265; Cases 133–136/85 *Rau v BALM* [1987] ECR 2289.
1 *R v Minister of Agriculture, Fisheries and Food ex p FEDESA* [1988] 3 CMLR 207.
2 Case 68/86 *UK v Council* [1988] 2 CMLR 543.

Chapter 4

Challenging Community acts

I. INTRODUCTION

This chapter will be concerned with the procedures and the grounds for challenging acts of Community institutions.[1] Two preliminary comments should be made. Firstly, references by national courts under art 177 of the EEC Treaty on the validity of Community acts have already been mentioned in the previous chapter; this has proved an effective and developing method of challenging Community acts. Secondly, although this chapter will be concerned primarily with the remedies available to private persons, natural and legal, no account of those remedies would be complete or comprehensible without a brief treatment of certain other remedies available to states and community institutions. Thus, the EEC Treaty provides for suits by the Commission against member states (art 169); by one member state against another (art 170); by member states against the Council and the Commission; and by the Council and the Commission against each other (arts 173 and 175). The effects of actions by the Commission against member states and the grounds of the actions against Community institutions are closely connected with the problem of the remedies available to private persons within the Community framework. It is for this reason that this chapter will deal with remedies open to parties other than private individuals and legal persons.

The remedies available to challenge administrative acts of the Community institutions were much influenced in their original formulation by French administrative law, as were the grounds for review. But the development of the grounds for review by the European Court has also been inspired by German legal concepts, and more recently the common law, especially with regard to the rules of natural justice, has begun to have some influence.[2]

The system of remedies described in this chapter shows some very marked contrasts to the administrative law of the United Kingdom.

---

1 See especially Schermers and Waelbroeck *Judicial Protection in the European Communities* (4th edn 1987) chs 2 and 3; Hartley *Foundations of European Community Law* (2nd edn 1988) chs 10 to 17.
2 See Akehurst (1981) 52 BYIL 29.

As Lord Diplock has put it, the application of the distinction, at least as regards substantive law, between private law and public law was a latecomer to the English legal system and was a consequence of the development since about 1950 of the procedures available for judicial control of administrative action.[3] Since then there has been 'progress towards a comprehensive system of administrative law that I regard as having been the greatest achievement of the English courts in my judicial lifetime'.[4] Despite these developments, the United Kingdom lawyer will be struck by certain basic features of the Community system which are absent from, or less developed in, the administrative law of the United Kingdom:[5] these include the rules relating to locus standi, the automatic right of view of administrative decisions addressed to private parties, the obligation to state reasons for administrative decisions and legislative regulations, the application of general principles of administrative law, and the right to damages for unlawful acts of the administration.

II. REMEDIES AGAINST MEMBER STATES UNDER COMMUNITY LAW

By art 169 of the EEC Treaty:

> If the Commission considers that a Member State has failed to fulfil an obligation under this Treaty, it shall deliver a reasoned opinion on the matter after giving the State concerned the opportunity to submit its observations.
>
> If the State concerned does not comply with the opinion within the period laid down by the Commission, the latter may bring the matter before the Court of Justice.[6]

The Commission views art 169 as one of the instruments for the achievement of the single internal market by requiring the strict application of Community law by the member states. Article 169 is a means of monitoring the application of Community law and ensuring

---

3 *O'Reilly v Mackman* [1983] 2 AC 237 at 277, [1982] 3 All ER 1124 at 1128.
4 *R v IRC, ex p National Federation of Self-Employed and Small Businesses Ltd* [1982] AC 617 at 641, [1981] 2 All ER 93 at 104 per Lord Diplock. See also *R v Lancashire County Council, ex p Huddleston* [1986] 2 All ER 941 at 945, per Sir John Donaldson MR.
5 See especially Wade *Administrative Law* (6th edn 1988); Justice-All Souls Committee *Administrative Justice: Some Necessary Reforms* (1988).
6 See generally Schermers and Waelbroeck, pp 251 et seq; Barav (1975) 12 CML Rev 369; Dashwood and White (1989) 14 EL Rev 388; Everling (1984) 9 EL Rev 215. The corresponding provision in the ECSC Treaty is art 88 and in the Euratom Treaty, art 141.

its observance by member states.⁷ The extent of the problem is revealed by the fact that of 65 directives which were to have been implemented by 1 January 1989 as part of the programme for the single market, only two had been implemented by all member states.⁸

The vast majority of complaints against member states do not reach the European Court. In recent years the Commission has initiated the infringement procedure in more than 500 cases in each year. In 1988 reasoned opinions were delivered in 227 cases, and proceedings brought before the European Court in 73 cases. In that year the Court delivered 54 judgments in cases under art 169 declaring member states in breach of their obligations, and 32 cases were removed from the Court register because member states had substantially complied with their obligations after proceedings were commenced.⁹

Virtually all of the proceedings under art 169 are for non-implementation of directives, or for failure to comply with provisions of the constitutive treaties, or with regulations or decisions. It has also been suggested that a breach by a member state of the general principles of law, at least if the breach is in connection with the performance of functions under Community law, would fall within the scope of an enforcement action.¹⁰ The obligations to which an art 169 proceeding may relate extend not only to the constitutive treaties and Community legislation under the treaties, but also to associated treaties concluded by the Community under arts 228 and 236 of the EEC Treaty. By art 228(2) these agreements are binding not only on the Community and its institutions, but also on member states. Member states are bound not only vis-à-vis the non-EEC member states who are party to these agreements, but also vis-à-vis the Community itself.¹¹ Thus Greece has been held to be in breach of the Second Lomé Convention of 1979 by restricting banana imports.¹²

The conditions for the application of art 169 are these: (i) the Commission has taken the view that a member state is in breach of its obligation; (ii) it has informed the state concerned of this view and given the state an opportunity to answer the allegation or repent of its

---

7 EC Commission *Fifth Annual Report to the European Parliament on Commission Monitoring of Community Law* OJ C No 310, 5 December 1988 at p 6.
8 EC Commission, *Sixth Annual Report*, not yet published. For a limited right of immediate access to the European Court for improper derogation from harmonisation directives see art 100A of the EEC Treaty, as introduced by the Single European Act, and see art 100B for a potentially more extensive right after 1992.
9 EC Commission *22nd General Report on the Activities of the European Communities 1988* (1989), pp 422–423.
10 Schermers and Waelbroeck, pp 261–262; Dashwood and White, op cit, n 6, supra, p 390 and contrast Hartley, p 288.
11 Case 104/81 *Hauptzollamt Mainz v Kupferberg* [1982] ECR 3641, [1983] 1 CMLR 1.
12 Cases 194 and 241/85 *Commission v Greece* 25 February 1988.

wrong; (iii) the state has actually been in breach of obligation; (iv) the Commission has delivered a reasoned opinion to that effect; (v) the state has failed within the time limit laid down by the Commission to comply with its treaty obligation; and (vi) the Commission has brought the matter before the Court.

Despite the widespread view that the United Kingdom is less than wholly supportive of the EEC, the number of infringement actions brought against the United Kingdom has been very low. Thus the total brought in the European Court against the United Kingdom between 1986 and 1988 was 3, compared to 53 for Italy.[13] In recent years proceedings against the United Kingdom have resulted in adverse judgments: for unlawful restrictions on the import of potatoes,[14] milk,[15] poultry and eggs,[16] clothes and other goods;[17] for failure to comply with a Council regulation requiring the use of the tachograph (or 'spy in the cab') in lorries;[18] for discriminatory taxation on wine;[19] for unlawful unilateral fishery conservation measures;[20] for failure to implement directives on VAT[1] and on motor vehicle lights;[2] for failure to comply with an 'invitation' from the Commission for earlier payment of 'own resources';[3] and for failure to comply with regulations.[4]

To take a recent example, in 1981 the government issued a statutory instrument, which entered into force at the beginning of 1982, prohibiting retailers from selling clothes, footwear, domestic electrical appliances and cutlery unless the goods indicated their country of manufacture. The Commission took the view that the measure had an effect equivalent to an import restriction contrary to art 30 of the

---

13 This is, of course, in part due to the internal political situation in Italy: see p 221, post.
14 Case 231/78 *Commission v UK* [1979] ECR 1447, [1979] 2 CMLR 427; cf Case 118/78 *Meijer BV v Department of Trade* [1979] ECR 1387, [1979] 2 CMLR 398.
15 Case 124/81 *Commission v UK* [1983] ECR 203, [1983] 2 CMLR 1; Case 261/85 *Commission v UK* [1988] 2 CMLR 11.
16 Case 40/82 *Commission v UK* [1982] ECR 2793, [1982] 3 CMLR 497; [1984] ECR 283.
17 Case 207/83 *Commission v UK* [1985] ECR 1201, [1985] 2 CMLR 259.
18 Case 128/78 *Commission v UK* [1979] ECR 419, [1979] 2 CMLR 45 (and see *Concorde Express Transport Ltd v Traffic Examiner Metropolitan Area* [1980] 2 CMLR 221; Case 133/83 *R v Thomas Scott & Sons (Bakers) Ltd* [1984] ECR 2863, [1985] 1 CMLR 188; Cases 91–92/84 *DPP v Sidney Hackett Ltd* [1985] ECR 1139, [1985] 2 CMLR 213).
19 Case 170/78 *Commission v UK* [1983] ECR 2265, [1983] 3 CMLR 512.
20 Case 804/79 *Commission v UK* [1981] ECR 1045, [1982] 1 CMLR 543.
1 Case 353/85 *Commission v UK* (1988) Times, 24 February 1988.
2 Case 60/86 *Commission v UK* [1988] 3 CMLR 437.
3 Case 93/85 *Commission v UK* [1986] ECR 4011, [1987] 1 CMLR 895.
4 Case 23/84 *Commission v UK* [1986] ECR 3581, [1987] 1 CMLR 607 (milk); Case 100/84 *Commission v UK* [1985] ECR 1169, [1985] 2 CMLR 199 (fish).

EEC Treaty, because it placed additional burdens on the production and distribution chain, and would necessarily increase the production costs of the imported articles. The Commission drew the attention of the United Kingdom government to its view in a letter in December 1981. The government replied in February 1982 that the order would not have the effects which the Commission feared, and that the origin information was of value to consumers; it offered, however, to allow retailers to choose between an indication of national origin or Community origin. The Commission disagreed, and issued its reasoned opinion in February 1983, and when the United Kingdom government maintained its position, the Commission brought proceedings in September 1983 in the European Court, which gave judgment against the United Kingdom in April 1985.[5] The Court declared that, by prohibiting the retail sale of goods imported from other member states unless they were marked with an indication of origin, the United Kingdom had failed to fulfil its obligations under art 30. The Order was repealed in March 1986.

The 'reasoned opinion' should contain 'a coherent statement of the reasons which led the Commission to believe that the state in question had failed to fulfil an obligation under the Treaty'.[6] The opinion must also contain a time limit within which the member state must desist from the breach. Sometimes the Commission requires compliance with its opinion within a very short period. When the Commission required Belgium to remove a property tax on Community officials within two weeks of the reasoned opinion, the European Court held that the time limit was reasonable because the Belgian government knew of (and had not contested) the Commission's position long before the art 169 procedure was initiated.[7] But when the Commission required Belgium to take measures to remove discriminatory higher education fees within 15 days, the Court held that the time limit was excessively short, and dismissed the action. The Commission must allow member states a reasonable time to reply to the letter of formal notice and to comply with a reasoned opinion or to prepare their defence. In determining what time is reasonable, all the circumstances of the case must be looked at, especially where there is an urgent need to remedy a breach and where the member state has been fully aware of the Commission's views.[8]

If the member state has not desisted within the time limit, then the Commission may bring the matter before the European Court and the Court may give a ruling that there has been a breach even if, in certain

---

5 Case 207/83 *Commission v UK* [1985] ECR 1201, [1985] 2 CMLR 259.
6 Case 7/61 *Commission v Italy* [1961] ECR 317 at 327, [1962] CMLR 39 at 54.
7 Case 85/85 *Commission v Belgium* [1986] ECR 1149, [1987] 1 CMLR 787.
8 Case 293/85 *Commission v Belgium* [1989] 2 CMLR 527.

circumstances, the particular breach originally complained of has been brought to an end by the time the complaint reaches the Court,[9] although frequently the Commission withdraws the proceedings when member states terminate the alleged infringement. The proceedings under art 169 must be confined to the complaints made during the pre-litigation phase.[10] But French restrictions on the importation of Italian table wines which were subsequent to the reasoned opinion and constituted the same conduct as that complained of in the opinion could be taken account of in art 169 proceedings.[11] The Court will not hear the complaint, if the real object of the Commission is to obtain a ruling of the Court on the compatibility with the Treaty of new (and different) legislation enacted in the course of the proceedings.[12]

The failure on the part of the member state to fulfil an obligation (which may be a matter of omission as well as commission[13]) will be a matter for the Court in the last resort. In particular, in accordance with well-recognised principles of international law, the respondent Government will not be heard to say that the executive has done everything it could but its legislature has refused to pass the necessary legislation.[14] Thus, in a case brought against Belgium,[15] alleging that it had imposed, in contravention of art 95, a discriminatory tax on imported pressed wood, the Belgian Government pleaded *force majeure*; it argued that, in order to remedy the breach, it had twice submitted to the legislature a bill revising the relevant law and had informed the legislature that the bill was designed to ensure compliance with art 95 and pointing to its great importance. The Court rejected this plea. It said:[16]

---

9 See Case 7/61 *Commission v Italy* [1961] ECR 317, [1962] CMLR 39; Case 26/69 *Commission v France* [1970] ECR 565, [1970] CMLR 444; Case 44/64 *Commission v Italy* [1965] ECR 857, [1966] CMLR 97; Case 39/72 *Commission v Italy* [1973] ECR 101, [1973] CMLR 439; Case 69/77 *Commission v Italy* [1978] ECR 1749 [1979] 1 CMLR 206; Case 103/84 *Commission v Italy* [1986] ECR 1759, [1987] 2 CMLR 825; Case 154/85 *Commission v Italy* [1987] ECR 2717, [1988] 2 CMLR 951; Case 240/86 *Commission v Greece* [1989] 3 CMLR 578.
10 See eg Case 7/69 *Commission v Italy* [1970] ECR 111, [1970] CMLR 97; Case 166/82 *Commission v Italy* [1984] ECR 459, [1985] 2 CMLR 615; Case 298/86 *Commission v Belgium* 14 July 1988.
11 Case 42/82 *Commission v France* [1983] ECR 1013, [1984] 1 CMLR 160.
12 Case 7/69 *Commission v Italy* [1970] ECR 111, [1970] CMLR 97.
13 Case 31/69 *Commission v Italy* [1970] ECR 25, [1970] CMLR 175. The mere *existence* of legislation contrary to the Treaty, even though it is not applied in practice, may be a breach of the Treaty: Case 167/73 *Commission v France* [1974] ECR 359, [1974] 2 CMLR 216; Case 159/78 *Commission v Italy* [1979] ECR 3247, [1980] 3 CMLR 446.
14 See Chapter 1, pp 20–21, ante.
15 Case 77/69 *Commission v Belgium* [1970] ECR 237, [1974] 1 CMLR 203.
16 [1970] ECR 237 at 243.

The obligations arising from article 95 of the Treaty devolve upon states as such and the liability of a member state under article 169 arises whatever the agency of the state whose action or inaction is the cause of the failure to fulfil its obligations, even in the case of a constitutionally independent institution.

The attitude of the Court was the same when the Italian Government had secured the passage of a bill through the Italian Senate but not the Chamber of Deputies.[17] As the European Court put it in a later case:[18]

> The grant made by member states to the Community of rights and powers in accordance with the provisions of the Treaty involves a definitive limitation on their sovereign rights and no provisions whatsoever of national law may be invoked to override this limitation.

This is no more than a general principle of the law of treaties. A state cannot rely on its municipal law to avoid its international obligations. There are many examples of this principle in the Court's decisions, too numerous to mention. The problem has arisen especially in proceedings brought against Italy, whose parliamentary system is such that the frequency of change in government means that legislation to implement Community law frequently lapses on a dissolution, and that the coalition governments cannot, or will not, secure the passage of legislation. As a result Italy has been held frequently in breach of its obligations to implement directives such as the Company Law Directives[19] or those implementing the environment programme.[20] Similarly Belgium relied, without success, on its institutional reforms on redistribution of powers to justify its failure to implement directives on the environment.[1] The problem has not yet presented itself in the United Kingdom, but it is possible that it may arise if there should be a minority or coalition government, or if the House of Lords does not support legislation passed by the House of Commons.

A member state is responsible for the acts of public authorities, and also in exceptional cases for acts of private parties under its control. Thus Ireland was condemned for the 'Buy Irish' campaign which was conducted by the Irish Goods Council, a body organised as a private limited company; but the Council was funded by the Irish

---

17 Case 8/70 *Commission v Italy* [1970] ECR 961.
18 Case 48/71 *Commission v Italy* [1972] ECR 527 at 532, [1972] CMLR 699 at 708.
19 Case 136/81 *Commission v Italy* [1982] ECR 3547; Case 17/85 *Commission v Italy* [1986] ECR 1199.
20 Eg Case 364/85 *Commission v Italy* [1987] ECR 487. For changes in the Italian system see *Petriccione* (1989) 14 EL Rev 456.
1 Cases 68–71/81 *Commission v Belgium* [1982] ECR 153 et seq; see also eg Case 9/86 *Commission v Belgium* [1987] ECR 1331; Case 134/86 *Commission v Belgium* [1987] ECR 2415.

Government, which appointed its management and defined its policies.[2]

A member state may also be responsible for the decisions of its courts. Advocate General Warner has expressed the view that mere judicial error does not engage the responsibility of the state, and that art 169 only applies in such cases where the courts of a member state deliberately ignore or disregard Community law.[3] It is because the independence of the judiciary is a cornerstone of the democratic ideal that the Commission has been reluctant to take action against member states on account of actions by courts of member states. But the Commission has initiated infringement proceedings against France in connection with a judgment of the Cour de Cassation in 1986 in which the court, without making reference to the European Court, refused to apply a Community customs regulation.[4]

A member state cannot rely on the excuse that the Community institutions,[5] or another member state,[6] are in breach of their obligations under the Treaty. France therefore could not justify its restrictions on imports of British mutton and lamb by pointing to the United Kingdom's own alleged restrictions.[7]

A member state may be in breach even if the provision which is not complied with is capable of having direct effect in municipal law, so that there would also be effective remedies in national courts. This is because 'the existence of remedies available through the national courts cannot in any way prejudice the making of the application referred to in article 169 since the two procedures have different objectives and effects'.[8] Conversely, the existence of a remedy under art 169 does not preclude a private party from raising an alleged violation indirectly through a reference in national proceedings pursuant to art 177.[9] There is therefore no room for the application of the rule in public international law that local remedies must be exhausted before the state can be brought before an international tribunal, at any rate where the gist of the action is damage to private parties who have a remedy in national courts.[10] Consequently, the fact that art 169 of the Treaty enables the Commission to complain of a breach of obligation by a member state does not mean that individuals may not plead those

---

2 Case 249/81 *Commission v Ireland* [1982] ECR 4005, [1983] 2 CMLR 104.
3 Case 30/77 *R v Bouchereau* [1977] ECR 1999 at 2019–2021, [1977] 2 CMLR 800 at 805–810.
4 *Sixth Annual Report to the European Parliament*, not yet published.
5 Cases 90 and 91/63 *Commission v Luxembourg and Belgium* [1964] ECR 625, [1965] CMLR 58.
6 Case 52/75 *Commission v Italy* [1976] ECR 277, [1976] 2 CMLR 320.
7 Case 232/78 *Commission v France* [1979] ECR 2729, [1980] 1 CMLR 418.
8 Case 31/69 *Commission v Italy* [1970] ECR 25 at 32, [1970] CMLR 175 at 188.
9 Cf pp 211–214, ante.
10 See eg *US v Italy (ELSI Case)* 1989 ICJ Rep 14 at 42–48.

obligations before a national court in proceedings in which the national court may make a reference under art 177.[11] In that reference the European Court may not, as has been seen above,[12] rule on the compatibility of national law with Community law, but the practical effect of a ruling under art 177 and under art 169 may not be significantly different. For example, the effect of the ruling under art 177 in *Meijer v Department of Trade* and of the Commission's proceedings under art 169[13] was equally that the restrictions on potato imports by the United Kingdom were contrary to the Treaty.

When a member state has failed to comply with a Community obligation, it cannot plead the unlawfulness of the act imposing the obligation as a defence in art 169 proceedings. It must comply with the obligation unless and until the European Court has annulled the act or granted an order suspending its operation. The only situation in which the member state could plead in art 169 proceedings that the act was unlawful was one in which the act involved contained such particularly serious and manifest defects that it could be regarded as non-existent.[14] The point becomes a practical one where the member state fails to take action to seek annulment of the act within the time limit laid down by art 173. The member state who fails to take action is not given another opportunity in art 169 proceedings to challenge the validity of the act.[15] But even if the member state has commenced proceedings for annulment, it is still under a duty to comply with the obligation pending the outcome of the annulment proceedings. Thus where Greece had failed to comply with a decision on state aids, and had commenced proceedings for its annulment but had failed in an interim application for suspension of the decision, it was held to have been in breach of the decision in a judgment delivered on the same day as a judgment dismissing its application for annulment.[16]

Once a judgment under art 169 has been given the legislative authorities of the member state concerned must amend the legislative provisions so as to make its law conform with Community law and its

---

11 Case 172/82 *Syndicat National des Fabricants Raffineurs d'Huile de Graissage v Interhuiles* [1983] ECR 555, [1983] 3 CMLR 485.
12 See pp 166–169, ante.
13 See cases at p 218, n 14, ante.
14 Case 226/87 *Commission v Greece* [1989] 3 CMLR 569. For a discussion of the concept of acts so tainted with irregularity that they are void see Case 15/85 *Consorzio Cooperative d'Abruzzo v Commission* [1987] ECR 1005 at 1019–1020, [1988] 1 CMLR 841 at 850–852 per Mischo AG. See also art 184, which would enable such a plea to be made in the case of illegal breach of a regulation.
15 See eg Case 156/77 *Commission v Belgium* [1978] ECR 1881; Case 52/83 *Commission v France* [1983] ECR 3707, [1985] 3 CMLR 278; Case 52/84 *Commission v Belgium* [1986] ECR 89.
16 Case 63/87 *Commission v Greece* 7 June, 1988.

courts are under a duty to secure compliance with the relevant Community law in actions involving individuals.[17] The judgment of the Court under art 169 is declaratory only, and the Court has no jurisdiction to order the member state to take steps to comply with its obligations, eg by implementing a directive or removing import restrictions. But it does seem that the Court has jurisdiction to declare that a member state is in breach of its obligations by not acceding to a requirement by the Commission that, for example, it should ensure the repayment of state aids.[18]

The Court has, however, decided that it has power to order interim measures in art 169 cases, the effect of which is that in interim proceedings it can grant more effective orders than it can at the final hearing. The power was first asserted in 1977 when the United Kingdom was ordered to desist from paying subsidies to pig producers[19] and has been exercised frequently since. Two examples illustrate this important practice. In the *Dundalk Water Supply* case,[20] an Irish local authority invited tenders for a new water supply scheme, which required compliance with an Irish technical standard. Only one firm was authorised to apply that standard, and that firm was Irish. Following complaints of unlawful discrimination made by a Spanish firm, the Commission instituted proceedings under art 169 against Ireland, and obtained an emergency *ex parte* interim order from the President of the European Court that, pending the *inter partes* application for interim measures, no award of the contract for the water supply scheme be made. But a month later the President was persuaded on the *inter partes* hearing that, although there was a prima facie case (later upheld by the European Court on the hearing of the merits), it would not be right to make the interim order because, among other reasons, there was evidence that the existing water shortage created a fire risk and even a risk to health for the inhabitants of Dundalk.

The second example is the important *Factortame* case, which has been discussed in earlier chapters.[1] In the English proceedings Spanish interests sought to argue that the British nationality and residence requirements of the Merchant Shipping Act 1988 were contrary to Community law. They failed to obtain an interim injunction against the Secretary of State for Transport. The Divisional

---

17 Cases 314–316/81 and 83/82 *Procureur de la République v Waterkeyn* [1982] ECR 4337, [1983] 2 CMLR 145, on the consequences of Case 152/78 *Commission v France* [1980] ECR 2299, [1981] 2 CMLR 743.
18 See Hartley, pp 310–313.
19 Cases 31 and 53/77R [1977] ECR 921, [1977] 2 CMLR 359.
20 Case 45/87R *Commission v Ireland* [1987] ECR 783 and 1369, [1987] 2 CMLR 197 and 563; Case 45/87 [1989] 1 CMLR 225.
1 See pp 38–39, 108–110, ante.

Court referred the substantive questions of EEC law to the European Court under art 177, and the House of Lords referred the question whether the English court had a duty to grant interim relief to the applicants pending the outcome of the reference to the European Court.[2] In the Court of Appeal (whose decision to refuse interim relief was upheld by the House of Lords) Bingham LJ expressed the view that it would be more appropriate for the European Court to grant interim relief in art 169 proceedings than for the English court to do so in the judicial review application, because, among other reasons, the European Court was better placed than the English court to assess whether the conditions for granting interim relief were met and whether the interests of the Community and its member states and citizens called for the grant of such relief.[3]

Subsequently, the Commission commenced proceedings against the United Kingdom, and in November 1989 the President of the European Court made an interim order requiring the United Kingdom to disapply the nationality requirements in the Merchant Shipping Act 1988. The Commission did not seek interim measures in relation to complaints about the residence and domicile requirements, and the Court held that the continued existence of the remaining registration requirements would adequately protect the United Kingdom policy (should it ultimately be held lawful) of ensuring a genuine link between the vessels fishing against the British quotas and the British fishing industry.[4]

There has been an increasing tendency for member states not to implement decisions of the European Court in art 169 proceedings. As at 31 January 1989 there were more than 50 judgments given prior to July 1988 with which there had not yet been compliance and where the member state had not indicated that steps were in hand to comply with the judgment, and in some of these cases judgment had been given as early as 1983.[5]

Art 171 provides:

> If the Court of Justice finds that a Member State has failed to fulfil an obligation under this Treaty, the State shall be required to take the necessary measures to comply with the judgment of the Court of Justice.

In the second case brought against Italy in connection with its export tax on art treasures,[6] the Commission claimed a declaration that

---

2 See *Factortame Ltd v Secretary of State for Transport* [1989] 2 WLR 997, [1989] 2 All ER 692, HL.
3 [1989] 2 CMLR 353 at 408.
4 Case 246/89R *Commission v UK* [1989] 3 CMLR 601.
5 *Sixth Annual Report to the European Parliament*, not yet published.
6 Case 48/71 *Commission v Italy* [1972] ECR 527, [1972] CMLR 699.

Italy was in breach of art 171 by not complying with the decision in the first case.[7] The Court held that Italy (which in fact remedied the breach before judgment) had failed to comply with the first judgment and had accordingly failed to fulfil the obligations imposed by art 171.

After France had failed to comply with the judgment of the Court condemning its ban on imports of British mutton and lamb,[8] the Commission brought new proceedings complaining that France was in breach of its obligations under art 171, but the Court refused to grant interim measures requiring France to comply with the earlier judgment because France was already under an obligation to comply with the judgment as a result of art 171.[9] Since then there have been several other cases in which several years elapsed between the original decision of the European Court and the judgment in the proceedings under art 171. Even then, there have been several cases in which the judgment in the later proceedings has not been complied with. One particularly important case is the continuing failure by Italy to comply with a judgment delivered in February 1987 under art 171 in relation to the failure to comply with a judgment originally delivered in 1983.[10]

Other member states can also bring alleged treaty violations before the Court under art 170, which provides:[11]

> A Member State which considers that another Member State has failed to fulfil an obligation under this Treaty may bring the matter before the Court of Justice.
>
> Before a Member State brings an action against another Member State for an alleged infringement of an obligation under this Treaty, it shall bring the matter before the Commission.
>
> The Commission shall deliver a reasoned opinion after each of the States concerned has been given the opportunity to submit its own case and its observations on the other party's case both orally and in writing.
>
> If the Commission has not delivered an opinion within three months of the date on which the matter was brought before it, the absence of such opinion shall not prevent the matter from being brought before the Court of Justice.

---

7 Case 7/68 [1968] ECR 423, [1969] CMLR 1.
8 Case 232/78 *Commission v France* [1979] ECR 2729, [1980] 1 CMLR 418.
9 Cases 24/80R and 97/80R *Commission v France* [1980] ECR 1319, [1981] 3 CMLR 25. The dispute was settled by the adoption in 1980 of a regulation setting up a common organisation of the market in mutton and lamb.
10 Case 69/86 *Commission v Italy* [1987] ECR 773.
11 See also ECSC Treaty, art 89(1), and Euratom Treaty, art 142.

The first case to reach the European Court under art 170 was a successful action by France to challenge the United Kingdom's unilateral fishery conservation measures.[12]

III. THE RELATIONSHIP BETWEEN ARTICLE 169 AND THE REMEDIES AVAILABLE TO PRIVATE PARTIES

The Commission often acts after complaints by private parties of infringements by member states. The increase in the number of proceedings brought by it is evidence of increasing public awareness of the duty of member states to comply with Community law, and the Commission has noted that complaints addressed to it are, apart from proceedings before national courts, the most direct and effective instrument available to the citizen to ensure the application of Community law.[13] In 1988 more than one thousand complaints were received by the Commission from private parties.[14] Early in 1989 the Commission published a standard complaint form in order to assist private parties to lodge complaints with the Commission so that the Commission could consider infringement proceedings.[15] But private parties are not entitled to intervene or be heard in art 169 proceedings.[16]

The question arises whether private parties who complain of breaches by member states have a remedy if the Commission fails to take action. To anticipate the topic to be treated in succeeding sections, arts 173 and 175 make available remedies to private parties to challenge acts and omissions of Community institutions. Under the former article, the European Court has jurisdiction to hear complaints by natural or legal persons challenging the legality on specified grounds of certain acts (largely, at the risk of oversimplification, decisions) of Community institutions. Under the latter article, again at the risk of oversimplification, private parties may complain that, in breach of the Treaty, a Community institution has failed to address to them 'any act other than a recommendation or an opinion'. Can these articles be used by private persons to evade the fact that the remedies in arts 169 and 170 are available only to Community institutions and

---

12 Case 141/78 *France v United Kingdom* [1979] ECR 2923, [1980] 1 CMLR 6. There have been several cases in which the procedure has been commenced and subsequently not proceeded with: eg in 1984 the Commission delivered a reasoned opinion following complaints by the French government against the Netherlands over preferential gas tariffs: see Case 169/84 *COFAZ v Commission* [1986] ECR 391, [1986] 3 CMLR 385.
13 OJ C 310, 5 December 1988, p 6.
14 *Sixth Annual Report to the European Parliament*, not yet published.
15 OJ C No 26, 1 February 1989, p 6; [1989] 1 CMLR 617.
16 Case 154/85R *Commission v Italy* [1985] ECR 1753, [1986] 2 CMLR 159.

states by complaining that the Commission has not instituted proceedings against a member state for violation of the Treaty?

In *Rhenania v Commission*[17] the first attempt was made by private parties to use art 175 (the remedy against inaction) to complain of the failure of the Commission to take action against Germany. The plaintiffs, who were German transport companies, alleged that the Commission had failed to respond to their requests to take action against the German Government. They alleged further that the German Government was in breach of a Council regulation by fixing intervention prices (ie prices below which subsidies would be payable) at too low a level in relation to trans-shipment centres. This was alleged to have caused grain producers to avoid such centres, thus causing loss to the plaintiff companies. On the same day, however, as the complaint to the European Court was made the Commission informed the plaintiffs that their complaints were being investigated and subsequently, during the proceedings, that it had instituted the procedure laid down by art 169 against Germany. The applicants accordingly accepted that their substantive objections had been met and the Court therefore, without deciding on the admissibility of the application, decided that there was no need to deliver judgment. Although most of the argument was concerned with costs in view of the factual developments, Advocate General Roemer submitted that art 175 could not be used to complain of inaction under art 169, because the art 175 procedure is designed to secure an act *addressed to the applicant* and all the proceedings in art 169 are between the Commission and the member state concerned.

The second attempt was made in *Lütticke v Commission*[18] where the plaintiffs were importers of powdered milk who were aggrieved at an adjustment tax on turnover imposed by the German government and who contended that the tax was a breach of art 95, which prohibits the imposition of taxes on imported products higher than those on products originating within the member state. They requested the Commission to initiate against Germany the procedure provided under art 169. The Commission declared by letter that it was satisfied that any violation of art 95 by the German Government had been brought to an end and that in any event it did not consider that the adjustment tax was in violation of art 95.

The Court held that the application by the plaintiffs to challenge the Commission's decision was inadmissible. As to the claim under art 173 to annul an act of the Commission, it held that in the preliminary stages of the art 169 procedure the Commission issues only a reasoned opinion which does not have any binding force and conse-

---

17 Case 103/63 [1964] ECR 425, [1965] CMLR 82.
18 Case 48/65 [1966] ECR 19, [1966] CMLR 378.

quently any application for annulment of the 'act' in which the Commission comes to a conclusion about the request is not admissible.[19] As to the complaint under art 175 in relation to inaction, that only applies if at the end of the period of two months from the request to act the relevant Community institution has not defined its position.[20] In this case, the Commission had defined its position clearly in its letter to the applicants. Therefore the application was inadmissible. The Court did not therefore have to consider the opinion of Advocate General Gand that in any event private persons had no legal interest in the Commission instituting proceedings under art 169.

IV. ACTIONS TO ANNUL COMMUNITY ACTS

Article 173 invests the European Court with jurisdiction to review the legality of Community acts[1] at the suit of member states and of Community institutions and also (although in more limited circumstances) at the suit of private parties. This section will deal with the article largely from the standpoint of private parties, but the text makes clear the close relationship between suits by member states and Community institutions on the one hand and private parties on the other:[2]

> The Court of Justice shall review the legality of acts of the Council and the Commission other than recommendations or opinions. It shall for this purpose have jurisdiction in actions brought by a Member State, the Council or the Commission on grounds of lack of competence, infringement of an essential procedural requirement, infringement of this Treaty or of any rule of law relating to its application, or misuse of powers.
>
> Any natural or legal person may, under the same conditions, institute proceedings against a decision addressed to that person or against a decision which, although in the form of a regulation or a decision

---

19 On the legal nature of the 'reasoned opinion' under art 169, see the arguments in Case 7/61 *Commission v Italy* [1961] ECR 317, [1962] CMLR 39 and in Cases 6 and 11/69 *Commission v France* [1969] ECR 523, [1970] CMLR 43.
20 See also 42/71 *Nordgetreide v Commission* [1972] ECR 105, [1973] CMLR 177. Hartley, pp 302–4, suggests that an individual affected by the Commission's failure to take action under art 169 may claim damages under art 215: but this is doubtful, since the real cause of any damage would be the unlawful act of the member state. Cf Case 9/75 *Meyer-Burckhardt v Commission* [1975] ECR 1171 at 1190–1191, per Warner AG; Case 14/78 *Denkavit v Commission* [1978] ECR 2497 at 2516, per Mayras AG.
1 Which includes acts of the European Parliament, even though it is not mentioned in art 173: Case 294/83 *Partie Ecologiste Les Verts v Parliament* [1986] ECR 1339, [1987] 2 CMLR 343. For acts adopted under all three Community treaties see Case 230/81 *Luxembourg v Parliament* [1983] ECR 255, [1983] 2 CMLR 726. The European Parliament has no standing to apply to annul Community acts: Case 302/87 *Parliament v Council* (1988) Times, 17 October.
2 See also ECSC Treaty, art 33(2), and Euratom Treaty, art 146(2).

addressed to another person, is of direct and individual concern to the former.

The proceedings provided for in this Article shall be instituted within two months of the publication of the measure, or of its notification to the plaintiff or, in the absence thereof, of the day on which it came to the knowledge of the latter, as the case may be.

The consequence of a successful action is that the Court declares the challenged act to be void.[3]

Thus the remedies open to private parties are in effect limited to challenge of essentially non-legislative acts individually concerning them. But, as may be expected, the concept of decisions (so designated or regulations having the same effect) addressed to other persons but affecting the plaintiff directly and individually has given rise to some difficulty.

1 The types of act which are open to challenge

In the first paragraph the only acts which are expressed not to be capable of review are recommendations and opinions. Thus in actions by member states or Community institutions, directives,[4] regulations, and decisions are subject to review. In addition, there is another, vaguer, group of acts which are none of the foregoing but which have sufficient legal effect to make them subject to annulment. In *Lütticke v Commission*[5] the Court held that a letter notifying the applicant that the Commission would not take steps under art 169 was not subject to review under art 173 because before a case against a member state is actually before the Court under art 169 the acts of the Commission do not have binding force. The Court in that case appears to have adopted the submission of Advocate General Gand that the exclusion of recommendations and opinions from the scope of review indicated that art 173 comprehended review only of acts of a compulsory nature. But in the *Noordwijks Cement Accoord* case[6] the Court went some way towards extending the notion of 'decision' to any act which alters the legal position. In that case the act complained of was a communication from the Commission informing the applicants that it considered that their agreements were within the prohibition of art 85(1) and not subject to exemption under art 85(3). That notification was not, at that stage, a formal decision not to grant an exemption under

---

3 Article 174.
4 See Cases 52 and 55/65 *Germany v Commission* [1966] ECR 159, [1967] CMLR 22.
5 Case 48/65 [1966] ECR 19, [1966] CMLR 378.
6 Cases 8–11/66 *Cimenteries v Commission* [1967] ECR 75, [1967] CMLR 77. Cf Case 59/77 *De Bloos v Bouyer* [1977] ECR 2359, [1978] 1 CMLR 511. See p 245, post, on locus standi in relation to restrictive practices.

art 85(3), but it had the intention and effect[7] of removing the temporary immunity from fines obtained by notifying the agreements. The Commission argued that the notification was not subject to review because it did not produce any final legal effects and did not finally terminate the internal administrative procedure since there had not yet been any decision by the Commission to impose fines. The Commission therefore suggested that since the communication did not oblige the applicants to put an end to the performance of their agreements, it did not impose any legal obligation and did not finally affect any individual interests. It was accordingly only an opinion. The Court, however, took a broader view and held that, although in any event Regulation 17 required in effect a provisional decision, there were wider grounds for the conclusion that the notification was a decision, since it:

> affected the interests of the undertakings by bringing about a distinct change in their legal position. It is unequivocally a measure which produces legal effects touching the interests of the undertakings concerned and which is binding on them. It thus constitutes not a mere opinion but a decision.[8]

In 1971, in the case brought by the Commission against the Council concerning the European Road Transport Agreement (ERTA),[9] the Court significantly extended the types of act which may be subject to review under art 173. This case concerned a challenge by the Commission to the authority of the Council to conduct discussions regarding the negotiation and conclusion of a revision to the European Road Transport Agreement of 1962. In March 1970 the Council of Ministers discussed the attitude to be adopted by the six member states of the EEC in the then current negotiations. Those negotiations were undertaken and concluded in accordance with the discussions held by the Council of Ministers and the new ERTA was open for signature as from 1 July 1970. The Commission took the view that since a matter involving common transport policy was involved only the Community (and not the individual member states whether acting individually or collectively) had the power to negotiate and conclude the new ERTA. In particular, it alleged that the Council had acted in breach of the EEC Treaty by failing to ensure the participation of the Commission in the matter of making proposals on transport policy and in negotiating treaties. The Court held on the merits (in a decision which is by no means clear) that the Commission was right in its argument that transport was now a matter for the Community but that in the unusual circumstances of the case the strictness of the rule

---

7 Regulation 17, art 15(6).
8 [1967] ECR 75 at 91. Cf Case 15/70 *Chevalley v Commission* [1970] ECR 975.
9 Case 22/70 *Commission v Council* [1971] ECR 263, [1971] CMLR 335.

must be relaxed to allow the negotiation of a multilateral convention which had been under negotiation from before that time. For present purposes, the interest of the case lies in the argument of the Council that the application was inadmissible because its deliberation was not an act subject to review under art 173, not being in form, purpose or context, a directive, regulation or decision, nor having binding legal effect.

The Court held that the acts subject to review are not limited to the acts declared by art 189 to have binding force, namely, regulations, directives and decisions. To put it differently, although both art 173 and art 189 expressly put recommendations and opinions in a separate category, the express mention of regulations, directives and decisions in art 189 is not a guide to the interpretation of the words 'acts . . . other than recommendations or opinions' in art 173. The previous practice of the Court had been to assimilate an act having legal effect to decisions, although not expressly so-called. The Court then went on to indicate what acts were subject to review in these words:[10]

> Since the only matters excluded from the scope of the action for annulment open to the member states and the institutions are 'recommendations or opinions'—which by the final paragraph of article 189 are declared to have no binding force—article 173 treats as acts open to review by the Court all measures adopted by the institutions which are intended to have legal force. The objective of this review is to ensure, as required by article 164, observance of the law in the interpretation and application of the Treaty. It would be inconsistent with this objective to interpret the conditions under which the action is admissible so restrictively as to limit the availability of this procedure merely to the categories of measures referred to by article 189. An action for annulment must therefore be available in the case of all measures adopted by the institutions, whatever their nature or form, which are intended to have legal effects.

This decision did not deal with a case involving an application by a private party under art 173(2). The question arose in *IBM v Commission*.[11] IBM had been for several years the subject of an enquiry by the Commission as to whether it had been guilty of an abuse of a dominant position under art 86 of the EEC Treaty in connection with its marketing of computers. In 1980 the Commission informed IBM that it was taking proceedings against IBM under Regulation 17 and sent a statement of objections. The procedure under Regulation 17 involves administrative hearings which may result in a decision imposing a fine.[12] IBM tried without success to persuade the Commission to withdraw the proceedings and the statement of objections. It then

---

10 [1971] ECR 263 at 276–7.
11 Case 60/81 [1981] ECR 2639, [1981] 3 CMLR 635.
12 On this procedure see p 246, post.

commenced an action under art 173(2) for a declaration that the Commission's actions were void because (inter alia) the Commission had not acted fairly and that the complaint was contrary to international law because the conduct of IBM occurred outside the Community. IBM argued that the initiation of the procedure and notification of the objections were 'decisions' by reason of their legal nature and their consequences. The Court disagreed and held the application to be inadmissible. It said:[13]

> According to the consistent case law of the Court any measure the legal effects of which are binding on, and capable of affecting the interests of, the applicant by bringing about a distinct change in his legal position is an act or decision which may be the subject of an action under Article 173 for a declaration that it is void. However, the form in which such acts or decisions are cast is, in principle, immaterial as regards the question whether they are open to challenge under that article. In the case of acts or decisions adopted by a procedure involving several stages, in particular where they are the culmination of an internal procedure, it is clear from the case law that in principle an act is open to review only if it is a measure definitively laying down the position of the Commission or the Council on the conclusion of that procedure, and not a provisional measure intended to pave the way for the final decision.

But some provisional measures may be subject to challenge, provided that they affect the legal position of the applicants, such as the opinion given by the Commission in the *Noordwijks Cement Accoord* Case, which had the effect of removing an exemption from fines.

These cases show, therefore, that for the purpose of considering whether an act is a 'decision' within the meaning of art 173(2), the expression should not be interpreted restrictively; the substance, and not the form, should be looked at; an act will be regarded as a decision if it is binding upon, and capable of affecting the interests of, the applicant. Thus where the Commission refuses to take action under Regulation 17 against a commercial undertaking for abuse of a dominant position, the complainant who is directly concerned by the alleged abuse may challenge the refusal.[14] But where the Commission has no power, or does not intend, to make a binding decision it is clear that its statement of position cannot found an action under art 173(2). Thus a telex from the Commission to a French intervention agency expressing the view that the applicant had no right to a refund could not be the subject of an application; this was because it was not

---

13 [1981] ECR at 2651-2, [1981] 3 CMLR at 659-661.
14 Case 210/81 *Demo-Studio Schmidt v Commission* [1983] ECR 3045, [1984] 1 CMLR 63. But the complainant must be directly and individually concerned: see Case 26/76 *Metro-SB-Grossmärkte GmbH & Co KG v Commission* [1977] ECR 1875, [1978] 2 CMLR 1; cf Case 246/81 *Lord Bethell v Commission* [1982] ECR 2277, [1982] 3 CMLR 300. See p 249, post.

capable of having legal effect since the Commission's view did not bind the national authorities.[15] A letter from the Commission refusing to give a contractor an assurance that it was eligible to tender for public works contracts could not be the subject of an action under art 173(2) because the Commission had no power to take a decision as to its eligibility.[16] An internal Commission instruction merely reflecting an intention to follow a policy in the selection of candidates for service contracts was not reviewable.[17] But a letter definitively refusing a claim to a payment may amount to a decision if the applicant is entitled to the payment.[18]

The holding[19] that acts of the European Parliament are reviewable under art 173 has made it necessary for the Court to deal with the concept of decision in the context of acts of the Parliament, where it has emphasised that for the decision to be reviewable it must have legal effects on third parties. It has held that internal measures of the Parliament to implement payments of campaign expenditure were not 'decisions' (even if the decisions they implemented had been annulled), because the measures only had legal effects within the administration and did not give rise to rights or obligations on the part of third parties.[20] Nor was the setting up of a committee of enquiry into racism and fascism a reviewable decision; the establishment of the committee, which had no right of subpoena, was not intended to, and did not, produce legal effects vis-à-vis third parties.[1]

2 The standing of private persons

The problem of standing is a familiar one in administrative law, probably because the duties of the administration contain so large an element of duty to the public, and the point at which the duty is owed not only to the public at large, but also to private parties, is blurred. In England an applicant for judicial review must have 'a sufficient interest in the matter to which the application relates',[2] but even after an important decision of the House of Lords it cannot be said to be clear

---

15 Case 133/79 *Sucrimex v Commission* [1980] ECR 1299, [1981] 2 CMLR 479.
16 Case 182/80 *Gauff v Commission* [1982] ECR 799, [1982] 3 CMLR 402.
17 Case 114/86 *UK v Commission* [1989] 1 CMLR 32. Contrast Case 34/86 *Council v Parliament* [1986] ECR 2155, [1986] 3 CMLR 94 (declaration by President of Parliament that budget adopted: reviewable).
18 Cf Case 44/81 *Germany v Commission* [1982] ECR 1855, [1983] 2 CMLR 656.
19 Case 294/83 *Partie Ecologiste Les Verts v Parliament* [1986] ECR 1339, [1987] 2 CMLR 343.
20 Case 190/84 *Partie Ecologiste Les Verts v Parliament* [1989] 2 CMLR 880.
1 Case 78/85 *Group of the European Right v Parliament* [1986] ECR 1753, [1988] 3 CMLR 645.
2 Supreme Court Act 1981, s 31(3); RSC, Ord 53, r 3(7).

what will constitute a sufficient interest.[3] In one respect, however, English law goes much further than Community law, in that (at least to a limited extent) it allows a form of *actio popularis*, ie an action brought in the public interest by a person without a direct personal interest. Thus Mr Smedley was held to have standing, merely because he was a taxpayer, to apply for judicial review of an Order in Council which purported to give effect to the government's undertaking to pay a contribution of £121 million to the European Community. Woolf J said that he would be surprised:

> . . . if the result of the authorities dealing with *locus standi* was such that they prevented a public spirited citizen coming before the courts, seeking to prevent what would be an unconstitutional and unauthorised disposal by the Government of moneys from the Consolidated Fund.[4]

In Community law, private parties (natural or legal persons)[5] may challenge the legality of certain Community acts but the types of act in respect of which a private person has a remedy are limited. In the first place, as has been seen in the preceding section, there is no question of all 'acts' of the Council and the Commission being expressed to be open to review at the instance of private persons. Article 173(2) limits the reviewable acts to decisions, whether issued as such or 'in the form of a regulation'. This is narrower than the right of member states, who may also challenge (inter alia) regulations and directives. Thus in *Asteris AE v Commission*[6] the Greek Government was held to have standing to challenge a Commission regulation, whereas the Greek tomato producers concerned were not able to do so because they failed to show that the act was in truth a decision in the guise of a regulation. In the second place, the applicant must have a legal interest, although such an interest is broadly interpreted. In *BP v Commission*[7] the Commission had found that the applicants had been guilty of an abuse of a dominant position under art 86, but in view of special circumstances had decided not to impose a penalty; the absence of pecuniary sanctions did not prevent the applicants from having an interest in obtaining a review by the Court of the legality of the decision under art 173. In the third place, although such review is

---

3 *IRC v National Federation of Self-Employed and Small Businesses Ltd* [1982] AC 617, [1981] 2 All ER 93; Wade, ch 19; Justice-All Souls Report, ch 8.
4 *R v HM Treasury, ex p Smedley* [1985] 1 CMLR 665 at 674; affd (but without full discussion of standing) [1985] QB 657, [1985] 1 All ER 589, CA; cf *R v A-G, ex p ICI plc* [1987] 1 CMLR 72, CA.
5 On the meaning of 'legal person' see Case 135/81 *Groupement des Agences de Voyages Asbl v Commission* [1982] ECR 3799.
6 Cases 97 etc/86 [1988] 3 CMLR 493.
7 Case 77/77 [1978] ECR 1513, [1978] 3 CMLR 174; cf Case 92/78 *Simmenthal SpA v Commission* [1979] ECR 777, [1980] 1 CMLR 25. For a case where there was no such interest see Case 88/76 *Exportation des Sucres v Commission* [1977] ECR 709.

not limited to decisions addressed to the applicant, if addressed to another the decision must be 'of direct and individual concern' to the applicant.

In the context of art 173(2) the most difficult question is that of the standing of private parties in relation to 'a decision which, although in the form of a regulation or a decision addressed to another person, is of direct and individual concern' to the applicant. The problem arises in its most acute form when an applicant alleges that a regulation or a decision addressed to a member state is in reality a decision directed to the applicant, and that in consequence the applicant has standing to seek to annul the measure. There have been more than 50 decisions of the European Court on the admissibility of such applications, and in these decisions there are inconsistencies of approach and reasoning, and of results. It is probably not possible (and certainly not within the confines of an introductory work) to reconcile all the decisions, but it is possible to extract some principles and see some trends.

(i) Article 173(2) and the annulment of regulations

In almost all of the cases where regulations have been challenged, the applicant is a trader whose commercial interests are adversely affected by the measure. These are not cases of *actio popularis*, but cases where traders complain of very specific and often highly technical (and often short term) measures taken by the Community which, for example, harm their business or remove or reduce subsidies. Frequently, although couched in general terms, the measure is taken with the specific case of the applicant in mind. It is such cases that have given rise to difficulty.

The starting point is that the purpose of the provision in art 173(2) which allows annulment of a 'decision which, although in the form of a regulation . . . is of direct and individual concern' to the applicant is, in particular:

> . . . to prevent the Community institutions from being able to deny an individual the right to institute proceedings against a decision which is of direct and individual concern to him simply by choosing to issue that decision in the form of a regulation; the provision is thus intended to make it clear that the choice of form cannot alter the nature of the measure.[8]

The first cases[9] involving this question concerned the efforts of associations of fruit and vegetable producers and of wholesalers in

---

8 Cases 233–235/86 *Champlor SA v Commission* [1987] ECR 2251 at 2254. For essentially the same formulation see eg Case 101/76 *Koninklijke Scholten Honig NV v Council and Commission* [1977] ECR 797 at 806, [1980] 2 CMLR 669 at 679; Cases 97 etc/86 *Asteris AE v Commission* [1988] 3 CMLR 493 at 505.
9 Cases 16–17, 19–22/62 *Producteurs de Fruits et Légumes v Council* [1962] ECR 471, [1963] CMLR 160.

various meat and agricultural products to annul portions of Council regulations providing for the gradual establishment of a common organisation of the markets in the fruit and vegetable sectors and for the application of competition rules to the production of and trading in agricultural products. The Court held, first, that the expression 'decision' in art 173(2) was used in the same technical sense as in art 189 where it is distinguished from the expression 'regulation'. Therefore the application would not be admissible if the challenged act was a regulation. But what it was called was not decisive. The Court said:[10]

> In examining this question the Court cannot restrict itself to considering the official title of the measure, but must first take into account its object and content.

The Court regarded the basic distinction as being between those acts which were of general scope (regulations) and those which were of limited scope (decisions):

> The essential characteristics of a decision arise from the limitation of the persons to whom it is addressed, whereas a regulation, being essentially of a legislative nature, is applicable not to a limited number of persons, defined or identifiable, but to categories of persons viewed abstractly and in their entirety.[11] The Court then went on to hold that, in order to determine in doubtful cases whether the Court was concerned with a decision or a regulation, it was necessary to ascertain whether the measure in question was of individual concern to specific individuals.

As a result the approach of the Court may be summarised as follows: first, it is the substance and not the form of the measure which is relevant;[12] secondly, the test for determining whether a regulation is truly a decision is whether or not it is truly legislative in character, ie whether it applies to objectively determined situations and has legal effects on classes of persons defined in a general and abstract manner;[13] thirdly, the legislative character of a measure is not affected by the fact that it may be possible more or less precisely to determine the number and even the identity of the persons to whom it applies so long as it is applied by virtue of an

---

10 [1962] ECR 471 at 478. See also Case 101/76 *Koninklijke Scholten Honig v Council and Commission* [1977] ECR 797 at 806.
11 [1962] ECR 471 at 478–9. This case, and subsequent cases, show that a provision in a regulation which is otherwise legislative in character may be regarded as a decision if it is severable from the 'legislative whole': Case 789/79 *Calpak SpA v Commission* [1980] ECR 1949 at 1971, [1981] 1 CMLR 26 at 38, per Warner AG.
12 Cases supra, n 8.
13 For recent applications of the principle see Case 147/83 *Binderer v Commission* [1985] ECR 257; Case 40/84 *Casteels Pvba v Commission* [1985] ECR 667, [1986] 2 CMLR 475; Case 26/86 *Deutz und Gelderman v Council* [1987] ECR 941, [1988] 1 CMLR 668; Cases 97 etc/86 *Asteris AE v Commission* [1988] 3 CMLR 493; Case 191/87 *Cooperativa Veneta Allevatori Equini v Commission* [1989] 3 CMLR 420; Case 253/86 *SAP Vicente Nobre v Council* [1990] 1 CMLR 105; Cases 250/86 and 11/87 *RAR v Council and Commission* 29 June 1989.

objective legal or factual situation defined by the measure (thus a regulation relating to only one product manufactured by a small number of producers is no less a regulation for that reason,[14] nor does the fact that it has an unequal effect on the persons affected by it prevent it being a true regulation);[15] fourthly, a measure is of individual concern[16] where the applicant has been:

> ... affected by the measure in question by reason of certain attributes which are peculiar to him or by reason of circumstances in which he is differentiated from all other persons and by virtue of these factors must have been distinguished individually just as in the case of the person addressed.[17]

Strictly, in determining whether a measure in the form of a regulation is truly a decision, the Court should first look to see whether it is legislative in character, and only then go on to consider whether it is of direct and individual concern to the applicant.[18] In the majority of cases where the Court has found the application inadmissible, it has adopted that approach, but it is noteworthy that in the majority of cases where the application has been found admissible the Court has merely decided that the measure is of direct and individual concern without first considering the question whether the measure is legislative in character. This suggests that a measure which is of direct and individual concern to a private party cannot be legislative in character.

If there is a common thread among those cases where a regulation, or a provision in a regulation, has been held to be of direct and individual concern it is that they 'concern a closed circle of persons who are determined at the time of its adoption',[19] or when (which may be another way of putting the same point) the regulation is directed at

---

14 Among many others see Case 6/68 *Zuckerfabrik Watenstedt v Council* [1968] ECR 409, [1969] CMLR 26; Case 101/76 *Koninklijke Scholten Honig NV v Council and Commission* [1977] ECR 797, [1980] 2 CMLR 669; Case 789/79 *Calpak SpA v Commission* [1980] ECR 1949, [1981] 1 CMLR 26; Case 64/80 *Giuffrida and Campogrande v Council* [1981] ECR 693; Case 45/81 *Moksel v Commission* [1982] ECR 1129; Case 242/81 *Roquette Frères SA v Council* [1982] ECR 3213; Case 26/86 *Deutz und Gelderman v Council* supra; Cases 97 etc/85 *Asteris AE v Commission* [1988] 3 CMLR 493.
15 Cases 63–65/69 *Cie Française Commerciale v Commission* [1970] ECR 205, [1970] CMLR 369; Case 101/76 *Koninklijke Scholten Honig NV v Council and Commission*, supra. The same principles apply where a directive rather than a regulation is under attack: Case 160/88R *FEDESA v Council* [1988] 3 CMLR 534.
16 On direct concern in the context of regulations see Case 55/86 *ARPOSOL v Council* [1988] ECR 13, [1989] 2 CMLR 508; Case 333/85 *Mannesmann-Röhrenwerke AG v Council* [1987] ECR 1381, [1988] 2 CMLR 627.
17 Case 40/64 *Sgarlata v Commission* [1965] ECR 215 at 226, [1966] CMLR 314 at 323. See also Case 30/67 *Industria Molitoria Imolese v Council* [1968] ECR 115; Case 250/81 *Greek Canners Association v Commission* [1982] ECR 3535, [1983] 2 CMLR 32.
18 See Case 333/85 *Mannesmann-Röhrenwerke AG v Council* [1987] ECR 1381 at 1390–1391, [1988] 2 CMLR 627 at 633–634, per Da Cruz Vilaça AG, with citations.
19 Cases 233–235/86 *Champlor SA v Commission* [1987] ECR 2251 at 2255.

a specific class of persons with existing rights. Thus a provision in a regulation which applied only to a closed group of importers who had applied for import licences for dessert apples by a particular date was not a provision of general application but a 'conglomeration of individual decisions taken by the Commission under the guise of a regulation . . . each of which decisions affects the legal position of each author of an application for a licence'.[20] The same was so when a regulation abolished the right of cancellation of export licences which had been issued but not used by the day immediately prior to the regulation;[1] or when a regulation altered exchange rates in relation to existing export licences;[2] or denied an increase in the amount of refunds for exports to exporters who had already applied for refunds, but not to those who had not so applied;[3] or when a regulation in terms specified a quota for individual producers of isoglucose;[4] or when a regulation set aside the sale of olive oil which had been allocated to the applicants.[5] A similar principle probably underlies the cases where anti-dumping regulations have been held to be of direct and individual concern to manufacturers and exporters of the allegedly dumped products.[6]

But there are several cases in which regulations have affected closed groups or been issued to deal with specific parties which have not been held susceptible to review. Thus a regulation which altered refunds which had been awarded to exporters before a particular date was held not to be a decision: it did not reduce the refund but altered its calculation.[7] The same result flowed where a regulation altered quotas which had already been allotted.[8] There are many cases in which the measure is of a very narrow legislative character, and where the lack of a remedy under art 173 will lead to injustice. When following a dispute between an importer of windscreen-wiper motors and the French customs authorities, the Commission issued a regulation reclassifying the goods for customs purposes, an application to annul

---

20 Case 41–44/70 *International Fruit Co NV v Commission* [1971] ECR 411 at 422, [1975] 2 CMLR 515 at 535.
1 Case 88/76 *Société pour Exportation des Sucres v Commission* [1977] ECR 709 (but the application was inadmissible on other grounds). Cf Case 123/77 *UNICME v Council* [1978] ECR 845.
2 Case 112/77 *Töpfer & Co GmbH v Commission* [1978] ECR 1019.
3 Case 100/74 *Société CAM v Commission* [1975] ECR 1393.
4 Case 138/79 *Roquetre Frères v Council* [1980] ECR 3333.
5 Case 232/81 *Agricola Commerciale Olio Srl v Commission* [1984] ECR 3881, [1987] 1 CMLR 363.
6 See pp 252–253, infra. Cf Cases 87 etc/77, 22/83, 9–10/84 *Salerno v Commission and Council* [1985] ECR 2523 (regulation laid down measures for transfer of specific staff of EAC to the EEC).
7 Case 162/78 *Wagner v Commission* [1979] ECR 3467.
8 Cases 103–109/78 *Société des Usines de Beauport v Council* [1979] ECR 17, [1979] 3 CMLR 1.

the regulation was inadmissible, even though the only alternative remedy for the applicant was long and laborious national proceedings involving a reference under art 177.[9]

(ii) Decisions addressed to member states

This section will deal with the problem of 'direct and individual concern' in the context of a decision which is addressed to 'another person', most often a member state.[10] But the problem has also arisen in less difficult and controversial areas. Thus, in deciding whether a decision is of direct and individual concern, the Court will not take a very technical approach to separate corporate personality. In *Ford of Europe Inc v Commission*,[11] a decision was addressed to Ford's German subsidiary requiring it to supply right-hand drive cars to its German dealers. The object was to facilitate exports to the United Kingdom. The Commission questioned the admissibility of the application of Ford of Europe Inc, which co-ordinated Ford's European operations, to annul the decision, on the ground that the decision was not of direct and individual concern to Ford of Europe, since it was addressed to the German subsidiary. The Court rejected that argument: if right-hand drive cars manufactured by the German subsidiary intended for sale on the British market were supplied directly to British consumers by German distributors, the problems to which this could give rise unquestionably came within the province of the activities for which Ford of Europe Inc was responsible in its capacity as co-ordinator of manufacture and sales for companies belonging to the Ford Group. The decision was, therefore, of direct and individual concern to Ford of Europe Inc. Similarly, in a case involving a decision denying duty free status to computers the Court was not troubled by the fact that the application was by a European subsidiary of an American company rather than by the parent.[12]

The expression 'direct' has given rise to some difficulty. In the earlier cases the Court avoided defining the expression by deciding that there was no 'individual concern' and that it was not therefore necessary to decide whether there was 'direct concern'.[13] The Court has drawn a

---

9 Case 40/84 *Casteels Pvba v Commission* [1985] ECR 667, [1986] 2 CMLR 475. Cf Case 147/83 *Binderer v Commission* [1985] ECR 257.
10 'Another person', contrary to the arguments of the Commission, has been held to include a member state: Case 25/62 *Plaumann & Co v Commission* [1963] ECR 95, [1964] CMLR 29. For other types of decision see eg Case 294/83 *Partie Ecologiste Les Verts v Parliament* [1986] ECR 1339, [1987] 2 CMLR 343; Case 197/86 *CIDA v Council* [1989] 3 CMLR 851.
11 Cases 228 and 229/82 [1984] 1 CMLR 649.
12 Case 294/81 *Control Data Belgium NV v Commission* [1983] ECR 911, [1983] 2 CMLR 357.
13 See eg *Plaumann & Co v Commission*, supra; Case 1/64 *Glucoseries Réunies v Commission* [1964] ECR 413, [1964] CMLR 596; Case 38/64 *Getreide-Import v Commission* [1965] ECR 203, [1965] CMLR 276.

distinction between those decisions which create a discretion in a member state on the one hand, and those which do not give any such discretion on the other. The former are not of direct concern, but the latter are.[14] The element of discretion is a crucial one. In rejecting a suggestion that a decision rejecting a request by Belgium and Luxembourg for an additional aluminium quota was of direct concern to the applicant aluminium refining companies, it was held that even where the Commission granted such a request:

> A decision taken by the Commission in pursuance of the provision quoted above has thus no effect other than to create a power in favour of the member states concerned, and does not confer any rights on possible beneficiaries of any measures to be taken subsequently by the said states.[15]

The same principles apply to acts of the European Parliament, so that decisions instituting and regulating a scheme for reimbursement of expenses were of direct concern to the Green Party because the contested measures were a complete set of rules which required no further implementing provisions.[16]

The element of 'individual concern' in the context of decisions addressed to member states is essentially the same as that discussed in the preceding section in relation to regulations. A decision addressed to a member state will not individually concern a private party unless it deals with a factual situation which differentiates it from other persons and distinguishes it individually. Thus in the 'Berlin Butter' case the Commission addressed a decision to the Federal Republic of Germany concerning measures to be adopted in West Berlin to promote consumption of butter and reduce the EEC butter surplus. The decision involved the sale of butter at (in effect) half price, by including with each packet of butter sold one free packet. The applicants were margarine producers who claimed that the decision was invalid and that they had standing because of the adverse consequences for the sale of margarine which was caused by the decision. Their application was inadmissible because they were not individually concerned. The decision affected them, but only because of the commercial effect it produced. They were 'not a closed circle of persons who were

---

14 Cases 106–107/63 *Toepfer v Commission* [1965] ECR 405, [1966] CMLR 111; Case 62/70 *Bock v Commission* [1971] ECR 897, [1972] CMLR 160.
15 Case 69/69 *Alcan v Commission* [1970] ECR 385 at 393, [1970] CMLR 337 at 376. See also Cases 10 and 18/68 *Eridania v Commission* [1969] ECR 459; Cases 89, 91/86 *L'Etoile Commerciale v Commission* [1987] ECR 3005, [1988] 3 CMLR 564; cf Case 222/83 *Commune de Differdange v Commission* [1984] ECR 2889, [1985] 3 CMLR 638.
16 Case 294/83 *Partie Ecologiste Les Verts v Parliament* [1986] ECR 1339, [1987] 2 CMLR 343.

known at the time of its adoption and whose rights the Commission intended to regulate'.[17]

But the notion of a 'closed circle' is by no means an easy one to apply. In four early cases the Court held that a decision addressed to a member state was not, on the facts, of individual concern to the applicants. In *Plaumann & Co v Commission*[18] the applicant was a German fruit importer which challenged a refusal of the Commission to authorise Germany to suspend a common tariff custom duty on clementines and replace it by a lower German customs duty. The Court held that the decision did not concern the applicant individually because it was only affected by the decision in its capacity as an importer of clementines, an activity which could be carried on by anyone at any time. In a second case, *Glucoseries Réunies v Commission*,[19] the applicant was the only substantial Belgian dextrose manufacturer; it sought to challenge a Commission decision authorising France to levy a countervailing import duty on dextrose from other member states (other than Italy) unless those states levied such a duty on exports. The Court held that the fact that the plaintiff was the only Belgian enterprise affected by the decision did not make it individually concerned. This was because the effects of the decision were not limited to exports from Belgium to France and because it had 'general economic scope' in that it was intended to protect a sector of the French economy against competition from imports from other member states. In *Getreide-Import v Commission*[20] the applicant sought to challenge a Commission decision, directed to Germany, setting the cif prices of feed-stuff. The applicant was a feed-stuff importer which applied for an import licence for certain feed-stuff on the day after the Commission decision. It was the only importer so to do during the limited period the decision was in effect. The Court, nevertheless, held that the decision was not of individual concern to the applicant. In the first place, the decision applied not only to imports but also to exports so that the applicant was not necessarily in a unique position. In the second place, the purely fortuitous fact that, subsequently to the attacked decision, only the applicant made a request for an import licence did not sufficiently distinguish it from other importers.

---

17 Case 97/85 *Union Deutsche Lebensmittelwerke v Commission* [1987] ECR 2265 at 2287. For other recent examples see Case 282/85 *DEFI v Commission* [1986] ECR 2469, [1988] 2 CMLR 156; Case 82/87R *Autexpo SpA v Commission* [1987] ECR 2131, [1988] 3 CMLR 541; Case 207/86 *APESCO v Commission* [1989] 3 CMLR 687.
18 Case 25/62 [1963] ECR 95, [1964] CMLR 29, applied in Case 231/82 *Spijker Kwasten BV v Commission* [1984] 2 CMLR 284.
19 Case 1/64 [1964] ECR 413, [1964] CMLR 596.
20 Case 38/64 [1965] ECR 203, [1965] CMLR 276. See also Cases 10 and 18/68 *Eridania v Commission* [1969] ECR 459.

The standing of private persons 243

In subsequent cases, however, the Court held decisions addressed to a member state to be of individual concern. In *Toepfer v Commission*[1] the applicants were German importers of, and wholesalers in, maize who had applied for import licences on a day which was a few days before a Commission decision addressed to Germany was made known to them and which had the result of their being refused licences. The Court held that the only persons concerned by the decision were the importers who had requested an import licence on a particular day, and went on:

> The number and identity of these importers had already become fixed and ascertainable before 4 October, when the contested decision was made. The Commission was in a position to know that its decision affected the interests and the position of the said importers alone. The factual situation thus created differentiates the said importers, including the applicants, from all other persons and distinguishes them individually just as in the case of the person addressed.[2]

The factual distinction between this case and the *Getreide-Import* case[3] is fine: the decision attacked in the former case was purely retroactive whereas it was not in the latter—therefore the number of individuals affected was determinable in the former and not in the latter. Secondly, the cases discussed above[4] on the distinction between decisions and regulations do not suggest that such importance is to be attached to the limited number of persons affected, provided that the act is of a general nature. *Bock v Commission*[5] is easier, because the facts showed that the German Government had requested a decision from the Commission authorising it to prohibit Chinese mushrooms with the purpose of denying an application by the plaintiff. The judgment is not clear on what amounts to individual concern, but it seems that because the decision applied to existing applications *pro tanto*, the number and identity of the importers were 'specified and ascertainable' within the meaning of the judgment in the *Toepfer* case. In *Control Data Belgium NV v Commission*,[6] a decision addressed to member states denying duty free status to computers manufactured by the US parent company of the applicant, which wished to import them into Belgium, was regarded as of direct and individual concern to the importer.

---

1 Cases 106–107/63 [1965] ECR 405, [1966] CMLR 111.
2 [1965] ECR 405 at 411–12.
3 Case 38/64 [1965] ECR 203, [1965] CMLR 276.
4 See pp 236–238, ante.
5 Case 62/70 [1971] ECR 897, [1972] CMLR 160, applied Case 1/84R *Ilford v Commission* [1984] 2 CMLR 475. See also Case 92/78 *Simmenthal v Commission* [1979] ECR 777, [1980] 1 CMLR 25. Cf Case 135/81 *Groupement des Agences de Voyages Asbl v Commission* [1982] ECR 3799.
6 Case 294/81 [1983] ECR 911, [1983] 2 CMLR 357.

Piraiki-Patraiki Cotton Industry v Commission[7] is an instructive illustration of the difference between 'direct concern' on the one hand, and 'individual concern' on the other. At the request of the French government, the Commission addressed a decision to France authorising it to impose import quotas on cotton yarn originating in Greece. The applicants were the principal Greek firms which produced and exported cotton yarn to France. The decision was held to be of 'direct concern' to the applicants. There was only a theoretical possibility that the French government would not take advantage of the power given by the decision to restrict imports. In fact there was no doubt whatsoever that the French authorities intended to implement the decision, and consequently the applicants were directly concerned. But not all of the applicants were individually concerned. Only those who had entered into contracts prior to the decision with French customers for the delivery of Greek cotton yarn during the period when the decision was in force were individually concerned. Those applicants were individually concerned because they were members of a limited category of enterprises which were identified or identifiable by the Commission and were especially affected by the decision because of those contracts.

(iii) Locus standi principles: restrictive practices, anti-dumping investigations, and state aids

The practical and commercial importance of restrictive practices and anti-dumping investigations and state aid decisions frequently causes the Commission's decisions to come under judicial scrutiny. Complainants may take the view that the Commission has not acted sufficiently to condemn restrictive practices or to mitigate the effects of dumping of products from non-member states; commercial undertakings accused of restrictive practices may seek to question the adequacy of the procedure adopted or to challenge fines imposed on them for unlawful agreements under art 85 of the EEC Treaty or for abuse of a dominant position under art 86; exporters may challenge the imposition of an anti-dumping duty on the ground that the procedure was unfair or that they have not been guilty of dumping, and importers may question the validity of the duty; businesses may seek to challenge state aids to their competitors which have been authorised by the Commission.

In each of these categories the Commission conducts investigations in which interested parties are heard, and which results in a determination. Private parties who seek annulment of acts made as a result of, or in the course of these proceedings, can only do so within the

---

7 [1985] ECR 207, [1985] 2 CMLR 4. Cf Case 197/86 *CIDA v Council* [1989] 3 CMLR 851.

framework of art 173(2). In the case of restrictive practices, the main decisions are addressed to parties who are guilty of restrictive practices or who seek to be exempted from sanctions for restrictive practices: the question arises whether other parties, such as complainants, have standing to seek to annul decisions not to proceed with a complaint or to grant an exemption. In anti-dumping cases, provisional and definitive anti-dumping duties can only be imposed by regulation: do complainants have standing to seek the annulment of decisions not to proceed? Can exporters on whose products a duty has been imposed challenge the regulation? In the case of state aids, the authorisation or disapproval of the state aid is in the form of a decision addressed to a member state: can the proposed recipient challenge the refusal, or can a competitor challenge the authorisation? In such cases the European Court[8] seeks to answer the question of whether the contested act is a decision of direct and individual concern to the applicant in accordance with the principles set out earlier. But, as Hartley has suggested, it is likely that in these cases the Court adopts a more liberal approach, on the basis that the proceedings are quasi-judicial, and that any private party which had an interest in the proceedings will have a sufficient interest to seek annulment under art 173(2).[9]

Restrictive practices. The relevant rules of the Common Market are contained in arts 85 to 90 of the EEC Treaty.[10] Art 85 prohibits as incompatible with the Common Market agreements and concerted practices which may affect trade between member states and which have as their object the prevention, restriction or distortion of competition within the Common Market; art 85(3) allows these prohibitions to be declared inapplicable in cases of agreements which contribute to improving production or distribution or promoting technical or economic progress. Art 86 prohibits any abuse of a dominant position which may affect trade between member states. Arts 87 and 89 make provision for the implementation of arts 85 and 86 by Council regulations and Commission decisions. Arts 85 and 86 were implemented by Council Regulation 17 of 1962, which, as subsequently amended and subject to Commission Regulation 99/63, regulates the investigation procedure. For present purposes it is sufficient to note that under Regulation 17 the Commission may give, on the application of undertakings concerned, a negative clearance to the effect that on the facts in its possession there are no grounds for

---

8 The new European Court of First Instance has jurisdiction in competition cases (Council Decision, art 3(1)(c) [1989] 3 CMLR 458), and in 1991 the Council will re-examine the proposal to give it jurisdiction in anti-dumping cases.
9 Hartley, pp 346, 354; see also Greaves (1986) 11 EL Rev 119.
10 See also ECSC Treaty, arts 65 and 66.

action under arts 85 or 86; the Commission grants the exemption under art 85(3) by decision, which may be subject to conditions (art 6); complaints about infringement may be made to the Commission by 'natural or legal persons who claim a legitimate interest' (art 3(2)); the Commission may require information and impose fines for failure to provide it, and may carry out on-the-spot investigations, to which undertakings must submit on pain of penalty (arts 11 and 14); the Commission may impose fines and periodic penalty payments, which are subject to review by the European Court (arts 16 and 17); undertakings which are the object of decisions have the right to be heard, as do other persons who show a sufficient interest (art 19). The rules on a right to a hearing were further implemented by Commission Regulation 99 of 1963. This provides that undertakings which are subject to investigation must be provided with a statement of objections, and have the right to make known their views (arts 2 to 4); if the Commission decides to take no action on a complaint, the complainants must be informed of the reasons for the decision and have a right to comment (arts 6 and 7). In addition to the powers granted directly by the EEC Treaty and the implementing regulations, the European Court has held that the Commission may, in urgent cases, take interim decisions. In *Camera Care Ltd v Commission*[11] distributors of Hasselblad cameras complained of Hasselblad's refusal to supply. The Commission refused to take urgent interim measures ordering Hasselblad to supply. The reason given for the refusal was that the Commission did not have the power to take the measures. The European Court held that the Commission did have the power to take interim measures if they were necessary to ensure the effectiveness of any final decision and provided the Commission had regard to the legitimate interests of the undertakings concerned. The measures must be temporary and the parties concerned must have a right to be heard, and the decisions must be in such a form that an action may be brought on them before the European Court by any injured party. An example of a successful challenge against an interim decision is *Ford v Commission*, where the Commission's interim order to Ford to supply right-hand drive cars to its German distributors was held void.[12]

In principle it is clear that undertakings which are the object of an investigation may challenge decisions taken by the Commission in the course of the investigation and decisions imposing fines. An undertaking may not challenge the opening of an investigation because the initiation of the procedure and the service of the statement of objections are not decisions within the meaning of art 173. Thus IBM

---

11 Case 792/79R [1980] ECR 119, [1980] 1 CMLR 334.
12 Cases 228 and 229/82 [1984] ECR 1129, [1984] 1 CMLR 649.

failed in its effort to have the Commission's investigation terminated. The European Court left open the question whether, in exceptional circumstances, where the measures concerned lacked the appearance of legality, a judicial review at an early stage might be possible.[13]

Decisions made by the Commission in the course of an investigation may be challenged by their addressees. Examples include the partially successful challenge against the production of documents on the ground of legal professional privilege in *AM and S Europe Ltd v Commission*;[14] the unsuccessful challenge against the on-the-spot investigation in *National Panasonic (UK) Ltd v Commission*;[15] the decision by the Commission to communicate to the complainant commercial information about the company whose conduct was under investigation;[16] and the many applications challenging the refusal of the Commission to grant exemptions.[17] Decisions of a preliminary character may be challenged, such as interim measures ordered by the Commission.[18] Where a preliminary decision materially affects the position of an undertaking, eg by removing the exemption from fines granted pending exemption of its restrictive agreements, it may be challenged even though Regulation 17 refers to it as an 'opinion'.[19] Where the Commission has made a decision finding an undertaking guilty of an abuse of a dominant position, but has not imposed a fine, the undertaking has a sufficient legal interest in seeking to annul the decision.[20] In these cases the grounds for review are those set out in art 173, which will be discussed in the next section. The powers of the European Court with regard to fines and periodic penalties are wider, because art 17 of Regulation grants to the European Court, pursuant to art 172 of the EEC Treaty, unlimited jurisdiction to review decisions fixing fines or periodic penalties. This is more akin to appeal than judicial review.[1]

Complainants have standing to seek the annulment of decisions provided that they have a legitimate interest. In terms of art 173, they must show that there is a decision addressed to them, or, if addressed to another person, that it is of direct and individual concern to the complainants. Where there is a decision of the Commission, eg granting an exemption to an undertaking, the complainant must show that

---

13 Case 60/81 *IBM v Commission* [1981] ECR 2639, [1981] 3 CMLR 635, p 233, ante.
14 Case 155/79 [1982] ECR 1575, [1982] 2 CMLR 264.
15 Case 136/79 [1980] ECR 2033, [1980] 3 CMLR 169, p 262, post.
16 Case 53/85 *AKZO Chemie BV v Commission* [1986] ECR 1965, [1987] 1 CMLR 231.
17 See eg Case 17/74 *Transocean Marine Paint Association v Commission* [1974] ECR 1063, [1974] 2 CMLR 459.
18 See p 246, ante.
19 *Noordwijks Cement Accoord* case, p 230, ante.
20 *BP v Commission*, p 235, ante.
 1 See eg Cases 100–103/80 *Musique Diffusion Française SA v Commission* [1983] ECR 1825, [1983] 3 CMLR 221.

it is directly and individually concerned. In *Metro v Commission*[2] Metro were 'Cash and Carry' wholesalers. They wanted to sell products manufactured by a company called SABA and sought recognition from SABA as a wholesaler for the distribution of SABA's electronic equipment. SABA refused this recognition because Metro were not exclusively wholesalers. Metro complained to the Commission under Regulation 17, asking it to find that the distribution system established by SABA was contrary to arts 85 and 86. SABA had notified to the Commission its conditions of sale for negative clearance. The Commission adopted a decision requiring SABA to discontinue certain of its conditions, but upheld the conditions in certain respects, the result of which was that Metro was prevented from becoming an approved distributor. Metro sought to have the decision annulled. The application was dismissed on the merits, but the European Court held that Metro had standing because the contested decision was adopted in particular as the result of the complaint submitted by Metro; it related to the provisions of SABA's distribution system, on which SABA relied as against Metro in order to justify its refusal to sell; it was in the interests of the satisfactory administration of justice and of the proper application of arts 85 and 86 that the persons who were entitled under Regulation 17 to request the Commission to find an infringement should be able, if their request was dismissed either wholly or in part, to institute proceedings in order to protect their legitimate interests. Consequently, Metro was directly and individually concerned within the meaning of art 173(2).

Almost ten years later the Court held that Metro had standing to challenge an exemption granted to SABA under art 85(3) in respect of its distribution system, which was essentially the same as the previous one.[3] SABA argued that the case was different from the first *Metro* case in that the new decision was not adopted after a complaint by Metro. The Court's view was that the decision was of direct and individual concern to Metro because Metro's application for admission to the SABA distribution system had been refused, Metro's interest has been recognised by the Commission, and it had submitted objections in the course of SABA's application for exemption. But Metro's case on the merits was again dismissed.

In the *Metro* case there were decisions in the strict sense by the Commission. In *Demo-Studio Schmidt v Commission*[4] the applicant was a retailer in television sets and loudspeakers; after he had been selling Revox equipment for some time, Revox introduced a new distribution

---

2 Case 26/76 [1977] ECR 1875, [1978] 2 CMLR 1. See Dinnage (1979) 4 EL Rev 15.
3 Case 75/84 *Metro SB-Grossmärkte GmbH & Co KG v Commission* [1986] ECR 3021, [1987] 1 CMLR 188.
4 Case 210/81 [1983] ECR 3045, [1984] 1 CMLR 63.

system, and refused to appoint him as a dealer under the new system for its specialist products on the ground that he did not open during normal hours. He then complained to the Commission that Revox had abused its dominant position and asked it to order Revox to supply him with the specialist equipment. The Commission, acting under art 6 of Regulation 99/63, notified the applicant of its intention not to follow up his complaint and asked him to submit his comments. The Commission notified the applicant, after receiving his comments, that there was no basis for concluding that Revox had abused a dominant position. The applicant sought the annulment of this notice. In the proceedings the Commission did not dispute the fact that its reply to the applicant on the complaint constituted a measure which might be referred to the Court under art 173(2), since the notice or communication was final, but left it to the Court to assess to what extent the applicant had an interest in taking legal proceedings. The Court held that the refusal to grant the applicant a dealership was capable of affecting his legitimate interests, particularly as the Court had held in the *Camera Care* case that the Commission had power to order the undertaking in question to take any measures necessary to bring the infringement to an end, which might include making the applicant a dealer. In the event, the complaint was dismissed because the Commission's decision was not based on a materially incorrect appreciation of the facts and was not vitiated by any manifest error of assessment. In *CICCE v Commission*[5] the Court held, applying *Demo-Schmidt*, that a letter from the Director-General of the Competition Directorate affirming the Commission's intention to close the file on a complaint was a decision in relation to which the complainant had standing to apply to annul.

It follows from the *Demo-Studio Schmidt* case that a complainant can challenge the failure to open an investigation, and from the *IBM* case that the undertaking being investigated cannot complain of the opening of the investigation. This apparently paradoxical result is explicable on the ground that the rejection of the complaint so far as the complainant is concerned is for all practical purposes a final decision affecting its interests if it has a direct concern; whereas, as the Court itself pointed out in the *IBM* case, the opening of an investigation is not a final decision in relation to the person being investigated. But not every complainant will have the requisite legal interest. In *Metro* and *Demo-Studio Schmidt* the applicant was a dealer who had been denied supplies by an undertaking subject to an investigation following the dealer's complaint. In *Lord Bethell v Commission*[6] Lord Bethell, who has long campaigned against restrictive practices in air

---

5 Case 298/83 [1985] ECR 1105, [1986] 1 CMLR 486.
6 Case 246/81 [1982] ECR 2777, [1982] 3 CMLR 300.

transport, complained to the Commission about fare-fixing on European scheduled routes, and asked the Commission to take action against the airlines. The Commission replied that there was no ground, in principle, for action under art 85 because the price-fixing was the final responsibility of the states concerned, and not of the airlines; that it was writing to the member states to inform them of its views, and warning them that excessive fares might involve an abuse of a dominant position under art 86. Lord Bethell brought proceedings for (inter alia) annulment of this communication. The application was held inadmissible because the Commission had no right or duty to adopt in respect of the applicant a decision saying either that the Commission was going to act or that it was not. The applicant was asking the Commission, not to take a decision in respect of him, but to open an enquiry with regard to third parties and to take decisions in respect of them. The applicant had an indirect interest in the proceedings and their possible outcome, but was not in the legal position of the addressee of a decision which might be declared void under art 173(2). Lord Bethell also failed in his complaint under art 175 against the Commission's failure to act because the Commission had no duty to adopt a decision with regard to him.[7]

Anti-dumping. Dumping is a special type of unfair competition involving price discrimination between markets, and occurs when goods are sold on an export market at a price below their normal value in the home market of the exporter. In order to avoid protectionism the General Agreement on Tariffs and Trade (GATT) contains provisions for limiting the extent to which states may impose anti-dumping duties (and countervailing duties to counteract foreign state subsidies). The Community has succeeded to the rights and duties of the member states under GATT,[8] and the Community rules providing for the imposition of anti-dumping duties and countervailing duties are now contained in Council Regulation 2423/88. This provides that any natural or legal person, or any association acting on behalf of a Community industry, which considers itself injured or threatened by dumped or subsidised imports may lodge a written complaint; where it becomes apparent, after consultation, that the complaint does not provide sufficient evidence to justify initiating an investigation, then the complainant is notified (art 5). If a proceeding is initiated, the complainant (among other persons) is informed, and the complainant

---

7 See p 280, post. Where the Commission rejects a complaint from a complainant with a direct interest, the appropriate remedy is not for failure to act under art 175 (Case 125/78 *GEMA v Commission* [1979] ECR 3173, [1980] 2 CMLR 177) but for annulment of the decision: see *Metro v Commission; Demo-Studio Schmidt v Commission*, supra.
8 See eg Case 266/81 *Soc Italiana per l'Oleodotto Transalpino v Ministero delle Finanze* [1983] ECR 731, [1984] 2 CMLR 231.

may inspect all information made available to the Commission by any party; the Commission may hear the interested parties, and must hear them if they have made a written request for a hearing showing that they are an interested party; the Commission is to give the parties directly concerned an opportunity to meet so that opposing views may be presented; a proceeding is concluded either by its termination or by definitive action (art 7). By article 9 the Commission is to inform the parties known to be concerned of the termination of proceedings where protective measures are unnecessary. If it finds that there has been dumping or subsidies have been granted and there is evidence of injury, the Commission may impose a provisional anti-dumping or countervailing duty, and a definitive duty may be imposed by Council Regulation. But if undertakings are given to revise prices or cease exports so that the injurious effects of dumping or subsidies are eliminated, the proceedings may be terminated without the imposition of a duty (art 10).

The consequences of an investigation may be very serious for interested parties. If the complaint is unsuccessful manufacturers in the Common Market may feel that their products continue to meet unfair competition from imports which are being sold at unfairly low prices because they are being dumped or because they are being subsidised. If the complaint is successful importers may feel that they are paying an unfairly high price for imports already ordered by them and which they may not be able to pass on to their customers; the exporters from outside the Community may feel that the duties imposed are really protectionist and designed to prevent them competing with producers in the Common Market. It is therefore complainants, exporters, and importers who are the persons most likely to seek to challenge the failure to impose duties on their imposition.

The duties can only be imposed by regulation, provisional duties by Commission regulation and definitive duties by Council regulation. These require collection of the duties by the authorities of the member states. If, therefore, exporters or importers wish to challenge the imposition of a duty, they have to show that the measure, notwithstanding that it is in form a regulation, is in truth a decision addressed to the member states which concerns the exporters or importers directly and individually. As regards independent importers, it was held in *Alusuisse v Council and Commission*[9] that regulations imposing a duty are not susceptible to judicial review because the regulations were measures having general application and not decisions of direct and individual concern. In that case the applicant was an Italian company engaged in the production of plasticisers and resins. It sought to challenge anti-dumping duties placed on a raw material required by it

---

9 Case 307/81 [1982] ECR 3463, [1983] 3 CMLR 388.

and originating from the United States. The Court emphasised that importers were not expressly named in the regulations. This was so notwithstanding that it was possible to determine the identities of the persons who would be affected. Nor was the position different because interested parties were heard before the decision was adopted: that did not change the character of the measure from a regulation to an administrative decision. The appropriate remedy for importers was to challenge the imposition of the duty in the national courts.[10]

Producers and exporters who are identified in the regulation or were concerned in the preliminary investigation have standing. The *Japanese Ball-Bearings* cases[11] were unusual in that a Council regulation had imposed anti-dumping duties on Japanese ball-bearings, but the duty was suspended subject to the observance of price undertakings given by the major Japanese producers; the regulation also provided for the definitive collection of provisional duties on ball-bearings exported by named Japanese manufacturers. The regulation was held to be void because it was not open to the Community both to accept price undertakings and to impose and collect a duty, since they were mutually exclusive remedies for the termination of an anti-dumping procedure. The applicants were the Japanese manufacturers and importers who were their subsidiaries or closely associated companies. Their applications were admissible because it was apparent on the face of the regulation that the suspended anti-dumping duty was intended to ensure the strict observance of the price undertakings by the creation of an additional penalty. Although drafted in general terms it concerned only the major Japanese manufacturers. The provision for the collection of the duty was a collective decision which was of direct and individual concern to those importers who had imported the products manufactured by the four major Japanese manufacturers, who were named in the regulation.

The *Japanese Ball-Bearings* cases were unusual because of the element of suspended duty, which only served to emphasise that the measures were directed at specific enterprises. But in the *Allied Corp* cases,[12] which involved the imposition of anti-dumping duties on

---

10 Followed, it would seem, by a reference on validity under art 177. See also Cases 239, 275/82 *Allied Corpn v Commission* [1984] ECR 1005 at 1031, [1985] 3 CMLR 572 at 614; Case 279/86 *Sermes v Commission* [1987] ECR 3109; Case 301/86 *Frimodt Pedersen v Commission* [1987] ECR 3123.
11 Cases 113, 118–121/77 [1979] ECR 1185, [1979] 2 CMLR 257.
12 Cases 239, 275/82 *Allied Corpn v Commission* [1984] ECR 1005, [1985] 3 CMLR 572; Case 53/83 *Allied Corpn v Commission* [1985] ECR 1622, [1986] 3 CMLR 605. See also Cases 240/84 *NTN Tokyo Bearing Co Ltd v Council* [1987] ECR 1809, [1989] 2 CMLR 76 (applicant only has standing in relation to the part of the regulation which affects it). On the position of importers who are associated with the exporters see also Cases 277 and 300/85 *Canon Inc v Council* [1989] 1 CMLR 915.

imports of United States chemical fertilisers, the Court accepted the view of the Commission (not supported by the Council) that exporters should have the right to challenge anti-dumping regulations, because (inter alia) it would help Community exporters to challenge anti-dumping measures in other countries (especially the United States) if there were reciprocity. The Court accepted that anti-dumping duties could only be imposed on the basis of findings resulting from an investigation concerning the production prices and export prices of identified undertakings. Consequently the measures imposing duties would be of direct and individual concern to producers and exporters who could establish that they were identified in the measures adopted by the Commission or the Council or were concerned by investigations.

The position with regard to complainants is clearer. In *FEDIOL v Commission*[13] the EEC Seed Crushers and Oil Processors Federation had lodged a complaint with the Commission about the subsidisation of exports of soya bean oil cake by Brazil and asked the Commission to initiate a subsidy proceeding and to impose a provisional countervailing duty. The Commission investigated the practices, and entered into negotiations with the Brazilian Government. FEDIOL subsequently served notice on the Commission, calling upon it to initiate a proceeding against Brazil without delay. By telex message the Commission informed the applicant that it did not, for the time being, intend to initiate a proceeding, and subsequently confirmed this conclusion by letter. FEDIOL sought to annul that communication under article 173. The Commission contested the admissibility of the application. The European Court held that it was admissible because the Council Regulation on dumping and subsidies recognised the existence of a legitimate interest on the part of producers in the adoption of an anti-subsidy measure, and gave them certain specific rights including the right to submit evidence, to see all information, the right to be heard, the opportunity to meet and the right to be informed if the Commission decided not to pursue a complaint. It was accepted by the Commission that where the Community authorities had disregarded specific rights in the regulation, including the right to lodge a complaint or the right to have it considered, there was a right of action. The Court held that complainants had the right to avail themselves, with regard both to the assessment of facts and to the adoption of protective measures, of a review by the Court appropriate to the nature of the powers reserved to the Community institutions; complainants should not be refused the right to put before the Court any matters which would facilitate a review as to whether the Commis-

---

13 Case 191/82 [1983] ECR 2913, [1984] 3 CMLR 244, applied in Case 264/82 *Timex Corpn v Council and Commission* [1985] ECR 849, [1985] 3 CMLR 550.

sion had observed the procedural guarantees granted to complainants by the regulation and whether or not it had committed manifest errors in its assessment of the facts, had omitted to take into consideration any essential matters or based the reasons for its decisions on considerations amounting to a misuse of powers. The regulation acknowledged that undertakings injured by subsidies by non-member states had a legitimate interest in the initiation of protective action, and they had, therefore, a right of action.

State aids. Because state aids to industry may distort competition, they are treated by art 92 of the EEC Treaty as incompatible with the Common Market. But certain types of aid are permitted if authorised by the Commission, and under art 93 the Commission may address decisions to member states authorising or prohibiting state aids after hearing the persons concerned. This semi-contentious procedure enables the view to be heard, not only of the aid-granting state, but of other member states and undertakings whose interests are liable to be affected by the grant or refusal of authorisation.

It is beyond doubt that the member state proposing to grant the aid, and other member states, have standing to challenge a decision of the Commission to refuse or grant authorisation. The European Court assumed (but did not decide) that a regional body which was empowered by the Belgian government to grant aid had standing to challenge the Commission's refusal,[14] but it has also held that a state-appointed quango which administered the aid did not have standing.[15] But in the latter case the French government itself was seeking annulment of the decision in other proceedings, and there was therefore an effective remedy. In proceedings brought by the member state to challenge a Commission decision that the member state should recover an unlawful state aid, the member state cannot obtain an order for the interim suspension of the order on the ground of damage to the recipient of the aid and its creditors; it must show damage to itself.[16]

The next class of persons who are affected by a Commission decision are the recipients or intended recipients of the aid. In *Philip Morris Holland BV v Commission*,[17] the Commission accepted that the Dutch subsidiary of an international cigarette group had standing to challenge the refusal by the Commission to authorise the Dutch government to grant aid to increase the production capacity of its factory. Similarly, in *Intermills SA v Commission*[18] the Commission

---

14 Cases 62 and 72/87 *Exécutif Régional Wallon v Commission* [1989] 2 CMLR 771.
15 Case 282/85 *DEFI v Commission* [1986] ECR 2469, [1988] 2 CMLR 156.
16 Case 142/87R *Belgium v Commission* [1988] 2 CMLR 601.
17 Case 730/79 [1980] ECR 2671, [1981] 2 CMLR 321.
18 Case 323/82 [1984] ECR 3809, [1986] 1 CMLR 614. Cf Case 223/85 *RSV v Commission* [1987] ECR 4617, [1989] 2 CMLR 259.

accepted that, where it had prohibited capital investment by the Belgian authorities in a paper-making group, the would-be recipient was directly and individually concerned by the Commission's decision. In 1985 the Commission ordered the Dutch Government to discontinue a tariff for natural gas sold to glasshouse growers, on the basis that it was an aid incompatible with the Common Market because it was lower than those charged to other Dutch industries. The Court held that the organisation set up to represent the interests of the growers had standing: although it was not directly and individually concerned as a recipient of the intended aid its position as a negotiator of gas tariffs was affected by the decision, and it had taken an active part in the procedure before the Commission; it was also one of the parties to the contract which established the preferential tariff. But individual growers who had benefited from the lower tariff did not have standing, because it was not of individual concern to them as distinct from being of concern to categories of persons envisaged in a general and abstract manner.[19] Recipients of state aid cannot obtain an interim suspension of a decision that the aid be repaid unless the remedies in the national court are inadequate to avoid serious irreparable harm from the effects of the member state rescinding its grant of aid.[20]

Finally, it is clear that the competing undertakings who are prejudiced by the grant of aid and who participate in the Commission's proceedings have standing to challenge a decision to authorise aid. In *COFAZ v Commission*[1] the applicants were French fertiliser manufacturers who objected to a Commission decision closing the file on their complaint against a Dutch natural gas tariff structure which, the French manufacturers alleged, constituted a state aid to Dutch manufacturers of ammonia. The Court applied the decisions in the antitrust and anti-dumping cases[2] to conclude that a party which had originated the complaint which led to the investigation procedure, whose views had been heard in that procedure, and whose observations had determined the conduct of that procedure, had standing, provided that its position on the market was significantly affected by the aid which was the subject of the contested decision. The decision to close the file was of direct concern to the applicants because it left all the potentially harmful effects of the tariff system in existence.

(iv) Conclusions

The following conclusions on standing may be drawn from this survey:

---

19 Cases 67 etc/85 *Kwekerij Gebr Van der Kooy BV v Commission* [1989] 2 CMLR 804.
20 Case 142/87R *Belgium v Commission* [1988] 2 CMLR 601.
 1 Case 169/84 [1986] ECR 391, [1986] 3 CMLR 385.
 2 *Metro, Demo-Studio Schmidt, FEDIOL* and *Timex*, pp 248–249, 253, ante.

(1) Private parties have standing to bring actions to annul decisions addressed to them. It is not material whether the decision is classified as such by the Commission. When an act addressed to a private party is not so classified, it will be regarded as a decision capable of annulment if its legal effects are binding upon, and capable of affecting the interests of, the applicant.

(2) An act of a preliminary nature may be the subject of annulment, but only if it definitively affects the legal position of the applicant.

(3) Private parties may also bring actions to annul regulations, or decisions addressed to others, but, in the case of regulations, only if they are in truth decisions, and in the case of both regulations and decisions, they are of direct and individual concern to the applicant.

(4) A regulation is not likely to be regarded as a decision but the label given to the act by the Community institution is not decisive. A regulation may be regarded as a decision (or a bundle of decisions) if it is limited in scope and is concerned with designated or identifiable persons individually rather than classes of persons defined in a general and abstract manner.

(5) A regulation or decision addressed to a member state will not be regarded as being of direct and individual concern unless it applies, without more, to the private party and unless the identity and individuality of the applicants are such that they must be treated as if they had been singled out for operation of the decision.

3 The substantive grounds for review

Article 173 specifies the following four substantive grounds for review:

(i) lack of competence (*incompétence*);
(ii) infringement of an essential procedural requirement (*violation des formes substantielles*);
(iii) infringement of the Treaty or of any rule of law relating to its application (*violation du présent Traité ou de toute règle de droit relative à son application*);
(iv) misuse of powers (*détournement de pouvoir*).

The substantive grounds for review all have some counterpart in United Kingdom law, although in a much less developed state. It is necessary to look at the rules relating to ultra vires and the control of abuse of discretion and to the rules of natural justice for the closest analogies. But there are major differences. There are no general principles, except perhaps in relation to principles of natural justice, which play as dynamic a role as those of the general principles of Community law applied by the European Court; and there are areas, such as the duty to give reasons for regulations and decisions, in which United Kingdom law is seriously deficient.[3]

Three preliminary comments are called for before the grounds are treated separately. In the first place, neither the Court nor the parties to proceedings before it have drawn narrow distinctions between the four headings. Whether a breach of treaty is to be classified as resulting in a lack of jurisdiction or an infringement of substantial procedural requirement does not have any real practical significance. Thus, there are cases turning on infringement of the Treaty which could well have turned on jurisdiction[4] and cases on infringement of Treaty which could well have turned on abuse of powers.[5] In the second place, although continental concepts of administrative law greatly influenced the structure of the remedies and the expressions used (particularly French administrative law) and German law has inspired many of the general principles applied by the Court, Community law is a separate legal system and reliance on technical concepts of national law has been discouraged. This is because to reintroduce technical concepts of national law would be to remove the flexibility and breadth of interpretation which have to be given to art 173.[6] In practice, of course, parties will tend to rely on all available legal authorities which support their cases and reliance on national law will continue wherever Community law is unclear or underdeveloped.[7] Thirdly, because art 177 provides for references on the validity of acts of the institutions, some very important cases on the substantive grounds for review have been decided under art 177 rather than art 173, and the relationship between these articles will be discussed below.[8]

(i) Lack of competence

This jurisdictional ground is in essence a complaint that the wrong body has acted or the right body has done something which it had no

---

3 See Wade, pp 547–548; Justice-All Souls Report, Ch 3.
4 See eg Case 22/70 *Re ERTA: Commission v Council* [1971] ECR 263, [1971] CMLR 335, and cf Case 48/69 *ICI v Commission* [1972] ECR 619, [1972] CMLR 557.
5 But see Case 34/62 *Germany v Commission* [1963] ECR 131, [1963] CMLR 369, for a stricter approach to classification. See also Case 41/69 *ACF Chemiefarma v Commission* [1970] ECR 661.
6 See submissions of Roemer AG in Case 6/68 *Zuckerfabrik Watenstedt GmbH v Council* [1968] ECR 409, [1969] CMLR 26. Cf Case 25/62 *Plaumann & Co v Commission* [1963] ECR 95, [1964] CMLR 29.
7 For examples, see the arguments in Case 40/64 *Sgarlata v Commission* [1965] ECR 215, [1966] CMLR 314, and in Cases 6–17, 19–22/62 *Producteurs de Fruits et Légumes v Council* [1962] ECR 471, [1963] CMLR 160; Case 155/79 *AM and S Europe Ltd v Commission* [1982] ECR 1575, [1982] 2 CMLR 264. Cf Case 81/72 *Commission v Council* [1973] ECR 575, [1973] CMLR 639.
8 See p 274, post.

power (in the jurisdictional sense) to do.⁹ Thus in the *Dyestuffs* case¹⁰ one of the main arguments of ICI was that the Commission had no power or jurisdiction over companies in non-member states. A recent example of a finding of a lack of competence was the decision in *Ford of Europe Inc v Commission*,¹¹ where the Court annulled an interim decision of the Commission requiring Ford's German subsidiary to withdraw its ban on sales of right-hand drive cars to its German dealers. The purpose of the ban was to prevent British customers buying right-hand drive Fords at German prices, which were lower than British prices, and the Commission's decision was designed to counteract this partition of the market. But the interim decision was taken in the context of its investigation of the Ford dealership agreements, and because the interim decision was not sufficiently related to any final decision the Commission could take in relation to those agreements, the Commission had 'exceeded the limit of its powers'.

In these cases, as it would be in most cases, it was academic whether the argument was put on the basis of lack of competence or violation of the Treaty. Similarly, the argument that the decision of the Commission was bad on the ground that it was signed on its behalf by the wrong official was treated on the basis that it went to procedure; whereas in another case¹² the same argument was put to the Court (although not decided) on the basis that the wrong person, namely, a person other than a Commission member, had made the decision and therefore there was a lack of competence or jurisdiction. Another example is *ACF Chemiefarma v Commission*,¹³ where the plaintiff made two objections based on lack of competence: the first was that because its agreement had been properly registered with the Dutch authorities, the jurisdiction of the Commission had been ousted; the second was that the Commission did not establish its jurisdiction because it had failed to furnish the information needed to prove the existence of the conditions required for the application of art 85. The first was dismissed on the ground that the competence of the Commission within the framework of the EEC Treaty was not affected by registration with national authorities; the second was dismissed but treated as a plea concerning violation of procedural rules and not as a plea going to the jurisdiction of the Commission.

---

9 See also Schermers and Waelbroeck, pp 175–178, who treat the question whether acts are invalid because Community institutions have unlawfully delegated their powers under this head.
10 Case 48/69 *ICI v Commission* [1972] ECR 619, [1972] CMLR 557.
11 Cases 228 and 229/82 [1984] ECR 1129, [1984] 1 CMLR 649.
12 Cases 8–11/66 *Cimenteries v Commission* [1967] ECR 75, [1967] CMLR 77.
13 Case 41/69 [1970] ECR 661.

(ii) Infringement of essential procedural requirement

This ground is concerned with those procedural defects which are capable of vitiating an otherwise lawful and effective act. In practice the most important areas under this head are the requirement of reasoning under art 190, which provides that regulations, directives and decisions must state the reasons on which they are based; and the requirement of natural justice, that a person be heard before an adverse decision is taken against him. It also includes those rules which require consultation before a decision is taken; the failure to observe a condition of consultation vitiates the decision.[14]

The procedural requirement must be 'essential' if its breach is to vitiate the act. In practice some requirements are essential in the sense that any breach of them vitiates the act, eg the failure to comply with consultation conditions, or with notification conditions. In other cases there must be such a procedural violation as to have deprived the person concerned of a basic safeguard. The notion gives some flexibility to the Court. Thus, in the *Dyestuffs* case,[15] two of the complaints related to matters which the Court found to be inessential on the facts. First, it was alleged that contrary to a Commission regulation minutes of statements made in the administrative proceedings were not sent promptly to the applicants. The Court held that the delay could only affect the legality of the decision if there were doubt as to the accuracy of the minutes; since there was no such doubt, the omission did not vitiate the decision. Second, it was alleged that in breach of art 191(2)[16] the decision had been notified not to the applicants but to their German subsidiary. The Court held that the decision was not vitiated by such a defect, because:[17]

> Irregularities in the procedure for notification of a decision are extraneous to that measure and cannot therefore invalidate it. In certain circumstances such irregularities may prevent the period within which an application must be lodged from starting to run . . . In the present case it is established that the applicant has had full knowledge of the text of the decision and that it has exercised its right to institute proceedings within the prescribed period. In these circumstances the question of possible irregularities concerning notification ceases to be relevant.

Even less significant procedural irregularities were pleaded in the *Continental Can* case:[18] that the decision of the Commission was

---

14 Case 138/79 *Roquette Frères SA v Council* [1980] ECR 3333.
15 Case 48/69 [1972] ECR 619, [1972] CMLR 557.
16 Which provides that '. . . decisions shall be notified to those to whom they are addressed and shall take effect upon such notification'.
17 [1972] ECR 619 at 652.
18 Case 6/72 *Europemballage & Continental Can v Commission* [1973] ECR 215, [1973] CMLR 199.

reported in the Official Journal under an inaccurate title; and that the applicant received notification of the decision by letter through diplomatic channels. Both complaints were dismissed on the ground that, even if well-founded, they were immaterial.

The right to a hearing. Where a Community instrument requires a hearing before a decision is taken, the absence of such a hearing would normally vitiate the decision. This is particularly important in restrictive practices investigations, where, as has been seen,[19] Council Regulation 17 and Commission Regulation 99/63 provide procedural safeguards. The essential elements of due process and natural justice are illustrated by the cases concerning the quinine cartel:[20] the plaintiffs argued (inter alia) that the statement of objections inadequately stated the points held against them and the evidence on which they were based; that the Commission had violated the right of due process by not permitting the plaintiffs to inspect the principal documents on which the contested decisions were based; that the Commission had failed to observe the general principle of law requiring it to allow the parties concerned to take an active part in the administrative proceedings. These arguments were rejected: the statement of objections was sufficiently full since the information contained in it served the purpose of furnishing the information necessary for the defence; the Court recognised that the Commission might have been at fault in not disclosing documents on the ground of confidentiality without asking the companies from whom those documents originated whether they objected to their production, but on the facts there had been no prejudice to the plaintiffs; the plaintiffs' claim that they had been denied a hearing was dismissed on the ground that the plaintiffs had had an adequate opportunity to submit oral and written comments on the Commission's complaints. Very similar conclusions were reached in the *Dyestuffs* case[1] and in the *Continental Can* case.[2]

In *Transocean Marine Paint Association v Commission*[3] the Commission had, pursuant to art 85(3), renewed an exemption in relation to an agreement restricting competition in the market in marine paints concluded between the members of the Association. A condition of the Commission's decision was that members of the Association had to inform the Commission without delay of any links (by way of common directors or managers) between a member of the Association and any other undertaking in the paints sector or any financial participation by a member of the Association in such outside companies.

---

19 See p 246, ante.
20 Case 41/69 *ACF Chemiefarma v Commission* [1970] ECR 661.
1 See p 259, n 15, ante.
2 See n 18, ante.
3 Case 17/74 [1974] ECR 1063, [1974] 2 CMLR 459.

This condition was at no time put to the applicants in the course of the proceedings which led up to the exemption. The Court inferred from the nature and objectives of the procedure for hearings under Regulation 17 and under Regulation 99/63[4] that they applied 'the general rule that a person whose interests were perceptibly affected by a decision taken by a public authority must be given the opportunity to make his point of view known'. The Court went on:[5]

> This rule requires that an undertaking be clearly informed, in good time, of the essence of conditions to which the Commission intends to subject an exemption and it must have the opportunity to submit its observations to the Commission. This is especially so in the case of conditions which . . . impose considerable obligations having far-reaching effects.

The Court annulled the condition because the requirement had not been fulfilled and was, therefore, imposed in breach of procedural requirements.

The consequence of these decisions, as the Court put it in *Hoffmann-La Roche v Commission*,[6] is that 'observance of the right to be heard is in all proceedings in which sanctions, in particular fines or penalty payments, may be imposed a fundamental principle of Community law which must be respected even if the proceedings in question are administrative proceedings'. This case involved Roche's challenge to fines imposed on it for an abuse of its dominant position in relation to supply of vitamins. The Court made it clear that in order to respect the principle of the right to be heard the undertaking concerned must, in competition investigations, have been afforded the opportunity during the administrative procedure to make known its view on the truth and relevance of the facts and circumstances alleged and on the documents used by the Commission to support its claim that there has been an infringement of the competition provisions of the Treaty. During the administrative procedure the Commission had refused to disclose material which it had obtained from competitors or customers of Roche which formed the basis of its assessment of Roche's market share and of the view that fidelity contracts relating to vitamins restricted competition; but they were disclosed during the proceedings before the Court, which held that the irregularities did not necessarily lead to the annulment of the decision because they had been remedied and therefore had not affected the right to be heard.

---

4 See p 246, ante.
5 [1974] ECR at 1080, [1974] 2 CMLR at 477. The submissions of Warner AG contain valuable material on similar rules in national law.
6 Case 85/76 [1979] ECR 461 at 511, [1979] 3 CMLR 211 at 268. See also Cases 100–103/80 *Musique Diffusion Française SA v Commission* [1983] ECR 1825, [1983] 3 CMLR 221; Case 40/85 *Belgium v Commission* [1986] ECR 2321, [1988] 2 CMLR 301.

The principle is that procedural irregularities will only vitiate the decision if, in the absence of those irregularities, the administrative proceedings could have led to a different result.[7] This confusion of the question of procedure (whether the undertaking had sufficient access) with substance (whether it would have made a difference) is also found in English administrative law, and is open to the same objection: if the principles of natural justice are violated it should be immaterial whether the same decision would have been arrived at in the absence of the departure from the essential principles of justice.[8]

In *National Panasonic (UK) Ltd v Commission*[9] the European Court refused to extend the principle to the investigative and preliminary stages of a restrictive practices investigation. In this case Commission officials, investigating alleged export bans on hi-fi and other electronic equipment, arrived at the UK subsidiary of the National Panasonic group without prior notice to carry out an on-the-spot investigation of the company's documents. The basis of the Commission's action was art 14 of Regulation 17, which provides that undertakings are to submit to investigations ordered by a Commission decision and which allows Commission officials to call for the production of documents without prior warning. National Panasonic sought to have the investigation set aside on the ground (inter alia) that by failing to communicate to it in advance the decision ordering an investigation, the Commission had infringed the fundamental right to receive advance notification and the right to be heard before a decision adversely affecting it was taken. While accepting the principle of the right to be heard in general, the Court held that in competition investigations it was limited to procedures which would result in the termination of an infringement or declaring an agreement to be incompatible with art 85, and it did not apply to the investigation stage whose sole object was to enable the Commission to gather information; only when the investigation justified the initiation of the opening of a procedure under Regulation 17 would the obligation to be heard come into play. This is the same as the principle in English administrative law, that the rules of natural justice do not apply at the preliminary stages of the opening of an investigation and the gathering of information.[10]

Reasoning. By far the greater number of cases involving allegations of infringement of procedural requirements concern the adequacy of the reasoning pursuant to art 190 of the EEC Treaty, which provides:

---

7 Case 30/78 *Distillers Co Ltd v Commission* [1980] ECR 2229 at 2264, [1980] 3 CMLR 121 at 167.
8 Wade, pp 533–535, citing *General Medical Council v Spackman* [1943] AC 627.
9 Case 136/79 [1980] ECR 2033, [1980] 3 CMLR 169.
10 *Norwest Holst Ltd v Secretary of State for Trade* [1978] Ch 201, [1978] 3 All ER 280, CA.

Regulations, directives and decisions of the Council and of the Commission shall state the reasons on which they are based and shall refer to any proposals or opinions which were required to be obtained pursuant to this Treaty.

The purpose of this provision was expressed by the European Court in *Tariff Quota on Wine* case as being:[11]

> to give an opportunity to the parties of defending their rights, to the Court of exercising its supervisory functions and to member states and to all interested nationals of ascertaining the circumstances in which the Commission has applied the Treaty.[12]

In essence the purpose is to ensure that on its face the act is lawful and that it can properly be reviewed on the merits. A failure to give adequate reasons will vitiate a Community act. According to the same case, the relevant decision must:

> set out, in a concise but clear and relevant manner, the principal issues of law and of fact upon which it is based and which are necessary in order that the reasoning which has led the Commission to its decision may be understood.

In that case the German Government challenged a Commission decision refusing in part authorisation for a tariff quota in relation to wine. The decision was almost in a standard form and the German Government complained that it hardly departed from the form of previous decisions and lacked specific wording. The Commission argued that its limited staff and the number of quota requests made it necessary to standardise the wording of the reasons for its decisions. The Court was not satisfied with this argument and annulled the decision because, except for general conditions and quotations from the Treaty, the Commission was content to rely on 'the information collected' (without giving details of what such information was) to reach the conclusion that the production of the relevant wines was sufficient (without indicating the source and amount of the surplus). In addition the partial grant of the quota was inconsistent with the reasons for the refusal of the rest. As a result, the inadequacy, the vagueness and the inconsistency of the reasoning of the decision justified the annulment of that part of it which had been challenged.[13]

In a later case,[14] however, the Court held that a decision altering the

---

11 Case 24/62 *Germany v Commission* [1963] ECR 63, [1963] CMLR 347.
12 [1963] ECR 63 at 69.
13 See also Case 34/62 *Germany v Commission* [1963] ECR 131, [1963] CMLR 369, for the effect of adding irrelevant considerations in the reasoning.
14 Case 16/65 *Schwarze v Einfuhr- und Vorratsstelle Getreide* [1965] ECR 877, [1966] CMLR 172. But cf Case 73/74 *Papiers Peints de Belgique v Commission* [1975] ECR 1491, [1976] 1 CMLR 589, where mere reference to a prior decision was insufficient.

effects of previous decisions was in sufficient form if it referred to the previous decision which contained the relevant reasoning. The speed and complexity of the decisions involved in that case (the weekly fixing of free frontier prices) led the Court to be less strict in its approach to the reasoning under art 190. It held that the duty to provide a statement of reasons must be interpreted in the light of the practical realities and the time and technical facilities available for making such a decision; a specific statement of reasons for each individual decision would have taken up so much time that the price fixing decisions might have been out of date before they were issued. The Court justified this conclusion in terms of the rationale behind art 190 in words which are not entirely consistent with the forthright expressions used in the *Tariff Quota on Wine* case.[15] In the later case it said:

> The need to protect the parties to whom the decision is addressed and nationals of member states affected by the decision, as also the need for proper judicial review, is sufficiently met as long as the Commission, as here, puts at the disposal of the parties the technical data used by it in fixing the free-at-frontier prices whenever the decision is challenged before a court having the appropriate jurisdiction.[16]

Where a decision is made in the course of administrative proceedings, such as a restrictive practices investigation, it is not necessary that the decision should deal with all the issues of fact and law which have been raised by every party in the proceedings;[17] and where a decision contains the essential elements required by enabling legislation, such as Regulation 17 on restrictive practices investigations, it will be regarded as sufficiently reasoned,[18] but not where it merely states a conclusion without any supporting reasoning.[19]

Where a decision appears on its face to have been arrived at as a result of a general policy without proper consideration of the actual case it will be annulled, both for violation of the procedural requirement, and on the merits. In *Control Data Belgium NV v Commission*[20] a Commission decision denied duty free status to computers manufactured by the US parent of the applicant. Duty free status depended on

---

15 Case 24/62 *Germany v Commission* [1963] ECR 63, [1963] CMLR 347.
16 [1965] ECR 877 at 889. See also Case 37/70 *Rewe-Zentrale* [1971] ECR 23, [1971] CMLR 238.
17 Cases 209 to 215 and 218/78 *Heintz van Landwyck Sàrl (FEDETAB) v Commission* [1980] ECR 3125, [1981] 3 CMLR 134; Case 86/82 *Hasselblad (GB) Ltd v Commission* [1984] 1 CMLR 559.
18 Case 136/79 *National Panasonic (UK) Ltd v Commission* [1980] ECR 2033, [1980] 3 CMLR 169.
19 Cases 8–11/66 *Cimenteries v Commission* [1967] ECR 75, [1967] CMLR 77.
20 Case 294/81 [1983] ECR 911, [1983] 2 CMLR 357. Cf Case 216/82 *Universität Hamburg v Hauptzollamt Hamburg* [1983] ECR 2771.

The substantive grounds for review 265

the computers being for exclusive use for scientific purposes. The Commission decision gave as reasons for the refusal a stereotyped formula used in all decisions concerning computers adopted since 1979 disallowing duty free status on the ground of scientific use. The decision was annulled on the ground (inter alia) that the Commission did not make it possible in the reasoning for the Court to conclude that the Commission had applied clear criteria which were in accordance with Community law, or that it had had sufficient regard for the characteristics of the computers involved.

The content of the reasoning will also be affected by the nature of the Community act involved. First, it must be an act which art 190 requires to be reasoned, namely, a regulation, directive or decision.[1] Secondly, a measure having normative character, namely a regulation, does not require the detailed reasoning that a decision does. The Court has said:[2]

> The extent of the requirement laid down by article 190 of the Treaty to state the reasons on which measures are based, depends on the nature of the measure in question. It is a question in the present case of a regulation, that is to say, a measure intended to have general application, the preamble to which may be confined to indicating the general situation which led to its adoption, on the one hand, and the general objectives which it is intended to achieve on the other. Consequently, it is not possible to require that it should set out the various facts, which are often very numerous and complex, on the basis of which the regulation was adopted, or *a fortiori* that it should provide a more or less complete evaluation of those facts.

In the case of a regulation, therefore, the reasoning may be short and may be inferred from the legal background.[3] In practice it is rarely that a regulation is likely to be annulled or ruled invalid for lack of reasoning. But in the *Butter Boats* case[4] German shipping companies were organising cruises from Germany, with a brief stop in Denmark (at a time when it was not in the Common Market) in order that passengers could take advantage on their return to Germany of

---

1 See Cases 8–11/66 *Cimenteries v Commission* [1967] ECR 75, [1967] CMLR 77, and cf Case 22/70 *Re ERTA: Commission v Council* [1971] ECR 263, [1971] CMLR 335.
2 Case 5/67 *Beus v Hauptzollamt München* [1968] ECR 83 at 95, [1968] CMLR 131 at 145. See also Case 18/62 *Barge v High Authority* [1963] ECR 259, [1965] CMLR 330; Case 87/78 *Welding v Hauptzollamt Hamburg* [1978] ECR 2457; Case 108/81 *Amylum v Council* (and other Isoglucose cases) [1982] ECR 3107; Cases 292 and 293/81 *Lion and Loiret & Haentjens v FIRS* [1982] ECR 3887.
3 See eg Case 92/77 *An Bord Bainne Co-operative Ltd v Minister for Agriculture* [1978] ECR 497, [1978] 2 CMLR 567; Cases 103 and 145/77 *Royal Scholten Honig (Holdings) Ltd v Intervention Board for Agricultural Produce* [1978] ECR 2037, [1979] 1 CMLR 675; Case 35/80 *Denkavit Nederland v Produktschap voor Zuivel* [1981] ECR 45.
4 Case 158/80 *Rewe v Hauptzollamt Kiel* [1981] ECR 1805, [1982] 1 CMLR 449. Cf Case 45/86 *Commission v Council* [1987] ECR 1493 [1988] 2 CMLR 131.

exemptions (for goods bought on the ships) from value added tax and excise duty on personal luggage of passengers coming from outside the Community. Although the effect of the Court's judgment was in part to remove this anomaly by holding that the exception only applied to cases of genuine international travel, it also held that a Council regulation designed to deal with this abuse was invalid because, although it made clear that the abuse existed, it nevertheless allowed its continuance at the discretion of member states. This contradiction in the statement of reasons meant that the statement provided no legal basis for the provisions of the regulation.

Thirdly, the extent of the duty to give reasons may depend on the context in which the act is adopted. A significant factor has therefore been held to be the knowledge of the party concerned of the reasons.[5] But where a decision is addressed to a member state and affects a private party directly and individually it is not sufficient that the member state knows the reasons for its adoption when the private party cannot deduce the reasons from the decision.[6]

(iii) Infringement of the Treaty or of a rule of law relating to its application

Although there is an obvious overlap between this head and the other heads of illegality, in practice it is most frequently the vehicle for complaints that a Community institution has violated general or fundamental principles of law in adopting decisions, or has misinterpreted the Treaty or a regulation, or has misapplied the facts.

Where the validity of the acts of the Commission in the economic sphere is in question the Court grants a latitude to the Commission and will not re-evaluate the Commission's factual findings or interfere with its discretion except within limited bounds. The Court has frequently said that in the case of an evaluation of a complex economic situation, the Commission enjoys a wide measure of discretion; in reviewing the legality of the exercise of such discretion, the Court will confine itself to examining whether it contains a manifest error or constitutes a misuse of power or clearly exceeds the bounds of the discretion.[7] For example, when the Court accepted the right of a complainant in an anti-subsidisation proceeding to challenge the decision of the Commission not to impose a countervailing duty it also

---

5 Case 13-72 *Netherlands v Commission* [1973] ECR 27, [1974] 1 CMLR 161; Case 1251/79 *Italy v Commission* [1981] ECR 205, [1981] 3 CMLR 110; Case 819/79 *Germany v Commission* [1981] ECR 21.
6 *Control Data Belgium v Commission*, n 20, supra. Cf Cases 296 and 318/82 *Netherlands and Leeuwarder Papierwaren-Fabriek v Commission* [1985] ECR 809, [1985] 3 CMLR 380.
7 See eg Case 29/77 *Roquette v France* [1977] ECR 1835; Cases 154 etc/78, 39 etc/79 *Valsabbia v Commission* [1980] ECR 907, [1981] 1 CMLR 613.

emphasised that the Commission had a wide discretion to decide, in the interests of the Community, on the measures needed to deal with the situation. Accordingly, the Court would only be able to consider whether the Commission had committed manifest errors in its assessment of the facts, had omitted to take into consideration any essential matters or had based its reasons on considerations amounting to a misuse of powers. The Court had no power to intervene in the exercise of the discretion.[8]

This ground also includes the violation of a rule of law relating to the application of the Treaty. There is no doubt that the violation may not only be of the Treaty itself and of rules derived from it, such as regulations, but also that there are general principles which apply to the operation of the Treaty. Whether breach of these principles is a violation of the Treaty itself or of the rules of law relating to its application is a verbal question devoid of practical significance. A detailed discussion of these principles is outside the scope of this work,[9] but an outline may be helpful. As has been seen above,[10] the European Court has drawn upon the constitutional traditions of the member states and the European Convention on Human Rights in holding that fundamental rights form an integral part of the general principles of Community law. But the content of these rights cannot be said to be clear, and no case has been decided solely on the ground of violation of fundamental rights.[11]

Some of the general principles of law which the Court applies, such as the right to be heard, are procedural in character and have been discussed in the previous section. Others have both procedural and substantive aspects, and may be included under a general heading of right of defence, such as the limited protection given to communications between independent lawyer and client in *A M and S Europe Ltd v Commission*;[12] and the protection against arbitrary or disproportionate searches recognised in *Hoechst AG v Commission*.[13] Those which are substantive in character include the 'fundamental requirement of legal certainty'.[14] In essence it is the principle that acts which have been relied on will not be altered to the detriment of a private party

---

8 Case 191/82 *FEDIOL v Commission* [1983] ECR 2913, [1984] 3 CMLR 244.
9 Schermers and Waelbroeck, pp 25–83; Akehurst (1981) 52 BYIL 29.
10 See p 8, ante.
11 See Mendelson (1981) 1 Yb Eur L 125, 152.
12 Case 155/79 [1982] ECR 1575, [1982] 2 CMLR 264. For the principle of confidentiality of medical records see Case 155/78 *Miss M v Commission* [1980] ECR 1797.
13 Cases 76/87, 277/88 (1989) Times, 23 October.
14 Case 48/69 *ICI v Commission* [1972] ECR 619 at 653, [1972] CMSLR 557 at 621. The concept is derived from German law, like the principles of legitimate expectation and proportionality: see Akehurst (1981) 52 BYIL at 38.

268 Challenging Community acts

and it is closely connected with principles of 'legitimate expectation' and non-retroactivity, or is the general principle of which they form part.

These concepts are more widely developed and used in European law than they are in the law of the United Kingdom. But the administrative law of the United Kingdom, probably under the unacknowledged influence of European law, is clearly moving in the direction of adopting them. Thus in England the doctrine of legitimate expectation is linked to the duty of the executive to act fairly: where there was an established practice of consultation between the management and unions about important alterations in the terms and conditions of staff at GCHQ, the government could not (prima facie) bar employees from trade union membership without consultation;[15] there was a legitimate expectation that the Home Secretary would follow guidelines on telephone tapping.[16]

There is no absolute guarantee of total respect for acquired rights in Community law,[17] but there is a general presumption against the retrospective alteration of rights, so that regulations are presumed not to be retrospective unless they are clearly so;[18] a regulation may not be retrospective unless the objects it seeks to achieve require it to be retrospective and it takes into account, to the extent possible, legitimate expectations, by making appropriate transitional arrangements.[19] But where traders or producers are likely to appreciate that their products are subject to changes in monetary compensatory amounts,[20] or in levies,[1] regulations altering them retrospectively may be upheld; nor is the application of new rules to existing situations a breach of the principle of non-retroactivity.[2] Similarly, the principle of legitimate expectation will operate as a type of estoppel to prevent the Community executive from acting against private parties who have reasonably relied on the Commission's failure to take action. Thus where the Commission took more than two years to issue a

---

15 *Council of Civil Service Unions v Minister for the Civil Service* [1985] AC 374, [1984] 3 All ER 935, HL (but national security was overriding).
16 *R v Secretary of State for the Home Department, ex p Ruddock* [1987] 2 All ER 518, [1987] 1 WLR 1482.
17 Cf Case 44/79 *Hauer v Land Rheinland-Pfalz* [1979] ECR 3727, [1980] 3 CMLR 42 (a case on interpretation).
18 See eg Case 21/81 *Openbaar Ministerie v Bout* [1982] ECR 381, [1982] 2 CMLR 371 and, generally, Lamoureux (1983) 20 CML Rev 269.
19 Case 74/74 *CNTA v Commission* [1975] ECR 533, [1977] 1 CMLR 171.
20 Ibid.
1 Case 98/78 *Racke v Hauptzollamt Mainz* [1979] ECR 69; Case 108/81 *Amylum v Council (Isoglucose)* [1982] ECR 3107.
2 Case 12/78 *Italy v Commission* [1979] ECR 1731, [1980] 2 CMLR 573; Case 112/80 *Dürbeck v Hauptzollamt Frankfurt am Main-Flughafen* [1981] ECR 1095, [1982] 3 CMLR 315.

decision holding Dutch government aid to shipbuilders to be unlawful and requiring repayment, the decision was annulled: there was no justification for the delay and in the circumstances the delay led the shipbuilders to believe that the aid was lawful.[3] But as in English law, practice of the Community or of a member state which is not in conformity with Community law cannot give rise to a legitimate expectation on the part of a private party that it will benefit from treatment which is inconsistent with Community law.[4]

The principle of equality requires that 'similar situations shall not be treated differently unless differentiation is objectively justified';[5] so that where production refunds for maize used in the manufacture of quellmehl and maize meal (or gritz) were abolished, but maintained for maize for processing into starch, the regulations were held to be discriminatory because there was no basis for distinguishing between quellmehl and gritz on the one hand, and starch on the other.[6] The principle of proportionality requires that the means used must not be excessive.[7] A Council Regulation on the compulsory purchase of skimmed milk powder was held to be invalid because the price was disproportionate to the objective of disposal of surplus stocks.[8] It has already been seen that the European Court annulled a provision in a Commission regulation which had the effect of forfeiting a security of £1.6 million merely because an export licence application was made four hours later than the regulation required.[9] The means employed by the regulation to ensure observance of the time limit were excessive in relation to the object sought.

---

3 Case 223/85 *RSV v Commission* [1987] ECR 4617, [1989] 2 CMLR 259. For another recent example see Case 84/85 *UK v Commission* [1987] ECR 3765, [1988] 1 CMLR 113.
4 Case 316/86 *Hauptzollamt Hamburg-Jonas v Krucken* 26 April 1988; cf *R v Board of Inland Revenue, ex p MFK Underwriting Agencies Ltd* [1990] 1 All ER 91.
5 Cases 117/76 and 16/77 *Ruckdeschel & Co v Hauptzollamt Hamburg-St Annen* [1977] ECR 1753 at 1769, [1979] 2 CMLR 445 at 481.
6 Ibid and Cases 124/76 and 20/77 *Moulins Pont-à-Mousson v Office Interprofessional des Céréales (Gritz)* [1977] ECR 1795, [1979] 2 CMLR 445.
7 Or that a steam hammer must not be used to crack a nut: *R v Goldstein* [1983] 1 All ER 434 at 436, [1983] 1 WLR 151 at 155, per Lord Diplock. In the *GCHQ* case, n 15, supra, Lord Diplock envisaged the adoption of the doctrine from European law, but Lord Donaldson MR (*R v Home Secretary, ex p Brind* [1990] 2 WLR 787, CA, has expressed the view that in English administrative law lack of proportionality is an aspect of the challenge based on perversity, or unreasonableness. See also Wade, p 429.
8 Case 114/76 *Bela-Mühle v Grows-Farm (Skimmed Milk Powder)* [1977] ECR 1211, [1979] 2 CMLR 83.
9 Case 181/84 *R v Intervention Board for Agricultural Produce, ex p E D & F Man (Sugar) Ltd* [1985] ECR 2889, [1985] 3 CMLR 759, p 211, ante. See also Case 66/82 *Fromançais SA v FORMA* [1983] ECR 395, [1983] 3 CMLR 453; Case 21/85 *Maas & Co NV v BALM* [1986] ECR 3537, [1987] 3 CMLR 794.

(iv) Misuse of powers

This expression is not defined but the concept is a very familiar one in the administrative law of civil law countries, although there are considerable differences in its application.[10] It comprehends largely, but not exclusively, the use of a power for a purpose other than that for which it was conferred.[11] In English law, although there is no separate concept to cover the situation, a similar result is achieved by an extended use of the notion of *ultra vires* and of the principle of reasonableness.[12]

Thus in the *Import Duties on Mutton* case[13] the German Government attacked two Commission directives ordering the abolition of certain import charges on mutton. One of its main arguments was that the Commission had not issued similar directives to France and Italy where, it was alleged, similar conditions existed. Advocate General Roemer suggested that the Commission had misused its powers by concentrating on the directive to the German Government as an attempt to carry out a test case. The Court rejected those arguments in words which illustrate the notion of misuse of powers and *détournement de pouvoir*. it said:[14]

> With regard to the complaint of misuse of powers by the Commission the applicant government has not established that the Commission has used its powers for a purpose other than that for which they were conferred upon it. Moreover the Treaty establishing the European Community imposes obligations upon all those persons to whom it applies, determines the extent of the powers, rights and obligations of these subjects and fixes the procedures for imposing sanctions in the event of any infringement. Any possible failure by the Commission to fulfil its obligations towards other member states cannot exempt one of them from performing the obligations which are legitimately placed upon it by measures taken in the application of the Treaty. If, in breach of the Treaty, the Commission were to fail to perform its task in calling attention by means of directives to obligations which certain member states have to fulfil, any other member state could invite it to take the necessary measures and, if necessary, apply to the Court for a ruling that there had been an infringement.

A similar understanding of the concept lay behind unsuccessful allegations that the real object of a Commission policy was the substitution of tangerines for clementines in the Common Market;[15] that the

---

10 See Case 3/54 *ASSIDER v High Authority* [1955] ECR at 75–85, per Lagrange AG.
11 Case 81/72 *Commission v Council* [1973] ECR 575, [1973] CMLR 639. See also Case 7/72 *Boehringer v Commission* [1972] ECR 1281, [1973] CMLR 864; Case 40/72 *Schroeder v Germany* [1973] ECR 125, [1973] CMLR 824.
12 For the position in English law, see Wade, ch 12.
13 Cases 52 and 55/65 *Germany v Commission* [1966] ECR 159, [1967] CMLR 22.
14 [1966] ECR 159 at 172.
15 In Case 25/62 *Plaumann & Co v Commission* [1963] ECR 95, [1964] CMLR 29.

real object of a Commission decision was to assist in the cover-up of an error of the German administrative authorities;[16] that the Commission used its powers to grant an authorisation to the French Government under art 226 as 'a disguised anti-dumping measure'.[17] Although wider uses of the term have been suggested,[18] in the *Import Duties on Sweet Oranges* case[19] the Court indicated that it would not extend the notion to include what in effect was a violation of treaty within the concept of *détournement de pouvoir*. It held that even if a refusal by the Commission to authorise the importation into Germany of sweet oranges from outside the Common Market did, as alleged, limit the free choice of consumers, such a charge could only be one of violation of treaty and not of *détournement de pouvoir*.

The charge of misuse of powers is particularly important in the area of discretionary powers, since in practice such powers are difficult to attack for violation of treaty *stricto sensu* or on their merits.

4 The time element

As a result of art 173(3) actions for annulment become time-barred two months after publication of the act, or of its notification to the applicant, or, in the absence of publication or notification, two months[20] after the applicant became aware of the act. Where the addressee of a decision knows about it before publication, time runs only from the date of publication.[1] Where a private party sought to annul a decision addressed to a member state, time ran from the day when the applicant was in a position to acquire knowledge of the text of the decision, or at any rate of the reasons on which it was based.[2]

It is not possible to start time running again by bringing an action to annul a refusal to accept a complaint relating to a time-barred act.[3] A confirmation of a previous decision is not a new decision which starts time running again, but a reconsideration of a decision may amount to

---

16 In Cases 106–107/63 *Toepfer v Commission* [1965] ECR 405, [1966] CMLR 111.
17 Case 13/63 *Italy v Commission* [1963] ECR 165, [1963] CMLR 289.
18 See eg Case 32/64 *Italy v Commission* [1965] ECR 365, [1967] CMLR 207; Case 32/65 *Italy v Council and Commission* [1966] ECR 389, [1969] CMLR 39.
19 Case 34/62 *Germany v Commission* [1963] ECR 131, [1963] CMLR 369.
20 On the method of calculating the time-limits see Cases 181 etc/85 *Germany v Commission* [1987] ECR 3203, [1988] 1 CMLR 11.
1 Case 76/79 *Könecke v Commission* [1980] ECR 665.
2 Case 59/84 *Tezi Textiel BV v Commission* [1986] ECR 887; see also Cases 31 and 33/62 *Wöhrmann v Commission* [1962] ECR 501, [1963] CMLR 152; Case 69/69 *Alcan v Commission* [1970] ECR 385, [1970] CMLR 337. As to date of publication see Case 99/78 *Decker v Hauptzollamt Landau* [1979] ECR 101.
3 Case 2/71 *Germany v Commission* [1971] ECR 669, [1972] CMLR 431. See also Cases 6 and 11/69 *Commission v France* [1969] ECR 523, [1970] CMLR 43.

a new decision.[4] If a statement of position by a Community institution is equivocal, its final statement will be regarded not as confirmation of a prior act but as the act whereby it notifies its definitive decision.[5]

5 The effects of annulment

If an application pursuant to art 173 is successful 'the Court of Justice shall declare the act concerned to be void' but in the case of regulations which may have had far-reaching effects while they were still in force the Court has power to specify that such effects may remain in force.[6] This power was used in the case involving Community staff salaries, when the Court held that a Council regulation setting out salary scales was unlawful because they were too low; but in order to avoid there being *no* salary scales the Court ruled that the annulment would only take effect when new scales were introduced by a new regulation.[7] Article 174(2) applies in terms only to regulations annulled in the course of annulment proceedings, but the Court has applied a similar principle to proceedings to annul decisions addressed to member states,[8] and to art 177 references from national courts on the validity of Community acts.[9] Thus it was reconfirmed that, despite the invalidity of a Commission regulation on the payment of monetary compensatory amounts, it would not be possible for private parties to challenge charges by national authorities prior to the date of the judgment declaring them invalid.[10] Once an administrative act has been annulled, a right of action for damages may arise under art 215 against its authors.[11] Where a regulation which deals with amounts payable to national authorities is annulled, the effects of the annulment as regards payments already made depend on national law.[12]

---

4 Cf Case 23/80 *Grasselli v Commission* [1980] ECR 3709; Case 54/77 *Herpels v Commission* [1978] ECR 585.
5 Case 44/81 *Germany v Commission* [1982] ECR 1855, [1983] 2 CMLR 656.
6 Article 174(2).
7 Case 81/72 *Commission v Council* [1973] ECR 575, [1973] CMLR 639.
8 Case 97/78 *Simmenthal SpA v Commission* [1979] ECR 777, [1980] 1 CMLR 25.
9 Case 4/79 *Société Coopérative Providence Agricole de la Champagne v ONIC* [1980] ECR 2823 (and associated cases).
10 Case 112/83 *Société de Produits de Maïs v Administration des Douanes* [1985] ECR 719, repeating the answer given in the cases in [n 9]. The French administrative courts, however, held that the French authorities were required to repay: see Hartley, p 235. See also Case 33/84 *Fragd v Amministrazione delle Finanze dello Stato* [1985] ECR 1605; Case 41/84 *Pinna v Caisse d'Allocations Familiales de la Savoie* [1986] ECR 1, [1988] 1 CMLR 350.
11 Case 26/62 *Plaumann & Co v Commission* [1963] ECR 95, [1964] CMLR 29. See p 282, post, on art 215.
12 See pp 76–77, ante.

6 Interim measures

By art 185 of the EEC Treaty the European Court has power to suspend the application of a contested act; and by art 186 it may prescribe interim measures in any case before it. Provision is made in the Statute and the Rules for the President of the Court to order interim measures on an interlocutory basis.[13] The new Court of First Instance may also order interim measures,[14] and this will be especially valuable in competition cases, where important interim orders have recently been made by the European Court.[15]

The request must be genuinely urgent and the applicant will normally have to show that it has a prima facie case on the merits and that irreparable harm would occur unless interim measures are granted.[16] In principle, the admissibility of the main application is not examined on the application for interim measures;[17] but where the defendant institution contends that the main application is manifestly inadmissible, then the President must consider whether there are any grounds for concluding prima facie that the main application is admissible. For example, an application directed at a decision addressed to a member state was dismissed because it was not of individual concern to the applicant;[18] similarly, the President dismissed an application for interim suspension of a directive, because prima facie the directive was a measure of general application.[19]

In deciding whether the interim measures should be granted, the Court must balance the interests of the applicant against the damage which would be caused if the order were made. Thus in anti-dumping cases the Court will consider not only the interests of manufacturers and exporters who claim that duty should not be imposed, but also the interests of Community industry to which damage is being caused by the continuance of the dumping.[20] The applicant must show that the damage suffered by it as a result of the anti-dumping duty is special to it, and is not inherent in the imposition of duties, such as a rise in its

---

13 EEC Statute, art 36, Euratom Statute, art 37, ECSC Statute, art 33, and Rules of Procedure, arts 83 et seq.
14 Council Decision, 24 October 1988, art 4: [1989] 3 CMLR 458.
15 Eg Cases 76 etc/89R *Radio Telefis Eireann v Commission* [1989] 4 CMLR 749; Cases 56/89R *Publishers Association v Commission* [1989] 4 CMLR 816. For an important decision in which interim measures were refused see Case 46/87R *Hoechst AG v Commission* [1987] ECR 1549, [1988] 4 CMLR 430.
16 See eg Case 3/75R *Johnson and Firth Brown Ltd v Commission* [1975] ECR 1, [1975] 1 CMLR 638; Case 119/77R *Japanese Ball Bearings (Nippon Seiko)* [1977] ECR 1867. See Usher *European Court Practice* (1983) pp 269–288; Gray (1979) 4 EL Rev 80; Borchardt (1985) 22 CML Rev 203.
17 See eg Case 65/87R *Pfizer International Inc v Commission* [1987] ECR 1691.
18 Case 82/87R *Autexpo SpA v Commission* [1987] ECR 2131, [1988] 3 CMLR 541.
19 Case 160/88R *FEDESA v Commission* [1988] 3 CMLR 534.
20 Case 273/85R *Silver Seiko Ltd v Council* [1985] ECR 3475, [1986] 1 CMLR 214.

prices and a consequent diminution of market share; the applicant must also show that the balance of interests is in its favour in the sense that grant of the measures would not cause appreciable injury to Community industry.[1]

The power to grant interim measures may not be exercised to prevent an administrative investigation because the obligation to participate in the investigation cannot cause serious and irreversible damage so as to justify interim measures.[2] In *Ford Werke AG v Commission*[3] the Commission had itself taken protective measures[4] in the course of its investigation of Ford's dealership arrangements; the protective measure was a decision addressed to Ford to sell right-hand drive cars to its German distributors. Ford sought and obtained an interim order from the European Court partially suspending the decision because there was a serious risk that the detrimental effects of the protective measures taken by the Commission would cause damage considerably in excess of the short-term necessary disadvantage from the protective measures. The Commission's protective measure was ultimately held to be invalid.[5]

V. THE RELATIONSHIP BETWEEN CHALLENGE UNDER ARTICLE 173 AND REFERENCES BY NATIONAL COURTS UNDER ARTICLE 177

Under art 177 national courts may (and, in certain circumstances, must) refer questions of (inter alia) the validity of acts of institutions of the Community to the European Court. The jurisdiction under art 177 to determine questions of validity is wider than that under the somewhat restricted art 173 jurisdiction. Thus in a case referred by the Finanzgericht, Munich,[6] the national court emphasised that a reference under art 177 to the European Court for a preliminary ruling would give the plaintiffs an opportunity not afforded to them by the narrow wording of art 173 to test the validity of a Commission regulation. When the case reached the European Court, the plaintiffs argued that another regulation was invalid. The Court considered these arguments, notwithstanding that the role of the litigants in an art 177 reference is limited, probably because the regulation which

---

1 Case 77/87R *Technointorg v Council* [1987] ECR 1793, [1987] 3 CMLR 491.
2 Cases 60, 190/81R *IBM v Commission* [1981] ECR 1857, [1981] 3 CMLR 93.
3 Cases 228–229/82R [1982] ECR 3091, [1982] 3 CMLR 673.
4 See Case 792/79R *Camera Care Ltd v Commission* [1980] ECR 119, [1980] 1 CMLR 334 for the power.
5 Cases 228, 229/82 [1984] ECR 1129, [1984] 1 CMLR 649.
6 Case 160/65 *Re Bulgarian Dessert Grapes* [1967] CMLR 156.

the plaintiffs belatedly argued was invalid was 'based' on the regulation the validity of which had been referred by the national court.[7]

The question arises whether a reference under art 177 can be used in effect as an independent means of attack on regulations and decisions by private parties. It is clear that the legal effects of an application for annulment under art 173 and a reference relating to validity under art 177 are not the same: a decision of annulment under art 173 renders an act void, but a judgment under art 177 declaring an act of a Community institution, such as a regulation, to be void is addressed only to the national court which made the reference. But the European Court has held that that is sufficient reason for any other national court to regard that act as void, although that other national court remains free to seek a further ruling from the European Court.[8] There may be cases where an application under art 173 is inadmissible, but a reference under art 177 will be possible; this arises most frequently in relation to regulations, where the scope for review at the instance of individuals under art 173 is very limited.[9]

In several decisions, the European Court deliberately refrained from deciding the question whether it would be permissible for a national court to make a reference under art 177 on the validity of a Community act, when the individual concerned by it had failed to make an application for annulment under art 173. Thus when a German court referred this very question, the Court held that it was not necessary to decide it because the contested decision (a decision addressed to member states on exemption of scientific apparatus from customs duties) was not of direct and individual concern to the plaintiff; accordingly, no application under art 173 could have been made, and the question did not arise.[10]

In the 'Berlin Butter' case[11] there was a reference by a German court on (inter alia) the validity of a Commission decision addressed to the Federal Republic of Germany on measures for the promotion of sales of surplus stocks of butter, which involved (in effect) the sale of butter

---

7 Case 5/67 *Beus v Hauptzollamt München* [1968] ECR 83, [1968] CMLR 131.
8 Case 66/80 *International Chemical Corpn v Amministrazione delle Finanze dello Stato* [1981] ECR 1191, [1983] 2 CMLR 593. See also pp 212–213, ante and Case 112/76 *Manzoni v FNROM* [1977] ECR 1647 at 1661–2, per Warner AG, [1978] 2 CMLR 416 at 428–31; cf Case 101/78 *Granaria* [1979] ECR 623 at 642, [1979] 3 CMLR 124 at 130 per Capotorti AG.
9 See eg Case 101/76 *Koninklijke Scholten Honig NV v Council and Commission* [1977] ECR 797 (action for annulment of regulation inadmissible); Case 125/77 *Koninklijke Scholten Honig v Hoofdproduktschap voor Akkerbouwprodukten* [1978] ECR 1991, [1979] 1 CMLR 675 (art 177 reference, regulation held valid).
10 Case 216/82 *Universität Hamburg v Hauptzollamt Hamburg* [1983] ECR 2771. See also Case 59/77 *Etablissements A De Bloos SpA v Bouyer* [1977] ECR 2359, [1978] 1 CMLR 511; cf Case 156/77 *Commission v Belgium* [1978] ECR 1881 at 1897.
11 Cases 133–136/85 *Rau v BALM* [1987] ECR 2289.

at half price to consumers in West Berlin. Margarine producers claimed they were prejudiced by the decision, and alleged that the measures were contrary to general principles of Community law. The German court also asked whether the possibility of bringing a direct action in the European Court under art 173(2) precluded actions in national courts against the implementation of the decision by national authorities. The Court answered that:

> ... there is nothing in Community law to prevent an action from being brought before a national court against a measure implementing a decision adopted by a Community institution where the conditions laid down by national law were satisfied. When such an action is brought, if the outcome of the dispute depends on the validity of that decision the national court may submit questions to the Court of Justice by way of a reference for a preliminary ruling, without there being any need to ascertain whether or not the plaintiff in the main proceedings has the possibility of challenging the decision directly before the Court.[12]

In that case, therefore, the Court clearly treated it as irrelevant whether the plaintiff would have had standing in art 173(2) proceedings, and indeed it is clear from the art 173 application decided on the same day (in which the plaintiffs were also among the applicants) that the plaintiff did not have standing.[13]

VI. THE PLEA OF ILLEGALITY—ARTICLE 184

The plea of illegality allows the validity of regulations (and, as will be seen, other acts of the Communities) to be attached collaterally:[14]

> Notwithstanding the expiry of the period laid down in the third paragraph of article 173, any party may, in proceedings in which a regulation of the Council or of the Commission is in issue, plead the grounds specified in the first paragraph of article 173, in order to invoke before the Court of Justice the inapplicability of that regulation.

Thus the plea may be made outside the two-month time limit imposed by art 173(3),[15] and 'any party' may raise it, including member states.[16] It applies in terms only to regulations—but the European Court has held that art 184 applies not only to regulations strictly

---

12 At p 2338.
13 Case 97/85 *Union Deutsche Lebensmittelwerke v Commission* [1987] ECR 2265.
14 In England regulations may usually (but not invariably) be attacked collaterally in proceedings in which they are relevant: see Wade pp 331–338, and for an example *Customs and Excise Comrs v Cure & Deeley Ltd* [1962] 1 QB 340, [1961] 3 All ER 641.
15 But it does not allow a member state to attack a *decision* outside the time limit: Case 156/77 *Commission v Belgium* [1978] ECR 1881.
16 Case 32/65 *Italy v Council and Commission* [1966] ECR 389, [1969] CMLR 39. Cf the expression 'another person' in art 173(2): Case 25/62 *Plaumann & Co v Commission* [1963] ECR 95, [1964] CMLR 29.

so-called, but also to acts of Community institutions which produce similar effects. In *Simmenthal SpA v Commission*[17] the action was for annulment of a Commission decision addressed to member states fixing minimum selling prices for beef put up for sale by tender by national intervention agencies. The Commission issued, pursuant to Council regulations, a general notice of invitations to tender. It was held that the applicant could, under art 184, challenge (in its proceedings to annul the decisions under art 173) the notices of invitation to tender. Art 184, said the Court:[18]

> gives expression to a general principle conferring upon any party to proceedings the right to challenge, for the purpose of obtaining the annulment of a decision of direct and individual concern to that party, the validity of previous acts of the institutions which form the legal basis of the decision which is being attacked, if that party was not entitled under Article 173 of the Treaty to bring a direct action challenging those acts by which it was thus affected without having been in a position to ask that they be declared void. The field of application of the said article must therefore include acts of the institutions which, although they are not in the form of a regulation, nevertheless produce similar effects and on those grounds may not be challenged under Article 173 by natural or legal persons other than Community institutions and Member States. This wide interpretation of Article 184 derives from the need to provide those persons who are precluded by the second paragraph of Article 173 from instituting proceedings directly in respect of general acts with the benefit of a judicial review of them at the time when they are affected by implementing decisions which are of direct and individual concern to them.

The plea only arises in a proceeding before the European Court and cannot be invoked as such in a national court, but in practice the validity of a regulation may be referred to the European Court by a national court under art 177 if its validity is put in issue in the national proceedings.[19]

Article 184, however, does not provide an independent cause of action. In *Wörhrmann v Commission*[20] the plaintiff applied directly to the European Court for a ruling that decisions of the Commission authorising Germany to impose duty on imports of powdered milk were invalid. This was a direct application and not a reference from a national court, although proceedings had been instituted in Germany challenging the validity of the additional duties imposed. The Court held, first, that art 184 does not of itself give rise to a cause of action;

---

17 Case 92/78 *Simmenthal SpA v Commission* [1979] ECR 777, [1980] 1 CMLR 25.
18 [1979] ECR at 800, (1980) 1 CMLR at 56.
19 Cf Case 44/65 *Hessische Knappschaft v Singer* [1965] ECR 965, [1966] CMLR 82.
20 Case 31/62 [1962] ECR 501, [1963] CMLR 152.

second, that it was without prejudice to the right of a national court to make a reference under art 177. The Court said:[1]

> It is clear from the wording and the general scheme of this article that a declaration of the inapplicability of a regulation is only contemplated in proceedings brought before the Court of Justice itself under some other provision of the Treaty, and then only incidentally and with limited effect. More particularly, it is clear from the reference to the time limit laid down in article 173 that article 184 is applicable only in the context of proceedings brought before the Court of Justice and that it does not permit the said time limit to be avoided. The sole object of article 184 is thus to protect an interested party against the application of an illegal regulation, without thereby in any way calling in issue the regulation itself, which can no longer be challenged because of the expiry of the time limit laid down in article 173.

But a regulation may only be attacked in this context if its validity is relevant to some issue in a matter in respect of which the Court is properly seised. It was because of the absence of such a relevant link that the Court refused to pass on the validity of a regulation in a case brought by Italy against the EEC Council and the Commission. The Court said that the intention of art 184:

> is not to allow a party to contest at will the applicability of any regulation in support of an application. The regulation of which the legality is called in question must be applicable, directly or indirectly, to the issue with which the application is concerned.[2]

VII. THE REMEDY AGAINST REFUSAL TO ACT—ARTICLE 175

The remedies available against Community institutions would be incomplete if they did not provide any remedy against inaction, and it is the purpose of art 175 to fill that gap. The equivalent in United Kingdom law is an application for judicial review by way of mandamus; this is a discretionary remedy, but there is an increasingly liberal attitude to standing, with the result that the House of Lords has almost accepted that there is, in some circumstances, an *actio popularis*, or citizen's action, to compel the executive to do its duty.[3] Article 175 provides:

> Should the Council or the Commission, in infringement of this Treaty, fail

---

1 [1962] ECR 501 at 506–7. See also Case 33/80 *Albini v Council and Commission* [1981] ECR 2141; Cases 87 etc/83 and 9 and 10/84 *Salerno v Commission and Council* [1985] ECR 2523; Cases 89 and 91/86 *L'Etoile Commerciale v Commission* [1987] ECR 3005, [1988] 3 CMLR 564.
2 Case 32/65 *Italy v Council and Commission* [1966] ECR 389 at 409, [1969] CMLR 39 at 65. Cf Euratom Treaty, art 156.
3 See *IRC v National Federation of Self Employed and Small Businesses* [1982] AC 617, [1981] 2 All ER 93; Wade, pp 700–705.

to act, the Member States and the other institutions of the Community may bring an action before the Court of Justice to have the infringement established.

The action shall be admissible only if the institution concerned has first been called upon to act. If, within two months of being so called upon, the institution concerned has not defined its position, the action may be brought within a further period of two months.

Any natural or legal person may, under the conditions laid down in the preceding paragraphs, complain to the Court of Justice that an institution of the Community has failed to address to that person any act other than a recommendation or an opinion.

The structure of art 175, therefore, is similar to that of art 173. There is a wide jurisdiction in relation to complaints by member states and Community institutions and a narrower jurisdiction in relation to complaints by individuals and there is a two-month time limitation.

The types of inaction in respect of which art 175 grants a remedy call for a few comments. First, there must be a failure to act in violation of the Treaty. Therefore there must be a *duty* to act which has not been fulfilled.[4] But this does not mean that there is no possibility of the control of discretionary powers under art 175 because a failure to exercise discretionary powers may involve an infringement of the Treaty if the failure is the result of improper motives constituting a misuse of powers.[5]

Secondly, the type of acts in respect of which private parties can complain of inaction is limited to 'any act other than a recommendation or an opinion'. The similarity of this expression with the equivalent expression in art 173(1) suggests that the acts in respect of which a private party may complain of inaction are the same as those which may be annulled under art 173, and the European Court has indicated that the concept of a measure giving rise to an action is identical in arts 173 and 175.[6] This would suggest that the extended notion of 'act' applies in proceedings under art 175, ie any act which would be intended to have legal force and which would affect the legal position of the applicant.[7] But there are differences. In the first place, although art 173(1) allows member states to bring actions for annulment of regulations, art 175 does not allow private parties to complain

---

4 Cf Cases 10 to 18/68 *Eridania v Commission* [1969] ECR 459; and Case 6/70 *Borromeo v Commission* [1970] ECR 815, [1970] CMLR 436; Cases 59 and 60/79 *Producteurs de Vins de Table et Vins de Pays v Commission* [1979] ECR 2425; Case 182/80 *Gauff v Commission* [1982] ECR 799, [1982] 3 CMLR 402.
5 Cf Schermers and Waelbroeck, p 223.
6 Case 15/70 *Chevalley v Commission* [1970] ECR 975; cf Case 792/79R *Camera Care Ltd v Commission* [1980] ECR 119, [1980] 1 CMLR 334.
7 See p 230, ante.

of the failure to adopt a regulation.[8] This is because there is no duty to adopt a regulation, and because a regulation cannot be regarded as 'addressed' to the applicant within the meaning of art 175(3). Secondly, for a private party to have standing to attack a decision, the decision must be addressed to that party, or, if addressed to another person, be of direct and individual concern to the applicant. Under art 175(3), the applicant can only complain of a failure to address an act to the applicant. Thus he will fail if he complains of a failure to address a decision to a member state, unless perhaps he can show that in substance he would be directly and individually concerned by the decision.[9] The complaint must relate to an act which would, if adopted, be binding on the applicant. If the complainant asks for a decision from the Commission, but in reality seeks advice or an opinion, the action under art 175 will be inadmissible.[10]

These principles inter-react with one another. Thus in *Lord Bethell v Commission*[11] Lord Bethell's proceedings against the Commission for (inter alia) failure to act on his complaint about price-fixing among the airlines were held to be inadmissible because the Commission had no duty to Lord Bethell to open an investigation and he was not the potential addressee of any decision.[12]

An important limitation on the types of inaction susceptible of being complained of was imposed as a result of the judgment of the European Court in *Lütticke v Commission*.[13] In that case the applicants complained of the failure by the Commission to take proceedings against a member state under art 169. In response to a request by the applicants to take such proceedings the Commission had expressed the view that the member state (France) had in fact complied with the Treaty. The application under art 175 could have been dismissed on the ground that taking proceedings under art 169 was not an act contemplated by art 175(3). But the Court held the application inadmissible on the ground that because the Commission had 'defined its position' within two months of being called upon to act pursuant to art 175(2), the action was barred. The Court said:[14]

> Under the terms of the second paragraph of article 175, proceedings for failure to act may only be brought if at the end of a period of two months from being called upon to act the institution has not defined its position. It is established that the Commission had defined its position and had notified this position to the applicants within the prescribed period.

---

8 Case 134/73 *Holtz and Willemsen GmbH v Council* [1974] ECR 1; Case 90/78 *Granaria BV v Council and Commission* [1979] ECR 1081; Cases 97 etc/86 *Asteris AE v Commission* [1988] 3 CMLR 493.
9 Case 15/71 *Mackprang v Commission* [1971] ECR 797, [1972] CMLR 52; cf Cases 59 and 60/79 *Producteurs de Vins de Table et Vins de Pays v Commission* [1979] ECR 2425.
10 Case 6/70 *Borromeo v Commission* [1970] ECR 815, [1970] CMLR 436.
11 Case 246/81 [1982] ECR 2277, [1982] 3 CMLR 300.
12 See p 250, ante.
13 Case 48/65 [1966] ECR 19, [1966] CMLR 378.
14 [1966] ECR 19 at 27.

In *GEMA v Commission*[15] the applicants were the German performing right society. They had complained to the Commission that Radio Luxembourg's broadcasting and publicity practices were such as to obtain for it an unfairly high proportion of the royalties, and that these practices were an abuse of a dominant position under art 86. When the Commission informed GEMA by letter that there were no grounds for adopting a decision finding that Radio Luxembourg was guilty of an abuse of a dominant position, GEMA complained under art 175 of the Commission's failure. The Court held that the Commission had acted in accordance with Regulation 17 by informing GEMA of its decision not to proceed and had addressed to GEMA an act which constituted a definition of its position under art 175.

Both *Lütticke* and *GEMA* show that there are cases where there will be a gap in the remedies available to private parties. They will not be able to secure the act they need by means of art 175 since all that the Commission may be required to do is to define its position; and yet the act defining the position may not be capable of annulment under art 173.[16] But this gap may not be substantial. If the applicant has a *right* to the act which he seeks then the definition of a position may be regarded as a decision, since it may affect his legal position; or the definition of position may not prevent reliance on art 175, to complain of the failure to address the act.[17] The position of the Court is that art 175 is concerned with 'a failure to act in the sense of failure to take a decision or to define a position'.[18]

The Court has on several occasions prevented art 175 from being used to open up new routes of challenge to state or community acts. Thus, in the *Lütticke* case it prevented individuals from using it to complain indirectly of violation of the Treaty by member states; the applicants sought, unsuccessfully, to bring direct complaints against the Commission for failing to take action against a member state in alleged default. Second, the Court has held that art 175 cannot be used to circumvent art 173 by complaining of the failure of a Community institution to revoke a decision which is not open to attack under art 173.[19] Third, if the Community institution has acted in response to a request by the applicant, the latter cannot use art 175

---

15 Case 125/78 [1979] ECR 3173, [1980] 2 CMLR 177.
16 GEMA was out of time under art 173. See p 249, ante, for remedies open to complainants.
17 Schermers and Waelbroeck, p 232.
18 Case 8/71 *Komponistenverband v Commission* [1971] ECR 705 at 710, [1973] CMLR 902 at 912. See also Case 42/71 *Nordgetreide v Commission* [1972] ECR 105, [1973] CMLR 177.
19 Cases 10 and 18/68 *Eridania v Commission* [1969] ECR 459, where the applicants sought to complain of the failure of the Commission to revoke a decision which was not of direct and individual concern. Another ground could have been that the decision would not have been addressed to the applicants.

to complain that the institution took the wrong decision by complaining of its failure to take the right one.[20] Thus in *Irish Cement Co Ltd v Commission*[1] the Commission refused to accede to a request by Irish Cement to open proceedings under art 93(2) of the EEC Treaty against an allegedly unlawful state aid to a rival. A year later Irish Cement made the same complaint and again the Commission refused to act. The application to annul the second refusal under art 173, and the action complaining of the refusal under art 175 were dismissed: the application under art 173 should have been brought within two months of the original decision, and was therefore out of time; the complaint under art 175 was ill-founded because the Commission had taken a position, and art 175 could not be used to complain of a refusal to take a decision different from that desired by the complainant.

VIII. DAMAGES AGAINST COMMUNITY INSTITUTIONS

By art 215(2) of the EEC Treaty:

> In the case of non-contractual liability, the Community shall, in accordance with the general principles common to the laws of the Member States, make good any damage caused by its institutions or by its servants in the performance of their duties.

Article 178 confers competence on the European Court to deal with damage claims under art 215. The damages remedy is more than an ordinary tort remedy and contains features which may appear novel at first sight to common lawyers. United Kingdom law with regard to damages against public authorities for acts other than those which would be torts if committed by private persons is very undeveloped,[2] and the claim to damages in an application for judicial review is not the creation of a new substantive right.

Article 215 confers a remedy in damages on individuals who are directly affected by illegal acts of Community institutions. It is possible, but not yet confirmed by the Court, that in certain circumstances a private party may be able to claim compensation for loss flowing from lawful acts. Under a concept known to French and German law, a private party may be entitled to compensation for injury suffered in consequence of a general measure which is lawful in itself but

---

20 Case 8/71 *Komponistenverband v Commission* [1971] ECR 705, [1973] CMLR 902, where the applicants had asked for an oral hearing during proceedings under reg 17 and had only been given the opportunity to submit their views in writing.
1 Cases 166 and 220/86 [1989] 2 CMLR 57.
2 Cf *Hoffman-La Roche v Secretary of State for Trade and Industry* [1975] AC 295 at 359, [1974] 2 All ER 1128 at 1148, per Lord Wilberforce; *Bourgoin SA v Ministry of Agriculture, Fisheries and Food* [1986] QB 716, [1985] 3 All ER 585, CA; Justice All Souls Report, ch 11.

particularly affects and harms the private party in a different way from, and much more seriously than, all other traders and producers.[3]

Although art 215 refers to the liability of the *Community* to make good damage, the normal practice is to name the Commission or, as the case may be, the Council as defendant. The Court held that where Community liability was involved by reason of the act of one of its institutions, the Community should be represented before the Court by the institution or institutions against which the matter giving rise to liability is alleged.[4]

Liability may arise under art 215 from activities of the institutions or their officials which amount to a 'faute de service'; for example, the Commission was held liable when, having given officials wrong advice about their pension entitlements, it did not correct the advice when it learned of its error.[5] For liability arising out of a wrongful administrative act,[6] the plaintiff does not have to show gross fault.[7]

The best-known example of the action for damages is *Adams v Commission*.[8] Stanley Adams was an employee of the Swiss company Hoffmann-La Roche. He gave the Commission information about Roche's anti-competitive practices in the sale of vitamins, and asked for his identity to be kept secret. The Commission subsequently fined Roche for breaches of arts 85 and 86, and its decision was upheld by the European Court.[9] Adams was arrested by the Swiss authorities and charged with the Swiss criminal offence of giving trade secrets to foreign authorities. He was at first held in solitary confinement, and following her interrogation by the Swiss authorities his wife committed suicide; Adams was sentenced to a suspended prison sentence

---

[3] See Case 59/83 *Biovilac NV v EEC* [1984] ECR 4057; Case 267/82 *Développement SA v Commission* [1986] ECR 1907; Case 265/85 *Van Den Bergh en Jurgens v Commission* [1987] ECR 1169; Bronkhorst, in Schermers et al, *Non-Contractual Liability of the European Communities* (1988) pp 13–22.
[4] Cases 63–69/72 *Werhahn v Council* [1973] ECR 1229.
[5] Cases 19 etc/69 *Richez-Parise v Commission* [1970] ECR 325.
[6] The Commission may be liable for a wrongful interference with the award procedure under the Lome Convention, so that the developing country is induced not to contract with the claimant: Case 267/82 *Développement SA v Commission* [1986] ECR 1907, [1989] 1 CMLR 309. But it is not possible to use art 215 as a means of obtaining damages for loss flowing from a treaty, such as the Spanish-Portuguese Act of Accession: Cases 31, 35/86 *Levantina Agricola Industrial SA v Council* [1988] 2 CMLR 420.
[7] Cases 5, 7 and 13–24/66 *Kampffmeyer v Commission* [1967] ECR 245; Case 30/66 *Becher v Commission* [1967] ECR 285, [1968] CMLR 169.
[8] Cases 145/83 and 53/84 [1985] ECR 3540, [1986] 1 CMLR 507. See March Hunnings (1987) 24 CML Rev 65.
[9] Case 85/76 *Hoffmann-La Roche & Co AG v Commission* [1979] ECR 461, [1979] 3 CMLR 211.

by the Swiss courts. In the course of the Swiss proceedings it emerged that Commission officials had given documents to Roche which enabled it to identify Adams as the main suspect in the complaint which Roche lodged with the Swiss authorities.

The European Court held that the Commission was in breach of duty[10] by not taking proper steps to keep Adams' identity confidential from Roche, and by not taking steps, after it knew that Roche was preparing to take criminal proceedings in Switzerland, to warn Adams of the risk. But the Court also came to the surprising conclusion that Adams was entitled only to one half of the damages suffered by him because he had contributed to his own damage by failing to inform the Commission that it was possible to discover his identity from the documents which he had handed over to the Commission; by failing to ask the Commission to keep him informed of the progress of the investigation, and in particular of any use that might be made of the documents; and by going back to Switzerland without making any enquiries about the investigation although he must have been aware of the risks involved. If the Commission was in breach of its duty, it does seem odd that the damages were reduced by such factors. Ultimately the quantification of damages was the subject of a settlement, and Adams received (including substantial costs) almost £400,000.

Liability extends not only to administrative acts or omissions, but also to acts of a legislative or normative character, such as regulations, provided that there is a sufficiently serious breach of a 'superior rule of law for the protection of the individual', such as the prohibition on discrimination.[11] Thus the Commission has been held liable to pay compensation for losses incurred as a result of a regulation which abolished with immediate effect and without warning the application of compensatory amounts: it was held to be a serious breach of the principle of 'legitimate expectation'.[12] Where Council regulations discriminated unlawfully against the producers of quellmehl and gritz at the expense of the producers of maize, the Community was held liable under art 215 because there had been a grave and manifest disregard of the limits on the exercise of discretionary

---

10 See EEC Treaty, art 214.
11 Case 5/71 *Zuckerfabrik Schöppenstedt v Council* [1971] ECR 975. For examples see cases in nn 13–15 below, and Cases 197 etc/80 *Ludwigshafener Walzemühle v Council and Commission* [1981] ECR 3211; Case 281/84 *Zuckerfabrik Bedburg AG v Council and Commission* [1987] ECR 49; Cases 194–206/83 *Asteris AE v Commission* [1985] ECR 2815. Nor can the plaintiff sue the national authorities in the national courts for having merely implemented the measure: Cases 106–120/87 *Asteris AE v Greece* 27 September 1988.
12 Case 74/74 *CNTA v Commission* [1975] ECR 533, [1977] 1 CMLR 171, but no damage was in fact proved: [1976] ECR 797.

powers.[13] This, the Court said, was because, among other reasons, the principle of nondiscrimination in the common agricultural policy occupied a particularly important place among the rules of Community law intended to protect the interests of the individual. But the producers of isoglucose (a sugar substitute) failed to obtain damages for the effects of a regulation imposing a production levy on isoglucose which was invalid[14] because it unlawfully discriminated against isoglucose; in that case the breach of the principle of equality had not been sufficiently serious.[15] In this case it was not the levy itself which was invalid; the method of calculation was vitiated by errors but the errors were not of such gravity that it could be said they verged on the arbitrary.

The 'general principles' do not mean principles common to the law of each member state—it may be enough to show a trend.[16] It was in reliance on the principles common to the law of member states that the Court held that the producers of maize gritz were entitled to interest.[17] The plaintiff must have suffered damage; but it is no bar to an action that they cannot be precisely quantified.[18] In the actions resulting from the discriminatory withdrawal of production refunds for quellmehl and gritz the European Court took a somewhat simplistic approach to the assessment of damages in holding that the measure of damages was the amount of production refunds which the producers would have received.[19]

The Court formerly took the view that a reviewable act which has not been annulled cannot form the basis of an action for damages.[20] But it was later held that the fact that an application for annulment of the measure under art 173 would not be admissible does not take away

---

13 Case 238/78 *Ireks-Arkady GmbH v Council and Commission* [1979] ECR 2955, and related cases (quellmehl); Cases 64 etc/76, 239/78, 27 etc/79 *Dumortier Frères SA v Council* [1979] ECR 3091 (gritz); Case 50/86 *Grands Moulins de Paris v Council and Commission* [1987] ECR 4833.
14 Cases 103 and 145/77 *Royal Scholten-Honig (Holdings) Ltd v Intervention Board for Agricultural Produce* [1978] ECR 2037, [1979] 1 CMLR 675.
15 Cases 116 and 124/77 *Amylum v Council and Commission* [1979] ECR 3497, [1982] 2 CMLR 590, and associated cases. See also Cases 83 and 94/76, 4, 15 and 40/77 *HNL v Council and Commission* [1978] ECR 1209, [1978] 3 CMLR 566.
16 See Akehurst (1981) 52 BYIL 29 at 32–38. Cf Cases 63–69/72 *Werhahn v Council* [1973] ECR 1229 at 1258–60 per Roemer AG; Case 68/77 *IFG v Commission* [1978] ECR 353, [1978] ECR 353, [1978] 2 CMLR 733; Cases 83 and 94/76, 4, 15 and 40/77 *HNL v Council and Commission* [1978] ECR 1209, [1978] 3 CMLR 566.
17 Cases 256 etc/80, 5 and 81/81, 282/82 *Birra Wührer SpA v Council and Commission* [1984] ECR 3693.
18 Cases 56–60/74 *Kampffmeyer v Commission and Council* [1976] ECR 711; Case 44/76 *Eier-Kontor v Council and Commission* [1977] ECR 393.
19 Case 23/78 *Ireks-Arkady GmbH v Council and Commission* [1979] ECR 2955 and related cases. From criticism see Rudden and Bishop (1981) 6 EL Rev 243.
20 Case 26/62 *Plaumann & Co v Commission* [1963] ECR 95, [1964] CMLR 29; Hartley, pp 470–472.

the right to damages under art 215, because the action for damages is an independent remedy,[1] and the current practice is, in appropriate cases, to claim in the alternative.[2] It has been held in several decisions that the action for damages under art 215(2) was established as an autonomous form of action, and is not subject to the same restrictions as art 173 and art 175. Thus it can be used to obtain damages for the effects of an unlawful regulation, even though the regulation is of a legislative nature and cannot be the subject of an action by a private party under art 173.[3] It can be used to obtain damages for an unlawful failure to act, even though the failure to act could not have been the subject of an application under art 175 because the failure did not relate to an act to be addressed to the applicant.[4]

But it does not follow that art 215 can be used to obtain damages for the effects of an unlawful decision addressed to the applicant which could have been, but was not, challenged within the two-month limitation period imposed under art 173.[5] In *Krohn & Co v Commission*[6] the plaintiffs claimed damages flowing from an instruction by the Commission addressed to the Federal Republic of Germany, as a result of which the plaintiffs were refused import licences for manioc from Thailand. The plaintiffs had taken no steps to challenge the decision under art 173(2), and the Commission objected to the admissibility of the damages claim on the basis of the decision in *Plaumann & Co v Commission*[7] that an application for compensation could not be brought if it would nullify the legal effects of a decision which had (by not being challenged under art 173) become definitive. Advocate General Mancini accepted that the subsequent decisions of the Court (that the action for damages is an independent action) wholly superseded the relevant part of the judgment in *Plaumann*, with the result that the fact that the plaintiff could have sought, but did not seek, annulment was wholly irrelevant to the claim for damages. The Court

---

1 Case 4/69 *Lütticke v Commission* [1971] ECR 325; Cases 9 and 11/71 *Cie d'Approvisionnement v Commission* [1972] ECR 391, [1973] CMLR 529; Case 43/72 *Merkur v Commission* [1973] ECR 1055; Case 175/84 *Krohn & Co v Commission* [1986] ECR 753, [1987] 1 CMLR 745.
2 See eg Case 112/77 *Toepfer v Commission* [1978] ECR 1019; Case 132/77 *Exportation des Sucres v Commission* [1978] ECR 1061, [1979] 1 CMLR 309; Case 64/82 *Tradax BV v Commission* [1984] ECR 1359; Case 59/84 *Tezi Textiel BV v Commission* [1986] ECR 887, [1987] 3 CMLR 64; Cases 89 and 91/86 *L'Etoile Commerciale v Commission* [1987] ECR 3005, [1988] 3 CMLR 564.
3 Cases 9 and 11/71 *Cie d'Approvisionnement v Commission* [1972] ECR 391; Case 43/72 *Merkur v Commission* [1973] ECR 1055; Cases 197 etc/80 *Ludwigshafener Walzmühle v Council and Commission* [1981] ECR 3211.
4 Case 153/73 *Holtz and Willemsen GmbH v Council and Commission* [1974] ECR 675, [1975] 1 CMLR 91; Case 4/69 *Lütticke v Commission* [1971] ECR 325.
5 Cf Schermers and Waelbroeck, pp 304–310.
6 Case 175/84 [1986] ECR 753, [1987] 1 CMLR 745.
7 Case 25/62 [1963] ECR 95, [1964] CMLR 29.

seems substantially to have accepted that view.[8] Although this case concerned a decision addressed to a member state (and therefore it would not have been by any means clear that the plaintiff would have had standing to apply for annulment) the terms of the judgment are not qualified, and it appears to be clear authority for the view that, provided the applicant seeks damages, and not merely restitution, the fact that an application for annulment could have been, but was not, made is irrelevant.

It seems, from a difficult and not entirely consistent line of cases, that art 215 cannot be used where the essence of the claim is essentially restitutionary. Certainly where the real complaint is about the conduct of national authorities a claim for damages against the Community is not admissible.[9] But even if the legality of a Community measure is in issue, a claim for damages under art 215 is inadmissible if the real object of the action is to obtain restitution of sums paid to national authorities.[10] In such a case the appropriate remedy is a claim in the national courts followed, if necessary, by a reference under art 177.[11] But where the real complaint is about the conduct of Community institutions, or where it is clear that national law can provide no remedy, an action under art 215 may be admissible.[12] The distinction between the cases in which actions were admissible and those in which they were not is fine, and not all of the decisions can be reconciled with each other.[13]

---

8 The *Plaumann* decision was said to relate only to cases where the essence of the claim was restitution of duty paid.
9 Cases 12, 18 and 21/77 *Debayser v Commission* [1978] ECR 553, [1978] 3 CMLR 361; Case 132/77 *Exportation des Sucres v Commission*, supra; Case 12/79 *Wagner v Commission* [1979] ECR 3657; Case 133/79 *Sucrimex SA v Commission* [1980] ECR 1299, [1981] 2 CMLR 479; Case 217/81 *Interagra SA v Commission* [1982] ECR 2233; Case 175/84 *Krohn & Co v Commission* [1986] ECR 753, [1987] 1 CMLR 745; Cases 89 and 91/86 *L'Etoile Commerciale v Commission* [1987] ECR 3005, [1988] 3 CMLR 564.
10 Cases 5, 7, 13–24/66 *Kampffmeyer v Commission* [1967] ECR 245; Case 96/71 *Haegeman v Commission* [1972] ECR 1005, [1973] CMLR 365; Case 46/75 *IBC v Commission* [1976] ECR 65; Case 26/74 *Roquette v Commission* [1976] ECR 677. See also Cases 106–120/87 *Asteris AE v Greece and EEC* 27 September 1988.
11 See Case 119/77 *Japanese Ball Bearings (Nippon Seiko)* [1979] ECR 1303 at 1272, [1979] 2 CMLR 257 at 328, per Warner AG.
12 Case 126/76 *Dietz v Commission* [1977] ECR 2431, [1978] 2 CMLR 608; Case 43/72 *Merkur v Commission* [1973] ECR 1055; Case 238/78 *Ireks-Arkady GmbH v Council and Commission* [1979] ECR 2955; Cases 197 etc/80 *Ludwigshafener Walzmühle v Council and Commission* [1981] ECR 3211; Case 281/82 *Unifrex v Council and Commission* [1984] ECR 1969; Case 175/84 *Krohn & Co v Commission* [1986] ECR 753; Case 251/84 *Zuckerfabrik Bedburg AG v Council and Commission* [1987] ECR 49. Cases 67–85/75 *Lesieur Cotelle v Commission* [1976] ECR 391, [1976] 2 CMLR 185, and contrast Case 99/74 *Grands Moulins v Commission* [1975] ECR 1531.
13 See Hartley, pp 483–492; Harding (1979) 16 CML Rev 389; Durand (1976) EL Rev 431.

Article 43 of the Statute of the Court provides for a five-year limitation period in the following terms:

> Proceedings against the Community in matters arising from non-contractual liability shall be barred after a period of five years from the occurrence of the event giving rise thereto. The period of limitation shall be interrupted if proceedings are instituted before the Court or if prior to such proceedings an application is made by the aggrieved party to the relevant institution of the Community. In the latter event the proceedings must be instituted within the period of two months provided for in article 173; the provisions of the second paragraph of article 175 shall apply where appropriate.

An action under art 215(2) may be brought before any damage has occurred, provided it is imminent and foreseeable.[14] But it has been held that for the purposes of art 43 of the Statute the five-year limitation period runs from the time of actual damage, and not from the earliest time the action could have been commenced.[15] In these cases the plaintiffs sued for damages caused by regulations abolishing production refunds which they argued were unlawful. The Court rejected the argument that the time began to run from the date on which the regulations were published, when damage was imminent and foreseeable, and held that time did not run before the injurious effects were produced. It follows from these two lines of authority that an action may be brought for a declaration before the limitation period has begun. But time does not run where the plaintiff could not reasonably have known of the wrongful act. In *Adams v Commission*, Adams did not become aware of the breach of confidentiality by the Commission until six years afterwards. The Court held that time did not run until the plaintiff could reasonably have become aware of the event giving rise to the damage.[16] The final sentence of art 43 is rather obscure, but it does not have the effect of cutting down the five-year period in the case of actions under art 215.[17] Its only effect is to prevent time running when an application is made under art 173 or when a request for action is made and then followed by an application under art 175.[18]

---

14 Cases 56–60/74 *Kampffmeyer v Commission and Council* [1976] ECR 711; Case 44/76 *Eier-Kontor v Commission and Council* [1977] ECR 393; Case 147/83 *Binderer v Commission* [1985] ECR 257.
15 Cases 256 etc/80 and 5/81 *Birra Wührer SpA v Council and Commission* [1982] ECR 85.
16 P 283, n 8, supra.
17 Cases 5, 7 and 13–24/66 *Kampffmeyer v Commission* [1967] ECR 245; Case 11/72 *Giordano v Commission* [1973] ECR 417. See also Case 44/76 *Eier-Kontor v Council and Commission* [1977] ECR 393 at 413–15, per Reischel AG.
18 See Heukels, in Schermers et al, p 283, n 3, ante, pp 83–103.

Appendix

European Communities Act 1972
(1972 c 68)

An Act to make provision in connection with the enlargement of the European Communities to include the United Kingdom, together with (for certain purposes) the Channel Islands, the Isle of Man and Gibraltar [17 October 1972]

PART I
GENERAL PROVISIONS

1 Short title and interpretation

(1) This Act may be cited as the European Communities Act 1972.

(2) In this Act . . .—

'the Communities' means the European Economic Community, the European Coal and Steel Community and the European Atomic Energy Community;

'the Treaties' or 'the Community Treaties' means, subject to subsection (3) below, the pre-accession treaties, that is to say, those described in Part I of Schedule 1 to this Act, taken with—

(a) the treaty relating to the accession of the United Kingdom to the European Economic Community and to the European Atomic Energy Community, signed at Brussels on the 22nd January 1972; and

(b) the decision, of the same date, of the Council of the European Communities relating to the accession of the United Kingdom to the European Coal and Steel Community; and

(c) the treaty relating to the accession of the Hellenic Republic to the European Economic Community and to the European Atomic Energy Community, signed at Athens on 28th May 1979; and

(d) the decision, of 24th May 1979, of the Council relating to the accession of the Hellenic Republic to the European Coal and Steel Community;

(e) the decisions, of 7th May 1985 and of 24th June 1988, of the Council on the Communities' system of own resources; and

(f) the undertaking by the Representatives of the Governments of the member States, as confirmed at their meeting within the Council on 24th June 1988 in Luxembourg, to make payments to finance the Communities' general budget for the financial year 1988; and

(g) the treaty relating to the accession of the Kingdom of Spain and the Portuguese Republic to the European Economic Community, signed at Lisbon and Madrid on 12th June 1985; and

(h) the decision, of 11th June 1985, of the Council relating to the accession of the Kingdom of Spain and the Portuguese Republic to the European Coal and Steel Community; and

(j) the following provisions of the Single European Act signed at Luxembourg and The Hague on 17th and 28th February 1986, namely Title II (amendment of the treaties establishing the Communities) and, so far as they relate to any of the Communities or any Community institution, the preamble and Titles I (common provisions) and IV (general and final provisions);

and any other treaty entered into by any of the Communities, with or without any of the member States, or entered into, as a treaty ancillary to any of the Treaties, by the United Kingdom;

and any expression defined in Schedule 1 to this Act has the meaning there given to it.

(3) If Her Majesty by Order in Council declares that a treaty specified in the Order is to be regarded as one of the Community Treaties as herein defined, the Order shall be conclusive that it is to be so regarded; but a treaty entered into by the United Kingdom after the 22nd January 1972, other than a pre-accession treaty to which the United Kingdom accedes on terms settled on or before that date, shall not be so regarded unless it is so specified, nor be so specified unless a draft of the Order in Council has been approved by resolution of each House of Parliament.

(4) For purposes of subsections (2) and (3) above, 'treaty' includes any international agreement, and any protocol or annex to a treaty or international agreement.

NOTES

The words omitted from sub-s (2) were repealed by the Interpretation Act 1978, s 25(1), Sch 3, paras (c) and (d) were inserted by the European Communities (Greek

Accession) Act 1979, s 1, paras (*e*) and (*f*) (which were originally inserted by the European Communities (Finance) Act 1985, s 1) were substituted by the European Communities (Finance) Act 1988, s 1, paras (*g*) and (*h*) were inserted by the European Communities (Spanish and Portuguese Accession) Act 1985, s 1, substituted by the European Communities (Finance) Act 1988, s 1, and para (*j*) was inserted by the European Communities (Amendment) Act 1986, s 1.

2 General implementation of Treaties

(1) All such rights, powers, liabilities, obligations and restrictions from time to time created or arising by or under the Treaties, and all such remedies and procedures from time to time provided for by or under the Treaties, as in accordance with the Treaties are without further enactment to be given legal effect or used in the United Kingdom shall be recognised and available in law, and be enforced, allowed and followed accordingly; and the expression 'enforceable Community right' and similar expressions shall be read as referring to one to which this subsection applies.

(2) Subject to Schedule 2 to this Act, at any time after its passing Her Majesty may by Order in Council, and any designated Minister or department may by regulations, make provision—

   (*a*) for the purpose of implementing any Community obligation of the United Kingdom, or enabling any such obligation to be implemented, or of enabling any rights enjoyed or to be enjoyed by the United Kingdom under or by virtue of the Treaties to be exercised; or
   (*b*) for the purpose of dealing with matters arising out of or related to any such obligation or rights or the coming into force, or the operation from time to time, of subsection (1) above;

and in the exercise of any statutory power or duty, including any power to give directions or to legislate by means of orders, rules, regulations or other subordinate instrument, the person entrusted with the power or duty may have regard to the objects of the Communities and to any such obligation or rights as aforesaid.

In this subsection 'designated Minister or department' means such Minister of the Crown or government department as may from time to time be designated by Order in Council in relation to any matter or for any purpose, but subject to such restrictions or conditions (if any) as may be specified by the Order in Council.

(3) There shall be charged on and issued out of the Consolidated fund or, if so determined by the Treasury, the National Loans Fund the amounts required to meet any Community obligation to make payments to any of the Communities or member States, or any Community obligation in respect of contributions to the capital or reserves of the European Investment Bank or in respect of loans to the

Bank, or to redeem any notes or obligations issued or created in respect of any such Community obligation; and, except as otherwise provided by or under any enactment,—

    (*a*) any other expenses incurred under or by virtue of the Treaties or this Act by any Minister of the Crown or government department may be paid out of moneys provided by Parliament; and

    (*b*) any sums received under or by virtue of the Treaties or this Act by any Minister of the Crown or government department, save for such sums as may be required for disbursements permitted by any other enactment, shall be paid into the Consolidated Fund or, if so determined by the Treasury, the National Loans Fund.

(4) The provision that may be made under subsection (2) above includes, subject to Schedule 2 to this Act, any such provision (or any such extent) as might be made by Act of Parliament, and any enactment passed or to be passed, other than one contained in this Part of this Act, shall be construed and have effect subject to the foregoing provisions of this section; but, except as may be provided by any Act passed after this Act, Schedule 2 shall have effect in connection with the powers conferred by this and the following sections of this Act to make Orders in Council and regulations.

(5) . . . and the references in that subsection to a Minister of the Crown or government department and to a statutory power or duty shall include a Minister or department of the Government of Northern Ireland and a power or duty arising under or by virtue of an Act of the Parliament of Northern Ireland.

(6) A law passed by the legislature of any of the Channel Islands or of the Isle of Man, or a colonial law (within the meaning of the Colonial Laws Validity Act 1865) passed or made for Gibraltar, if expressed to be passed or made in the implementation of the Treaties and of the obligations of the United Kingdom thereunder, shall not be void or inoperative by reason of any inconsistency with or repugnancy to an Act of Parliament, passed or to be passed, that extends to the Island of Gibraltar or any provision having the force and effect of an Act there (but not including this section), nor by reason of its having some operation outside the Island or Gibraltar; and any such Act or provision that extends to the Island or Gibraltar shall be construed and have effect subject to the provisions of any such law.

NOTES

The words omitted from sub-s (5) were repealed by the Northern Ireland Constitution Act 1973, s 41(1), Sch 6, Pt 1.

3 Decisions on, and proof of, Treaties and Community instruments, etc

(1) For the purposes of all legal proceedings any question as to the meaning or effect of any of the Treaties, or as to the validity, meaning or effect of any Community instrument, shall be treated as a question of law (and, if not referred to the European Court, be for determination as such in accordance with the principles laid down by and any relevant decision of the European Court [or any court attached thereto]).

(2) Judicial notice shall be taken of the Treaties, of the Official Journal of the Communities and of any decision of, or expression of opinion by, the European Court [or any court attached thereto] on any such question as aforesaid; and the Official Journal shall be admissible as evidence of any instrument or other act thereby communicated of any of the Communities or of any Community institution.

(3) Evidence of any instrument issued by a Community institution, including any judgment or order of the European Court [or any court attached thereto], or of any document in the custody of a Community institution, or any entry in or extract from such a document, may be given in any legal proceedings by production of a copy certified as a true copy by an official of that institution; and any document purporting to be such a copy shall be received in evidence without proof of the official position or handwriting of the person signing the certificate.

(4) Evidence of any Community instrument may also be given in any legal proceedings—

(a) by production of a copy purporting to be printed by the Queen's Printer;
(b) where the instrument is in the custody of a government department (including a department of the Government of Northern Ireland), by production of a copy certified on behalf of the department to be a true copy by an officer of the department generally or specially authorised so to do;

and any document purporting to be such a copy as is mentioned in paragraph (b) above of an instrument in the custody of a department shall be received in evidence without proof of the official position or handwriting of the person signing the certificate, or of his authority so to do, or of the document being in the custody of the department.

(5) In any legal proceedings in Scotland evidence of any matter given in a manner authorised by this section shall be sufficient evidence of it.

NOTES

The words in square brackets in sub-ss (1)–(3) were substituted or inserted by the European Communities (Amendment) Act 1986, s 2.

Part II

Amendment of Law

* * * * *

11 Community offences

(1) A person who, in sworn evidence before the European Court [or any court attached thereto], makes any statement which he knows to be false or does not believe to be true shall, whether he is a British subject or not, be guilty of an offence and may be proceeded against and punished—

- (*a*) in England and Wales as for an offence against section 1(1) of the Perjury Act 1911; or
- (*b*) in Scotland as for an offence against section 1 of the False Oaths (Scotland) Act 1933; or
- (*c*) in Northern Ireland as for an offence against [Article 3(1) of the Perjury (Northern Ireland) Order 1979].

Where a report is made as to any such offence under the authority of the European Court [or any court attached thereto], then a bill of indictment for the offence may . . . in Northern Ireland, be preferred as in a case where a prosecution is ordered under . . . [Article 13 of the Perjury (Northern Ireland) Order 1979], but the report shall not be given in evidence on a person's trial for the offence.

(2) Where a person (whether a British subject or not) owing either—

- (*a*) to his duties as a member of any Euratom institution or committee, or as an officer or servant of Euratom; or
- (*b*) to his dealings in any capacity (official or unofficial) with any Euratom institution or installation or with any Euratom joint enterprise;

has occasion to acquire, or obtain cognisance of, any classified information, he shall be guilty of a misdemeanour if, knowing or having reason to believe that it is classified information, he communicates it to any unauthorised person or makes any public disclosure of it, whether in the United Kingdom or elsewhere and whether before or after the termination of those duties or dealings; and for this purpose 'classified information' means any facts, information, knowledge, documents or objects that are subject to the security rules of a member State or of any Euratom institution.

This subsection shall be construed, and the Official Secrets Acts 1911 to 1939 shall have effect, as if this subsection were contained in the Official Secrets Act 1911, but so that in that Act sections 10 and 11, except section 10(4), shall not apply.

(3) This section shall not come into force until the entry date.

NOTES

The words in the first and third pairs of square brackets in sub-s (1) were inserted by the European Communities (Amendment) Act 1986, s 2(*b*), and the words in the second and fourth pairs of square brackets were substituted by the Perjury (Northern Ireland) Order 1979, SI 1979/1714, Art 19(1), Sch 1, para 24. The words omitted were repealed by the Prosecution of Offences Act 1985, s 31(6), Sch 2.

* * * * *

SCHEDULE 2

Section 2

PROVISIONS AS TO SUBORDINATE LEGISLATION

1.—(1) The powers conferred by section 2(2) of this Act to make provision for the purposes mentioned in section 2(2)(*a*) and (*b*) shall not include power—
- (a) to make any provision imposing or increasing taxation; or
- (b) to make any provision taking effect from a date earlier than that of the making of the instrument containing the provision; or
- (c) to confer any power to legislate by means of orders, rules, regulations or other subordinate instrument, other than rules of procedure for any court or tribunal; or
- (d) to create any new criminal offence punishable with imprisonment for more than two years or punishable on summary conviction with imprisonment for more than three months or with a fine of more than [level 5 on the standard scale] (if not calculated on a daily basis) or with a fine of more than [£100 a day].

(2) Sub-paragraph (1)(c) above shall not be taken to preclude the modification of a power to legislate conferred otherwise than under section 2(2), or the extension of any such power to purposes of the like nature as those for which it was conferred; and a power to give directions as to matters of administration is not to be regarded as a power to legislate within the meaning of sub-paragraph (1)(c).

2.—(1) Subject to paragraph 3 below, where a provision contained in any section of this Act confers power to make regulations (otherwise than by modification or extension of an existing power), the power shall be exercisable by statutory instrument.

(2) Any statutory instrument containing an Order in Council or regulations made in the exercise of a power so conferred, if made without a draft having been approved by resolution of each House of Parliament, shall be subject to annulment in pursuance of a resolution of either House.

3. Nothing in paragraph 2 above shall apply to any Order in Council made by the Governor of Northern Ireland or to any regulations made by a Minister or department of the Government of Northern Ireland; but where a provision contained in any section of this Act confers power to make such an Order in Council or regulations, then any

Order in Council or regulations made in the exercise of that power, if made without a draft having been approved by resolution of each House of the Parliament of Northern Ireland, shall be subject to negative resolution within the meaning of section 41(6) of the Interpretation Act (Northern Ireland) 1954 as if the Order or regulations were a statutory instrument within the meaning of that Act.

[4.—(1) The power to make orders under section 5(1) or (2) of this Act shall be exercisable in accordance with the following provisions of this paragraph.

(2) The power to make such orders shall be exercisable by statutory instrument and includes power to amend or revoke any such order made in the exercise of that power.

(3) Any statutory instrument containing any such order shall be subject to annulment in pursuance of a resolution of the House of Commons except in a case falling within sub-paragraph (4) below.

(4) Subject to sub-paragraph (6) below, where an order imposes or increases any customs duty, or restricts any relief from customs duty under the said section 5, the statutory instrument containing the order shall be laid before the House of Commons after being made and, unless the order is approved by that House before the end of the period of 28 days beginning with the day on which it was made, it shall cease to have effect at the end of that period, but without prejudice to anything previously done under the order or to the making of a new order.

In reckoning the said period of 28 days no account shall be taken of any time during which Parliament is dissolved or prorogued or during which the House of Commons is adjourned for more than 4 days.

(5) Where an order has the effect of altering the rate of duty on any goods in such a way that the new rate is not directly comparable with the old, it shall not be treated for the purposes of sub-paragraph (4) above as increasing the duty on those goods if it declares the opinion of the Treasury to be that, in the circumstances existing at the date of the order, the alteration is not calculated to raise the general level of duty on the goods.

(6) Sub-paragraph (4) above does not apply in the case of an instrument containing an order which states that it does not impose or increase any customs duty or restrict any relief from customs duty otherwise than in pursuance of a Community obligation.

5. As soon as may be after the end of each financial year the Secretary of State shall lay before each House of Parliament a report on the exercise during that year of the powers conferred by section 5(1) and (2) of this Act with respect to the imposition of customs duties and the allowance of exemptions and reliefs from duties so imposed (including the power to amend or revoke orders imposing customs duties or providing for any exemption or relief from duties so imposed).]

NOTES

The words in the first pair of square brackets in para 1(1)(*d*) are substituted by virtue of the Criminal Justice Act 1982, ss 40, 46. The words in the second pair of square brackets in that sub-paragraph were substituted by the Criminal Law Act 1977, ss 32(3), 65(10).

Paras 4, 5 were added by the Customs and Excise Duties (General Reliefs) Act 1979, s 19(1), Sch 2, para 5.

* * * * *

Index

Administrative tribunal
  European Court, reference to, 145–147
Agriculture
  directly effective provisions, 124
Annulment actions. *See* REMEDIES
Anti-dumping
  investigation, 250–254
Appeal
  lower court, decision to refer, 194–200
Arbitral tribunal
  European Court, reference to, 148–150

Capital
  free movement of, 124–125
Challenging Community acts. *See* REMEDIES
Commission
  complaints to or by. *See* REMEDIES
  decisions of. *See* DECISIONS
Common Market
  EEC Treaty, activities under, 114–115
Community law
  common law presumption, 117–120
  decisions. *See* DECISIONS
  direct applicability. *See* DIRECT APPLICABILITY
  direct effect. *See* DIRECT EFFECT
  directives. *See* DIRECTIVES
  enforceable Community rights, 36–51
  human rights and, 8–13
  individuals, and, 7–8
  international law, and, 1, 2–7
  interpretation. *See* INTERPRETATION
  national law and. *See* NATIONAL LAW
  nature of, 1–2
  reference. *See* REFERENCE
  regulations. *See* REGULATIONS
  remedies. *See* REMEDIES
  scrutiny, 120–121
  sovereignty, problem of, 15, 22–23, 26–43
  status of, 128–130
  statutes and, 137–142

Community law—*contd*
  supremacy of,
    EEC view of, 15–22
    generally, 2, 70–71
    national view of, 22–23
    treaties as source of, 1, 2, 23–26
Competition
  rules on, 125
  state aids, 254–255
Costs
  reference, of, 207–209
Council
  decisions of. *See* DECISIONS
  directives of. *See* DIRECTIVES
Court of Justice. *See* EUROPEAN COURT

Decisions
  annulment actions concerning, 236–240
  authorised by regulation, 82
  direct applicability of,
    authorised by regulation, 82
    generally, 77–82
    individuals, to, 82
    member states, to, 77–82
  direct effect of,
    arguments against, 79–80
    arguments for, 80
  individuals, addressed to, 82
  member states, addressed to, 77–82
  regulations compared with, 237
Delegated legislation. *See* SUBORDINATE LEGISLATION
Direct applicability
  decisions, of,
    authorised by regulation, 82
    generally, 77–82
    individuals, to, 82
    member states, to, 77–82
  direct effect distinguished from, 45
  directives, of, 83–99
  European Communities Act 1972, effect of, 46
  generally, 44–46

297

Direct applicability—*contd*
provisions, of,
approach to be adopted, 100–101
generally, 99
summary, 122–126
regulations, of,
constitutional problems, 70–73
direct effect, 73–74
generally, 8, 18–21, 69–77
limits on implementing, 74–77
pecuniary penalties, 117
summary, 77
subordinate legislation, rights and obligations, 112 *et seq.*
summary, 99–112

Direct effect
decisions, of,
arguments against, 79–80
arguments for, 80
direct applicability distinguished from, 45
other treaties, of, 67–69
partial, precision and, 53
principle of,
alternative remedies irrelevant, 59–60
clearness and precision, 49–53
discretion excluded, 56–59
further measures not required, 53–56
generally, 46–67, 122
member states only, provision must not concern, 48–49
precision and partial direct effect, 53
remedies, 62–67
temporal effect, 60–62
unconditional and unqualified, 53–56
subordinate legislation, rights and obligations, 112 *et seq.*
Treaty, of, 41

Directives
annulment actions, in, 230–234
direct applicability of, 83–99
generally, 83–88
horizontal effect, 88–91
national reaction, 94–99
remedies, 92–94
review of, 230–234

Disciplinary tribunal
European Court, reference to, 147–148

EEC Treaty
direct applicability, 122–126

EEC Treaty—*contd*
direct effect, 41

Euratom
treaty setting up, 1

European Coal and Steel Community
treaty setting up, 1

European Communities Act 1972
direct applicability of Community law, 44
European Court, on, 128–129
generally, 26–27
incorporation of Community law, 26–43
intention, 128–130
interpretation of Community law, 46, 130–134
rights and duties under, 46
subordinate legislation. *See* SUBORDINATE LEGISLATION
text, 289–296

European Court
annulment actions. *See* REMEDIES
complaints, rulings on. *See* REMEDIES
European Communities Act 1972 on, 128–129
facts of case, will not rule on, 163
guidelines, 172–174
human rights, 8–13
interpretation techniques, 130–134
national court which may refer questions,
administrative tribunal, 145–147
arbitral tribunal, 148–150
disciplinary tribunal, 147–148
generally, 144–145
national law, will not rule on, 163
preliminary rulings by. *See* REFERENCE
procedure. *See* PROCEDURE
reference to. *See* REFERENCE

General Agreement on Tariffs and Trade (GATT)
EEC, recognition of, 5

Goods
free movement of, 123–124

Human rights
Community law and, 8–13
European Convention, 9–13

Immunity
EEC, of, 4

Individuals
common law presumptions, 117–120
Community law and, 7–8

Individuals—*contd*
  decisions addressed to, 82
  free movement of, 124–125
  remedies available to. *See* REMEDIES
  rights of,
    decisions, created by, 82
    generally, 8
    independent of legislation, 16–22
    treaty provisions, under, 36–51
  standing of,
    annulment of regulations, 236–240
    anti-dumping, 244–245, 250–254
    conclusions on, 255–256
    generally, 234–236
    member states, decisions addressed to, 240–244
    restrictive practices, 244–250
    state aids, 254–255
Industry
  state aids, 254–255
Injunction. *See* REFERENCE
Interlocutory proceeding. *See* REFERENCE
International Tin Council
  insolvency of, litigation arising out of, 4
International law
  Community law and, 1, 2–7
  dualistic theory, 14
  legal personality in, 2–7
  public, position of European Communities in, 5–7
  yields to statute, 135
Interpretation
  ambiguity, 135–136
  delegated legislation, 117–120
  European Communities Act 1972, under, 46, 127 *et seq.*
  European Court, methods of, 130–134
  general Community rules, exceptions to, 132
  implementing legislation not directly applicable, of, 135–142
  preliminary rulings. *See* REFERENCE
  problems of, 127 *et seq.*
  purposes and objectives of Treaties, 132–133
  regulations, 74–77
  ruling on, 17
  statutes,
    Community law and, 137–142
    treaties and, 135–137

Legal aid
  reference, for, 208

Legal personality
  EEC, of, 3
  international law, in, 2–7
  United Nations, of, 3

Movement
  goods, of, 123–124
  persons, service and capital, of, 124–125
Municipal law. *See* NATIONAL LAW

National court
  reference by. *See* REFERENCE
National law
  common law presumptions, 117–120
  Community law and, 1, 14–15, 135–142
  constitutional problems, 70–73
  dualistic theory, 14
  incorporation of Community law, mode of, 26–43
  interpretation of,
    ambiguity, 135–136
    implementing legislation not directly applicable, 135–142
    problems of, 127 *et seq.*
    statutes,
      Community law and, 137–142
      treaties and, 135–137
  reference to European Court. *See* REFERENCE
  regulations, limits on implementing, 74–77
  Sovereignty,
    Parliament, of, 22, 27–43
    problem of, 15, 22–23, 27
    subordinate legislation. *See* SUBORDINATE LEGISLATION
  treaties, need for legislation, 14–15, 128

Parliament
  sovereignty of, 22, 27–43
Persons. *See* INDIVIDUALS
Preliminary ruling. *See* REFERENCE
Private persons. *See* INDIVIDUALS
Procedure
  infringement of, in annulment actions, 259–266
  reference to European Court. *See* REFERENCE
  subordinate legislation, 116

Quantitative restrictions
  elimination of, 56–57, 123–124

Reference
acte clair principle, 156–162, 178–179
administrative tribunal, by, 145–147
annulment actions and, relationship, 274–276
appeals from decisions of lower courts, 194–200
arbitral tribunal, by, 148–150
article 177,
  provisions, 142–143
  purpose, 143–144
authority of ruling, 209–211
Bulmer v Bollinger, 176 *et seq.*
costs, 174–175, 207–209
decision, when necessary, 176–183
disciplinary tribunal, by, 147–148
effect of ruling, 209–211
European Court's guidelines, 172–174
final court,
  identification of, 150–154
  interlocutory appeals, 154–156
Foglia v Novello, 169–172
form of, 201–203
generally, 44, 144–145
High Court, by, 200–201
identification of final court, 150–154
interlocutory appeals, final courts and, 154–156
interlocutory proceedings, 189–194
invalidity rulings, 211–214
legal aid, 208
lower courts, role of article 177 before, 174–176
national court,
  obligation to refer, 150
  power of, 144
national courts which may refer,
  administrative tribunal, 145–147
  arbitral tribunal, 148–150
  disciplinary tribunal, 147–148
  generally, 144–145
non-appealable decisions, 151
parties, role of, 203–207
preliminary rulings by European Court,
  article 177, purpose of, 143–144
  generally, 142–143
  national courts,
    article 177, which must make reference under,
      acte clair, 156–162
      generally, 150
      identification of final court, 150–154
      interlocutory appeal, 154–156

Reference—*contd*
preliminary rulings by European Court—*contd*
  national courts—*contd*
    questions, which may refer,
      administrative tribunals, 145–147
      arbitral tribunals, 148–150
      disciplinary tribunals, 147–148
      generally, 144–145
    questions which may be referred,
      application, 165–166
      generally, 162–163
      interpretation, 165–166
      national law and Community law, compatibility of, 166–169
      relevance, 163–165
    refusal to give, 169–172
  procedural aspects,
    costs, 207–209
    form, 201–203
    High Court, references by, 200–201
    legal aid, 208
    parties, role of, 203–207
  questions,
    generally, 162–163, 176–183
    interpretation and application, 165–166
    national and Community law, compatibility of, 166–169
    relevance, 163–165
    rules, 163
    whether necessary, 176–183
  United Kingdom practice, 183–189
  validity of acts of Community, 142–143
  validity rulings, 211–214
  when obligatory, 142–143

Regulations
annulment actions, in, 230–234
decisions and, comparison of, 237
direct applicability of,
  constitutional problems, 70–73
  direct effect, 73–74
  generally, 8, 18–21, 69–77
  limits on implementing, 74–77
  pecuniary penalties, 117
  summary, 77
interpretation of, 74–77

Remedies
annulment actions,
  acts open to challenge, 230–234
  decisions,
    detournement de pouvoir, 270–271
    generally, 230–234, 236–240
    hearing, right to, 260–262

Remedies—*contd*
annulment actions—*contd*
decisions—*contd*
jurisdiction, lack of, 257–258
member states, addressed to, 240–244
misuse of powers, 270–271
procedural infringement, 259–266
reasoning, 262–266
treaty infringement, 266–269
ultra vires acts, 270–271
directives, 230–234
effects of, 272
generally, 229–230
interim measures, 273–274
private parties,
anti-dumping, 244–245, 250–254
available to, 227–229, 234–256
restrictive practices, 244–250
standing of, 234–256
state aids, 254–255
recommendations and opinions, 230–234
references and, relationship, 274–276
regulations, 230–234
review of Community acts, 229
substantive grounds for review,
competence, lack of, 257–258
generally, 256–257
misuse of powers, 270–271
procudural infringement, 259–266
treaty infringement, 266–269
time infringement, 271–272
Community acts, actions to annul,
generally, 222–230
private persons, standing of,
annulment of regulations, 236–240
anti-dumping, 244–245, 250–254
conclusions on, 255–256
generally, 234–236
member states, decisions addressed to, 240–244
restrictive practices, 244–250
state aids, 254–255
types of act open to challenge, 234–235
damages against Community institutions,
generally, 282–285
time-limit, 285–288
directives, 92–94
directly effective treaty provisions, 62–67

Remedies—*contd*
generally, 215–216
illegality, plea of, 276–278
inaction, against, 278–282
individuals. *See* private parties *below*
member states, against,
Commission, at suit of,
force majeure, plea of, 220
matter brought before Court, 218
reasoned opinion, 216
generally, 216–227
private parties,
available to, 227–229, 234–256
Community institutions, against, 227–229
refusal to act, against, 278–282
refusal to act, against, 278–282
time-limits, 219, 271–272, 285–288
Restrictive practices
arts 85 and 86, direct applicability of, 102
locus standi principles, application of, 244–250

Service
free movement of, 124–125
Sovereignty
Community law, limitation by, 2, 22
meaning, 22
Parliament, of, 22, 27–43
problem of, 15, 22–23, 26–43
Statute
Community law and, 137–142
international law yields to, 135
treaties and, 135–137
Subordinate legislation
authority for, 113
challenge to, 117–120
direct applicability. *See* DIRECT APPLICABILITY
European Communities Act 1972, under, 44, 112–122
interpretation of, 117–120
powers,
generally, 114–116
limitations on,
additional taxation, 116
generally, 26–27, 113
new criminal offences, 117
retrospective legislation, 117
sub-delegation, 117
practice, in, 121–122
procedure, 116
rights and obligations, 112 *et seq.*

Subordinate legislation—*contd*
    scrutiny of European legislation, 120–121
    ultra vires acts, 77, 119

Transport
    directly effective provisions, 125

Treaties
    activities of Common Market under, 114–115
    ambiguity of legislation, resolving, 43
    Crown, treaty-making power of, 23–24
    direct effect, 41, 67–69
    EEC Treaty provisions directly applicable, summary, 122–126

Treaties—*contd*
    executive acts, as, 25
    legislation, need for, 14–15, 23–26
    source of Community law, as, 1, 2, 23–26

Tribunal
    reference by. *See* REFERENCE

Ultra vires
    annulment action, as grounds for, 270–271
    subordinate legislation, in, 77, 119

United Kingdom law. *See* NATIONAL LAW

United Nations
    legal personality of, 3